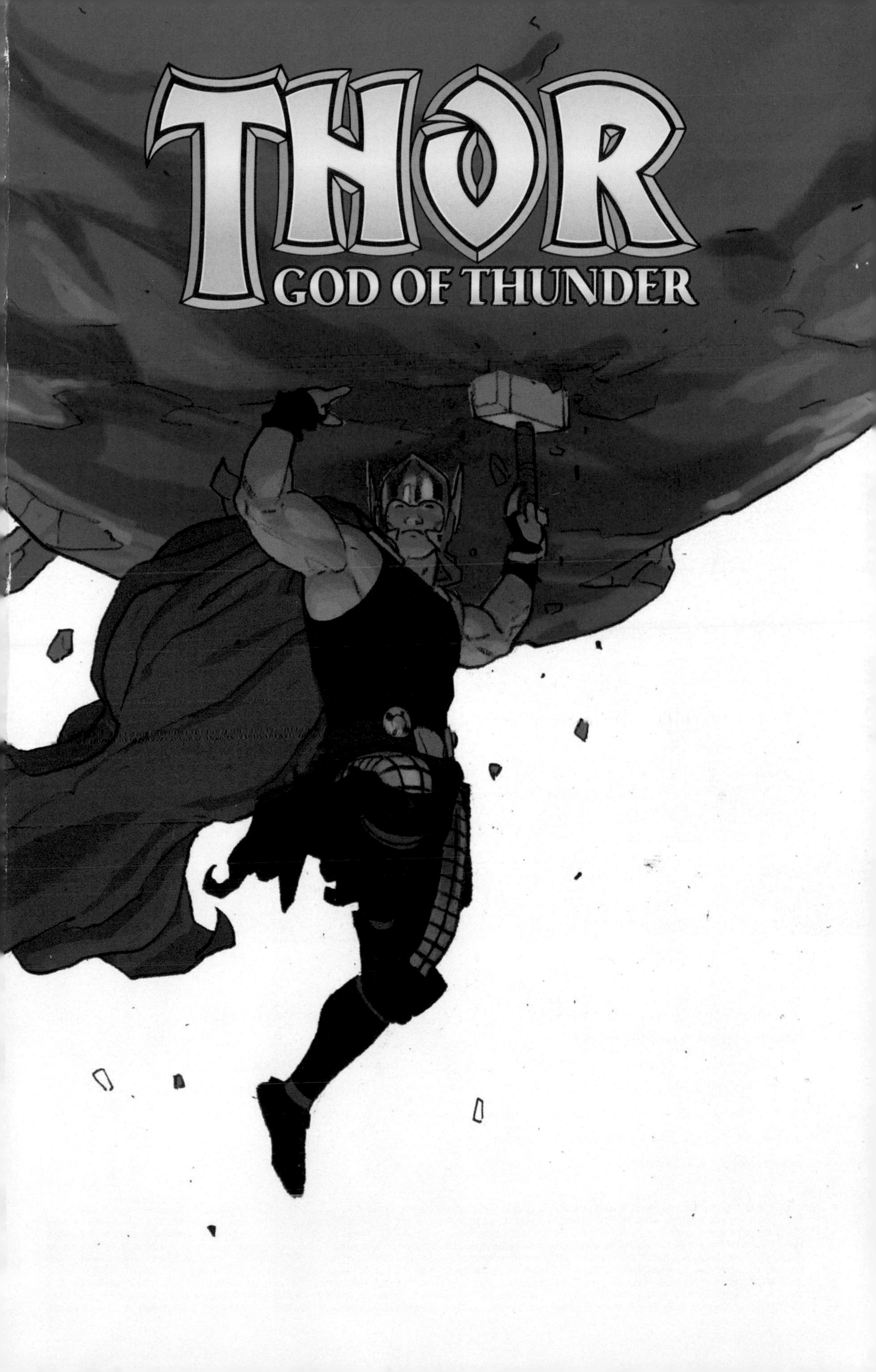
THOR
GOD OF THUNDER

Collection Editor: **Jennifer Grünwald**

Assistant Editor: **Sarah Brunstad**

Associate Managing Editor: **Alex Starbuck**

Editor, Special Projects: **Mark D. Beazley**

Senior Editor, Special Projects: **Jeff Youngquist**

SVP Print, Sales & Marketing: **David Gabriel**

Book Design: **Joe Frontirre**

Editor in Chief: **Axel Alonso**

Chief Creative Officer: **Joe Quesada**

Publisher: **Dan Buckley**

Executive Producer: **Alan Fine**

THOR: GOD OF THUNDER VOL. 4 — **THE LAST DAYS OF MIDGARD.** Contains material originally published in magazine form as THOR: GOD OF THUNDER #19-25. First printing 2014. ISBN# 978-0-7851-5488-4. Published by MARVEL WORLDWIDE, INC., a subsidiary of MARVEL ENTERTAINMENT, LLC. OFFICE OF PUBLICATION: 135 West 50th Street, New York, NY 10020. Copyright © 2014 Marvel Characters, Inc. All rights reserved. All characters featured in this issue and the distinctive names and likenesses thereof, and all related indicia are trademarks of Marvel Characters, Inc. No similarity between any of the names, characters, persons, and/or institutions in this magazine with those of any living or dead person or institution is intended, and any such similarity which may exist is purely coincidental. **Printed in the U.S.A.** ALAN FINE, EVP - Office of the President, Marvel Worldwide, Inc. and EVP & CMO Marvel Characters B.V.; DAN BUCKLEY, Publisher & President - Print, Animation & Digital Divisions; JOE QUESADA, Chief Creative Officer; TOM BREVOORT, SVP of Publishing; DAVID BOGART, SVP of Operations & Procurement, Publishing; C.B. CEBULSKI, SVP of Creator & Content Development; DAVID GABRIEL, SVP Print, Sales & Marketing; JIM O'KEEFE, VP of Operations & Logistics; DAN CARR, Executive Director of Publishing Technology; SUSAN CRESPI, Editorial Operations Manager; ALEX MORALES, Publishing Operations Manager; STAN LEE, Chairman Emeritus. For information regarding advertising in Marvel Comics or on Marvel.com, please contact Niza Disla, Director of Marvel Partnerships, at ndisla@marvel.com. For Marvel subscription inquiries, please call 800-217-9158. **Manufactured between 9/19/2014 and 11/3/2014** by R.R. DONNELLEY, INC., SALEM, VA, USA.

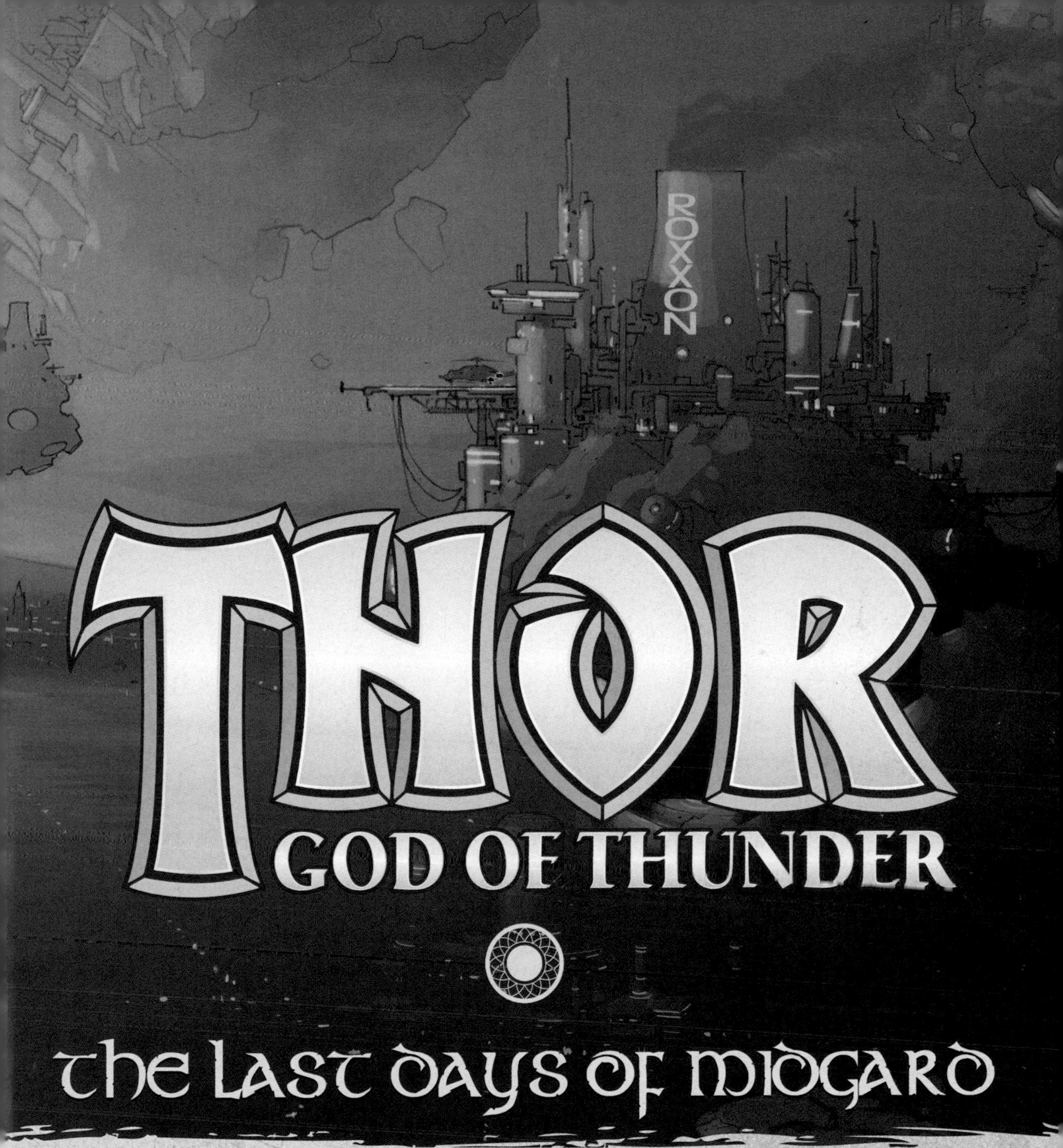
ROXXON

THOR
GOD OF THUNDER

THE LAST DAYS OF MIDGARD

WRITER
JASON AARON

ISSUES #19-24

ARTIST
ESAD RIBIC
with AGUSTIN ALESSIO
(#24, pp. 1-18)

COLOR ARTIST
IVE SVORCINA
with AGUSTIN ALESSIO
(#24, pp. 1-18)

ISSUE #25

"THE 13TH SON OF A 13TH SON"
ARTIST
R.M. GUERA
COLOR ARTIST
GIULIA BRUSCO

"BLOOD AND ICE"
ARTIST
SIMON BISLEY

"UNWORTHY"
ARTIST
ESAD RIBIC
COLOR ARTIST
IVE SVORCINA

LETTERER
VC'S JOE SABINO

COVER ART
ESAD RIBIC (#19-21 & #25), **JEE-HYUNG** (#22)
and AGUSTIN ALESSION (#23-24)

ASSISTANT EDITOR
JON MOISAN

EDITOR
WIL MOSS

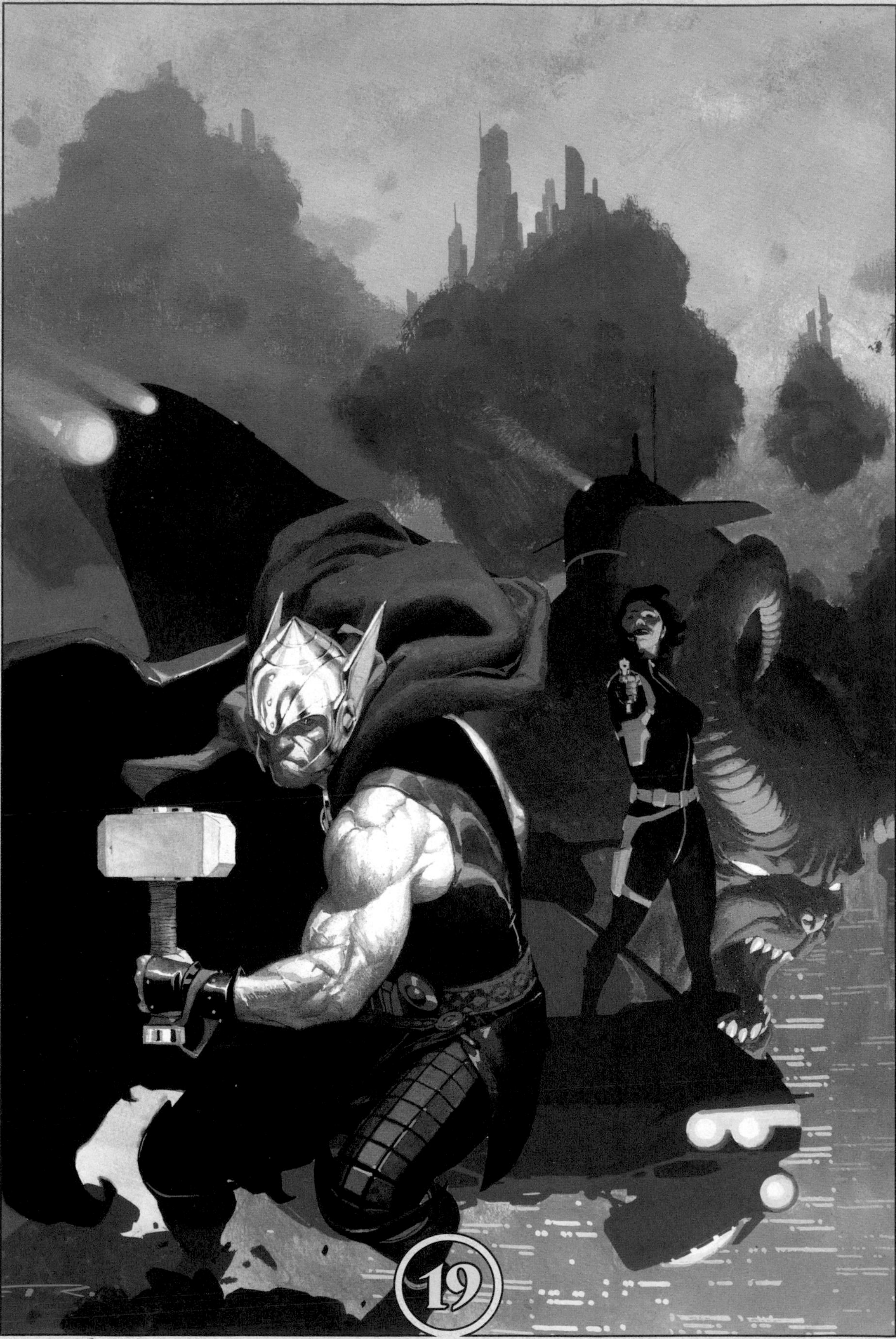
19

THE LAST DAYS OF MIDGARD – PART 1:
GODS AND CEOS

THOR IS THE ASGARDIAN GOD OF THUNDER AND AN AVENGER. AS THE WEILDER OF MJOLNIR, A MYSTICAL URU HAMMER OF IMMENSE POWER, HE HAS SWORN TO PROTECT OUR WORLD, MIDGARD, FOR THE REST OF HIS DAYS. WHICH IS WHY, SEVERAL MILLENIA FROM NOW WHEN HE HAS BECOME KING THOR, HE LABORS TO REVIVE THE RUINED PLANET...

ROXXON ENERGY CORPORATION

To: All Staff
Date: 02/12/2014
Subject: Public Relations

It has been a hard road, but we are all the stronger for it. ROXXON is its own master once again. As we prepare to take the corporate world by storm, we must guard our good reputation as the world's wealthiest, most powerful super-corporation with all due diligence.

With that in mind, there are a couple pieces of related business to address:

1.) As you may know, recently a S.H.I.E.L.D. environmental investigation team claimed that the unfortunate deaths of some sea life in the Southern Ocean were due to our underwater mining station there. It was a completely fraudulent claim, as was soon proven in a court of law. However, we continue to be dogged by a member of that team, a rookie S.H.I.E.L.D. agent named Roz Solomon. As is our policy, please continue to forward any and all communications from Agent Solomon to our PR team. She will be dealt with accordingly.

2.) On a more positive note, we are about to send out a press release inviting the media tothe grand unveiling of the Pipeline project in Glacier Bay National Park, Alaska. When the public gets their first glimpse of the gift we are bestowing upon them, I believe that the reaction will be "out of this world." But please, do keep the details under wraps until then.

I trust you all understand the importance of these matters. I look forward to working with you in our mission to make the world a better place through ROXXON.

Braxton Agger

Braxton Agger
CEO

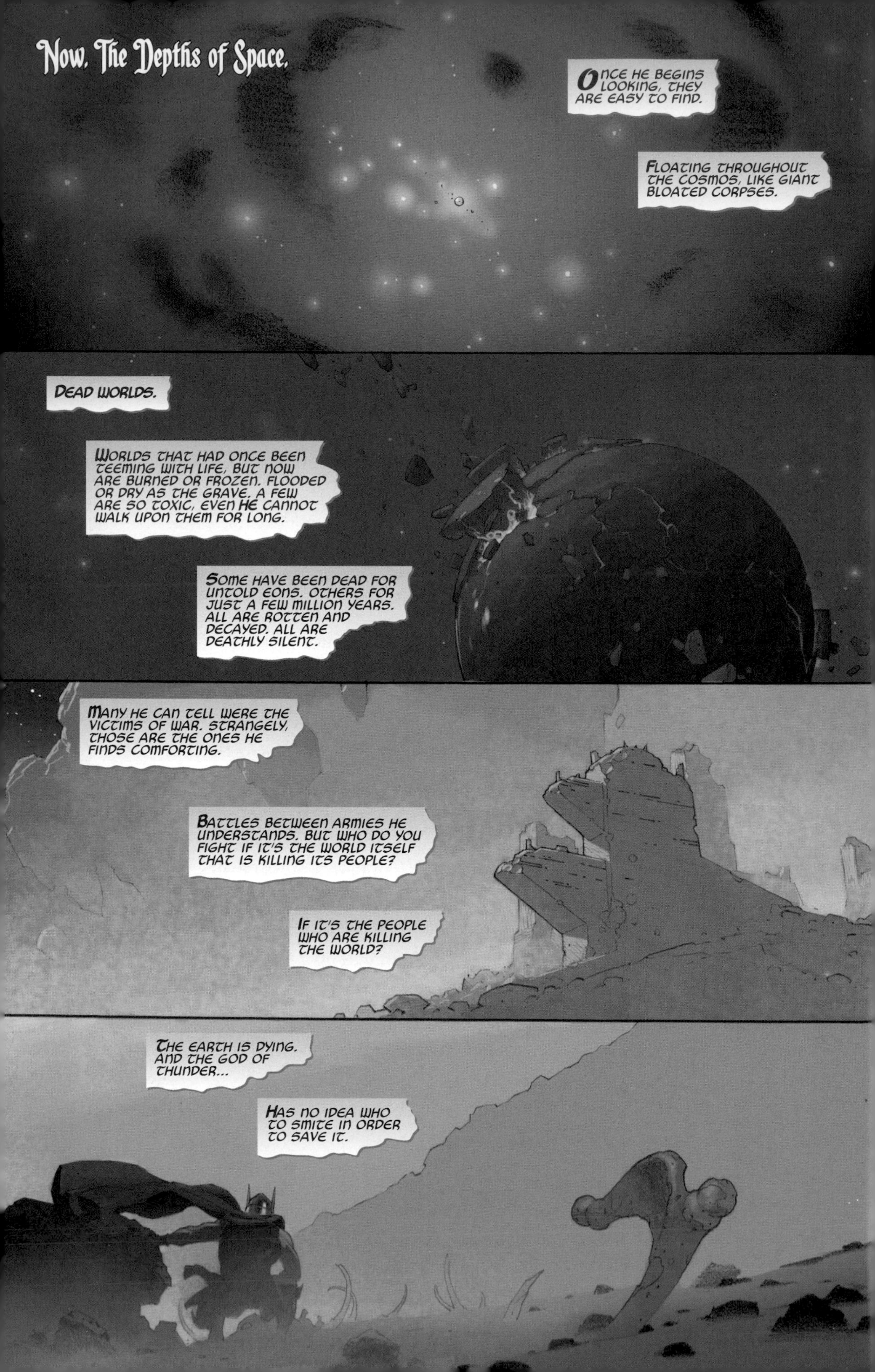
Now, The Depths of Space.
ONCE HE BEGINS LOOKING, THEY ARE EASY TO FIND.
FLOATING THROUGHOUT THE COSMOS, LIKE GIANT BLOATED CORPSES.
DEAD WORLDS.
WORLDS THAT HAD ONCE BEEN TEEMING WITH LIFE, BUT NOW ARE BURNED OR FROZEN. FLOODED OR DRY AS THE GRAVE. A FEW ARE SO TOXIC, EVEN HE CANNOT WALK UPON THEM FOR LONG.
SOME HAVE BEEN DEAD FOR UNTOLD EONS. OTHERS FOR JUST A FEW MILLION YEARS. ALL ARE ROTTEN AND DECAYED. ALL ARE DEATHLY SILENT.
MANY HE CAN TELL WERE THE VICTIMS OF WAR. STRANGELY, THOSE ARE THE ONES HE FINDS COMFORTING.
BATTLES BETWEEN ARMIES HE UNDERSTANDS. BUT WHO DO YOU FIGHT IF IT'S THE WORLD ITSELF THAT IS KILLING ITS PEOPLE?
IF IT'S THE PEOPLE WHO ARE KILLING THE WORLD?
THE EARTH IS DYING. AND THE GOD OF THUNDER...
HAS NO IDEA WHO TO SMITE IN ORDER TO SAVE IT.

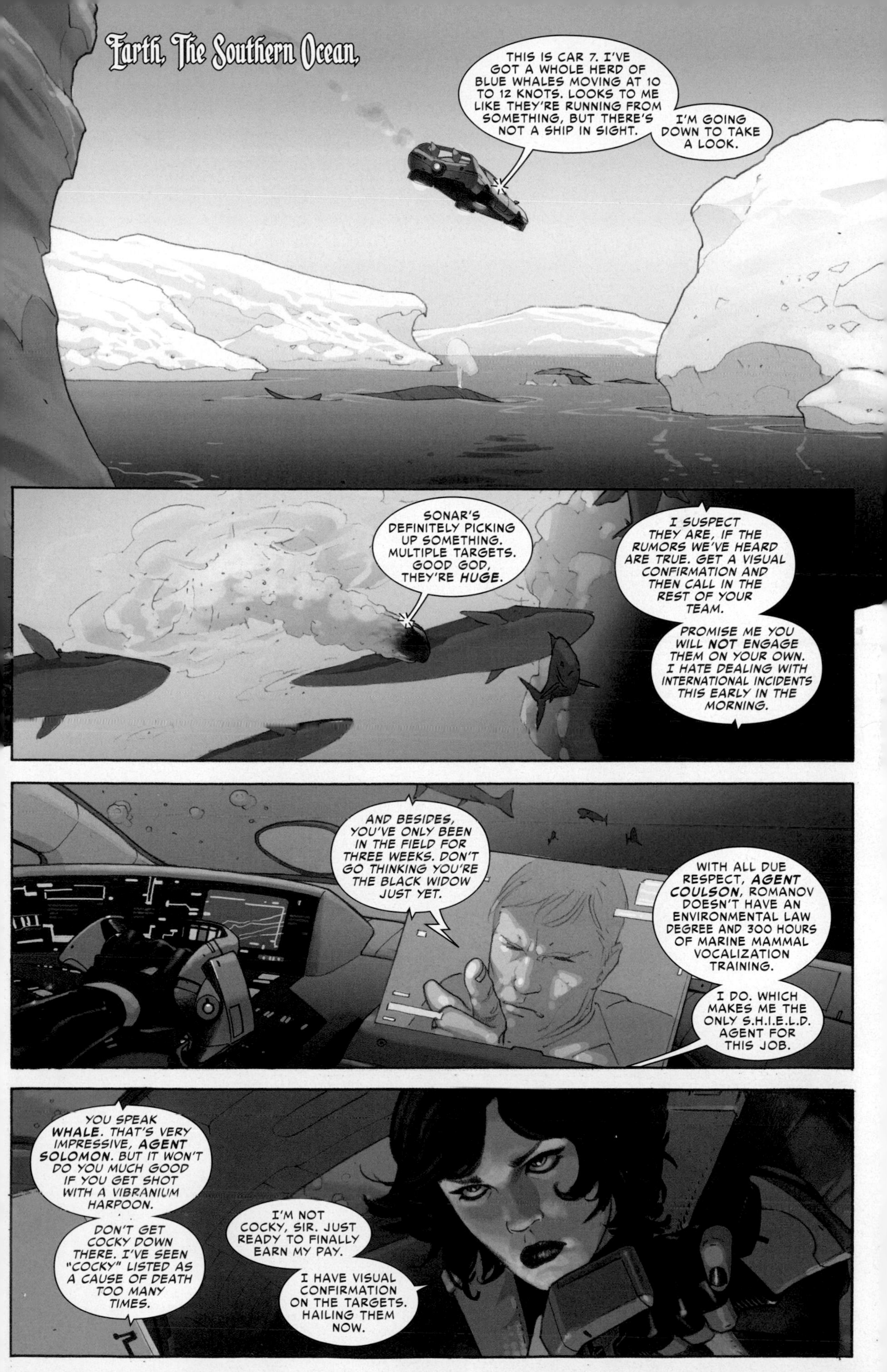
Earth, The Southern Ocean.
THIS IS CAR 7. I'VE GOT A WHOLE HERD OF BLUE WHALES MOVING AT 10 TO 12 KNOTS. LOOKS TO ME LIKE THEY'RE RUNNING FROM SOMETHING, BUT THERE'S NOT A SHIP IN SIGHT.
I'M GOING DOWN TO TAKE A LOOK.
SONAR'S DEFINITELY PICKING UP SOMETHING. MULTIPLE TARGETS. GOOD GOD, THEY'RE HUGE.
I SUSPECT THEY ARE, IF THE RUMORS WE'VE HEARD ARE TRUE. GET A VISUAL CONFIRMATION AND THEN CALL IN THE REST OF YOUR TEAM.
PROMISE ME YOU WILL NOT ENGAGE THEM ON YOUR OWN. I HATE DEALING WITH INTERNATIONAL INCIDENTS THIS EARLY IN THE MORNING.
AND BESIDES, YOU'VE ONLY BEEN IN THE FIELD FOR THREE WEEKS. DON'T GO THINKING YOU'RE THE BLACK WIDOW JUST YET.
WITH ALL DUE RESPECT, AGENT COULSON, ROMANOV DOESN'T HAVE AN ENVIRONMENTAL LAW DEGREE AND 300 HOURS OF MARINE MAMMAL VOCALIZATION TRAINING.
I DO. WHICH MAKES ME THE ONLY S.H.I.E.L.D. AGENT FOR THIS JOB.
YOU SPEAK WHALE. THAT'S VERY IMPRESSIVE, AGENT SOLOMON. BUT IT WON'T DO YOU MUCH GOOD IF YOU GET SHOT WITH A VIBRANIUM HARPOON.
DON'T GET COCKY DOWN THERE. I'VE SEEN "COCKY" LISTED AS A CAUSE OF DEATH TOO MANY TIMES.
I'M NOT COCKY, SIR. JUST READY TO FINALLY EARN MY PAY.
I HAVE VISUAL CONFIRMATION ON THE TARGETS. HAILING THEM NOW.

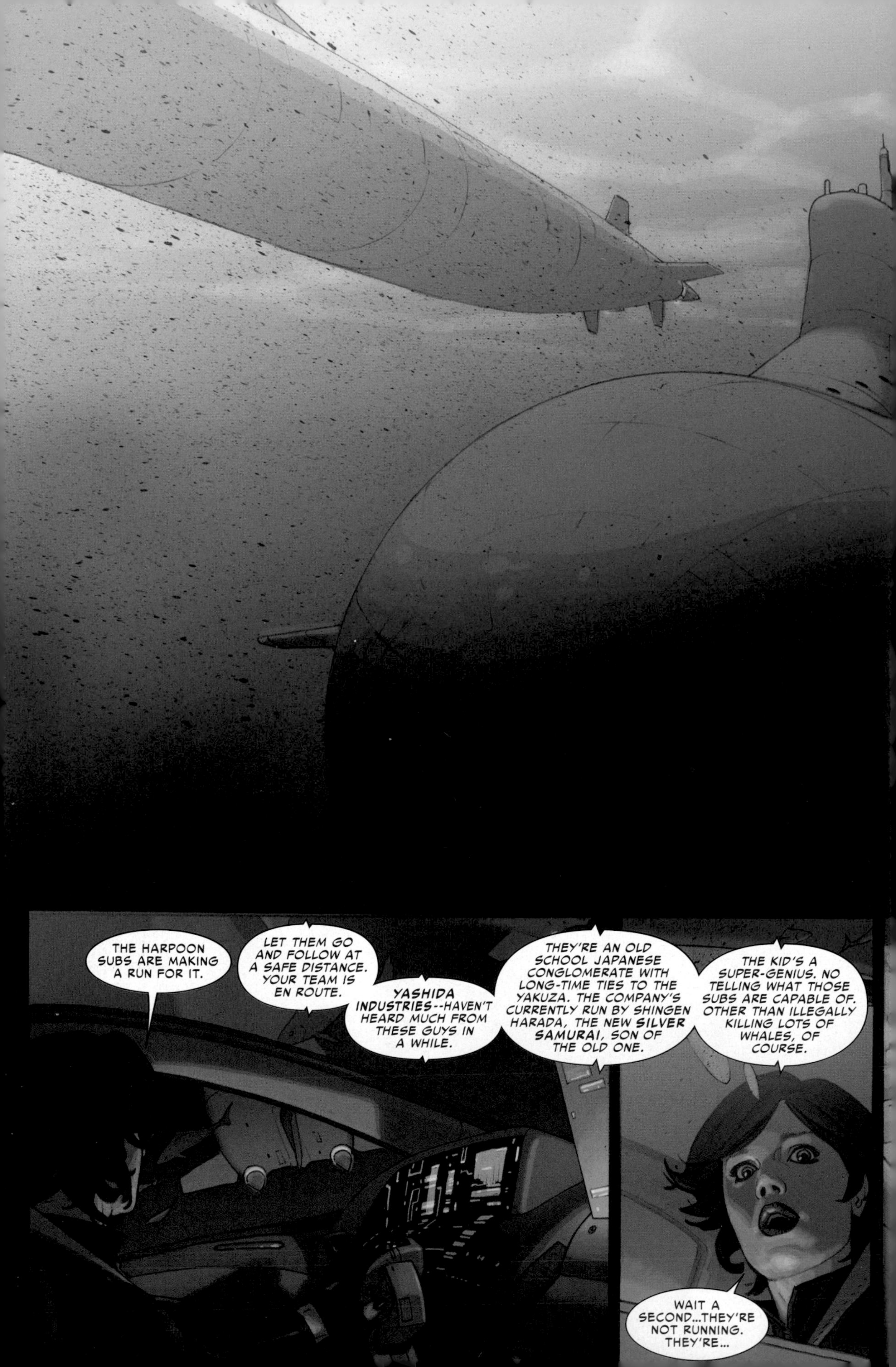
THE HARPOON SUBS ARE MAKING A RUN FOR IT.
LET THEM GO AND FOLLOW AT A SAFE DISTANCE. YOUR TEAM IS EN ROUTE.
YASHIDA INDUSTRIES--HAVEN'T HEARD MUCH FROM THESE GUYS IN A WHILE.
THEY'RE AN OLD SCHOOL JAPANESE CONGLOMERATE WITH LONG-TIME TIES TO THE YAKUZA. THE COMPANY'S CURRENTLY RUN BY SHINGEN HARADA, THE NEW SILVER SAMURAI, SON OF THE OLD ONE.
THE KID'S A SUPER-GENIUS. NO TELLING WHAT THOSE SUBS ARE CAPABLE OF. OTHER THAN ILLEGALLY KILLING LOTS OF WHALES, OF COURSE.
WAIT A SECOND...THEY'RE NOT RUNNING. THEY'RE...

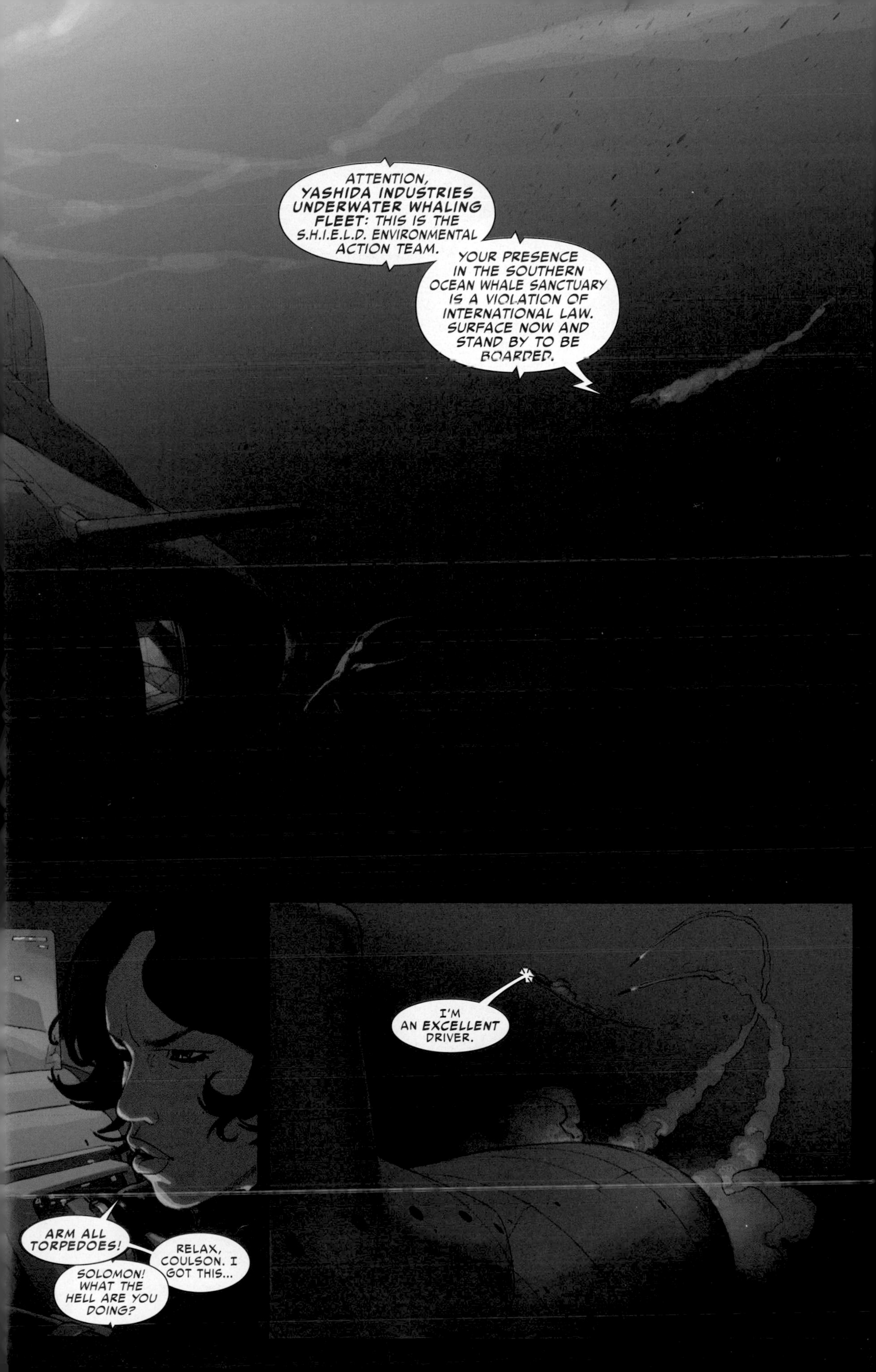
ATTENTION, YASHIDA INDUSTRIES UNDERWATER WHALING FLEET: THIS IS THE S.H.I.E.L.D. ENVIRONMENTAL ACTION TEAM.
YOUR PRESENCE IN THE SOUTHERN OCEAN WHALE SANCTUARY IS A VIOLATION OF INTERNATIONAL LAW. SURFACE NOW AND STAND BY TO BE BOARDED.
I'M AN EXCELLENT DRIVER.
ARM ALL TORPEDOES!
SOLOMON! WHAT THE HELL ARE YOU DOING?
RELAX, COULSON. I GOT THIS...

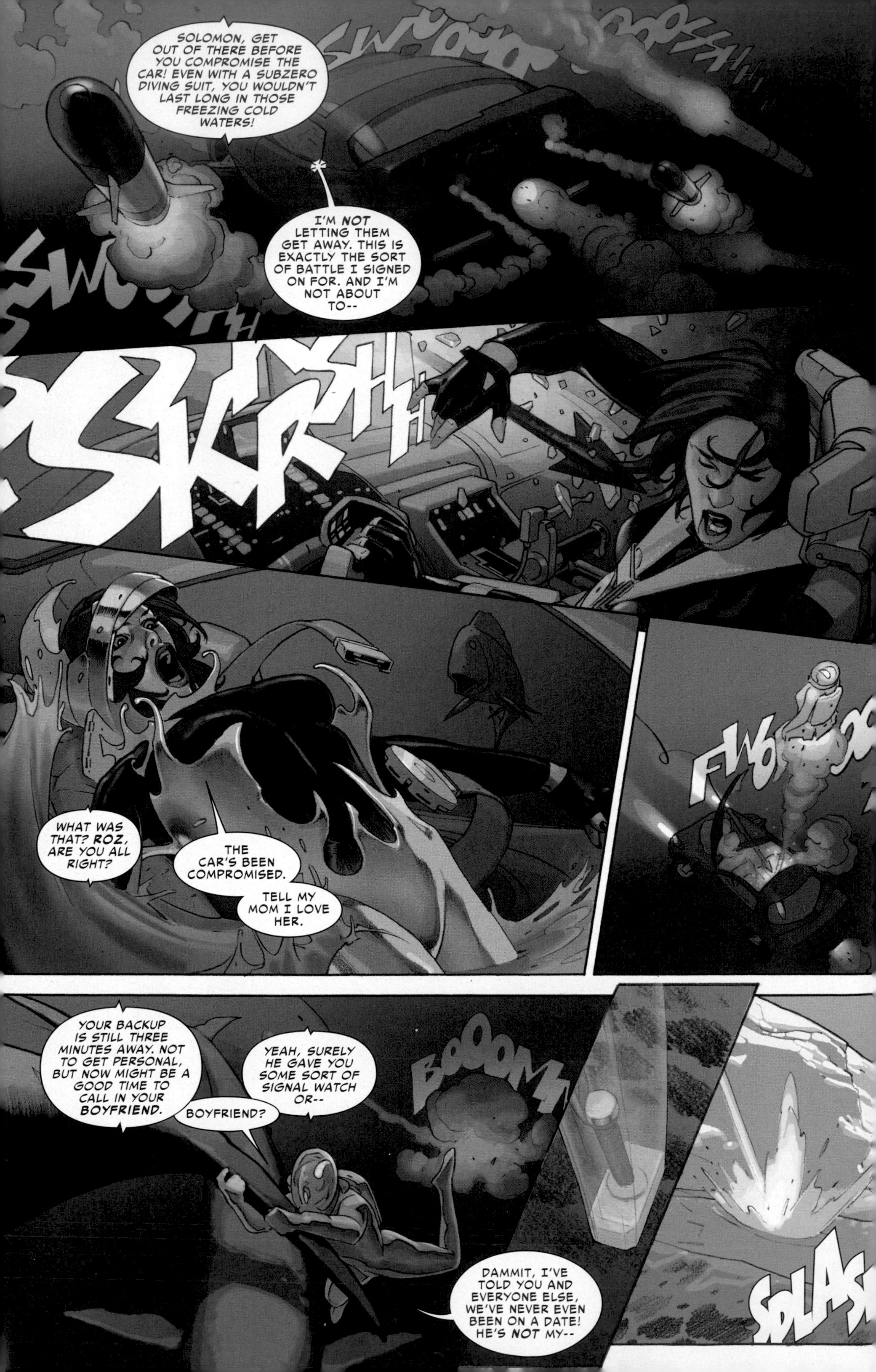
SOLOMON, GET OUT OF THERE BEFORE YOU COMPROMISE THE CAR! EVEN WITH A SUBZERO DIVING SUIT, YOU WOULDN'T LAST LONG IN THOSE FREEZING COLD WATERS!
I'M NOT LETTING THEM GET AWAY. THIS IS EXACTLY THE SORT OF BATTLE I SIGNED ON FOR. AND I'M NOT ABOUT TO--
SKRSH
WHAT WAS THAT? ROZ, ARE YOU ALL RIGHT?
THE CAR'S BEEN COMPROMISED.
TELL MY MOM I LOVE HER.
YOUR BACKUP IS STILL THREE MINUTES AWAY. NOT TO GET PERSONAL, BUT NOW MIGHT BE A GOOD TIME TO CALL IN YOUR BOYFRIEND.
BOYFRIEND?
YEAH, SURELY HE GAVE YOU SOME SORT OF SIGNAL WATCH OR--
BOOOM
DAMMIT, I'VE TOLD YOU AND EVERYONE ELSE, WE'VE NEVER EVEN BEEN ON A DATE! HE'S NOT MY--

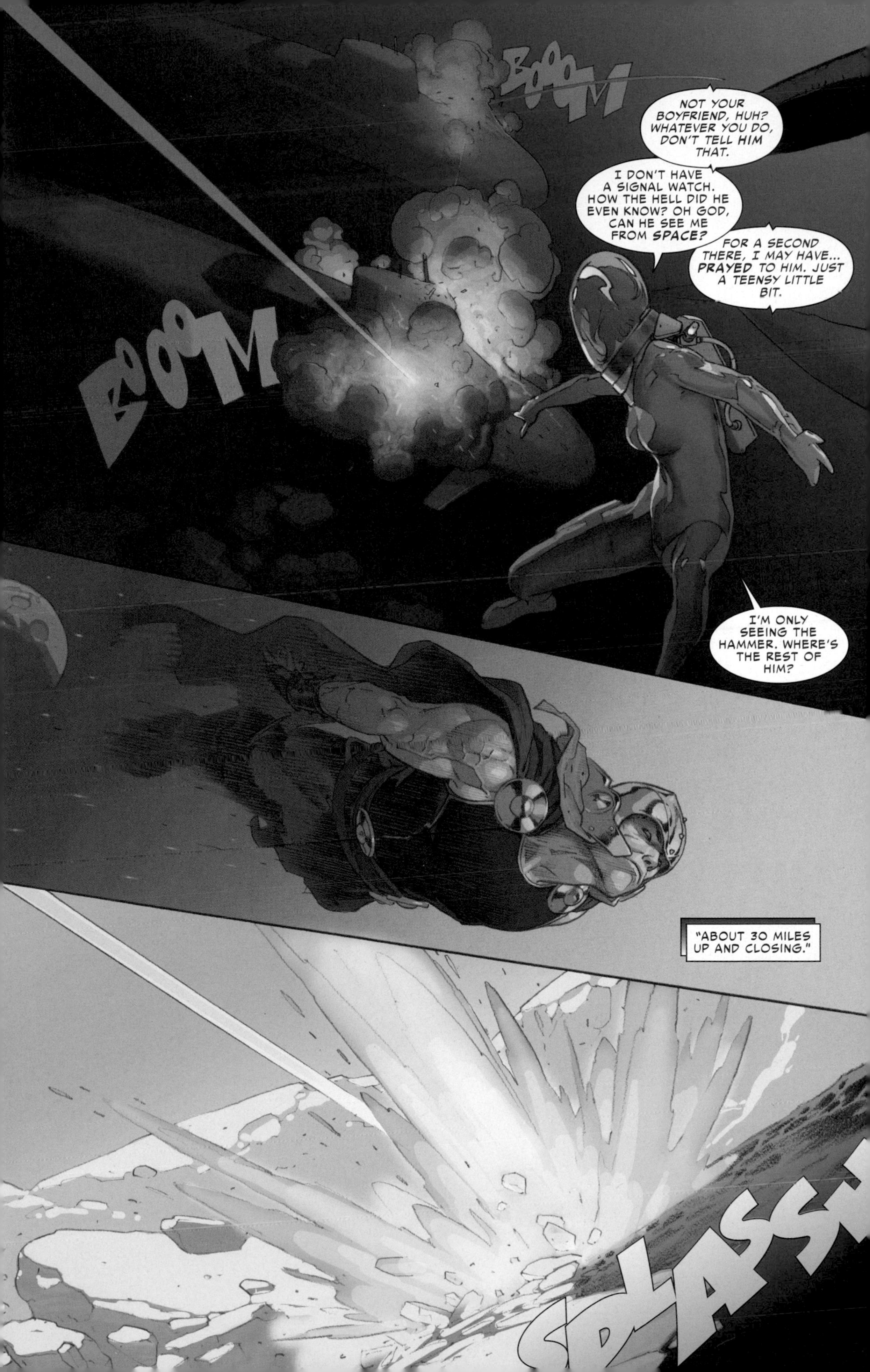
BOOOM
NOT YOUR BOYFRIEND, HUH? WHATEVER YOU DO, DON'T TELL HIM THAT.
I DON'T HAVE A SIGNAL WATCH. HOW THE HELL DID HE EVEN KNOW? OH GOD, CAN HE SEE ME FROM SPACE?
FOR A SECOND THERE, I MAY HAVE... PRAYED TO HIM. JUST A TEENSY LITTLE BIT.
BOOOM
I'M ONLY SEEING THE HAMMER. WHERE'S THE REST OF HIM?
"ABOUT 30 MILES UP AND CLOSING."

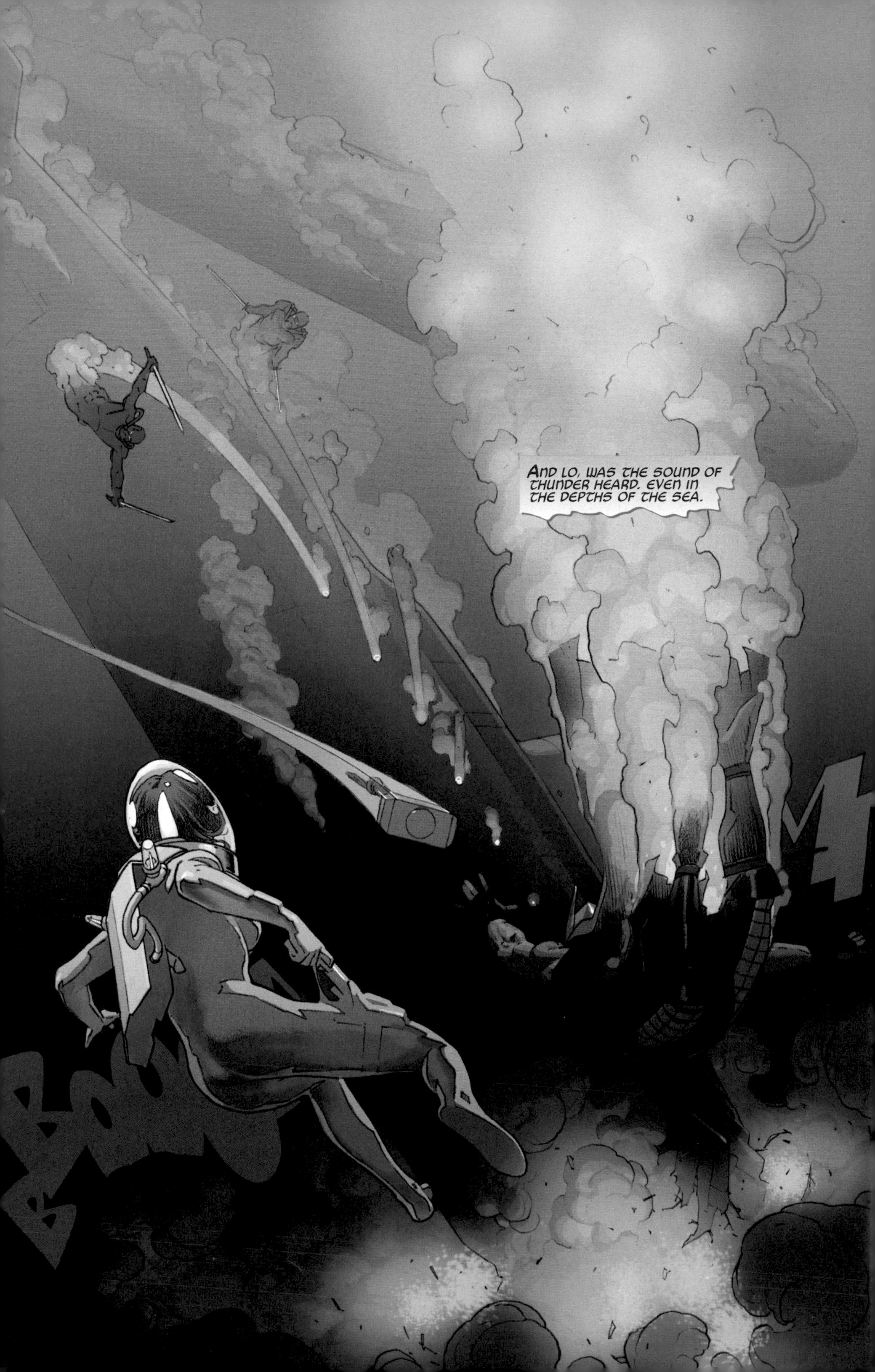
And lo, was the sound of thunder heard. Even in the depths of the sea.

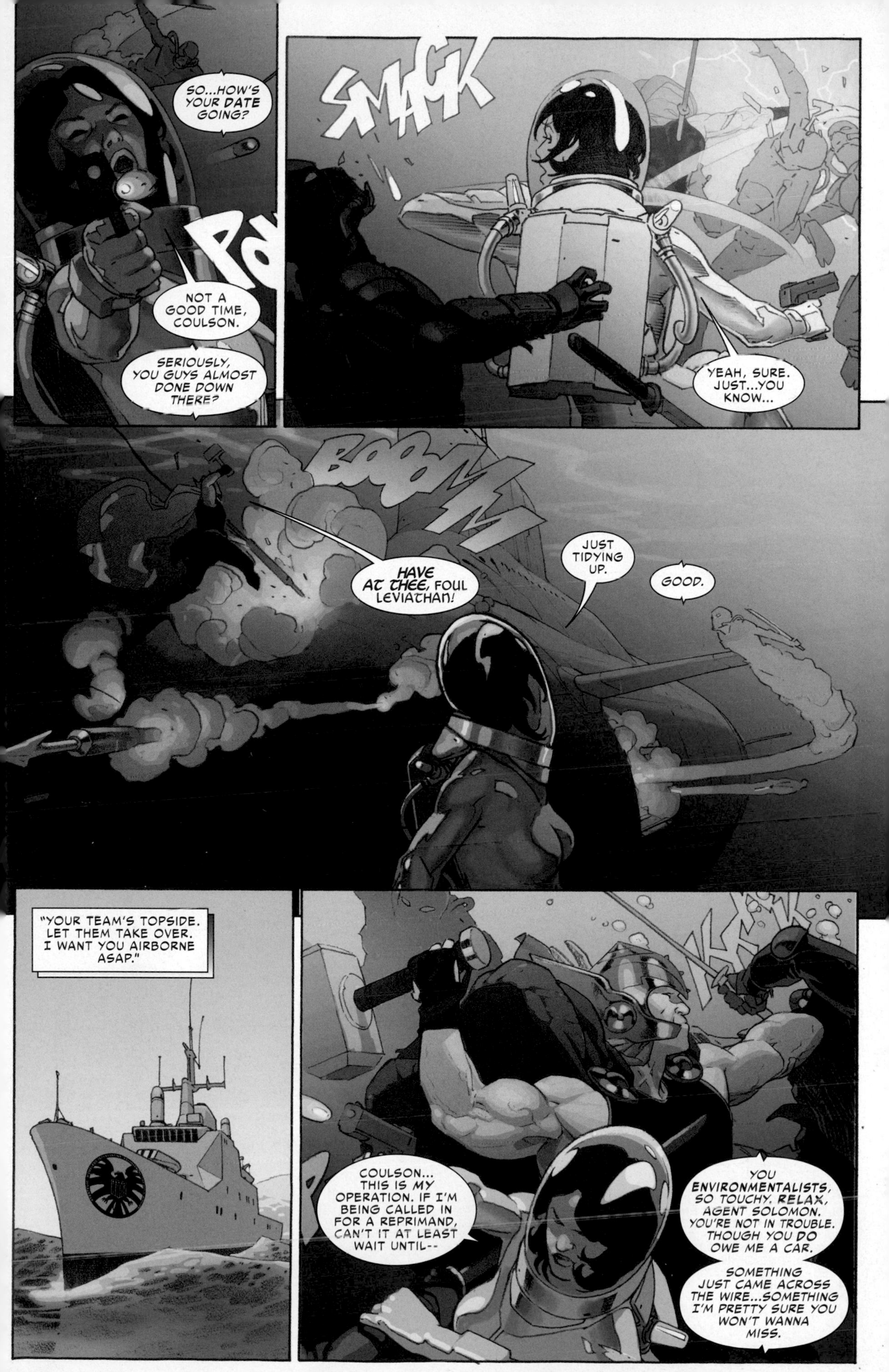
SO...HOW'S YOUR DATE GOING?
PA
NOT A GOOD TIME, COULSON.
SERIOUSLY, YOU GUYS ALMOST DONE DOWN THERE?
SMACK
YEAH, SURE. JUST...YOU KNOW...
BOOM
HAVE AT THEE, FOUL LEVIATHAN!
JUST TIDYING UP.
GOOD.
"YOUR TEAM'S TOPSIDE. LET THEM TAKE OVER. I WANT YOU AIRBORNE ASAP."
COULSON... THIS IS MY OPERATION. IF I'M BEING CALLED IN FOR A REPRIMAND, CAN'T IT AT LEAST WAIT UNTIL--
YOU ENVIRONMENTALISTS, SO TOUCHY. RELAX, AGENT SOLOMON. YOU'RE NOT IN TROUBLE. THOUGH YOU DO OWE ME A CAR.
SOMETHING JUST CAME ACROSS THE WIRE...SOMETHING I'M PRETTY SURE YOU WON'T WANNA MISS.

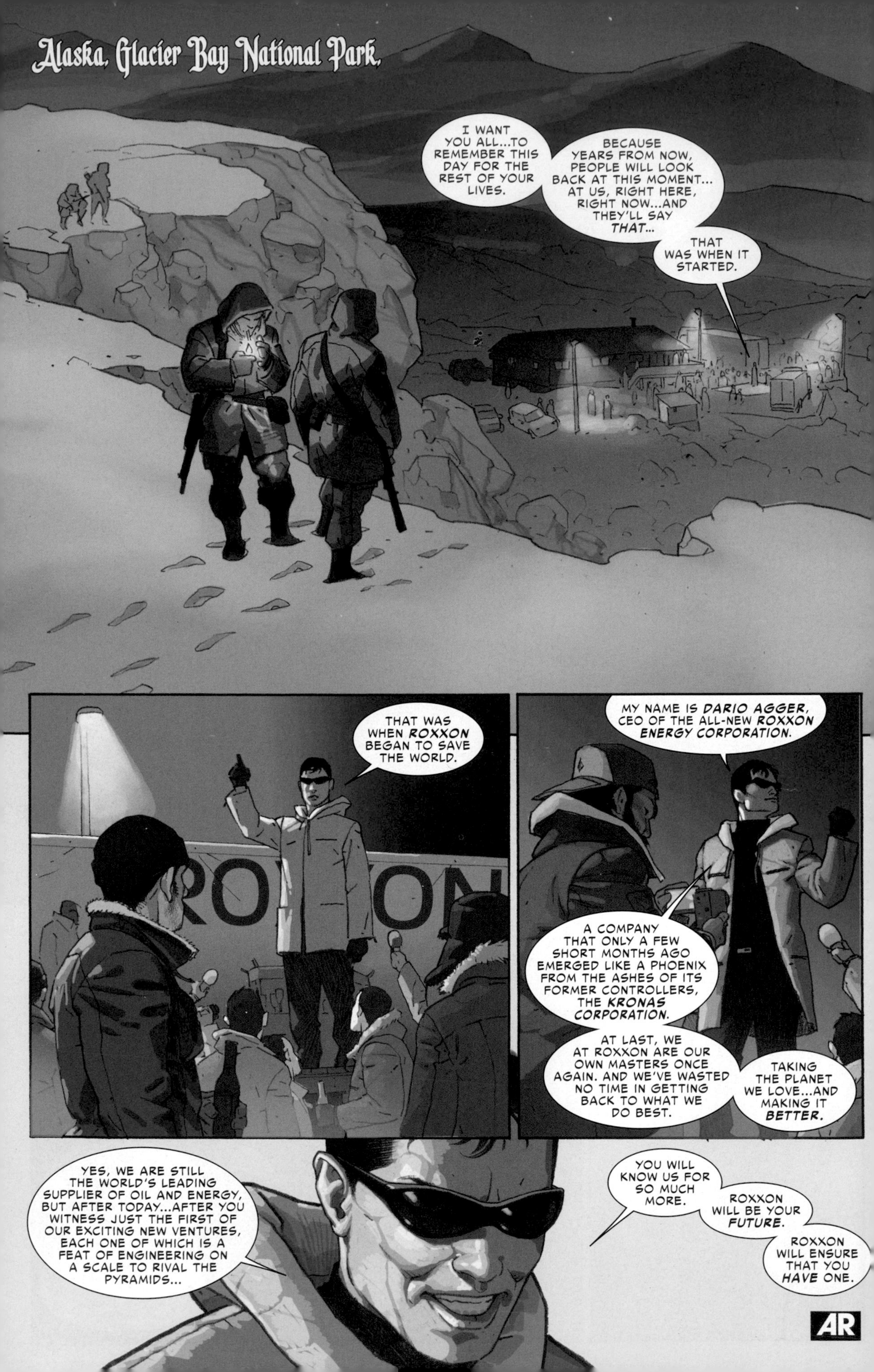
Alaska, Glacier Bay National Park.
I WANT YOU ALL...TO REMEMBER THIS DAY FOR THE REST OF YOUR LIVES.
BECAUSE YEARS FROM NOW, PEOPLE WILL LOOK BACK AT THIS MOMENT... AT US, RIGHT HERE, RIGHT NOW...AND THEY'LL SAY THAT...
THAT WAS WHEN IT STARTED.
THAT WAS WHEN ROXXON BEGAN TO SAVE THE WORLD.
ROXXON
MY NAME IS DARIO AGGER, CEO OF THE ALL-NEW ROXXON ENERGY CORPORATION.
A COMPANY THAT ONLY A FEW SHORT MONTHS AGO EMERGED LIKE A PHOENIX FROM THE ASHES OF ITS FORMER CONTROLLERS, THE KRONAS CORPORATION.
AT LAST, WE AT ROXXON ARE OUR OWN MASTERS ONCE AGAIN. AND WE'VE WASTED NO TIME IN GETTING BACK TO WHAT WE DO BEST.
TAKING THE PLANET WE LOVE...AND MAKING IT BETTER.
YES, WE ARE STILL THE WORLD'S LEADING SUPPLIER OF OIL AND ENERGY, BUT AFTER TODAY...AFTER YOU WITNESS JUST THE FIRST OF OUR EXCITING NEW VENTURES, EACH ONE OF WHICH IS A FEAT OF ENGINEERING ON A SCALE TO RIVAL THE PYRAMIDS...
YOU WILL KNOW US FOR SO MUCH MORE.
ROXXON WILL BE YOUR FUTURE.
ROXXON WILL ENSURE THAT YOU HAVE ONE.
AR

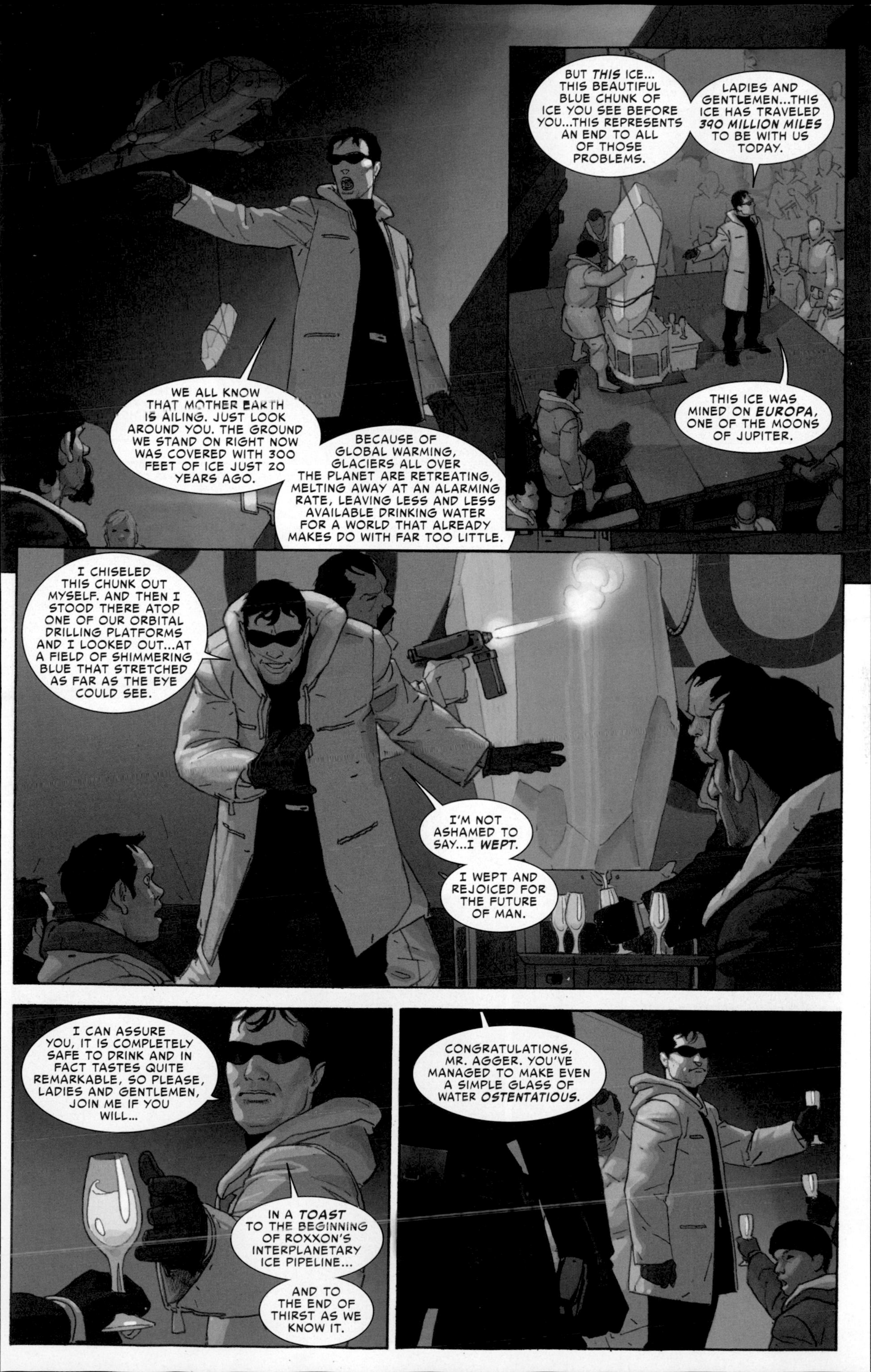
WE ALL KNOW THAT MOTHER EARTH IS AILING. JUST LOOK AROUND YOU. THE GROUND WE STAND ON RIGHT NOW WAS COVERED WITH 300 FEET OF ICE JUST 20 YEARS AGO.
BECAUSE OF GLOBAL WARMING, GLACIERS ALL OVER THE PLANET ARE RETREATING, MELTING AWAY AT AN ALARMING RATE, LEAVING LESS AND LESS AVAILABLE DRINKING WATER FOR A WORLD THAT ALREADY MAKES DO WITH FAR TOO LITTLE.
BUT THIS ICE... THIS BEAUTIFUL BLUE CHUNK OF ICE YOU SEE BEFORE YOU...THIS REPRESENTS AN END TO ALL OF THOSE PROBLEMS.
LADIES AND GENTLEMEN...THIS ICE HAS TRAVELED 390 MILLION MILES TO BE WITH US TODAY.
THIS ICE WAS MINED ON EUROPA, ONE OF THE MOONS OF JUPITER.
I CHISELED THIS CHUNK OUT MYSELF. AND THEN I STOOD THERE ATOP ONE OF OUR ORBITAL DRILLING PLATFORMS AND I LOOKED OUT...AT A FIELD OF SHIMMERING BLUE THAT STRETCHED AS FAR AS THE EYE COULD SEE.
I'M NOT ASHAMED TO SAY...I WEPT.
I WEPT AND REJOICED FOR THE FUTURE OF MAN.
I CAN ASSURE YOU, IT IS COMPLETELY SAFE TO DRINK AND IN FACT TASTES QUITE REMARKABLE, SO PLEASE, LADIES AND GENTLEMEN, JOIN ME IF YOU WILL...
IN A TOAST TO THE BEGINNING OF ROXXON'S INTERPLANETARY ICE PIPELINE...
AND TO THE END OF THIRST AS WE KNOW IT.
CONGRATULATIONS, MR. AGGER. YOU'VE MANAGED TO MAKE EVEN A SIMPLE GLASS OF WATER OSTENTATIOUS.

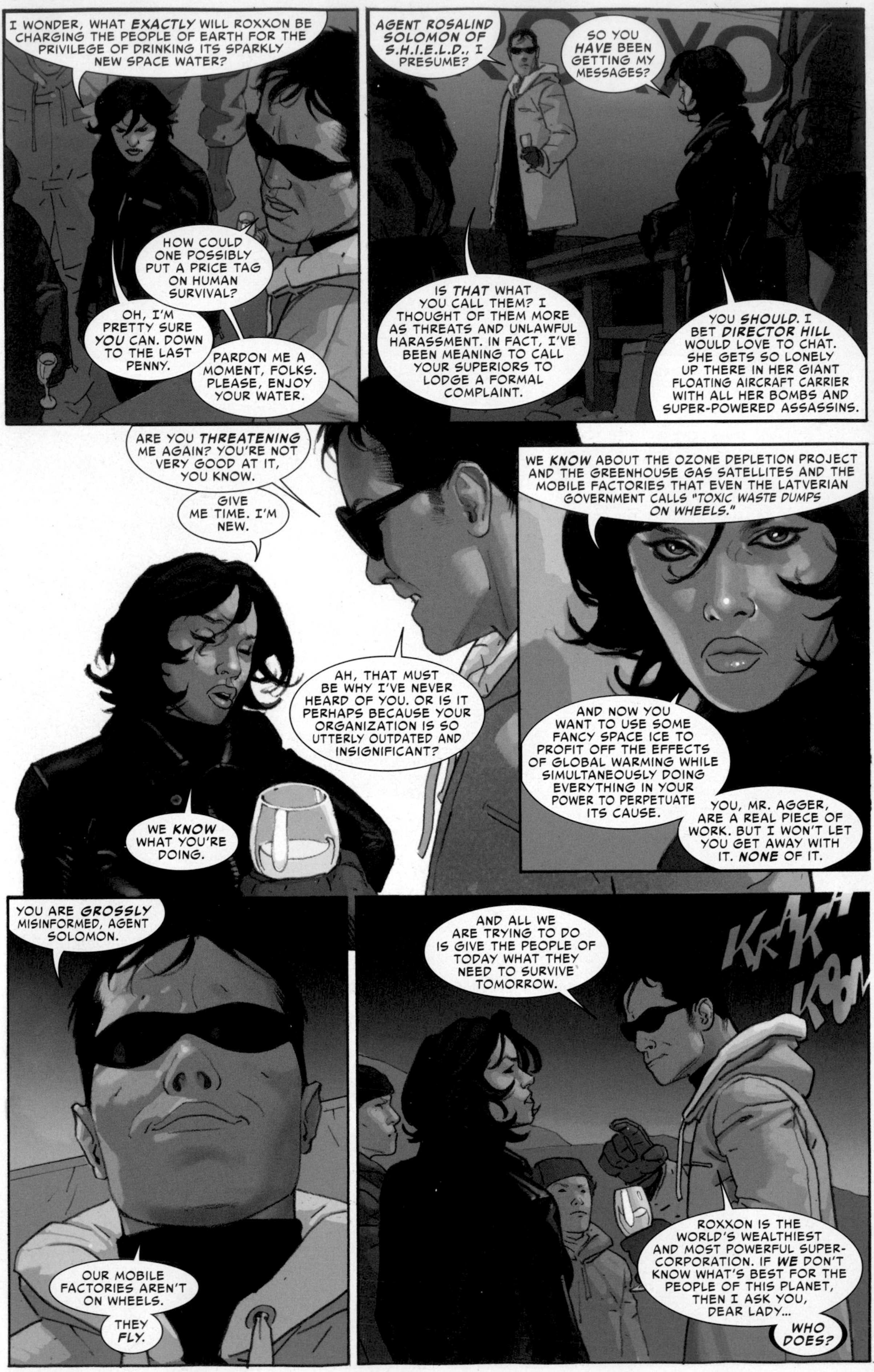
I WONDER, WHAT EXACTLY WILL ROXXON BE CHARGING THE PEOPLE OF EARTH FOR THE PRIVILEGE OF DRINKING ITS SPARKLY NEW SPACE WATER?
HOW COULD ONE POSSIBLY PUT A PRICE TAG ON HUMAN SURVIVAL?
OH, I'M PRETTY SURE YOU CAN. DOWN TO THE LAST PENNY.
PARDON ME A MOMENT, FOLKS. PLEASE, ENJOY YOUR WATER.
AGENT ROSALIND SOLOMON OF S.H.I.E.L.D., I PRESUME?
SO YOU HAVE BEEN GETTING MY MESSAGES?
IS THAT WHAT YOU CALL THEM? I THOUGHT OF THEM MORE AS THREATS AND UNLAWFUL HARASSMENT. IN FACT, I'VE BEEN MEANING TO CALL YOUR SUPERIORS TO LODGE A FORMAL COMPLAINT.
YOU SHOULD. I BET DIRECTOR HILL WOULD LOVE TO CHAT. SHE GETS SO LONELY UP THERE IN HER GIANT FLOATING AIRCRAFT CARRIER WITH ALL HER BOMBS AND SUPER-POWERED ASSASSINS.
ARE YOU THREATENING ME AGAIN? YOU'RE NOT VERY GOOD AT IT, YOU KNOW.
GIVE ME TIME. I'M NEW.
AH, THAT MUST BE WHY I'VE NEVER HEARD OF YOU. OR IS IT PERHAPS BECAUSE YOUR ORGANIZATION IS SO UTTERLY OUTDATED AND INSIGNIFICANT?
WE KNOW WHAT YOU'RE DOING.
WE KNOW ABOUT THE OZONE DEPLETION PROJECT AND THE GREENHOUSE GAS SATELLITES AND THE MOBILE FACTORIES THAT EVEN THE LATVERIAN GOVERNMENT CALLS "TOXIC WASTE DUMPS ON WHEELS."
AND NOW YOU WANT TO USE SOME FANCY SPACE ICE TO PROFIT OFF THE EFFECTS OF GLOBAL WARMING WHILE SIMULTANEOUSLY DOING EVERYTHING IN YOUR POWER TO PERPETUATE ITS CAUSE.
YOU, MR. AGGER, ARE A REAL PIECE OF WORK. BUT I WON'T LET YOU GET AWAY WITH IT. NONE OF IT.
YOU ARE GROSSLY MISINFORMED, AGENT SOLOMON.
OUR MOBILE FACTORIES AREN'T ON WHEELS.
THEY FLY.
AND ALL WE ARE TRYING TO DO IS GIVE THE PEOPLE OF TODAY WHAT THEY NEED TO SURVIVE TOMORROW.
KRAKA
KOOM
ROXXON IS THE WORLD'S WEALTHIEST AND MOST POWERFUL SUPER-CORPORATION. IF WE DON'T KNOW WHAT'S BEST FOR THE PEOPLE OF THIS PLANET, THEN I ASK YOU, DEAR LADY...
WHO DOES?

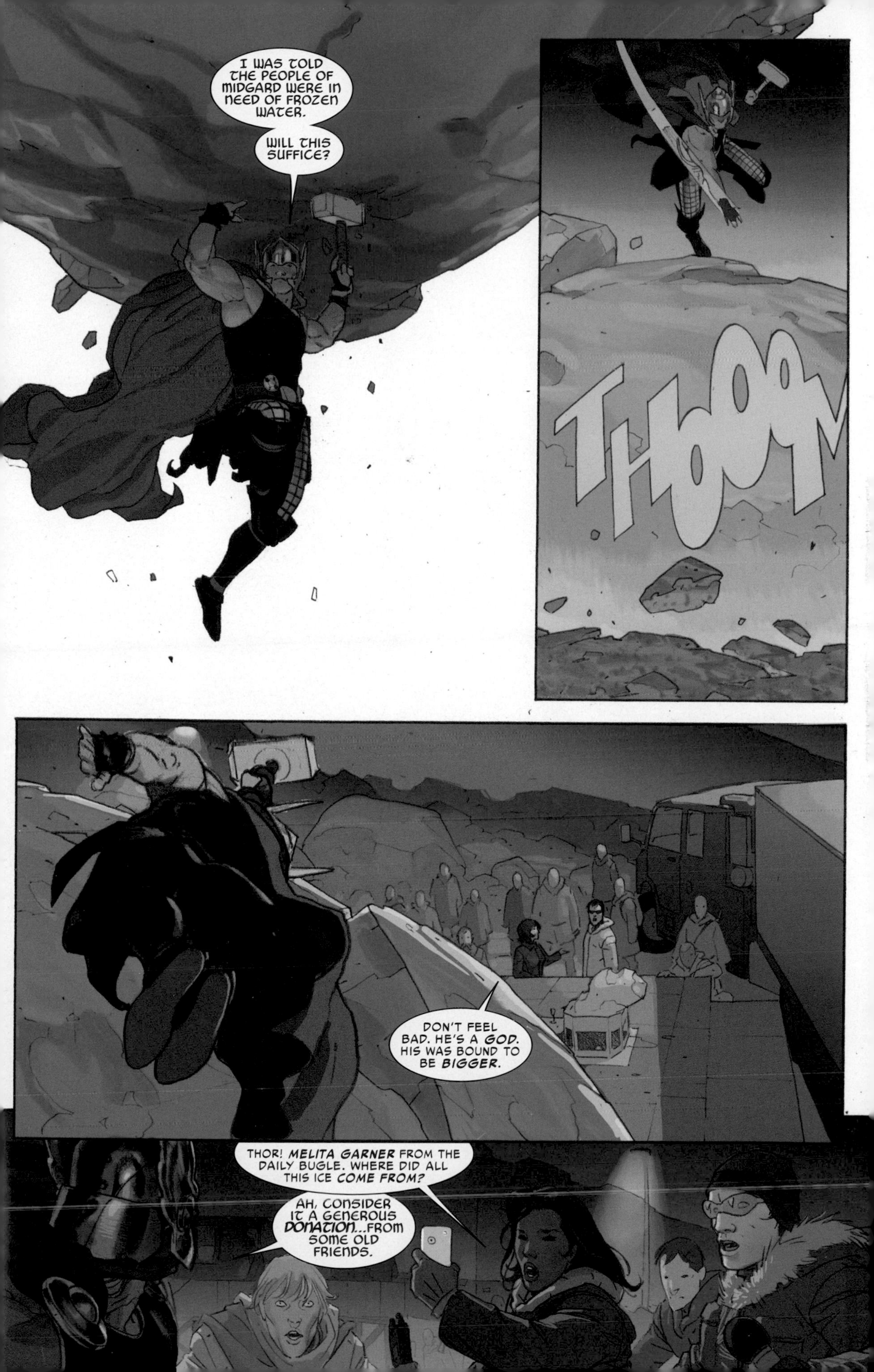
I WAS TOLD THE PEOPLE OF MIDGARD WERE IN NEED OF FROZEN WATER.
WILL THIS SUFFICE?
THOOM
DON'T FEEL BAD. HE'S A *GOD*. HIS WAS BOUND TO BE *BIGGER*.
THOR! *MELITA GARNER* FROM THE DAILY BUGLE. WHERE DID ALL THIS ICE *COME FROM?*
AH, CONSIDER IT A GENEROUS ***DONATION***...FROM SOME OLD FRIENDS.

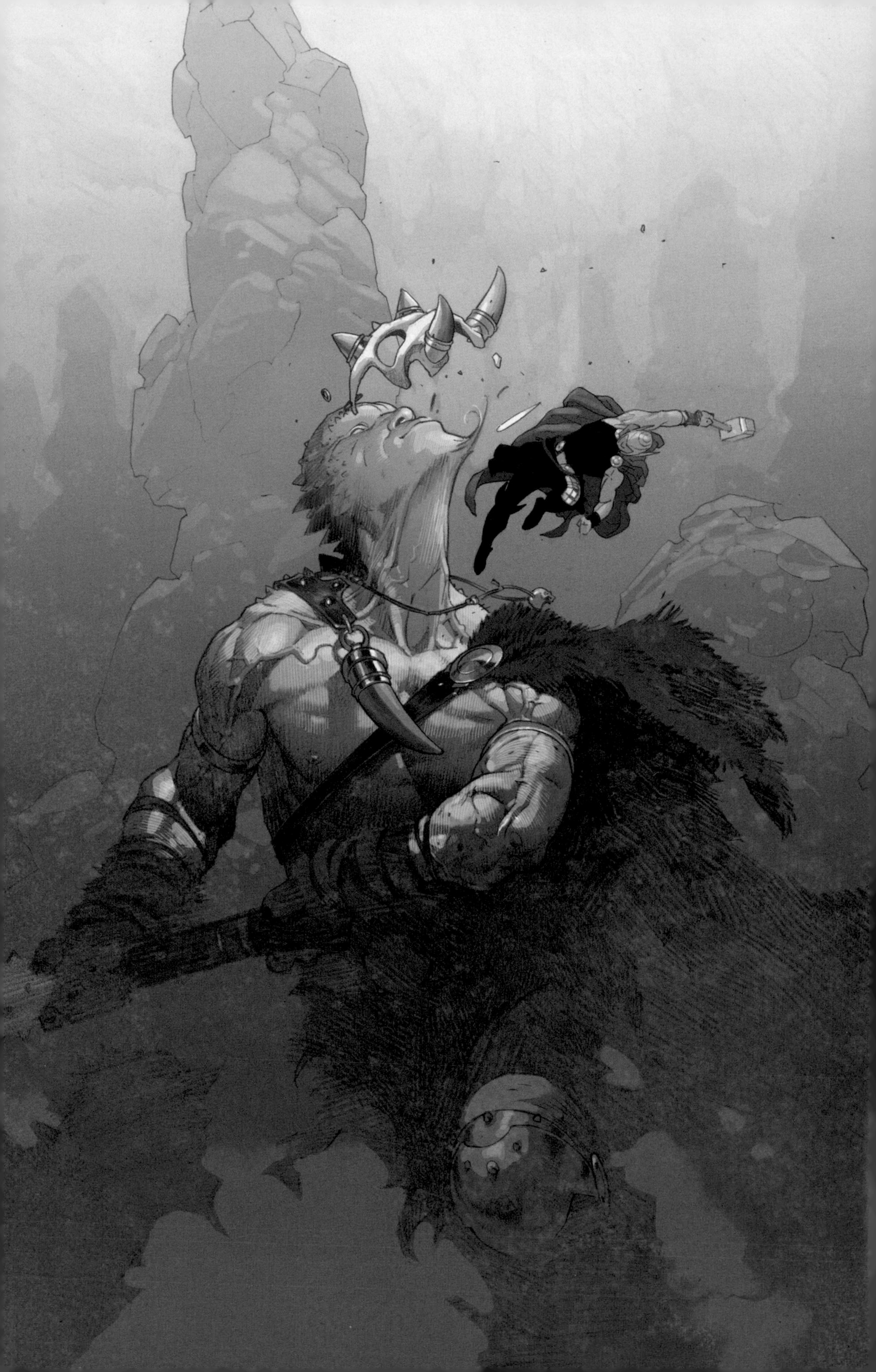

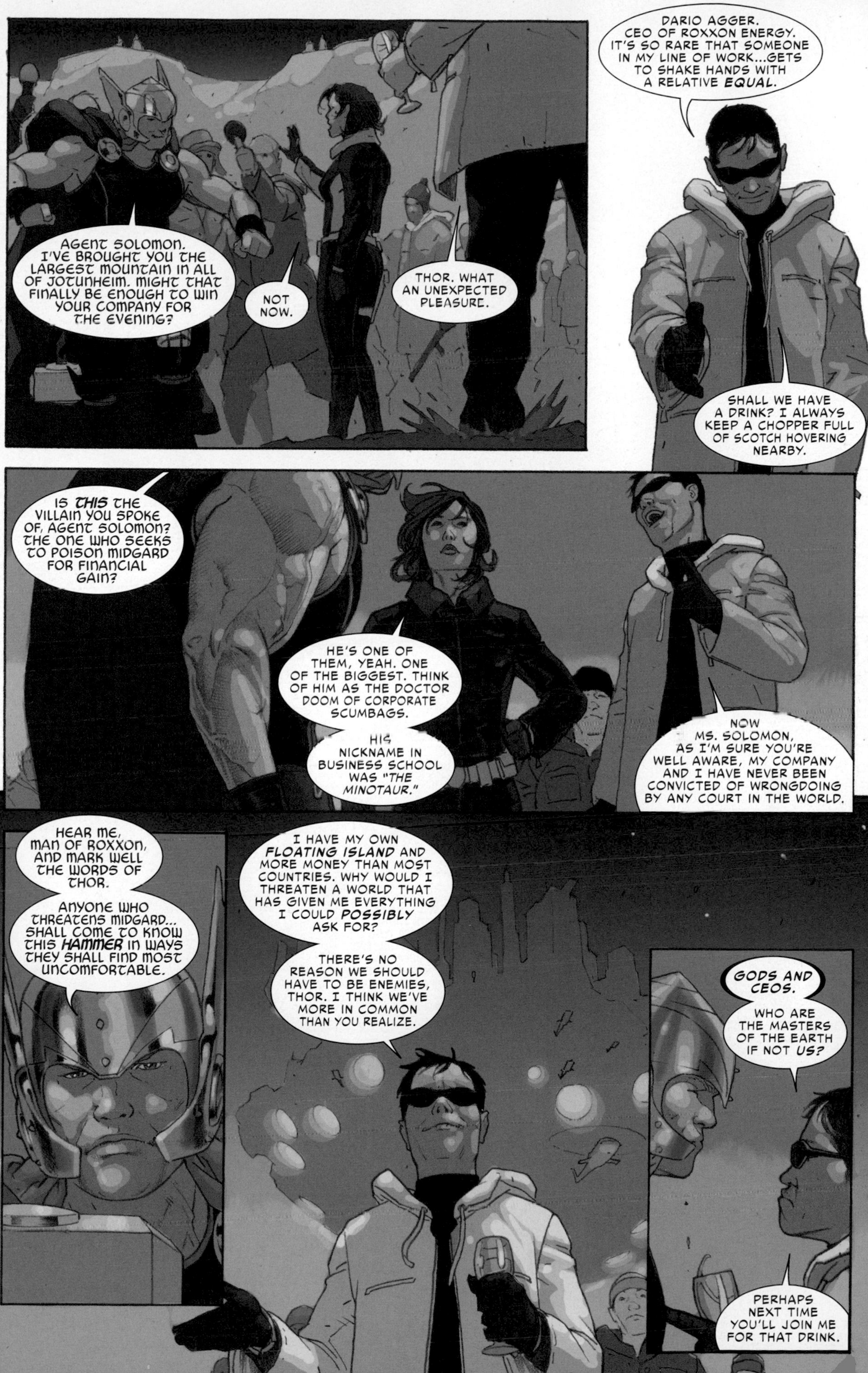
AGENT SOLOMON. I'VE BROUGHT YOU THE LARGEST MOUNTAIN IN ALL OF JOTUNHEIM. MIGHT THAT FINALLY BE ENOUGH TO WIN YOUR COMPANY FOR THE EVENING?
NOT NOW.
THOR. WHAT AN UNEXPECTED PLEASURE.
DARIO AGGER. CEO OF ROXXON ENERGY. IT'S SO RARE THAT SOMEONE IN MY LINE OF WORK...GETS TO SHAKE HANDS WITH A RELATIVE EQUAL.
SHALL WE HAVE A DRINK? I ALWAYS KEEP A CHOPPER FULL OF SCOTCH HOVERING NEARBY.
IS THIS THE VILLAIN YOU SPOKE OF, AGENT SOLOMON? THE ONE WHO SEEKS TO POISON MIDGARD FOR FINANCIAL GAIN?
HE'S ONE OF THEM, YEAH. ONE OF THE BIGGEST. THINK OF HIM AS THE DOCTOR DOOM OF CORPORATE SCUMBAGS.
HIS NICKNAME IN BUSINESS SCHOOL WAS "THE MINOTAUR."
NOW MS. SOLOMON, AS I'M SURE YOU'RE WELL AWARE, MY COMPANY AND I HAVE NEVER BEEN CONVICTED OF WRONGDOING BY ANY COURT IN THE WORLD.
HEAR ME, MAN OF ROXXON, AND MARK WELL THE WORDS OF THOR.
ANYONE WHO THREATENS MIDGARD... SHALL COME TO KNOW THIS HAMMER IN WAYS THEY SHALL FIND MOST UNCOMFORTABLE.
I HAVE MY OWN FLOATING ISLAND AND MORE MONEY THAN MOST COUNTRIES. WHY WOULD I THREATEN A WORLD THAT HAS GIVEN ME EVERYTHING I COULD POSSIBLY ASK FOR?
THERE'S NO REASON WE SHOULD HAVE TO BE ENEMIES, THOR. I THINK WE'VE MORE IN COMMON THAN YOU REALIZE.
GODS AND CEOS.
WHO ARE THE MASTERS OF THE EARTH IF NOT US?
PERHAPS NEXT TIME YOU'LL JOIN ME FOR THAT DRINK.

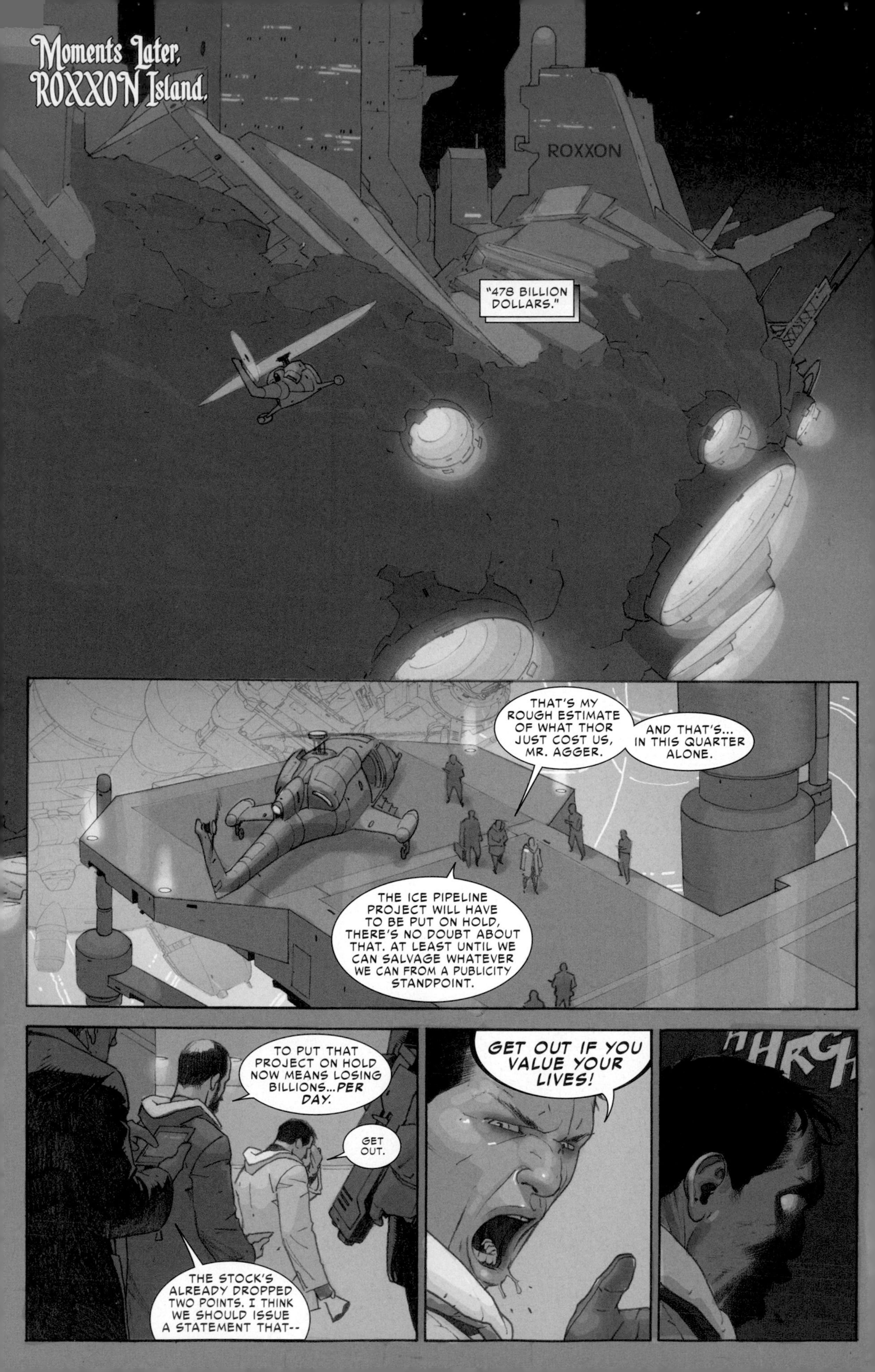
Moments Later, ROXXON Island.
ROXXON
"478 BILLION DOLLARS."
THAT'S MY ROUGH ESTIMATE OF WHAT THOR JUST COST US, MR. AGGER.
AND THAT'S... IN THIS QUARTER ALONE.
THE ICE PIPELINE PROJECT WILL HAVE TO BE PUT ON HOLD, THERE'S NO DOUBT ABOUT THAT. AT LEAST UNTIL WE CAN SALVAGE WHATEVER WE CAN FROM A PUBLICITY STANDPOINT.
TO PUT THAT PROJECT ON HOLD NOW MEANS LOSING BILLIONS...PER DAY.
GET OUT.
THE STOCK'S ALREADY DROPPED TWO POINTS. I THINK WE SHOULD ISSUE A STATEMENT THAT--
GET OUT IF YOU VALUE YOUR LIVES!

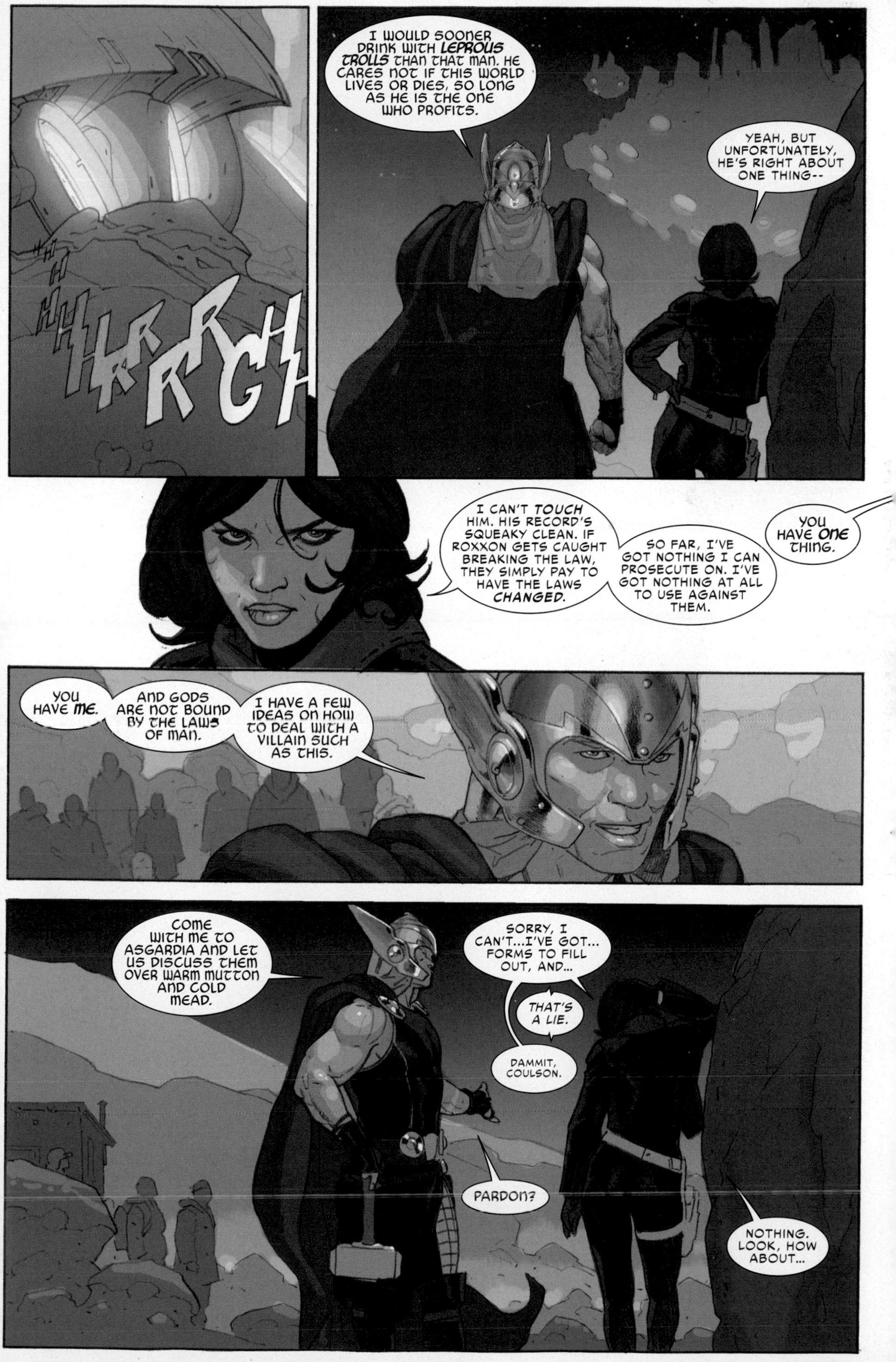
HHHHRRRRRGH
I WOULD SOONER DRINK WITH LEPROUS TROLLS THAN THAT MAN. HE CARES NOT IF THIS WORLD LIVES OR DIES, SO LONG AS HE IS THE ONE WHO PROFITS.
YEAH, BUT UNFORTUNATELY, HE'S RIGHT ABOUT ONE THING--
I CAN'T TOUCH HIM. HIS RECORD'S SQUEAKY CLEAN. IF ROXXON GETS CAUGHT BREAKING THE LAW, THEY SIMPLY PAY TO HAVE THE LAWS CHANGED.
SO FAR, I'VE GOT NOTHING I CAN PROSECUTE ON. I'VE GOT NOTHING AT ALL TO USE AGAINST THEM.
YOU HAVE ONE THING.
YOU HAVE ME.
AND GODS ARE NOT BOUND BY THE LAWS OF MAN.
I HAVE A FEW IDEAS ON HOW TO DEAL WITH A VILLAIN SUCH AS THIS.
COME WITH ME TO ASGARDIA AND LET US DISCUSS THEM OVER WARM MUTTON AND COLD MEAD.
SORRY, I CAN'T...I'VE GOT... FORMS TO FILL OUT, AND...
THAT'S A LIE.
DAMMIT, COULSON.
PARDON?
NOTHING. LOOK, HOW ABOUT...

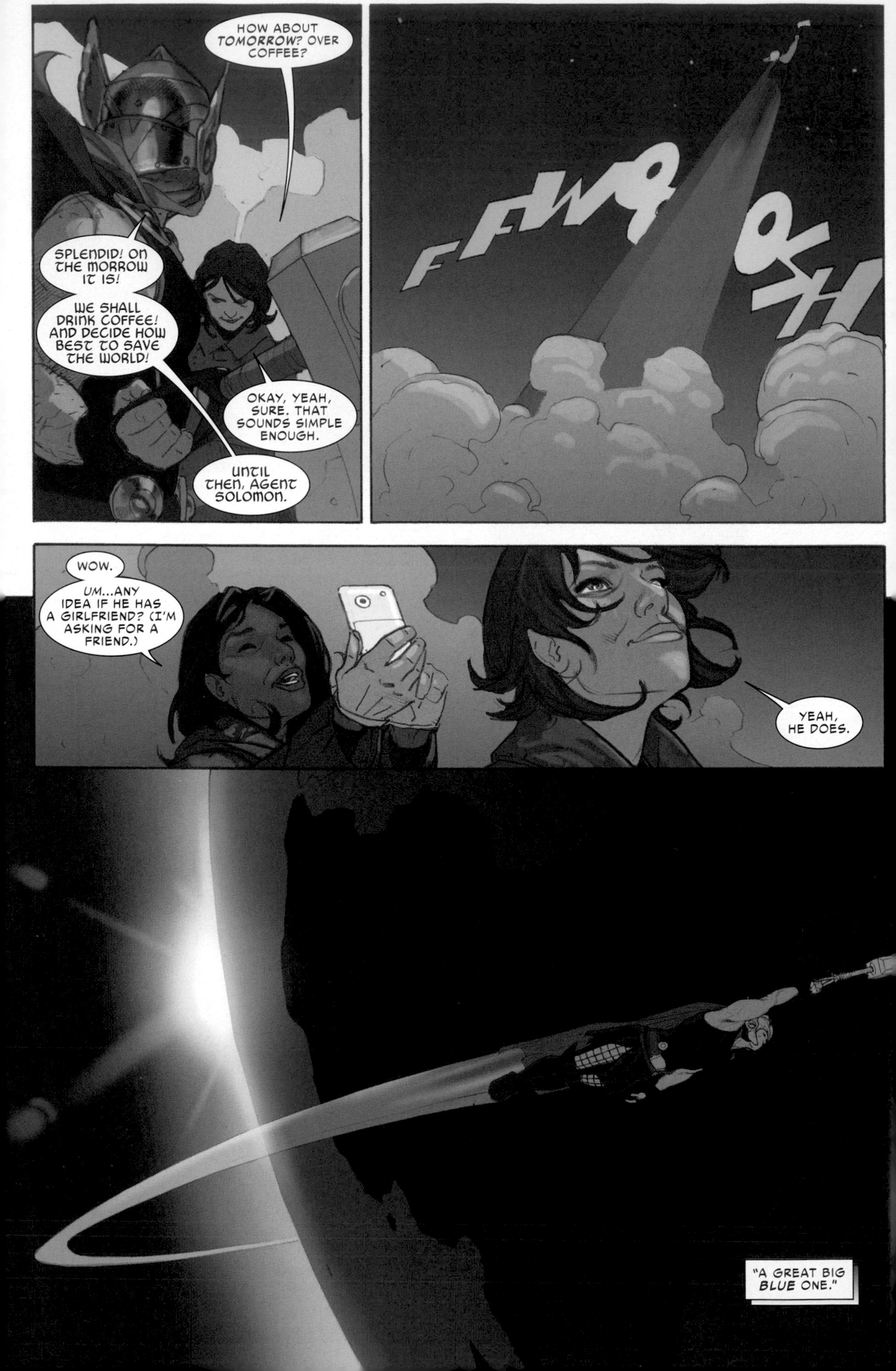
HOW ABOUT TOMORROW? OVER COFFEE?
SPLENDID! ON THE MORROW IT IS!
WE SHALL DRINK COFFEE! AND DECIDE HOW BEST TO SAVE THE WORLD!
OKAY, YEAH, SURE. THAT SOUNDS SIMPLE ENOUGH.
UNTIL THEN, AGENT SOLOMON.
FFWOOOH
WOW.
UM...ANY IDEA IF HE HAS A GIRLFRIEND? (I'M ASKING FOR A FRIEND.)
YEAH, HE DOES.
"A GREAT BIG BLUE ONE."

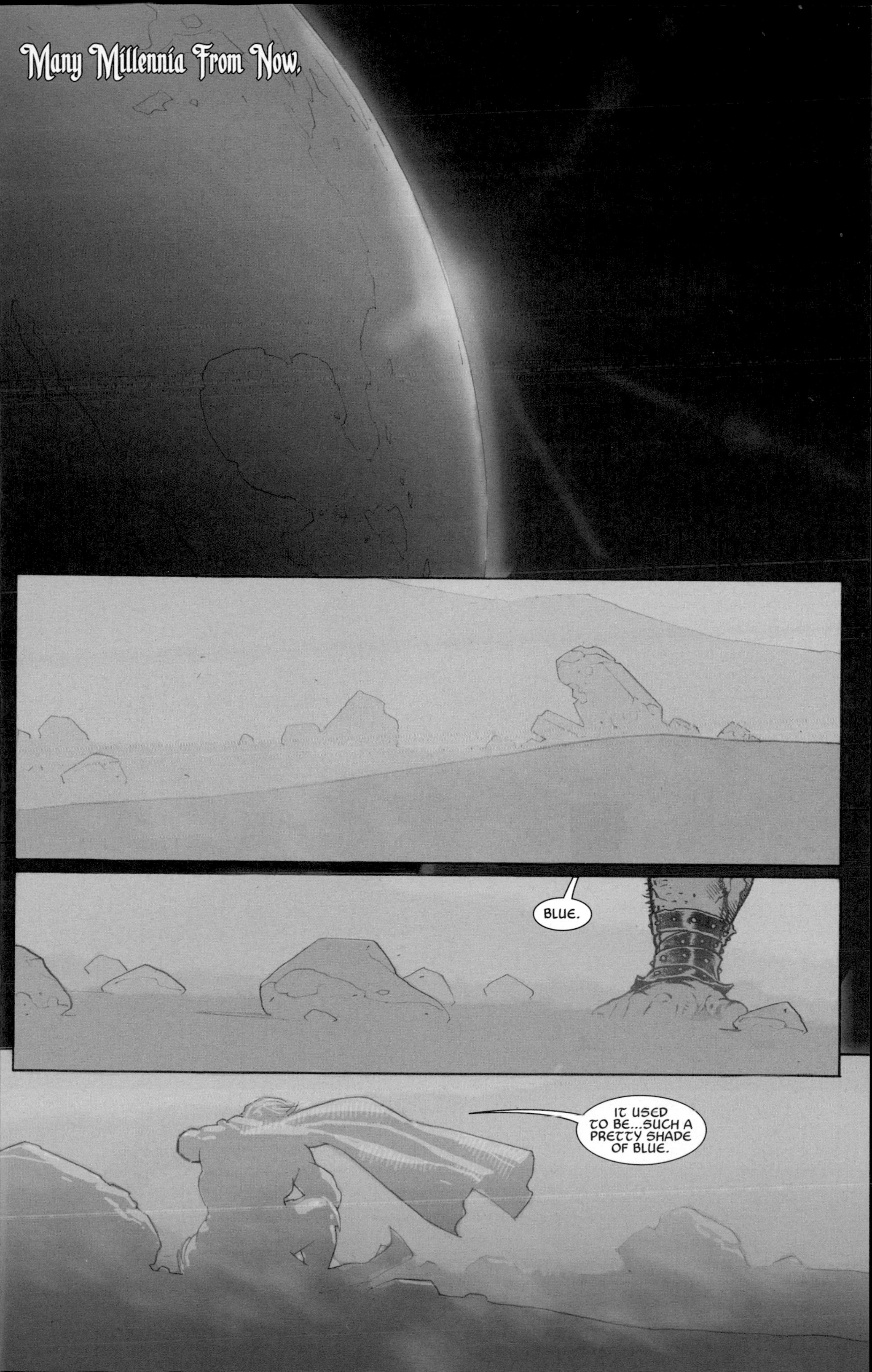
Many Millennia From Now,
BLUE.
IT USED TO BE...SUCH A PRETTY SHADE OF BLUE.

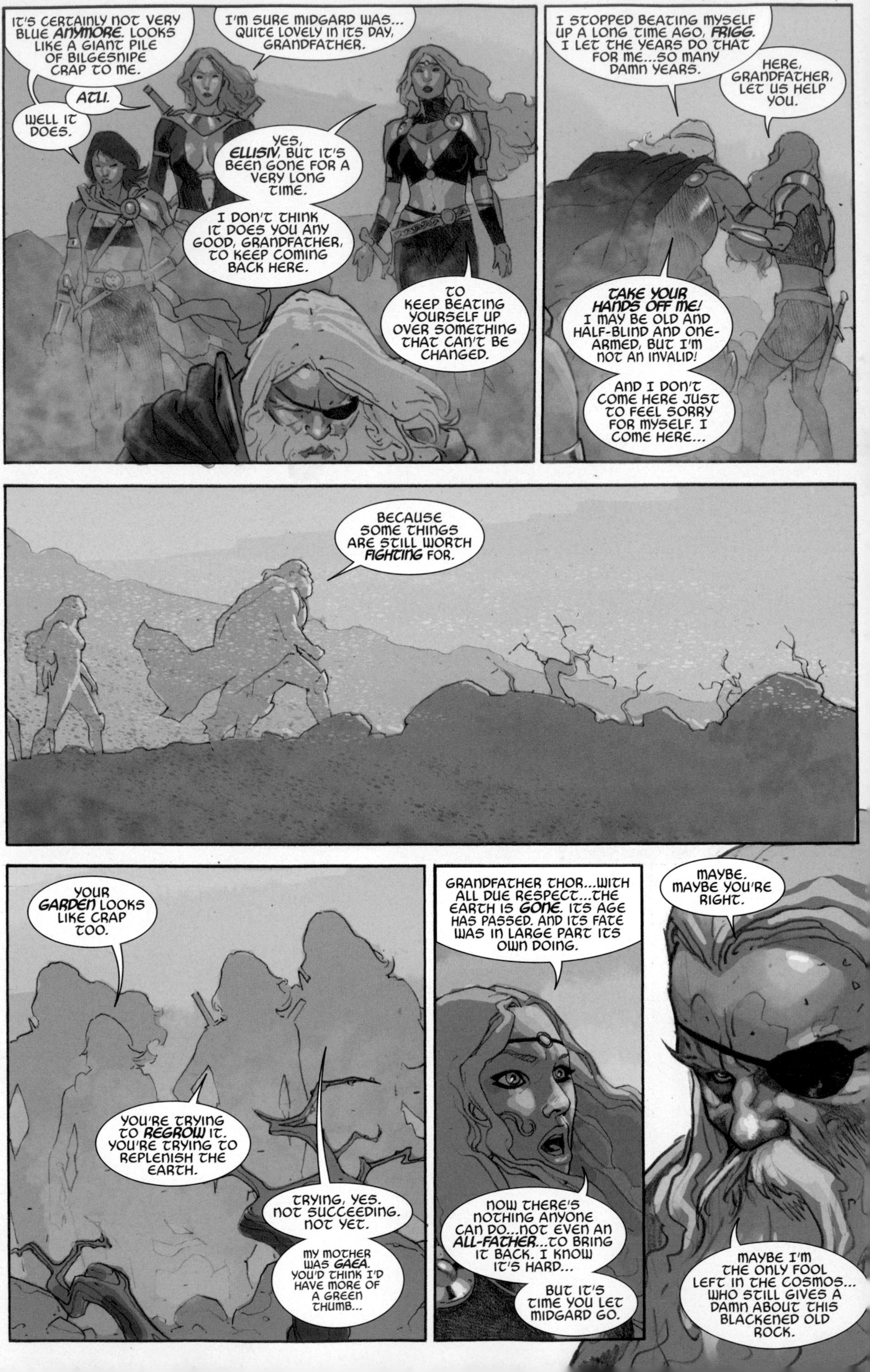
IT'S CERTAINLY NOT VERY BLUE ANYMORE. LOOKS LIKE A GIANT PILE OF BILGESNIPE CRAP TO ME.
I'M SURE MIDGARD WAS... QUITE LOVELY IN ITS DAY, GRANDFATHER.
ATLI.
WELL IT DOES.
YES, ELLISIV, BUT IT'S BEEN GONE FOR A VERY LONG TIME.
I DON'T THINK IT DOES YOU ANY GOOD, GRANDFATHER, TO KEEP COMING BACK HERE.
TO KEEP BEATING YOURSELF UP OVER SOMETHING THAT CAN'T BE CHANGED.
I STOPPED BEATING MYSELF UP A LONG TIME AGO, FRIGG. I LET THE YEARS DO THAT FOR ME...SO MANY DAMN YEARS.
HERE, GRANDFATHER, LET US HELP YOU.
TAKE YOUR HANDS OFF ME! I MAY BE OLD AND HALF-BLIND AND ONE-ARMED, BUT I'M NOT AN INVALID!
AND I DON'T COME HERE JUST TO FEEL SORRY FOR MYSELF. I COME HERE...
BECAUSE SOME THINGS ARE STILL WORTH FIGHTING FOR.
YOUR GARDEN LOOKS LIKE CRAP TOO.
YOU'RE TRYING TO REGROW IT. YOU'RE TRYING TO REPLENISH THE EARTH.
TRYING, YES. NOT SUCCEEDING. NOT YET.
MY MOTHER WAS GAEA. YOU'D THINK I'D HAVE MORE OF A GREEN THUMB...
GRANDFATHER THOR...WITH ALL DUE RESPECT...THE EARTH IS GONE. ITS AGE HAS PASSED. AND ITS FATE WAS IN LARGE PART ITS OWN DOING.
NOW THERE'S NOTHING ANYONE CAN DO...NOT EVEN AN ALL-FATHER...TO BRING IT BACK. I KNOW IT'S HARD...
BUT IT'S TIME YOU LET MIDGARD GO.
MAYBE. MAYBE YOU'RE RIGHT.
MAYBE I'M THE ONLY FOOL LEFT IN THE COSMOS... WHO STILL GIVES A DAMN ABOUT THIS BLACKENED OLD ROCK.

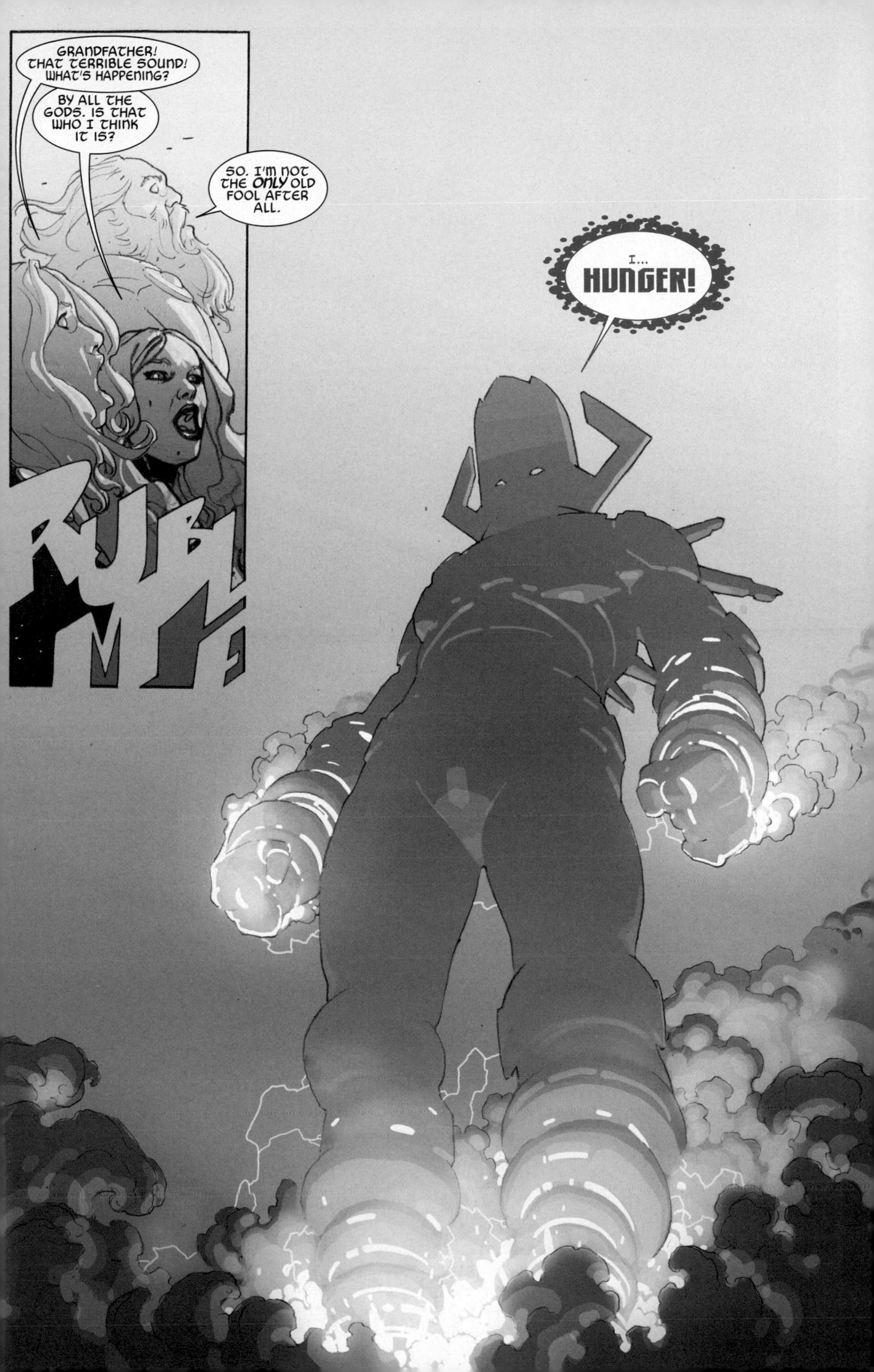
GRANDFATHER! THAT TERRIBLE SOUND! WHAT'S HAPPENING?
BY ALL THE GODS. IS THAT WHO I THINK IT IS?
SO. I'M NOT THE ONLY OLD FOOL AFTER ALL.
I... HUNGER!

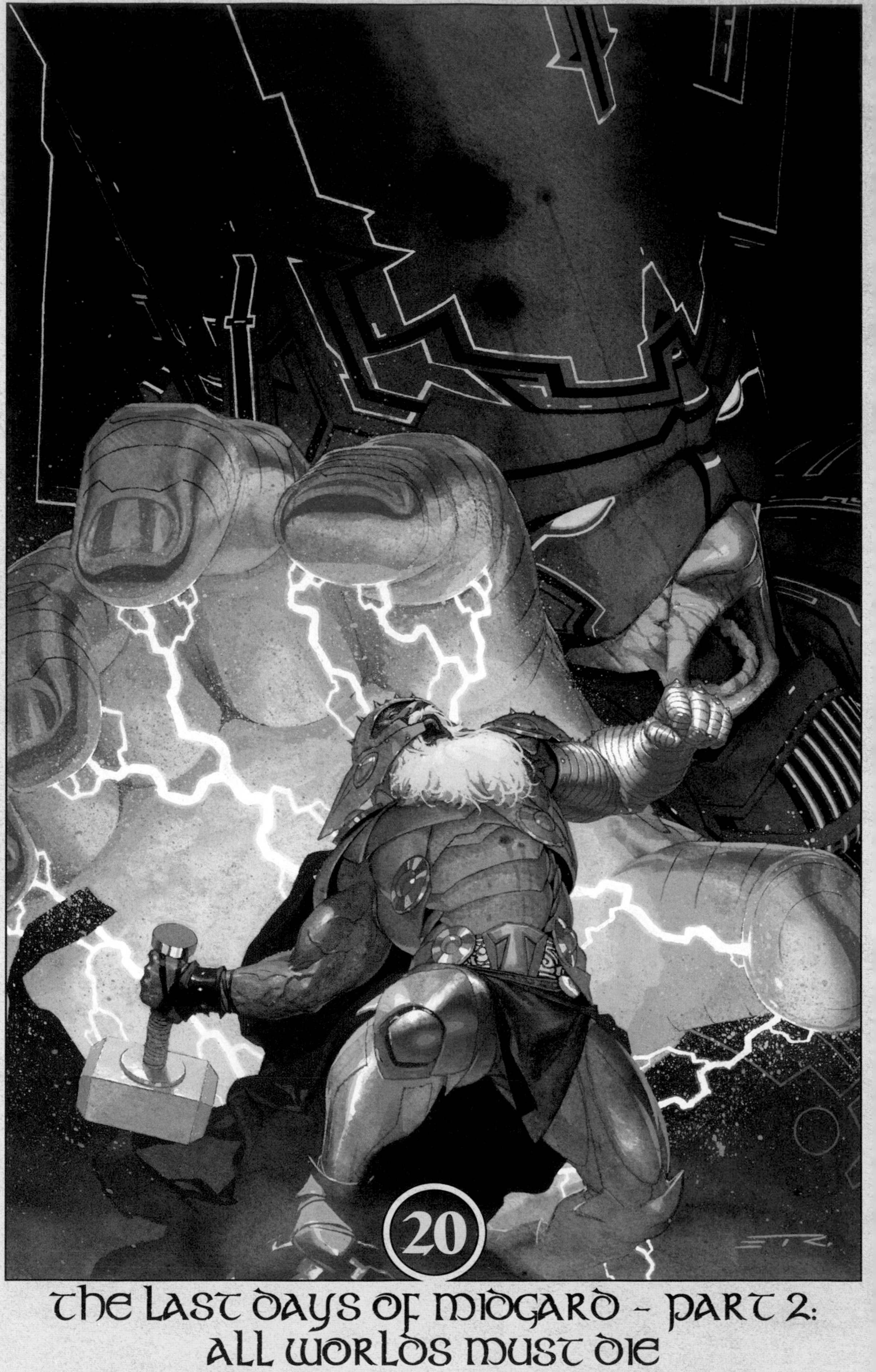
20

THE LAST DAYS OF MIDGARD – PART 2:
ALL WORLDS MUST DIE

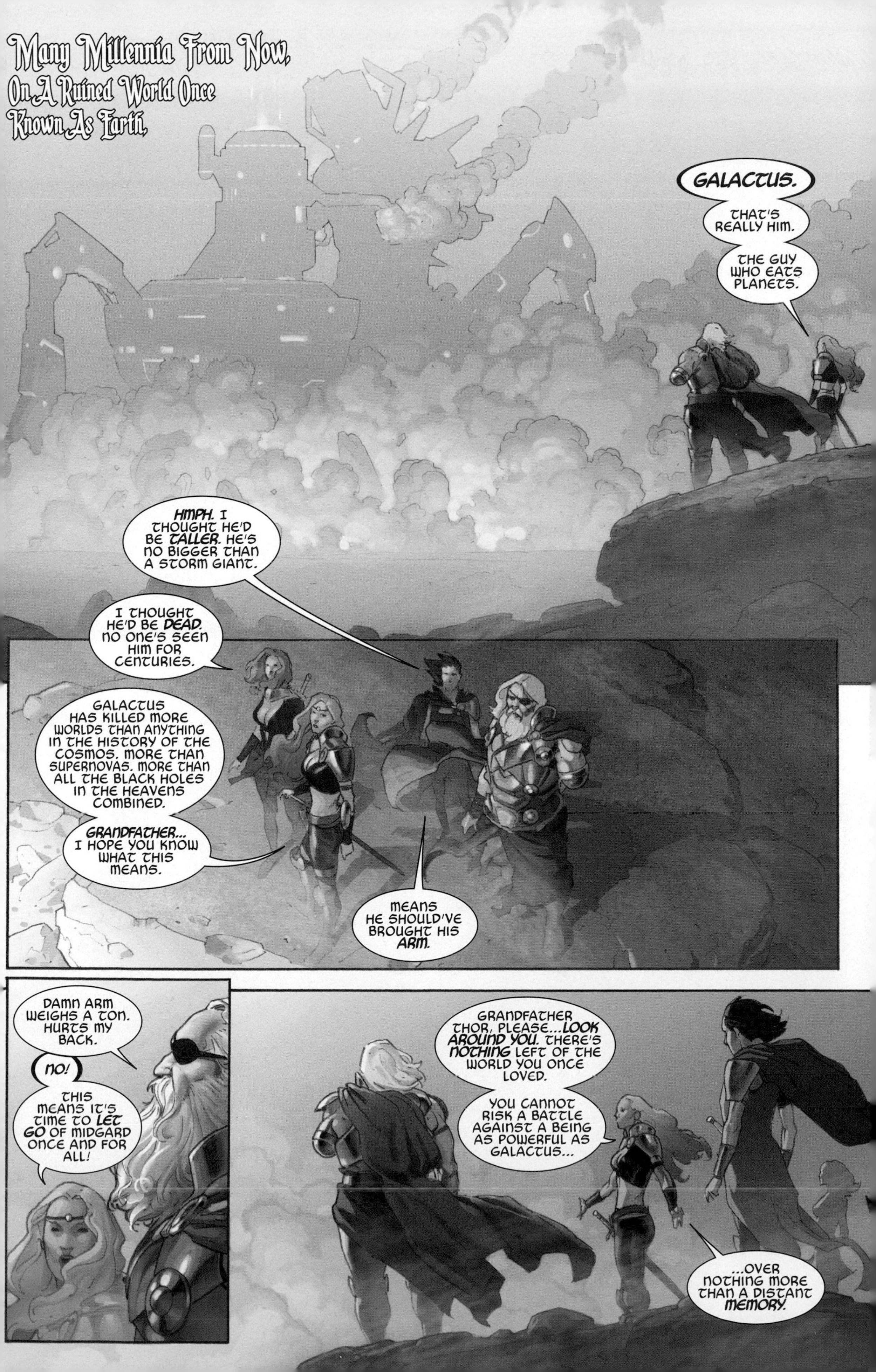
Many Millennia From Now, On A Ruined World Once Known As Earth,
GALACTUS.
THAT'S REALLY HIM.
THE GUY WHO EATS PLANETS.
HMPH. I THOUGHT HE'D BE TALLER. HE'S NO BIGGER THAN A STORM GIANT.
I THOUGHT HE'D BE DEAD. NO ONE'S SEEN HIM FOR CENTURIES.
GALACTUS HAS KILLED MORE WORLDS THAN ANYTHING IN THE HISTORY OF THE COSMOS. MORE THAN SUPERNOVAS. MORE THAN ALL THE BLACK HOLES IN THE HEAVENS COMBINED.
GRANDFATHER... I HOPE YOU KNOW WHAT THIS MEANS.
MEANS HE SHOULD'VE BROUGHT HIS ARM.
DAMN ARM WEIGHS A TON. HURTS MY BACK.
NO!
THIS MEANS IT'S TIME TO LET GO OF MIDGARD ONCE AND FOR ALL!
GRANDFATHER THOR, PLEASE...LOOK AROUND YOU. THERE'S NOTHING LEFT OF THE WORLD YOU ONCE LOVED.
YOU CANNOT RISK A BATTLE AGAINST A BEING AS POWERFUL AS GALACTUS...
...OVER NOTHING MORE THAN A DISTANT MEMORY.

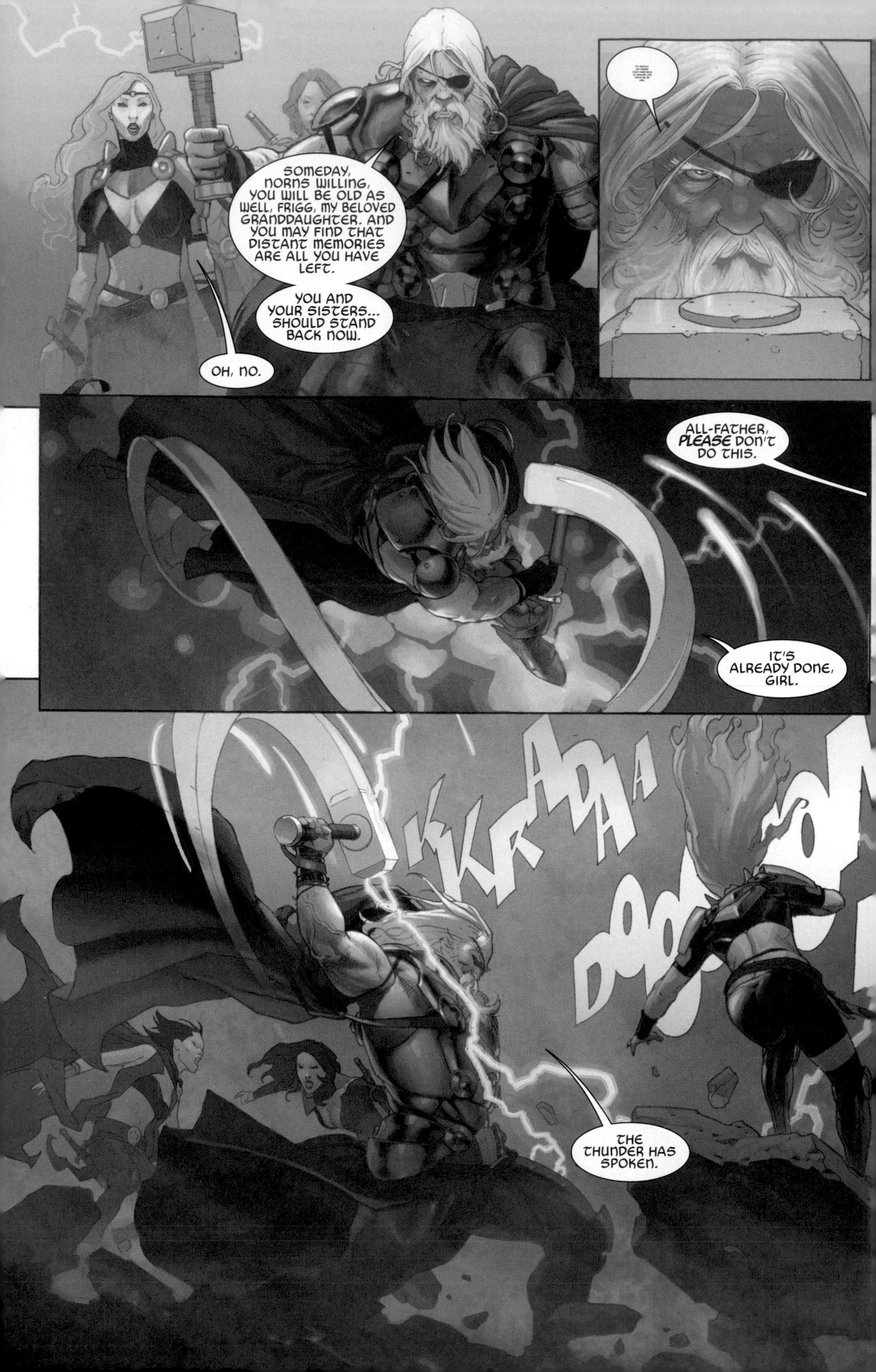
SOMEDAY, NORNS WILLING, YOU WILL BE OLD AS WELL, FRIGG, MY BELOVED GRANDDAUGHTER. AND YOU MAY FIND THAT DISTANT MEMORIES ARE ALL YOU HAVE LEFT.
YOU AND YOUR SISTERS... SHOULD STAND BACK NOW.
OH, NO.
ALL-FATHER, PLEASE DON'T DO THIS.
IT'S ALREADY DONE, GIRL.
KKRADAAA
THE THUNDER HAS SPOKEN.

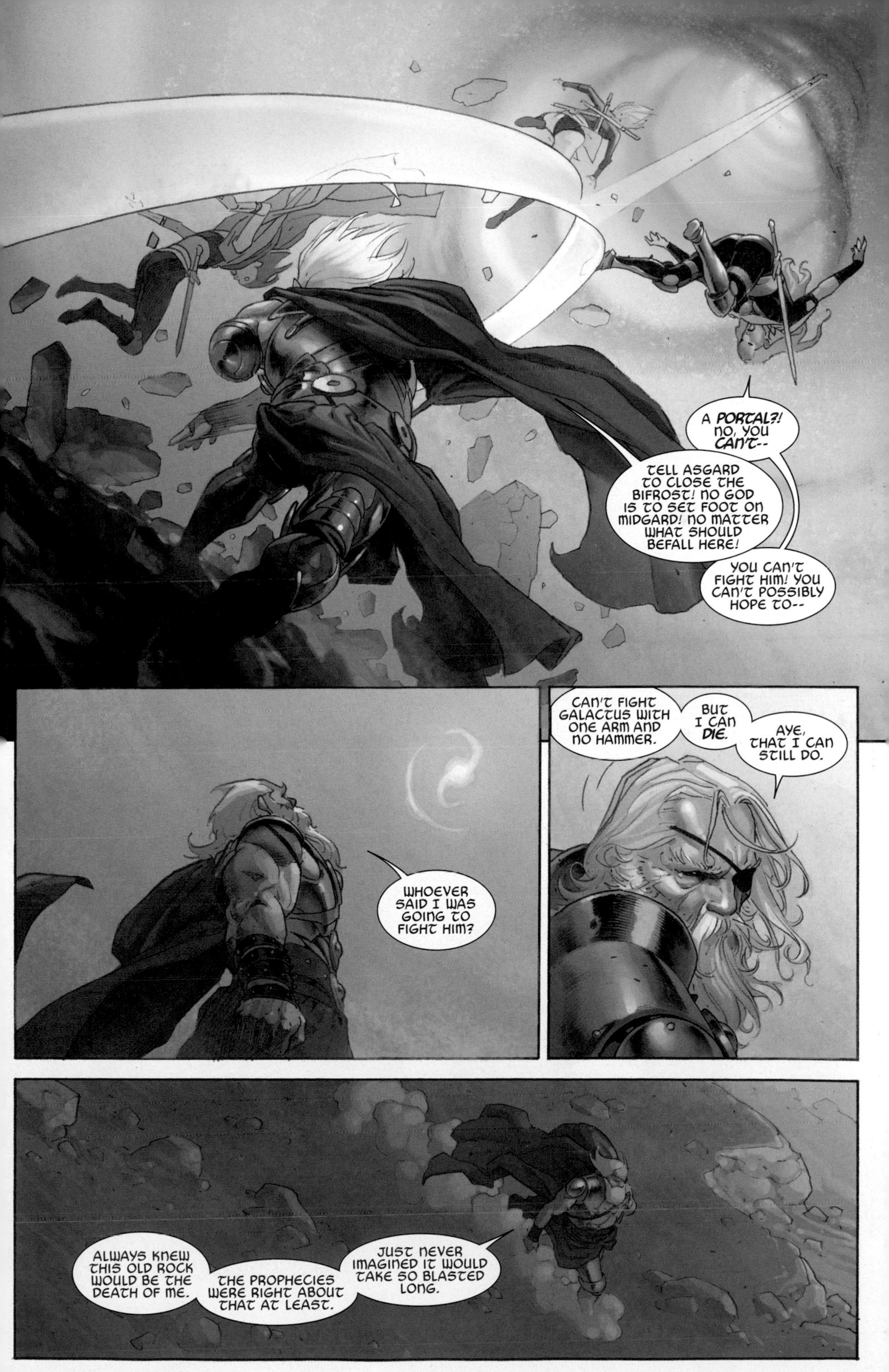
A **PORTAL?!** NO, YOU **CAN'T**--
TELL ASGARD TO CLOSE THE BIFROST! NO GOD IS TO SET FOOT ON MIDGARD! NO MATTER WHAT SHOULD BEFALL HERE!
YOU CAN'T FIGHT HIM! YOU CAN'T POSSIBLY HOPE TO--
WHOEVER SAID I WAS GOING TO FIGHT HIM?
CAN'T FIGHT GALACTUS WITH ONE ARM AND NO HAMMER.
BUT I CAN **DIE**.
AYE, THAT I CAN STILL DO.
ALWAYS KNEW THIS OLD ROCK WOULD BE THE DEATH OF ME.
THE PROPHECIES WERE RIGHT ABOUT THAT AT LEAST.
JUST NEVER IMAGINED IT WOULD TAKE SO BLASTED LONG.

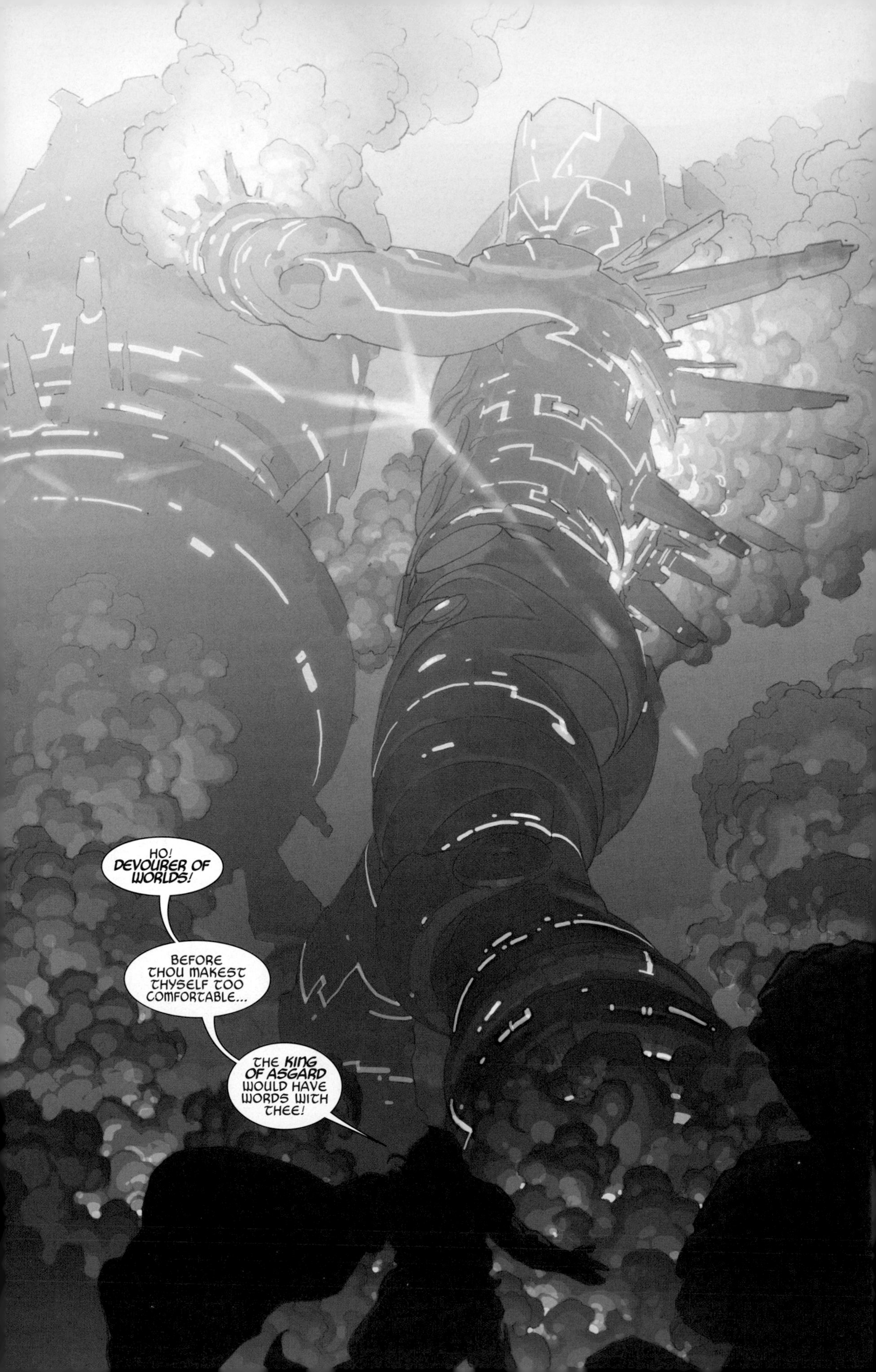
HO! DEVOURER OF WORLDS!
BEFORE THOU MAKEST THYSELF TOO COMFORTABLE...
THE KING OF ASGARD WOULD HAVE WORDS WITH THEE!

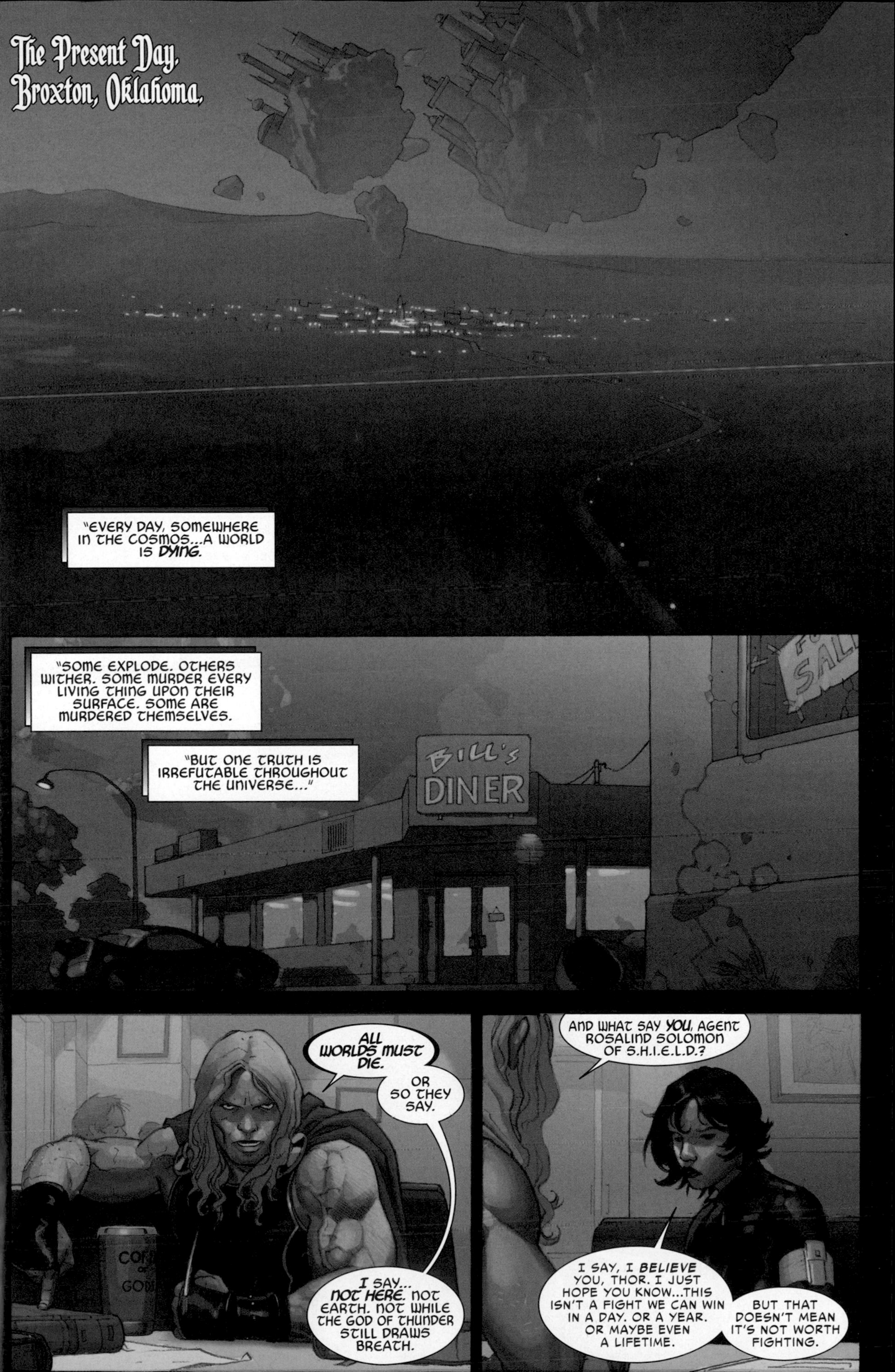
The Present Day, Broxton, Oklahoma,
"EVERY DAY, SOMEWHERE IN THE COSMOS...A WORLD IS DYING.
"SOME EXPLODE. OTHERS WITHER. SOME MURDER EVERY LIVING THING UPON THEIR SURFACE. SOME ARE MURDERED THEMSELVES.
"BUT ONE TRUTH IS IRREFUTABLE THROUGHOUT THE UNIVERSE..."
BILL's DINER
ALL WORLDS MUST DIE.
OR SO THEY SAY.
I SAY... NOT HERE. NOT EARTH. NOT WHILE THE GOD OF THUNDER STILL DRAWS BREATH.
AND WHAT SAY YOU, AGENT ROSALIND SOLOMON OF S.H.I.E.L.D.?
I SAY, I BELIEVE YOU, THOR. I JUST HOPE YOU KNOW...THIS ISN'T A FIGHT WE CAN WIN IN A DAY. OR A YEAR. OR MAYBE EVEN A LIFETIME.
BUT THAT DOESN'T MEAN IT'S NOT WORTH FIGHTING.

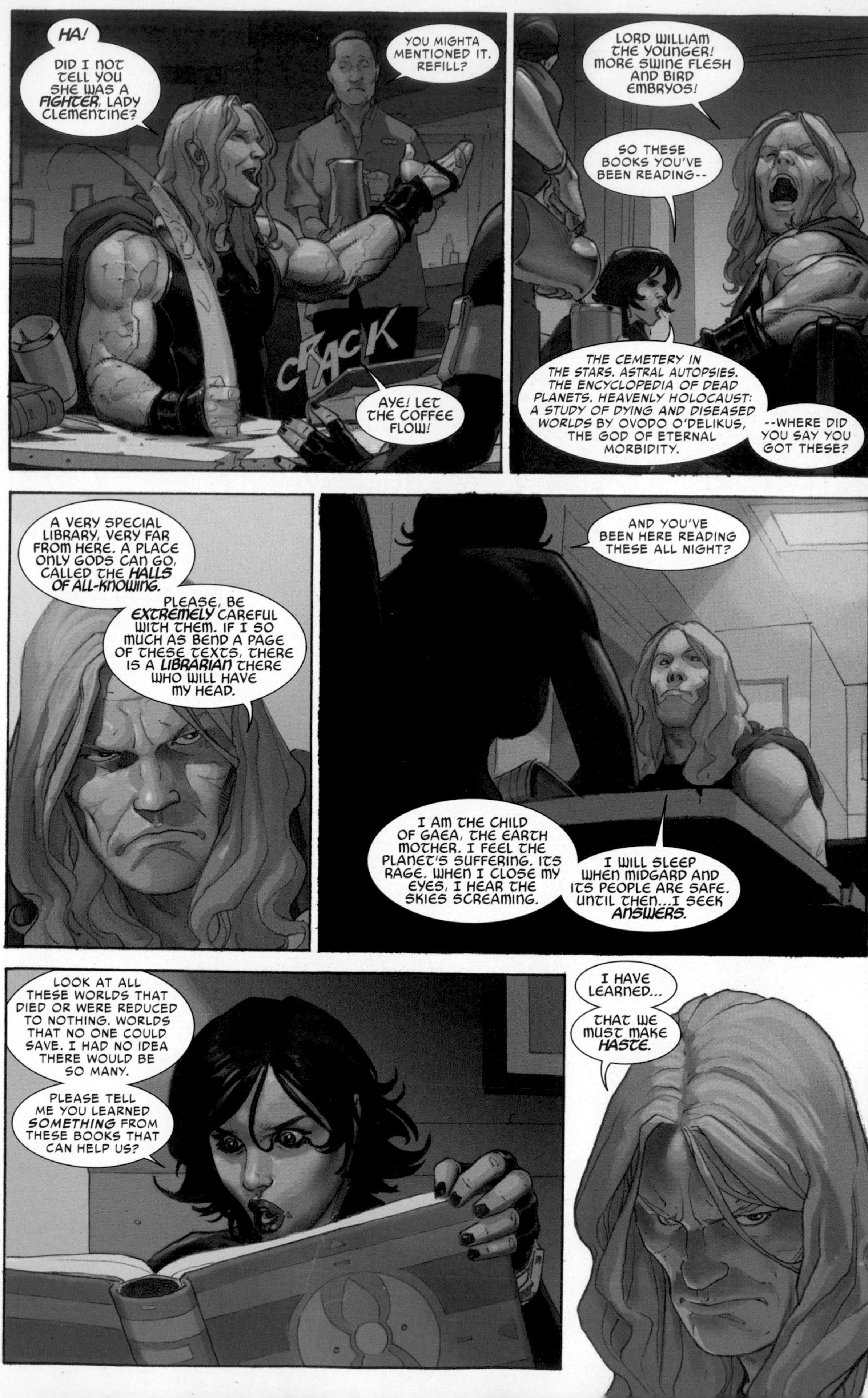

HA!
DID I NOT TELL YOU SHE WAS A FIGHTER, LADY CLEMENTINE?
YOU MIGHTA MENTIONED IT. REFILL?
CRACK
AYE! LET THE COFFEE FLOW!
LORD WILLIAM THE YOUNGER! MORE SWINE FLESH AND BIRD EMBRYOS!
SO THESE BOOKS YOU'VE BEEN READING--
THE CEMETERY IN THE STARS. ASTRAL AUTOPSIES. THE ENCYCLOPEDIA OF DEAD PLANETS. HEAVENLY HOLOCAUST: A STUDY OF DYING AND DISEASED WORLDS BY OVODO O'DELIKUS, THE GOD OF ETERNAL MORBIDITY.
--WHERE DID YOU SAY YOU GOT THESE?
A VERY SPECIAL LIBRARY, VERY FAR FROM HERE. A PLACE ONLY GODS CAN GO, CALLED THE HALLS OF ALL-KNOWING.
PLEASE, BE EXTREMELY CAREFUL WITH THEM. IF I SO MUCH AS BEND A PAGE OF THESE TEXTS, THERE IS A LIBRARIAN THERE WHO WILL HAVE MY HEAD.
AND YOU'VE BEEN HERE READING THESE ALL NIGHT?
I AM THE CHILD OF GAEA, THE EARTH MOTHER. I FEEL THE PLANET'S SUFFERING. ITS RAGE. WHEN I CLOSE MY EYES, I HEAR THE SKIES SCREAMING.
I WILL SLEEP WHEN MIDGARD AND ITS PEOPLE ARE SAFE. UNTIL THEN...I SEEK ANSWERS.
LOOK AT ALL THESE WORLDS THAT DIED OR WERE REDUCED TO NOTHING. WORLDS THAT NO ONE COULD SAVE. I HAD NO IDEA THERE WOULD BE SO MANY.
PLEASE TELL ME YOU LEARNED SOMETHING FROM THESE BOOKS THAT CAN HELP US?
I HAVE LEARNED...
THAT WE MUST MAKE HASTE.

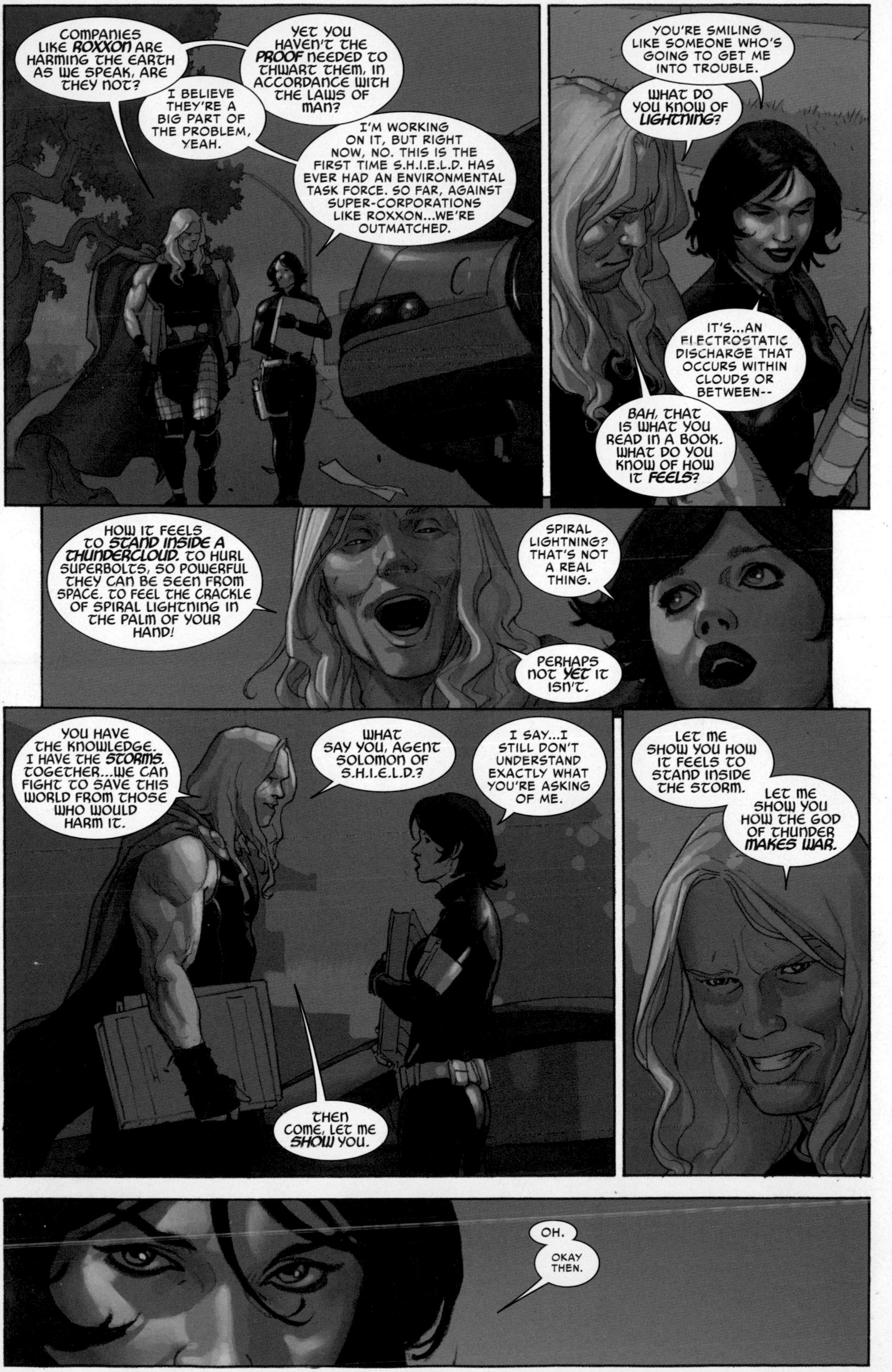
COMPANIES LIKE ROXXON ARE HARMING THE EARTH AS WE SPEAK, ARE THEY NOT?
I BELIEVE THEY'RE A BIG PART OF THE PROBLEM, YEAH.
YET YOU HAVEN'T THE PROOF NEEDED TO THWART THEM, IN ACCORDANCE WITH THE LAWS OF MAN?
I'M WORKING ON IT, BUT RIGHT NOW, NO. THIS IS THE FIRST TIME S.H.I.E.L.D. HAS EVER HAD AN ENVIRONMENTAL TASK FORCE. SO FAR, AGAINST SUPER-CORPORATIONS LIKE ROXXON...WE'RE OUTMATCHED.
YOU'RE SMILING LIKE SOMEONE WHO'S GOING TO GET ME INTO TROUBLE.
WHAT DO YOU KNOW OF LIGHTNING?
IT'S...AN ELECTROSTATIC DISCHARGE THAT OCCURS WITHIN CLOUDS OR BETWEEN--
BAH, THAT IS WHAT YOU READ IN A BOOK. WHAT DO YOU KNOW OF HOW IT FEELS?
HOW IT FEELS TO STAND INSIDE A THUNDERCLOUD. TO HURL SUPERBOLTS, SO POWERFUL THEY CAN BE SEEN FROM SPACE. TO FEEL THE CRACKLE OF SPIRAL LIGHTNING IN THE PALM OF YOUR HAND!
SPIRAL LIGHTNING? THAT'S NOT A REAL THING.
PERHAPS NOT YET IT ISN'T.
YOU HAVE THE KNOWLEDGE. I HAVE THE STORMS. TOGETHER...WE CAN FIGHT TO SAVE THIS WORLD FROM THOSE WHO WOULD HARM IT.
WHAT SAY YOU, AGENT SOLOMON OF S.H.I.E.L.D.?
I SAY...I STILL DON'T UNDERSTAND EXACTLY WHAT YOU'RE ASKING OF ME.
THEN COME, LET ME SHOW YOU.
LET ME SHOW YOU HOW IT FEELS TO STAND INSIDE THE STORM.
LET ME SHOW YOU HOW THE GOD OF THUNDER MAKES WAR.
OH.
OKAY THEN.

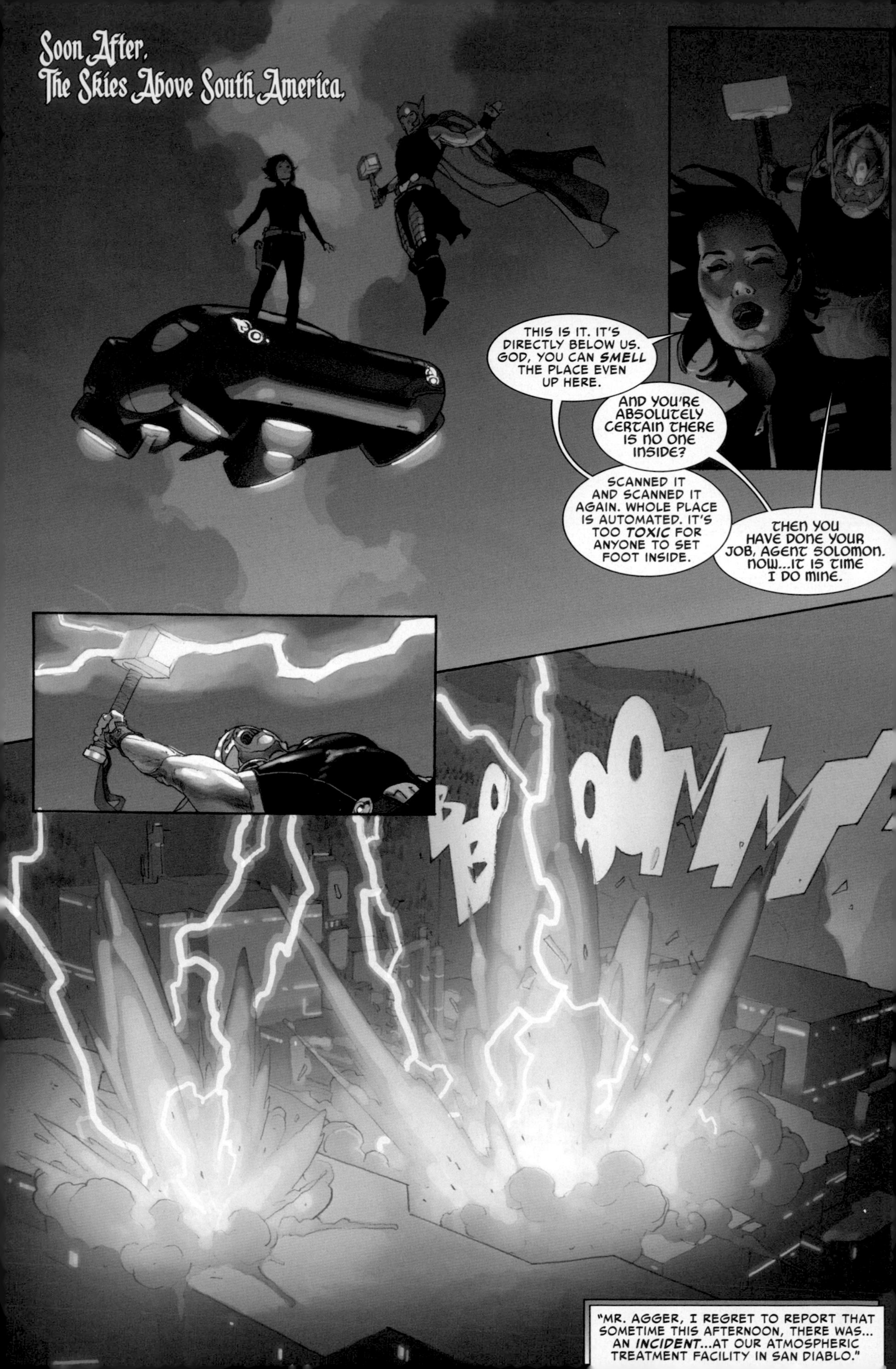
Soon After, The Skies Above South America.
THIS IS IT. IT'S DIRECTLY BELOW US. GOD, YOU CAN SMELL THE PLACE EVEN UP HERE.
AND YOU'RE ABSOLUTELY CERTAIN THERE IS NO ONE INSIDE?
SCANNED IT AND SCANNED IT AGAIN. WHOLE PLACE IS AUTOMATED. IT'S TOO TOXIC FOR ANYONE TO SET FOOT INSIDE.
THEN YOU HAVE DONE YOUR JOB, AGENT SOLOMON. NOW...IT IS TIME I DO MINE.
BOOM
"MR. AGGER, I REGRET TO REPORT THAT SOMETIME THIS AFTERNOON, THERE WAS... AN INCIDENT...AT OUR ATMOSPHERIC TREATMENT FACILITY IN SAN DIABLO."

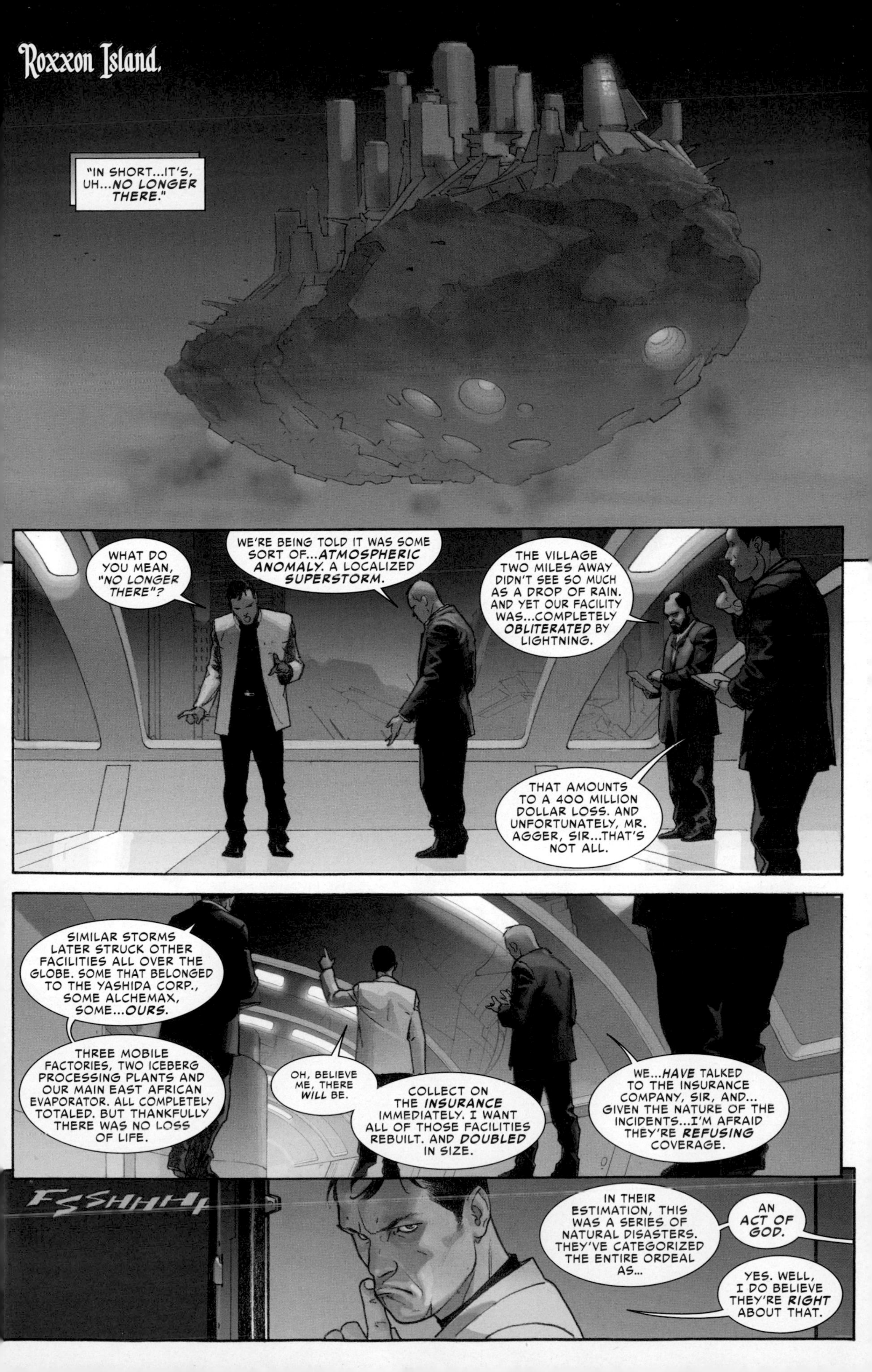
Roxxon Island.
"IN SHORT...IT'S, UH...NO LONGER THERE."
WHAT DO YOU MEAN, "NO LONGER THERE"?
WE'RE BEING TOLD IT WAS SOME SORT OF...ATMOSPHERIC ANOMALY. A LOCALIZED SUPERSTORM.
THE VILLAGE TWO MILES AWAY DIDN'T SEE SO MUCH AS A DROP OF RAIN. AND YET OUR FACILITY WAS...COMPLETELY OBLITERATED BY LIGHTNING.
THAT AMOUNTS TO A 400 MILLION DOLLAR LOSS. AND UNFORTUNATELY, MR. AGGER, SIR...THAT'S NOT ALL.
SIMILAR STORMS LATER STRUCK OTHER FACILITIES ALL OVER THE GLOBE. SOME THAT BELONGED TO THE YASHIDA CORP., SOME ALCHEMAX, SOME...OURS.
THREE MOBILE FACTORIES, TWO ICEBERG PROCESSING PLANTS AND OUR MAIN EAST AFRICAN EVAPORATOR. ALL COMPLETELY TOTALED. BUT THANKFULLY THERE WAS NO LOSS OF LIFE.
OH, BELIEVE ME, THERE WILL BE.
COLLECT ON THE INSURANCE IMMEDIATELY. I WANT ALL OF THOSE FACILITIES REBUILT. AND DOUBLED IN SIZE.
WE...HAVE TALKED TO THE INSURANCE COMPANY, SIR, AND... GIVEN THE NATURE OF THE INCIDENTS...I'M AFRAID THEY'RE REFUSING COVERAGE.
FSSHHHP
IN THEIR ESTIMATION, THIS WAS A SERIES OF NATURAL DISASTERS. THEY'VE CATEGORIZED THE ENTIRE ORDEAL AS...
AN ACT OF GOD.
YES. WELL, I DO BELIEVE THEY'RE RIGHT ABOUT THAT.

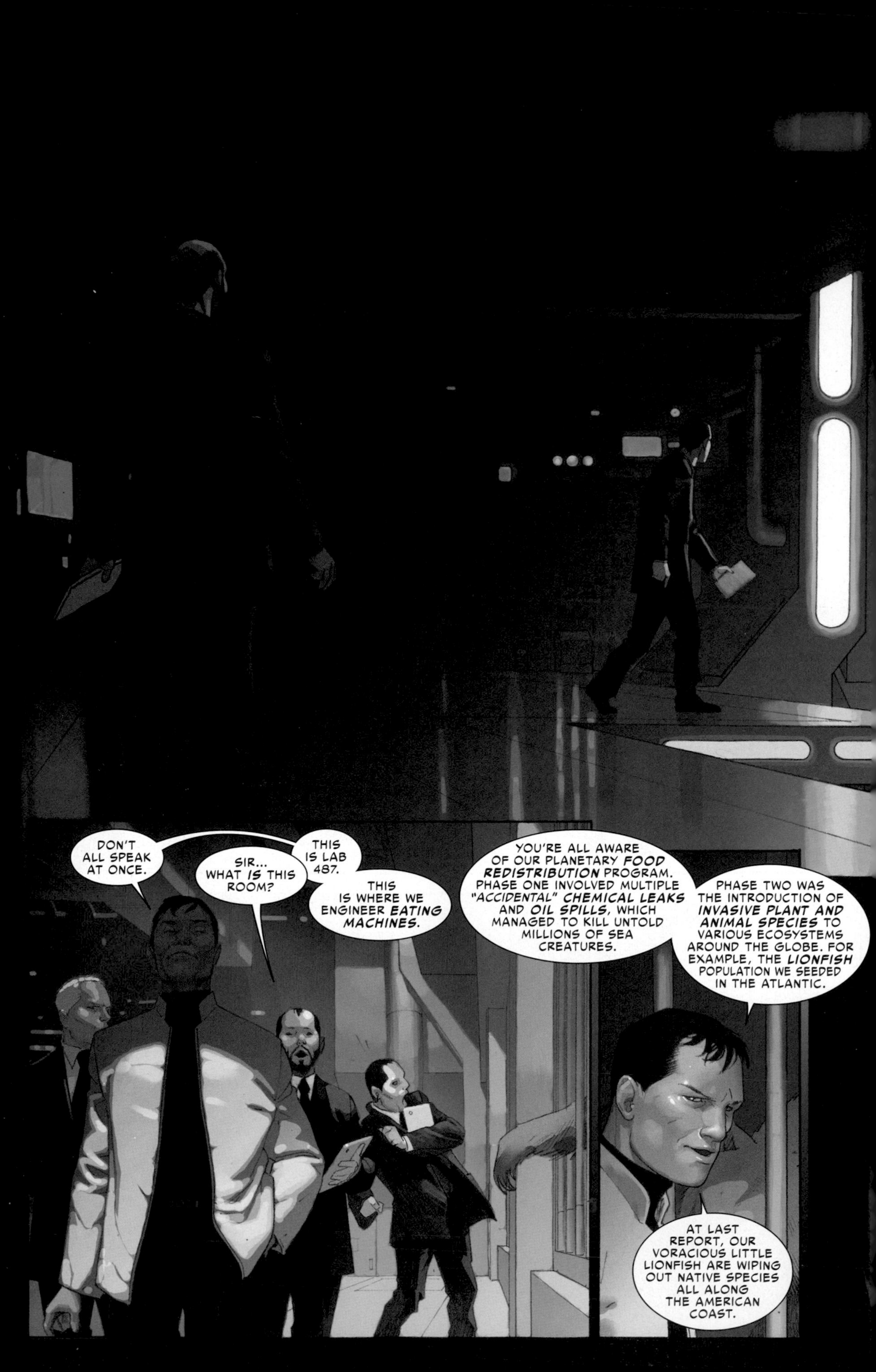
DON'T ALL SPEAK AT ONCE.
SIR... WHAT IS THIS ROOM?
THIS IS LAB 487.
THIS IS WHERE WE ENGINEER EATING MACHINES.
YOU'RE ALL AWARE OF OUR PLANETARY FOOD REDISTRIBUTION PROGRAM. PHASE ONE INVOLVED MULTIPLE "ACCIDENTAL" CHEMICAL LEAKS AND OIL SPILLS, WHICH MANAGED TO KILL UNTOLD MILLIONS OF SEA CREATURES.
PHASE TWO WAS THE INTRODUCTION OF INVASIVE PLANT AND ANIMAL SPECIES TO VARIOUS ECOSYSTEMS AROUND THE GLOBE. FOR EXAMPLE, THE LIONFISH POPULATION WE SEEDED IN THE ATLANTIC.
AT LAST REPORT, OUR VORACIOUS LITTLE LIONFISH ARE WIPING OUT NATIVE SPECIES ALL ALONG THE AMERICAN COAST.

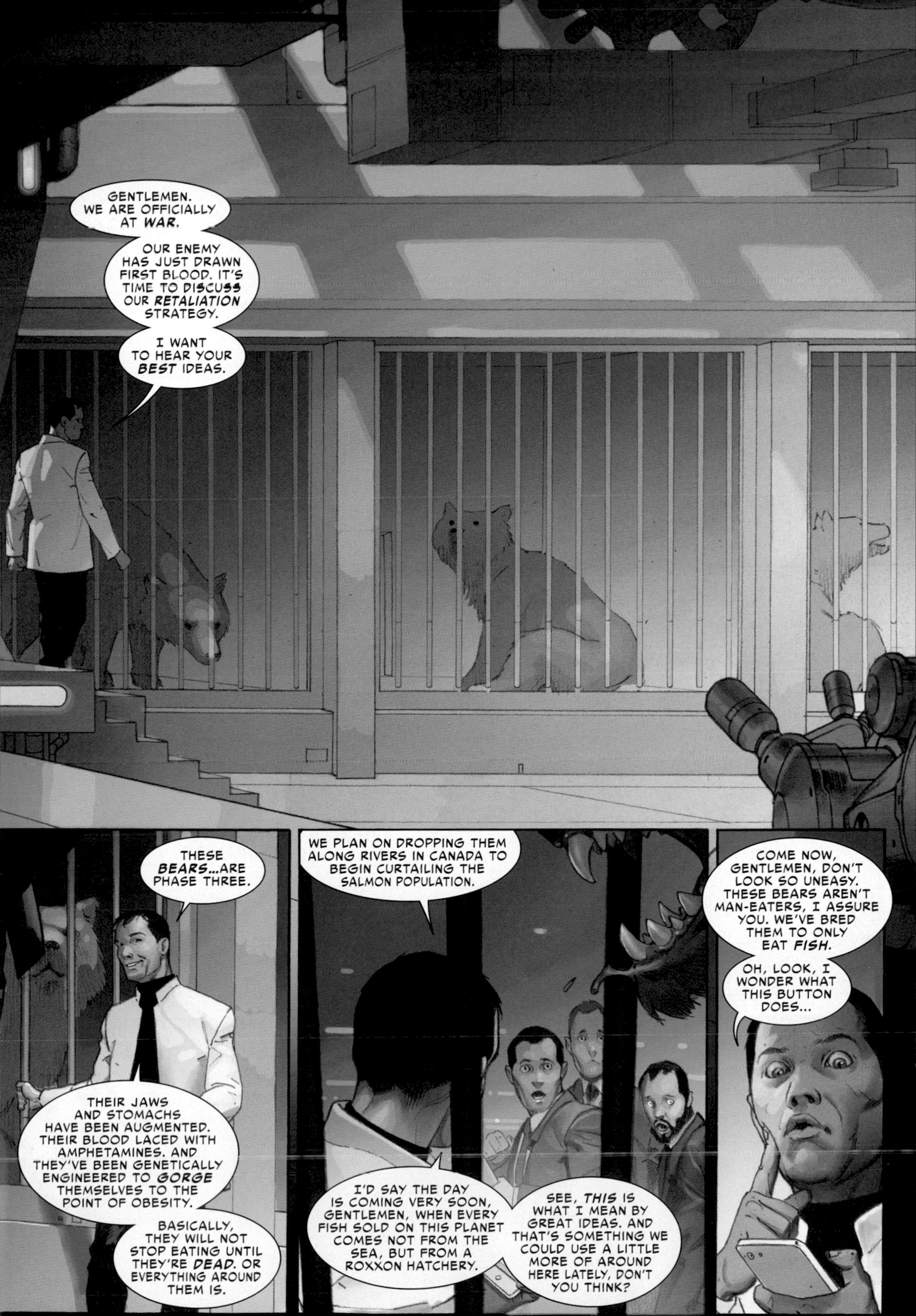
GENTLEMEN. WE ARE OFFICIALLY AT WAR.
OUR ENEMY HAS JUST DRAWN FIRST BLOOD. IT'S TIME TO DISCUSS OUR RETALIATION STRATEGY.
I WANT TO HEAR YOUR BEST IDEAS.
THESE BEARS...ARE PHASE THREE.
THEIR JAWS AND STOMACHS HAVE BEEN AUGMENTED. THEIR BLOOD LACED WITH AMPHETAMINES. AND THEY'VE BEEN GENETICALLY ENGINEERED TO GORGE THEMSELVES TO THE POINT OF OBESITY.
BASICALLY, THEY WILL NOT STOP EATING UNTIL THEY'RE DEAD. OR EVERYTHING AROUND THEM IS.
WE PLAN ON DROPPING THEM ALONG RIVERS IN CANADA TO BEGIN CURTAILING THE SALMON POPULATION.
I'D SAY THE DAY IS COMING VERY SOON, GENTLEMEN, WHEN EVERY FISH SOLD ON THIS PLANET COMES NOT FROM THE SEA, BUT FROM A ROXXON HATCHERY.
SEE, THIS IS WHAT I MEAN BY GREAT IDEAS. AND THAT'S SOMETHING WE COULD USE A LITTLE MORE OF AROUND HERE LATELY, DON'T YOU THINK?
COME NOW, GENTLEMEN, DON'T LOOK SO UNEASY. THESE BEARS AREN'T MAN-EATERS, I ASSURE YOU. WE'VE BRED THEM TO ONLY EAT FISH.
OH, LOOK, I WONDER WHAT THIS BUTTON DOES...

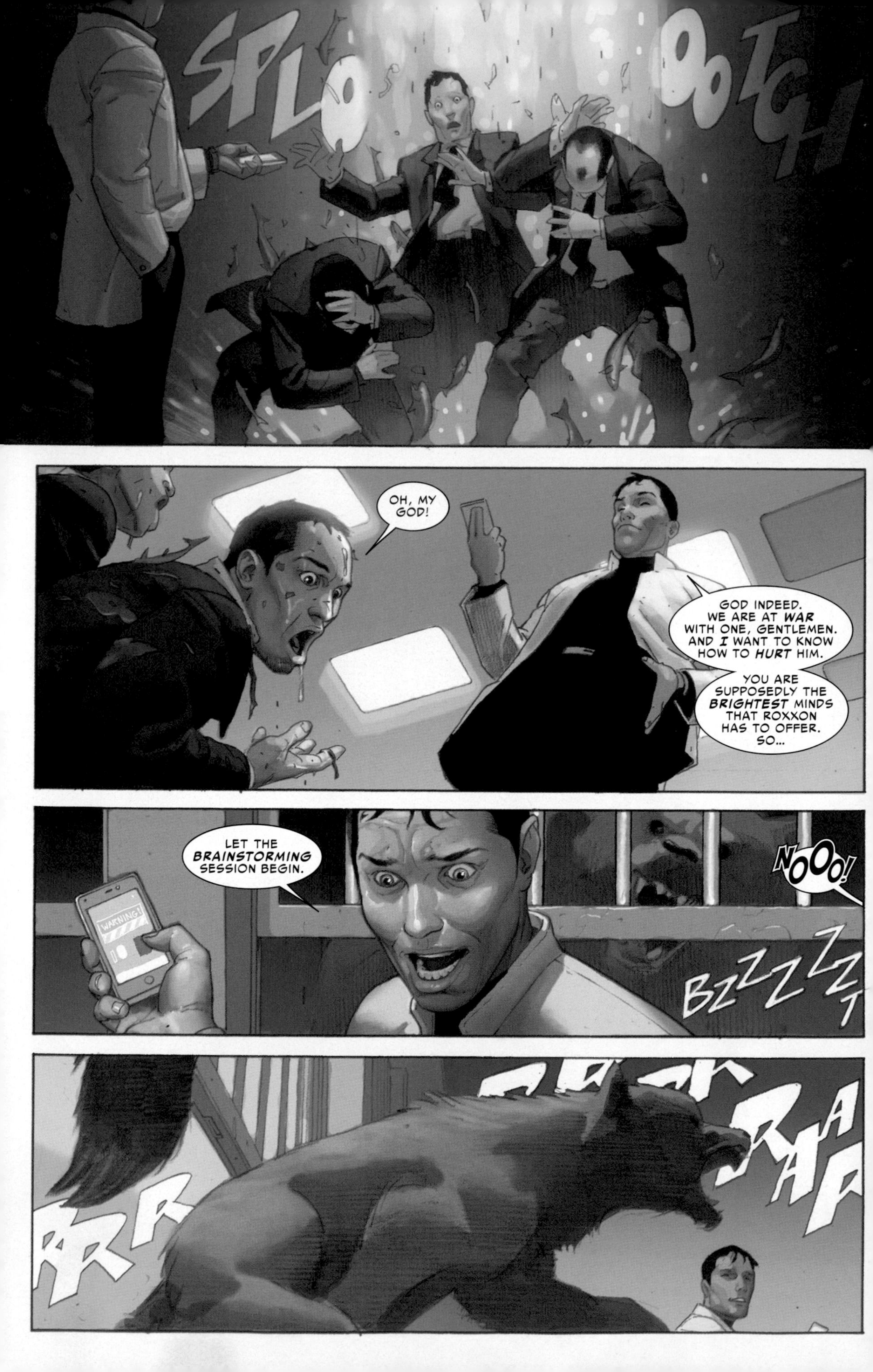
SPLOOOTCH
OH, MY GOD!
GOD INDEED. WE ARE AT WAR WITH ONE, GENTLEMEN. AND I WANT TO KNOW HOW TO HURT HIM.
YOU ARE SUPPOSEDLY THE BRIGHTEST MINDS THAT ROXXON HAS TO OFFER. SO...
LET THE BRAINSTORMING SESSION BEGIN.
WARNING!
NOOO!
BZZZZZT
RRR
RAAA

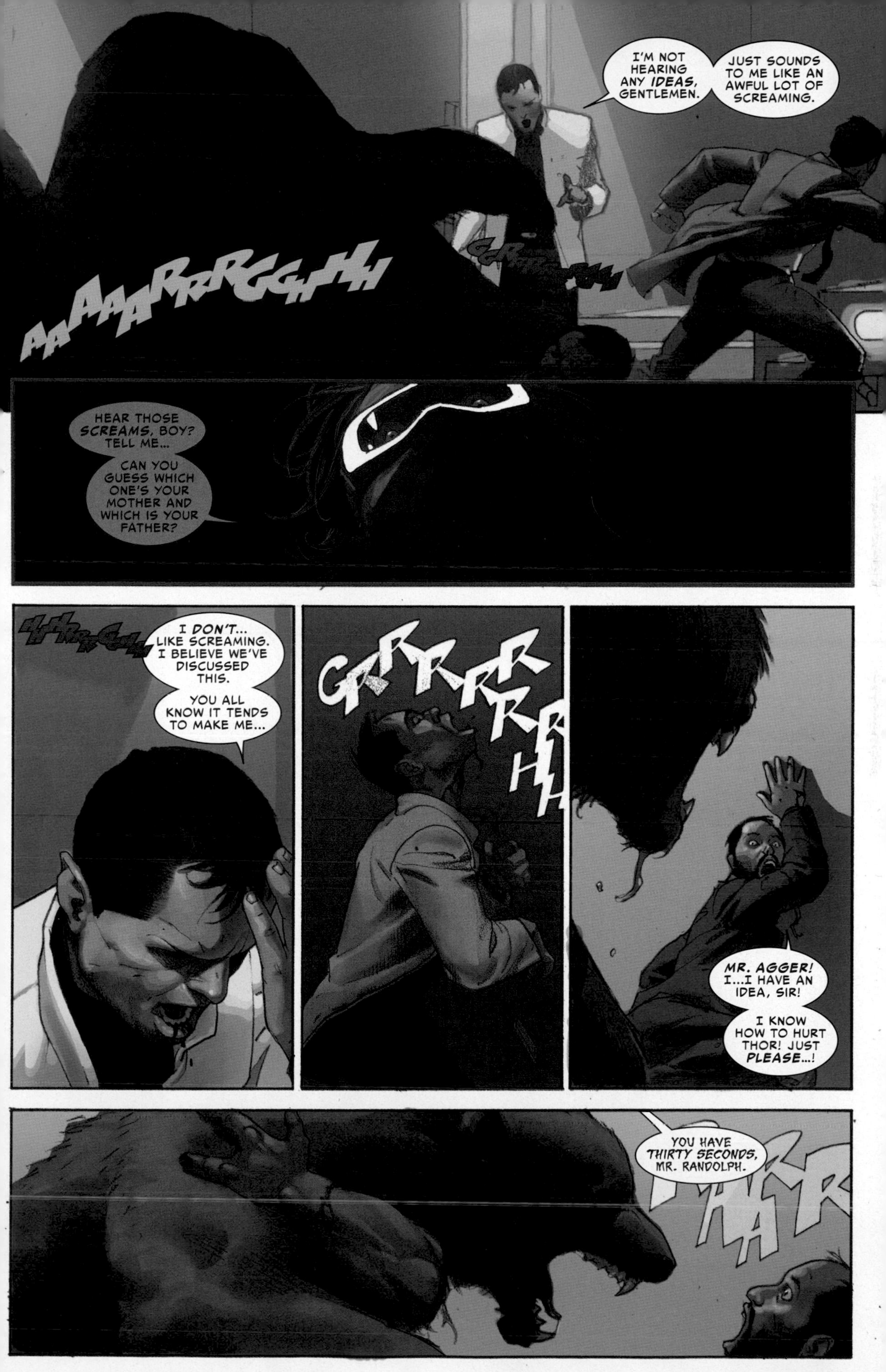
I'M NOT HEARING ANY IDEAS, GENTLEMEN.
JUST SOUNDS TO ME LIKE AN AWFUL LOT OF SCREAMING.
AAAAARRRGGHHHH
HEAR THOSE SCREAMS, BOY? TELL ME...
CAN YOU GUESS WHICH ONE'S YOUR MOTHER AND WHICH IS YOUR FATHER?
I DON'T... LIKE SCREAMING. I BELIEVE WE'VE DISCUSSED THIS.
YOU ALL KNOW IT TENDS TO MAKE ME...
GRRRRRR
MR. AGGER! I...I HAVE AN IDEA, SIR!
I KNOW HOW TO HURT THOR! JUST PLEASE...!
YOU HAVE THIRTY SECONDS, MR. RANDOLPH.

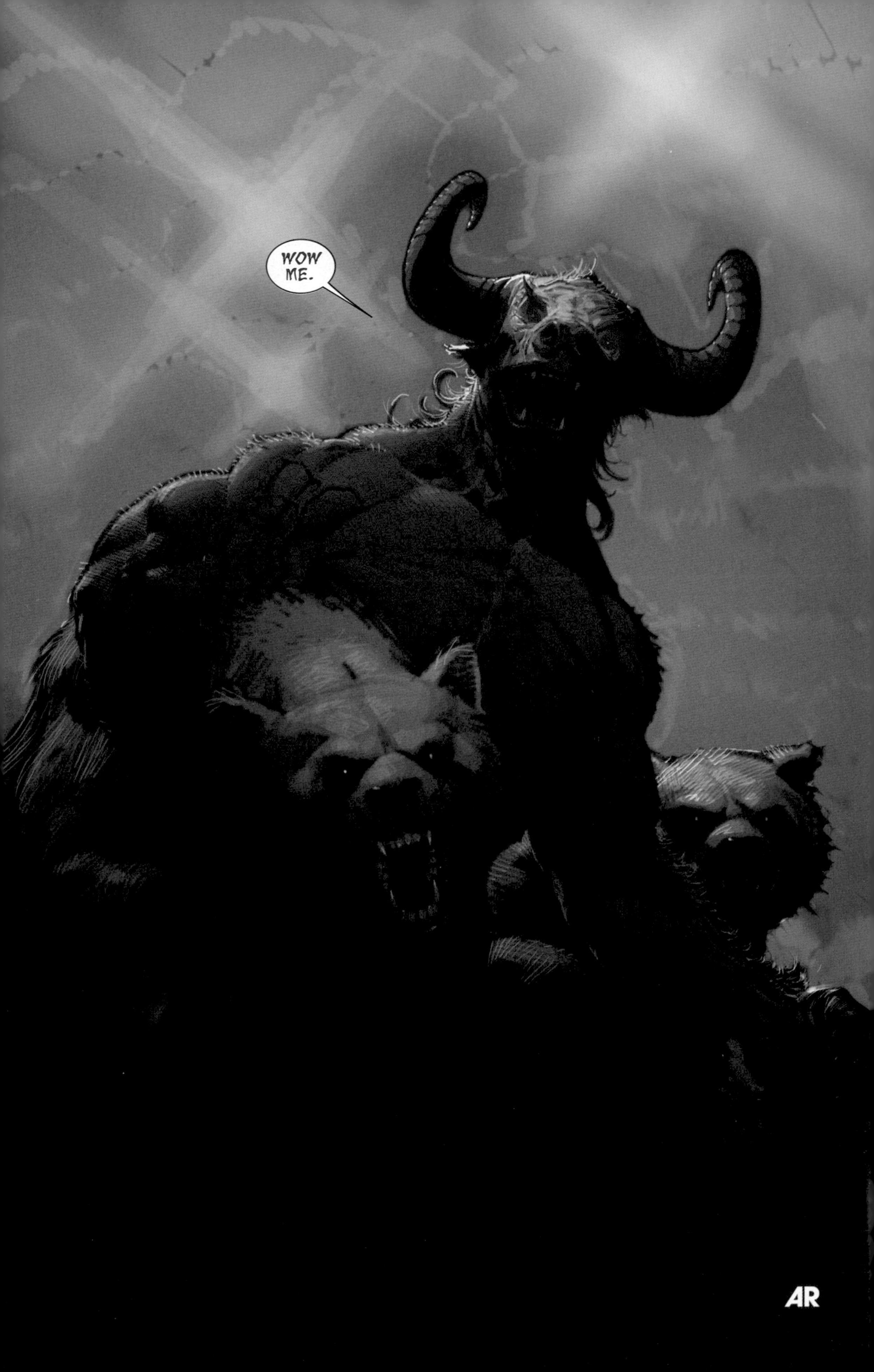
WOW ME.
AR

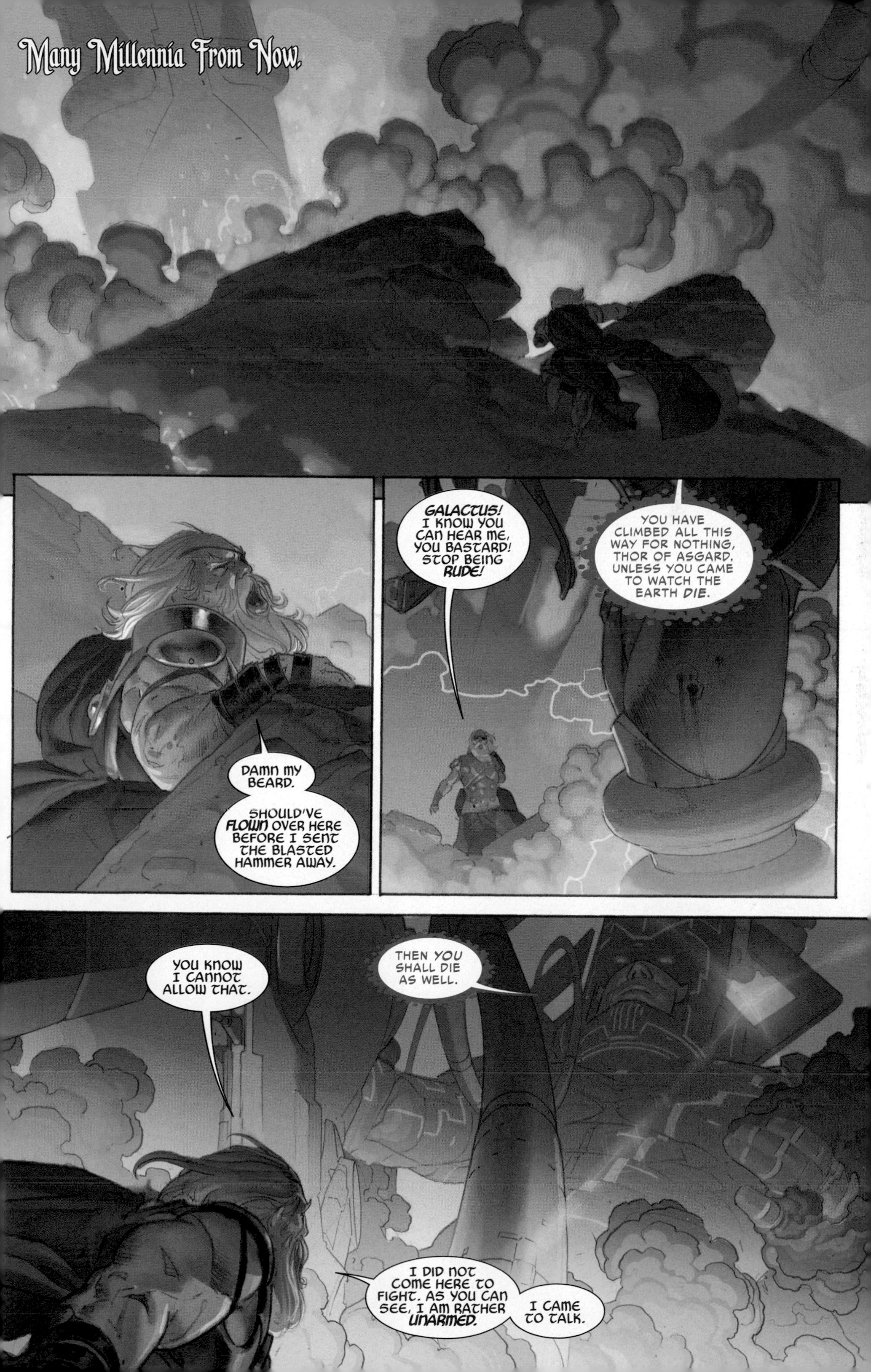
Many Millennia From Now.
DAMN MY BEARD.
SHOULD'VE FLOWN OVER HERE BEFORE I SENT THE BLASTED HAMMER AWAY.
GALACTUS! I KNOW YOU CAN HEAR ME, YOU BASTARD! STOP BEING RUDE!
YOU HAVE CLIMBED ALL THIS WAY FOR NOTHING, THOR OF ASGARD. UNLESS YOU CAME TO WATCH THE EARTH DIE.
YOU KNOW I CANNOT ALLOW THAT.
THEN YOU SHALL DIE AS WELL.
I DID NOT COME HERE TO FIGHT. AS YOU CAN SEE, I AM RATHER UNARMED.
I CAME TO TALK.

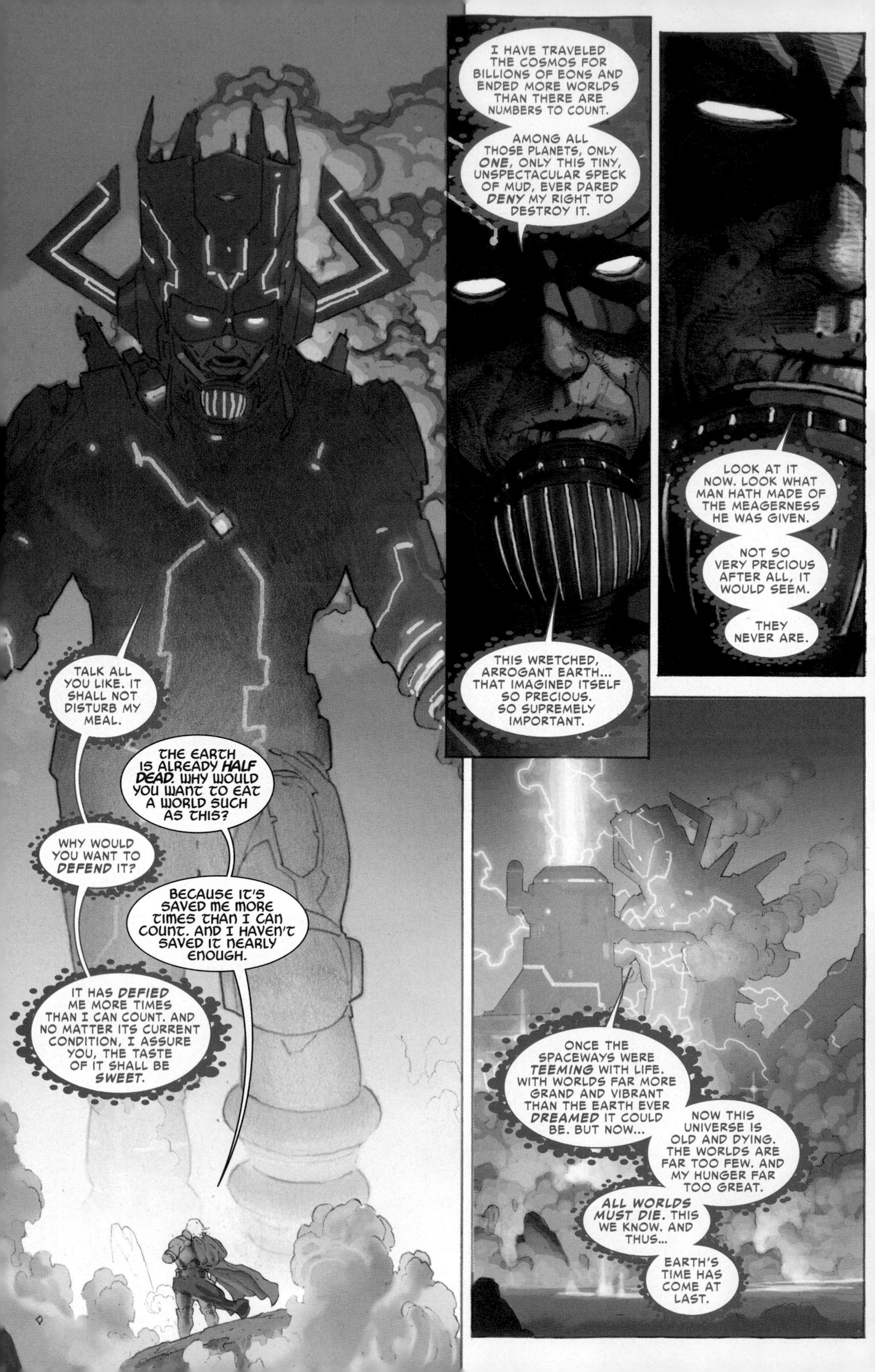

TALK ALL YOU LIKE. IT SHALL NOT DISTURB MY MEAL.
THE EARTH IS ALREADY HALF DEAD. WHY WOULD YOU WANT TO EAT A WORLD SUCH AS THIS?
WHY WOULD YOU WANT TO DEFEND IT?
BECAUSE IT'S SAVED ME MORE TIMES THAN I CAN COUNT. AND I HAVEN'T SAVED IT NEARLY ENOUGH.
IT HAS DEFIED ME MORE TIMES THAN I CAN COUNT. AND NO MATTER ITS CURRENT CONDITION, I ASSURE YOU, THE TASTE OF IT SHALL BE SWEET.
I HAVE TRAVELED THE COSMOS FOR BILLIONS OF EONS AND ENDED MORE WORLDS THAN THERE ARE NUMBERS TO COUNT.
AMONG ALL THOSE PLANETS, ONLY ONE, ONLY THIS TINY, UNSPECTACULAR SPECK OF MUD, EVER DARED DENY MY RIGHT TO DESTROY IT.
THIS WRETCHED, ARROGANT EARTH... THAT IMAGINED ITSELF SO PRECIOUS. SO SUPREMELY IMPORTANT.
LOOK AT IT NOW. LOOK WHAT MAN HATH MADE OF THE MEAGERNESS HE WAS GIVEN.
NOT SO VERY PRECIOUS AFTER ALL, IT WOULD SEEM.
THEY NEVER ARE.
ONCE THE SPACEWAYS WERE TEEMING WITH LIFE. WITH WORLDS FAR MORE GRAND AND VIBRANT THAN THE EARTH EVER DREAMED IT COULD BE. BUT NOW...
NOW THIS UNIVERSE IS OLD AND DYING. THE WORLDS ARE FAR TOO FEW. AND MY HUNGER FAR TOO GREAT.
ALL WORLDS MUST DIE. THIS WE KNOW. AND THUS...
EARTH'S TIME HAS COME AT LAST.

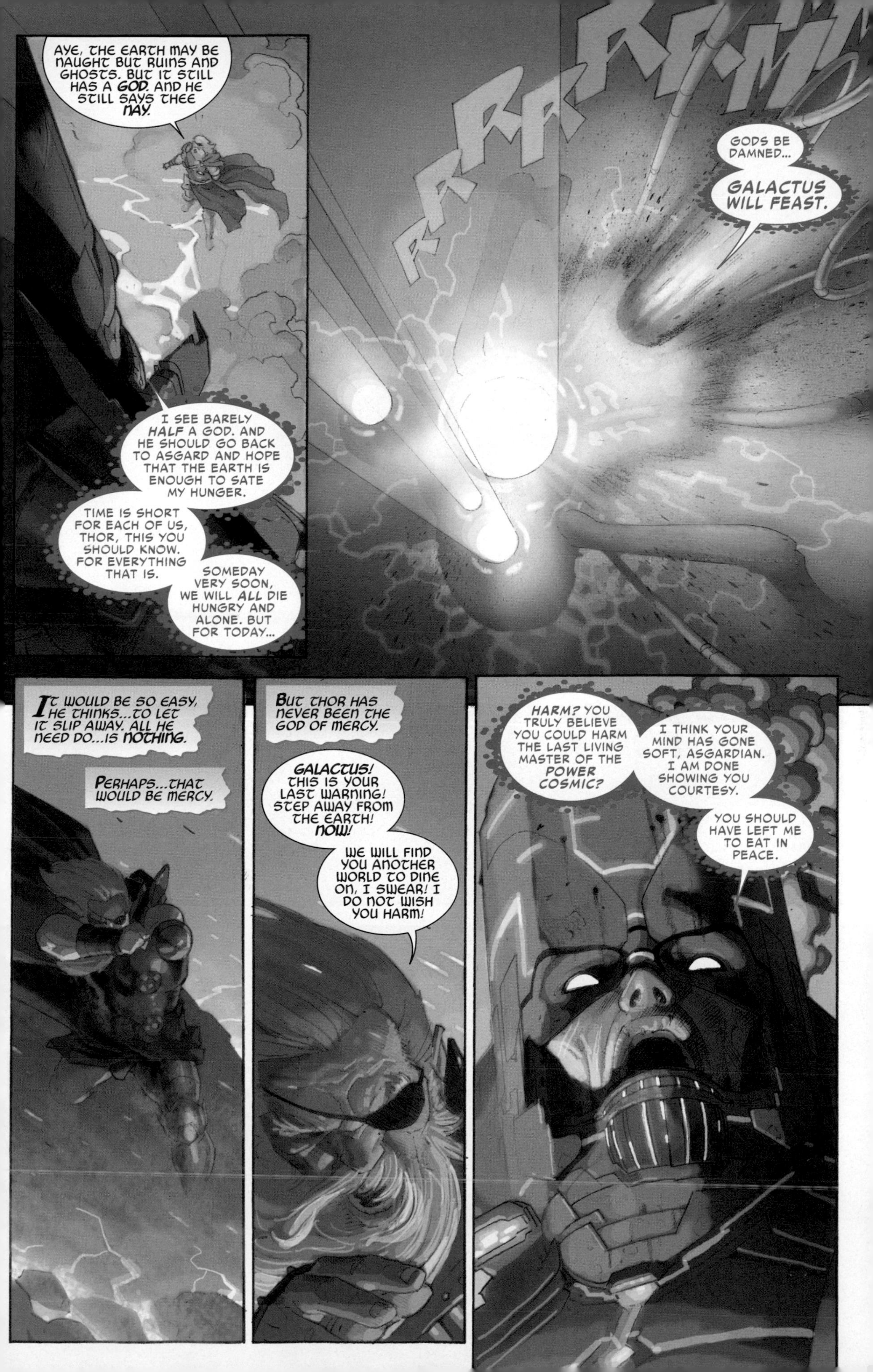
AYE, THE EARTH MAY BE NAUGHT BUT RUINS AND GHOSTS. BUT IT STILL HAS A GOD. AND HE STILL SAYS THEE NAY.
I SEE BARELY HALF A GOD. AND HE SHOULD GO BACK TO ASGARD AND HOPE THAT THE EARTH IS ENOUGH TO SATE MY HUNGER.
TIME IS SHORT FOR EACH OF US, THOR, THIS YOU SHOULD KNOW. FOR EVERYTHING THAT IS.
SOMEDAY VERY SOON, WE WILL ALL DIE HUNGRY AND ALONE. BUT FOR TODAY...
RRRRRR-MM
GODS BE DAMNED...
GALACTUS WILL FEAST.
IT WOULD BE SO EASY, HE THINKS...TO LET IT SLIP AWAY. ALL HE NEED DO...IS NOTHING.
PERHAPS...THAT WOULD BE MERCY.
BUT THOR HAS NEVER BEEN THE GOD OF MERCY.
GALACTUS! THIS IS YOUR LAST WARNING! STEP AWAY FROM THE EARTH! NOW!
WE WILL FIND YOU ANOTHER WORLD TO DINE ON, I SWEAR! I DO NOT WISH YOU HARM!
HARM? YOU TRULY BELIEVE YOU COULD HARM THE LAST LIVING MASTER OF THE POWER COSMIC?
I THINK YOUR MIND HAS GONE SOFT, ASGARDIAN. I AM DONE SHOWING YOU COURTESY.
YOU SHOULD HAVE LEFT ME TO EAT IN PEACE.

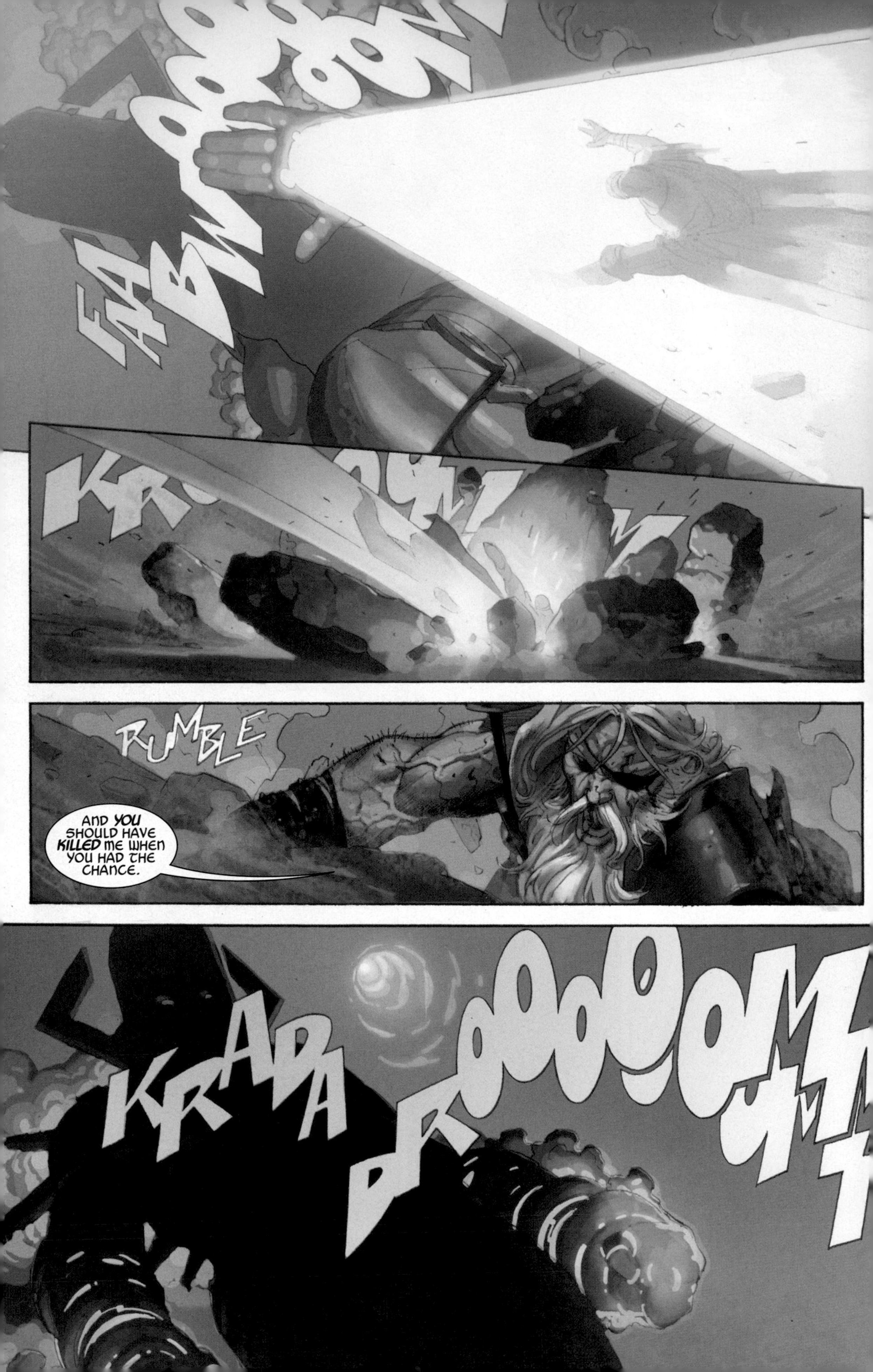
RUMBLE
AND YOU SHOULD HAVE KILLED ME WHEN YOU HAD THE CHANCE.

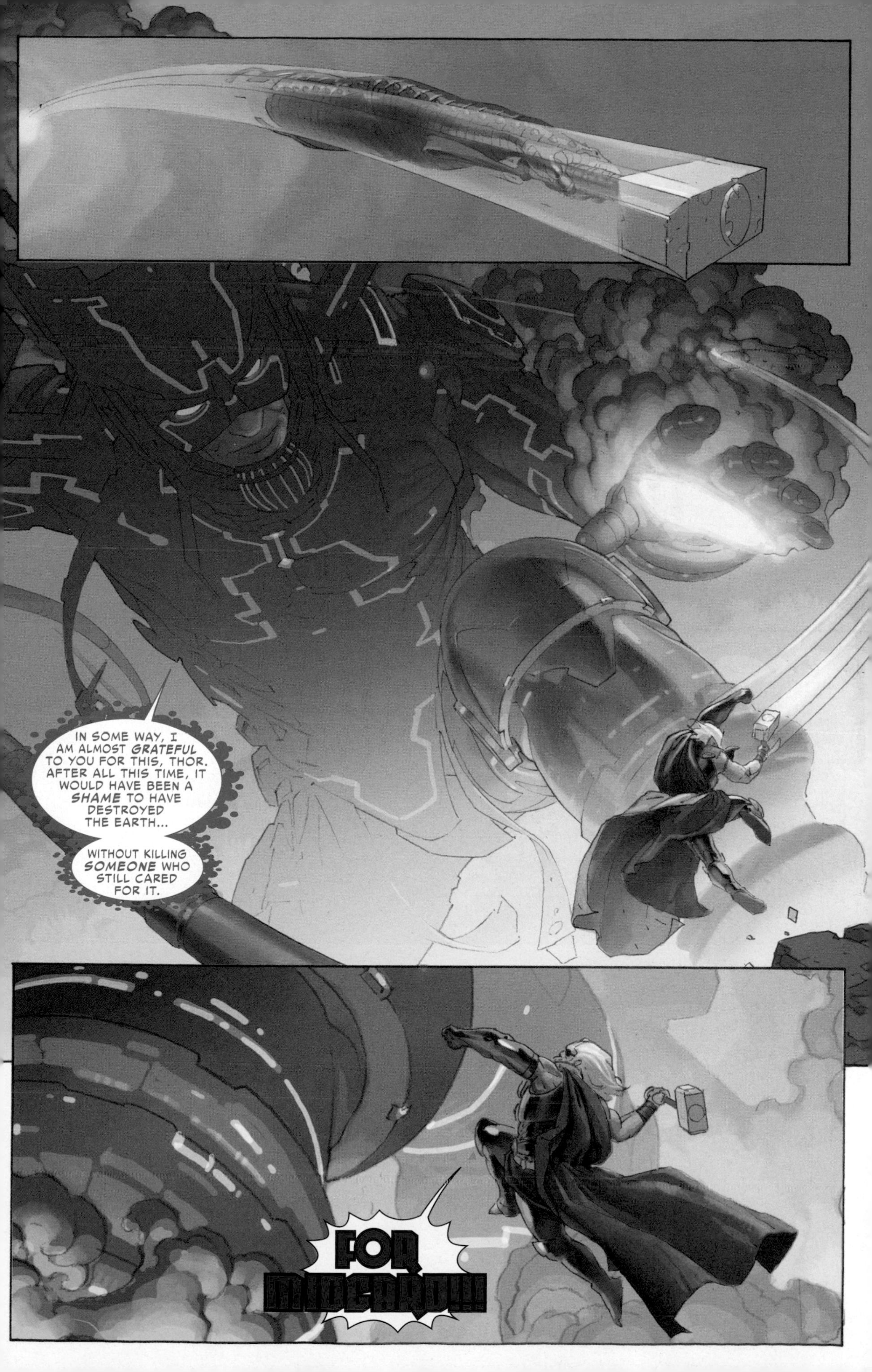

IN SOME WAY, I AM ALMOST GRATEFUL TO YOU FOR THIS, THOR. AFTER ALL THIS TIME, IT WOULD HAVE BEEN A SHAME TO HAVE DESTROYED THE EARTH...
WITHOUT KILLING SOMEONE WHO STILL CARED FOR IT.
FOR MIDGARD!!!

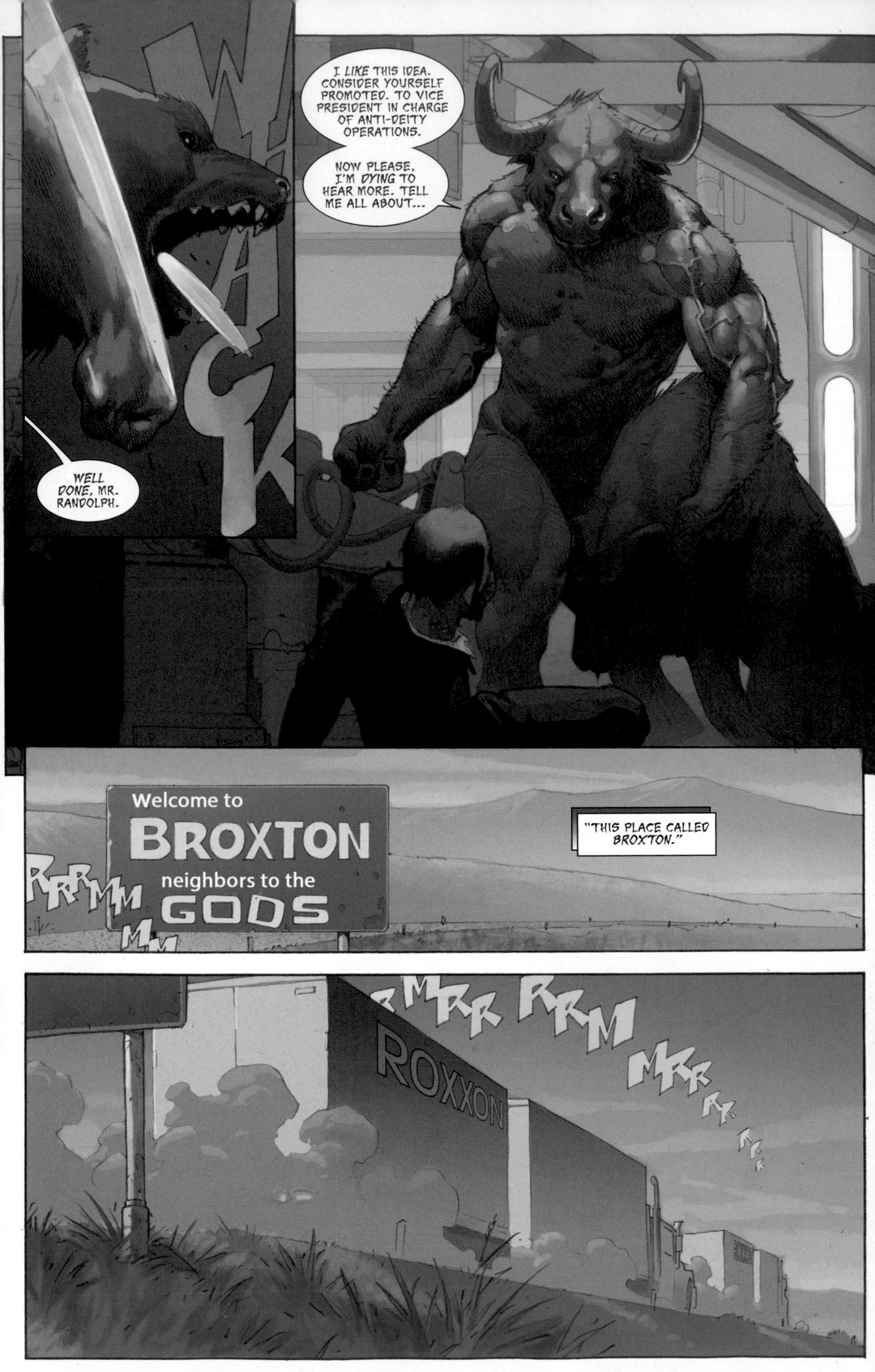
WHAK
WELL DONE, MR. RANDOLPH.
I LIKE THIS IDEA. CONSIDER YOURSELF PROMOTED. TO VICE PRESIDENT IN CHARGE OF ANTI-DEITY OPERATIONS.
NOW PLEASE, I'M DYING TO HEAR MORE. TELL ME ALL ABOUT...
Welcome to BROXTON neighbors to the GODS
RRRMMMM
"THIS PLACE CALLED BROXTON."
ROXXON
RMRR RRRM MRRRRRR

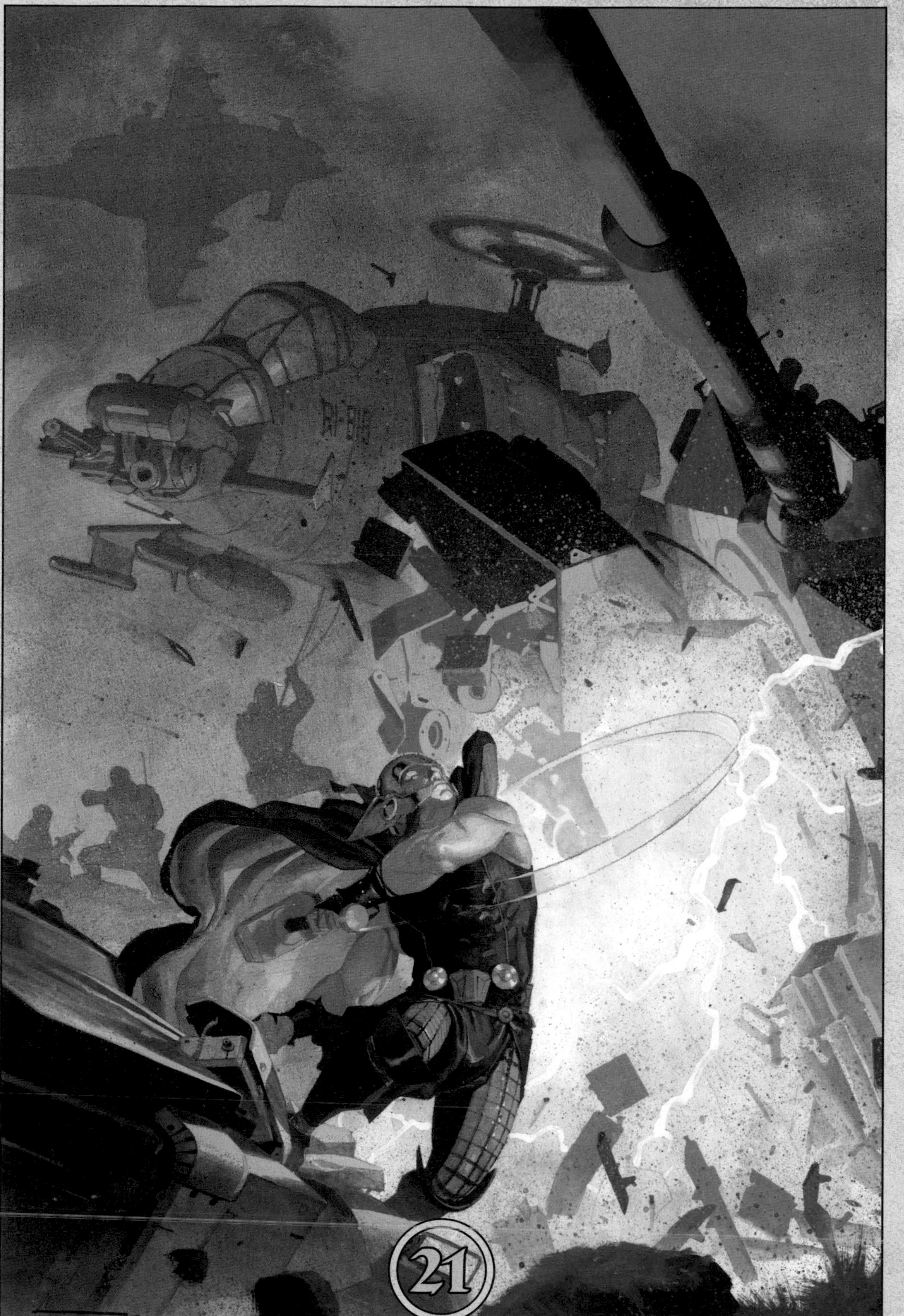

RF 819
21

THE LAST DAYS OF MIDGARD – PART 3:
GOD, INC.

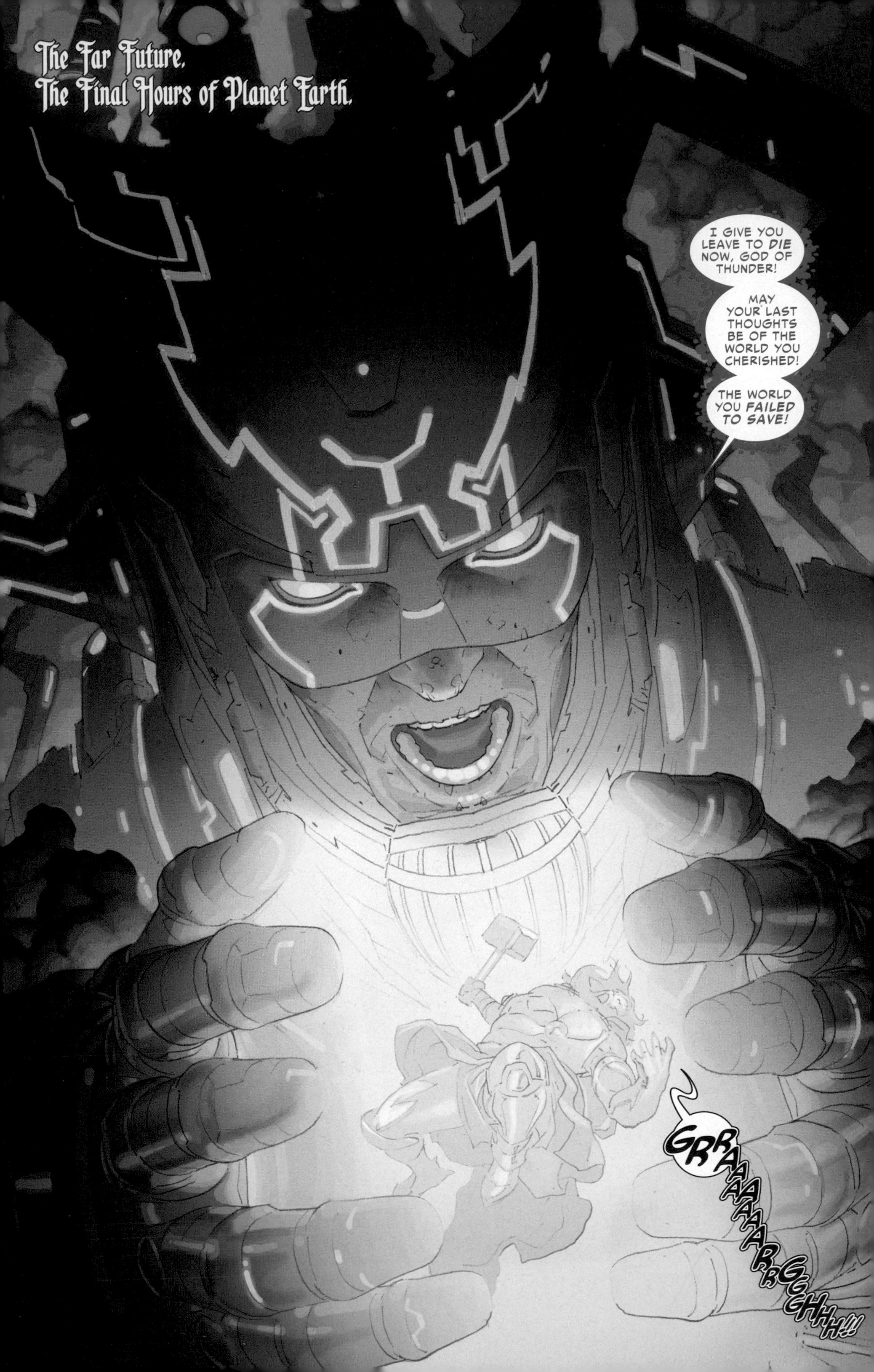
The Far Future.
The Final Hours of Planet Earth.
I GIVE YOU LEAVE TO *DIE* NOW, GOD OF THUNDER!
MAY YOUR LAST THOUGHTS BE OF THE WORLD YOU CHERISHED!
THE WORLD YOU *FAILED* TO *SAVE!*
GRRAAAAAARRGGHHH!!

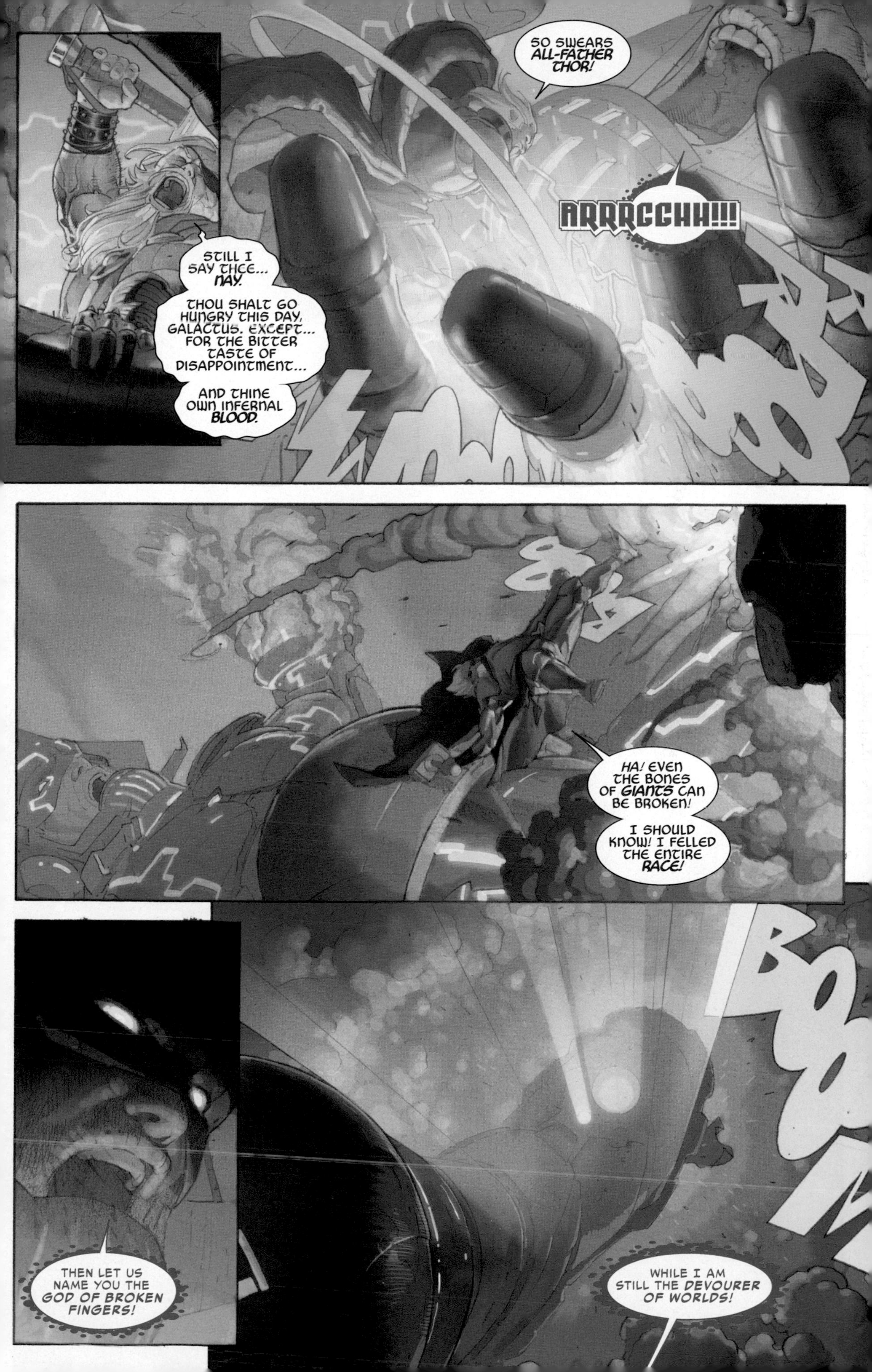
STILL I SAY THEE... NAY.
THOU SHALT GO HUNGRY THIS DAY, GALACTUS. EXCEPT... FOR THE BITTER TASTE OF DISAPPOINTMENT...
AND THINE OWN INFERNAL BLOOD.
SO SWEARS ALL-FATHER THOR!
ARRRGGHH!!!
HA! EVEN THE BONES OF GIANTS CAN BE BROKEN!
I SHOULD KNOW! I FELLED THE ENTIRE RACE!
THEN LET US NAME YOU THE GOD OF BROKEN FINGERS!
WHILE I AM STILL THE DEVOURER OF WORLDS!

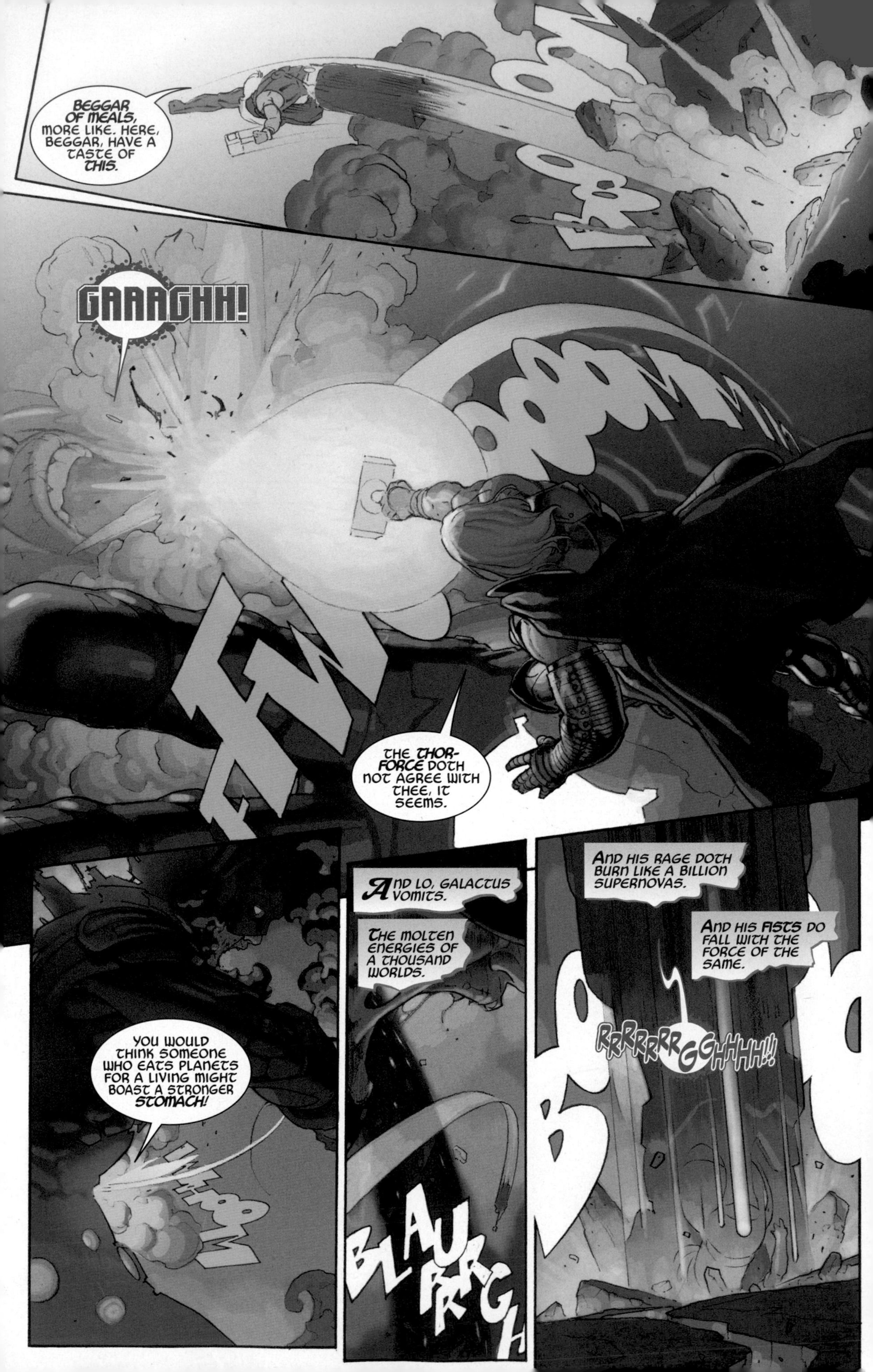

BEGGAR OF MEALS, MORE LIKE. HERE, BEGGAR, HAVE A TASTE OF THIS.
BOOOM
GAAAGHH!
BOOOOM!!
THE THOR-FORCE DOTH NOT AGREE WITH THEE, IT SEEMS.
YOU WOULD THINK SOMEONE WHO EATS PLANETS FOR A LIVING MIGHT BOAST A STRONGER STOMACH!
AND LO, GALACTUS VOMITS.
THE MOLTEN ENERGIES OF A THOUSAND WORLDS.
BLAURRRGH
AND HIS RAGE DOTH BURN LIKE A BILLION SUPERNOVAS.
AND HIS FISTS DO FALL WITH THE FORCE OF THE SAME.
RRRRRRRGGHHHH!!!

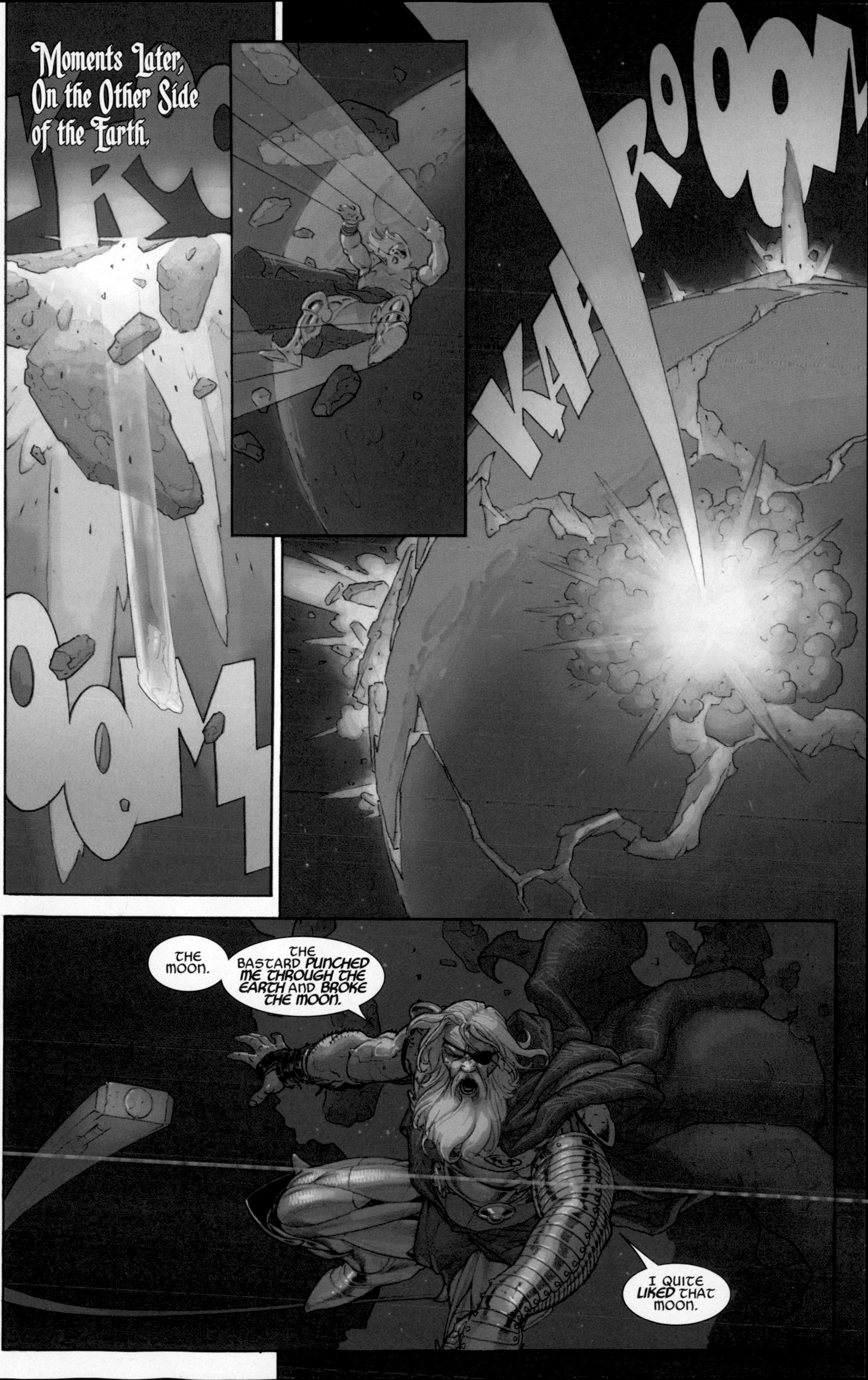

Moments Later, On the Other Side of the Earth,
KAROOOM
THE MOON.
THE BASTARD PUNCHED ME THROUGH THE EARTH AND BROKE THE MOON.
I QUITE LIKED THAT MOON.

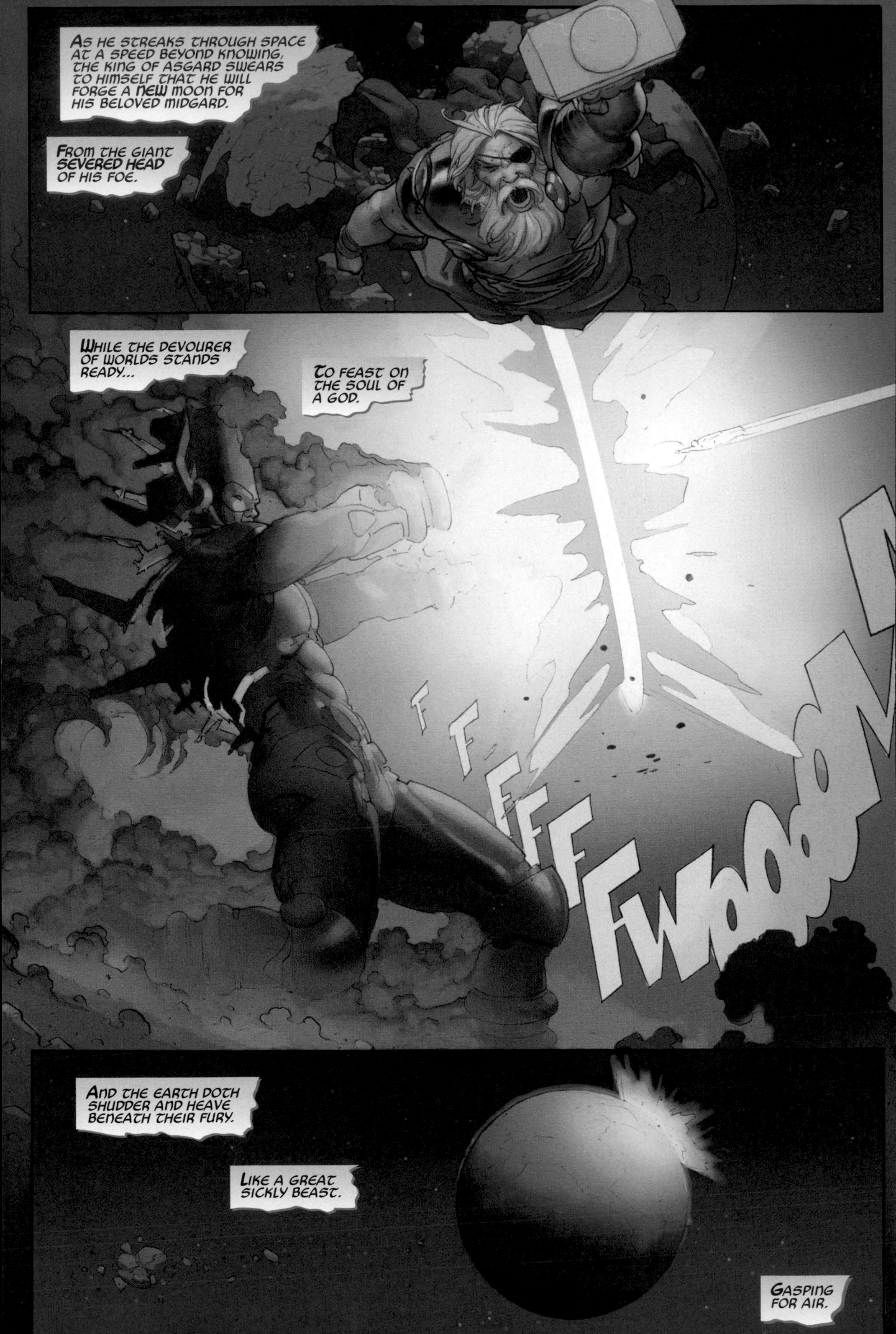
AS HE STREAKS THROUGH SPACE AT A SPEED BEYOND KNOWING, THE KING OF ASGARD SWEARS TO HIMSELF THAT HE WILL FORGE A **NEW** MOON FOR HIS BELOVED MIDGARD.
FROM THE GIANT **SEVERED HEAD** OF HIS FOE.
WHILE THE DEVOURER OF WORLDS STANDS READY...
TO FEAST ON THE SOUL OF A GOD.
FFFFFFWOOOOM
AND THE EARTH DOTH SHUDDER AND HEAVE BENEATH THEIR FURY.
LIKE A GREAT SICKLY BEAST.
GASPING FOR AIR.

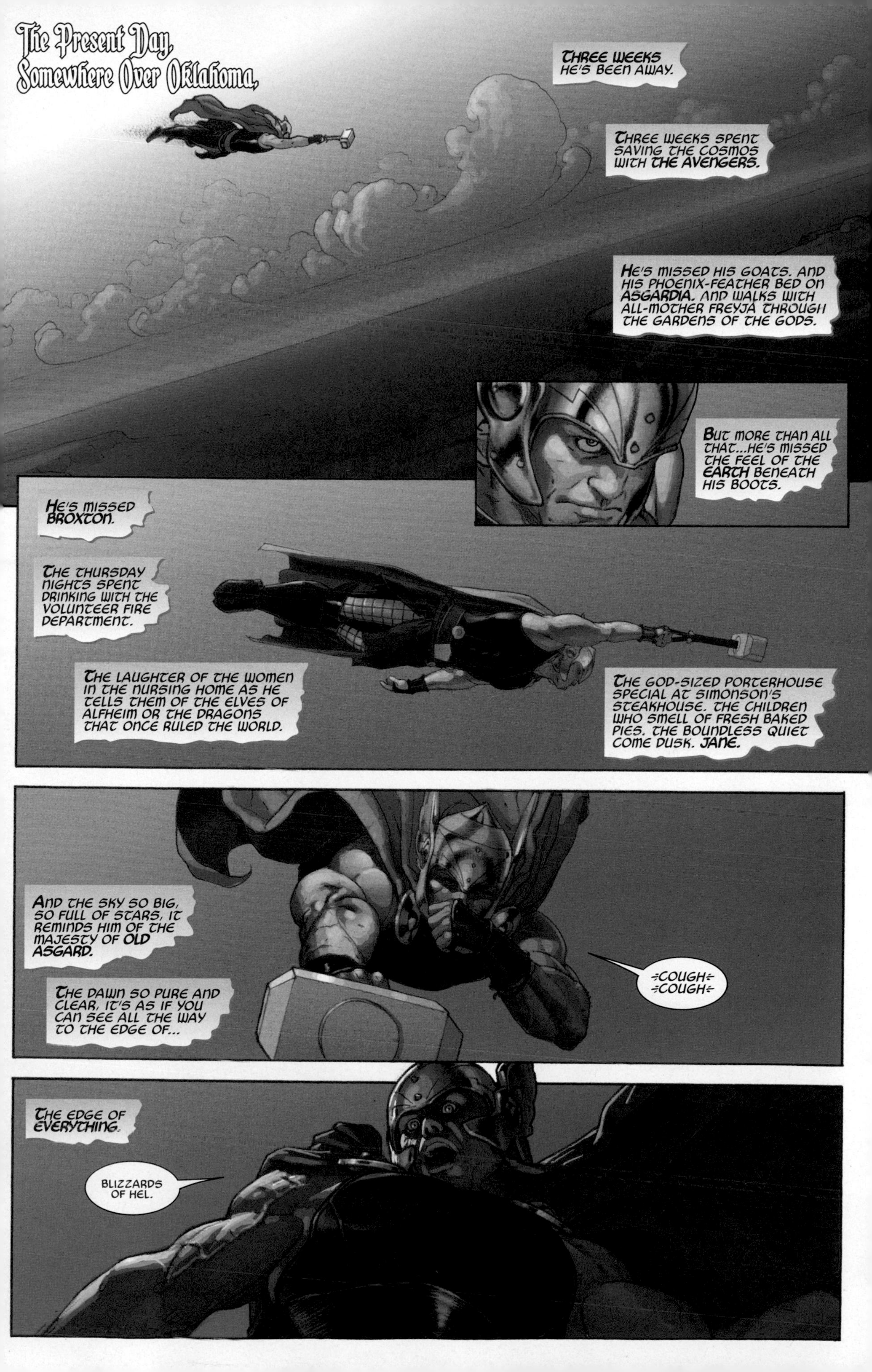
The Present Day, Somewhere Over Oklahoma,
THREE WEEKS HE'S BEEN AWAY.
THREE WEEKS SPENT SAVING THE COSMOS WITH THE AVENGERS.
HE'S MISSED HIS GOATS. AND HIS PHOENIX-FEATHER BED ON ASGARDIA. AND WALKS WITH ALL-MOTHER FREYJA THROUGH THE GARDENS OF THE GODS.
BUT MORE THAN ALL THAT...HE'S MISSED THE FEEL OF THE EARTH BENEATH HIS BOOTS.
HE'S MISSED BROXTON.
THE THURSDAY NIGHTS SPENT DRINKING WITH THE VOLUNTEER FIRE DEPARTMENT.
THE LAUGHTER OF THE WOMEN IN THE NURSING HOME AS HE TELLS THEM OF THE ELVES OF ALFHEIM OR THE DRAGONS THAT ONCE RULED THE WORLD.
THE GOD-SIZED PORTERHOUSE SPECIAL AT SIMONSON'S STEAKHOUSE. THE CHILDREN WHO SMELL OF FRESH BAKED PIES. THE BOUNDLESS QUIET COME DUSK. JANE.
AND THE SKY SO BIG, SO FULL OF STARS, IT REMINDS HIM OF THE MAJESTY OF OLD ASGARD.
THE DAWN SO PURE AND CLEAR, IT'S AS IF YOU CAN SEE ALL THE WAY TO THE EDGE OF...
=COUGH= =COUGH=
THE EDGE OF EVERYTHING.
BLIZZARDS OF HEL.

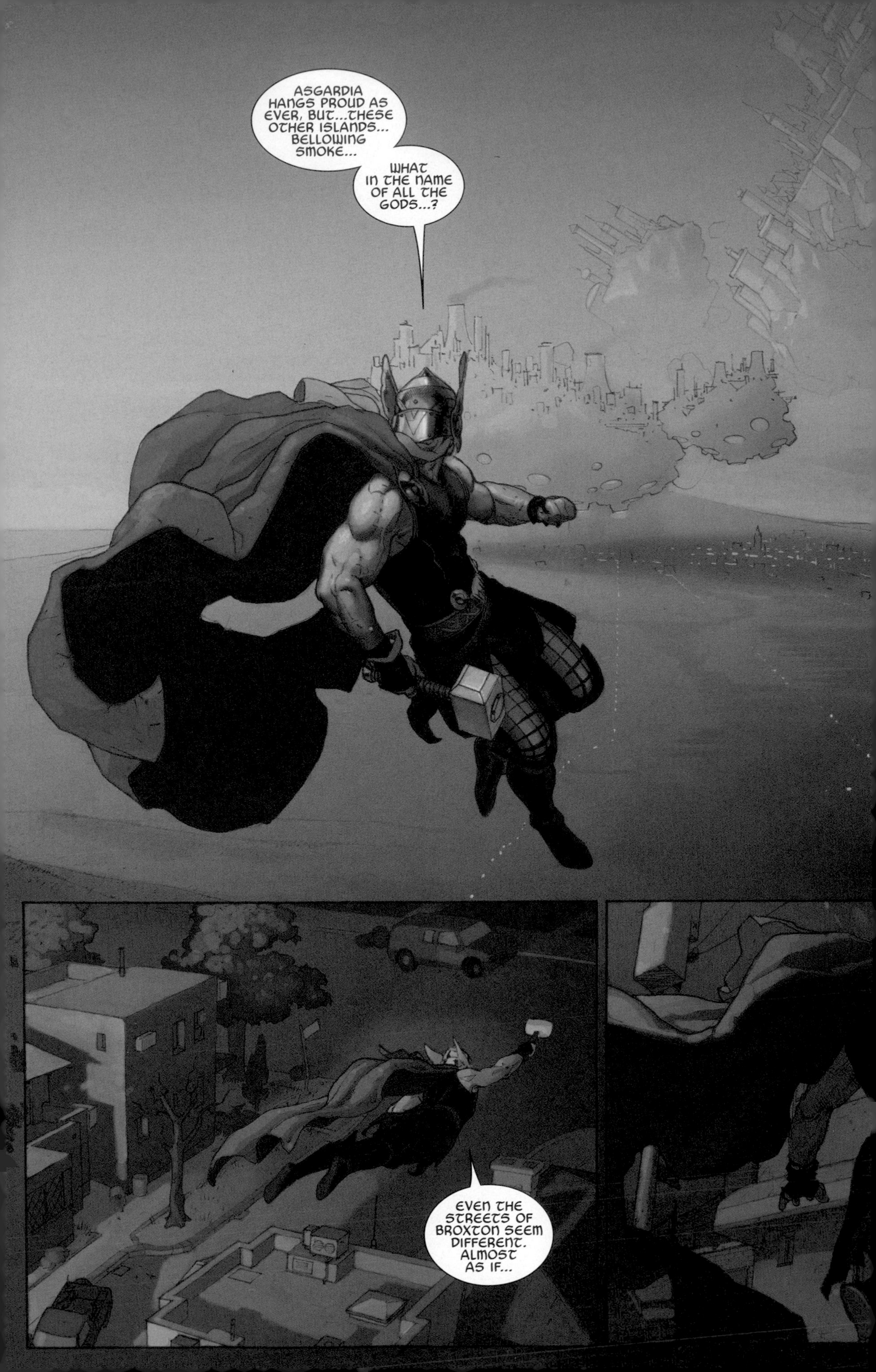
ASGARDIA HANGS PROUD AS EVER, BUT...THESE OTHER ISLANDS... BELLOWING SMOKE...
WHAT IN THE NAME OF ALL THE GODS...?
EVEN THE STREETS OF BROXTON SEEM DIFFERENT. ALMOST AS IF...

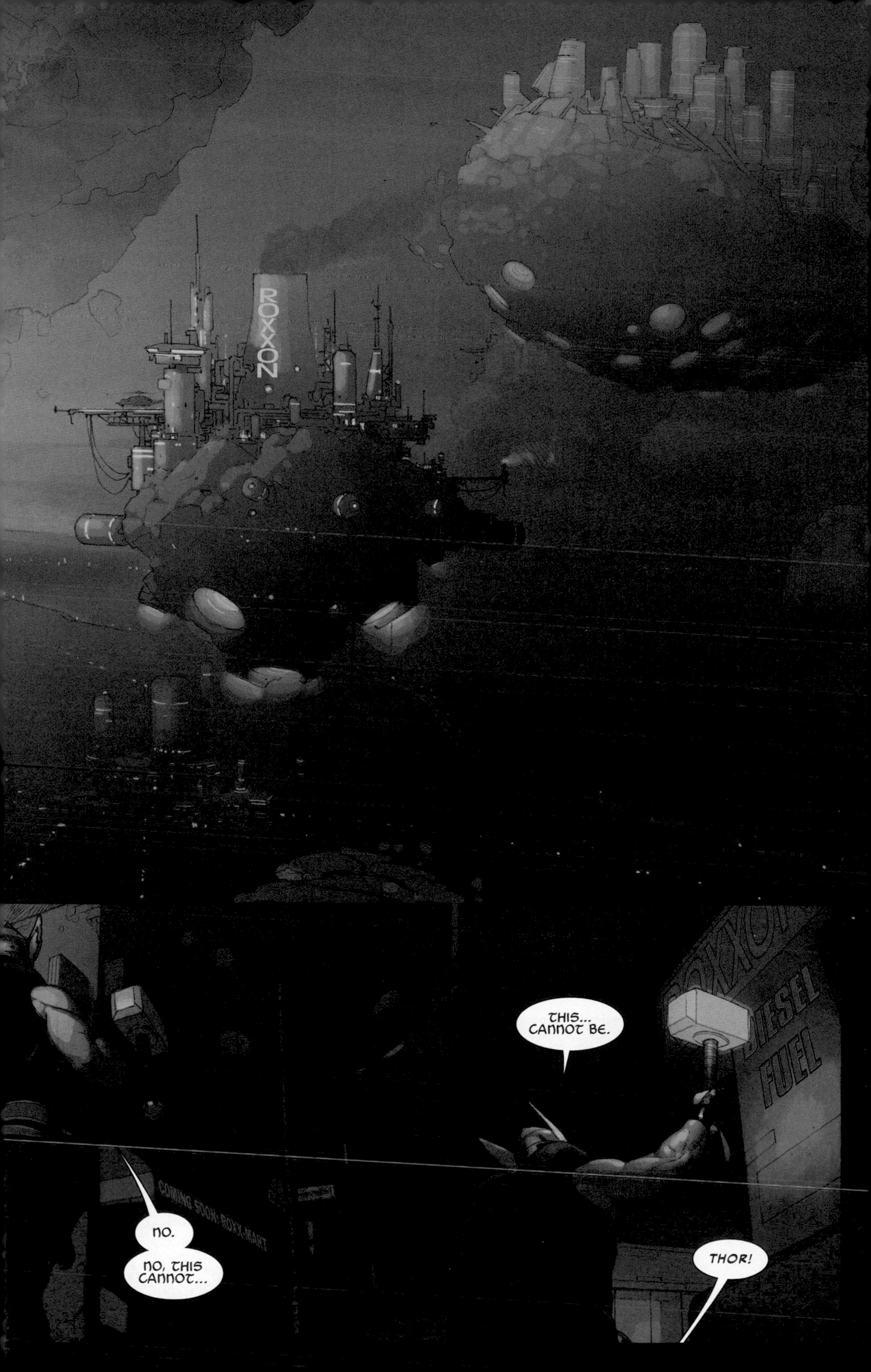
ROXXON
THIS... CANNOT BE.
DIESEL FUEL
COMING SOON: ROXX-MART
NO.
NO, THIS CANNOT...
THOR!

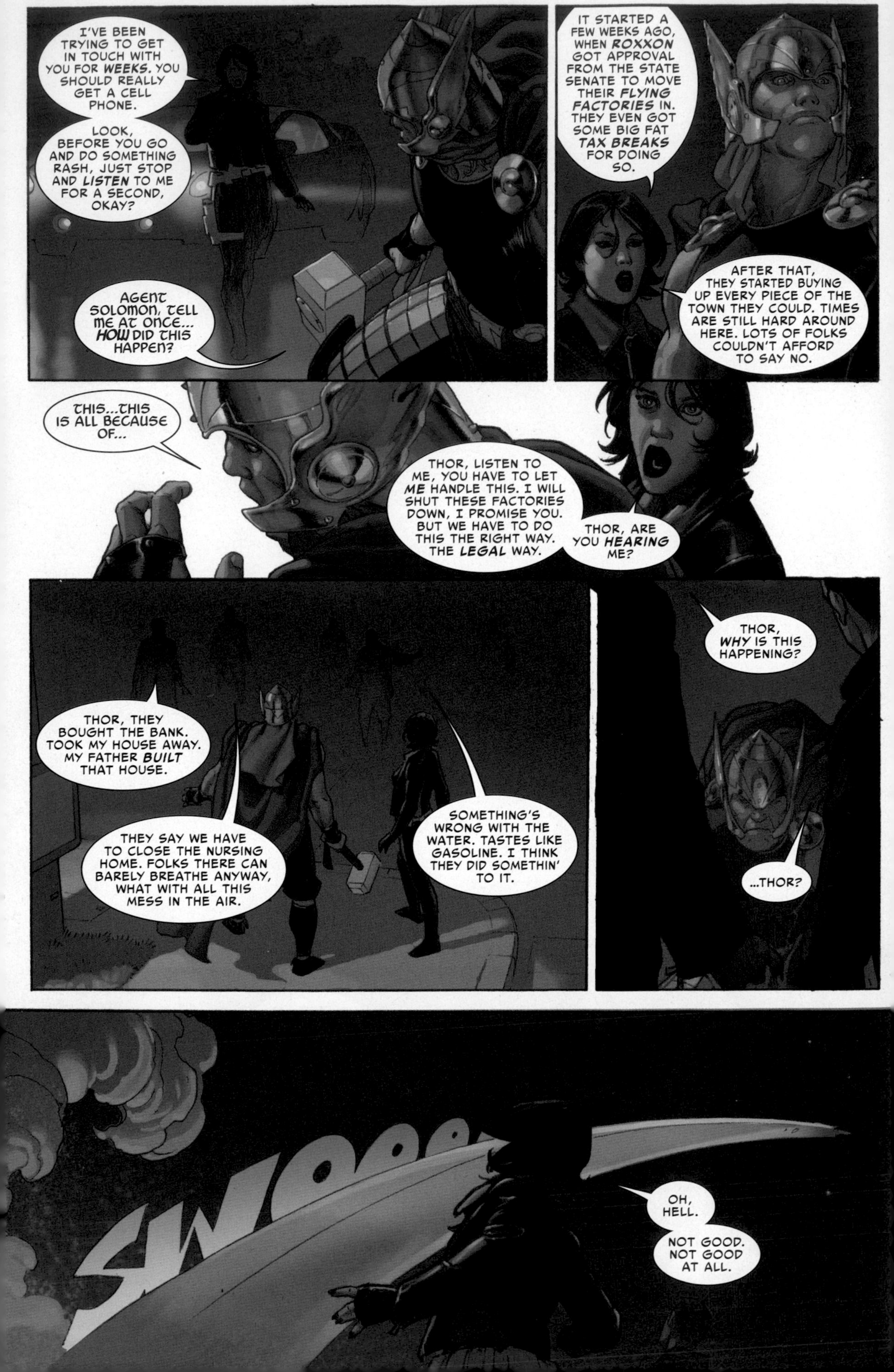
I'VE BEEN TRYING TO GET IN TOUCH WITH YOU FOR WEEKS. YOU SHOULD REALLY GET A CELL PHONE.
LOOK, BEFORE YOU GO AND DO SOMETHING RASH, JUST STOP AND LISTEN TO ME FOR A SECOND, OKAY?
AGENT SOLOMON, TELL ME AT ONCE... HOW DID THIS HAPPEN?
IT STARTED A FEW WEEKS AGO, WHEN ROXXON GOT APPROVAL FROM THE STATE SENATE TO MOVE THEIR FLYING FACTORIES IN. THEY EVEN GOT SOME BIG FAT TAX BREAKS FOR DOING SO.
AFTER THAT, THEY STARTED BUYING UP EVERY PIECE OF THE TOWN THEY COULD. TIMES ARE STILL HARD AROUND HERE. LOTS OF FOLKS COULDN'T AFFORD TO SAY NO.
THIS...THIS IS ALL BECAUSE OF...
THOR, LISTEN TO ME, YOU HAVE TO LET ME HANDLE THIS. I WILL SHUT THESE FACTORIES DOWN, I PROMISE YOU. BUT WE HAVE TO DO THIS THE RIGHT WAY. THE LEGAL WAY.
THOR, ARE YOU HEARING ME?
THOR, THEY BOUGHT THE BANK. TOOK MY HOUSE AWAY. MY FATHER BUILT THAT HOUSE.
THEY SAY WE HAVE TO CLOSE THE NURSING HOME. FOLKS THERE CAN BARELY BREATHE ANYWAY, WHAT WITH ALL THIS MESS IN THE AIR.
SOMETHING'S WRONG WITH THE WATER. TASTES LIKE GASOLINE. I THINK THEY DID SOMETHIN' TO IT.
THOR, WHY IS THIS HAPPENING?
...THOR?
SWOOO
OH, HELL.
NOT GOOD. NOT GOOD AT ALL.

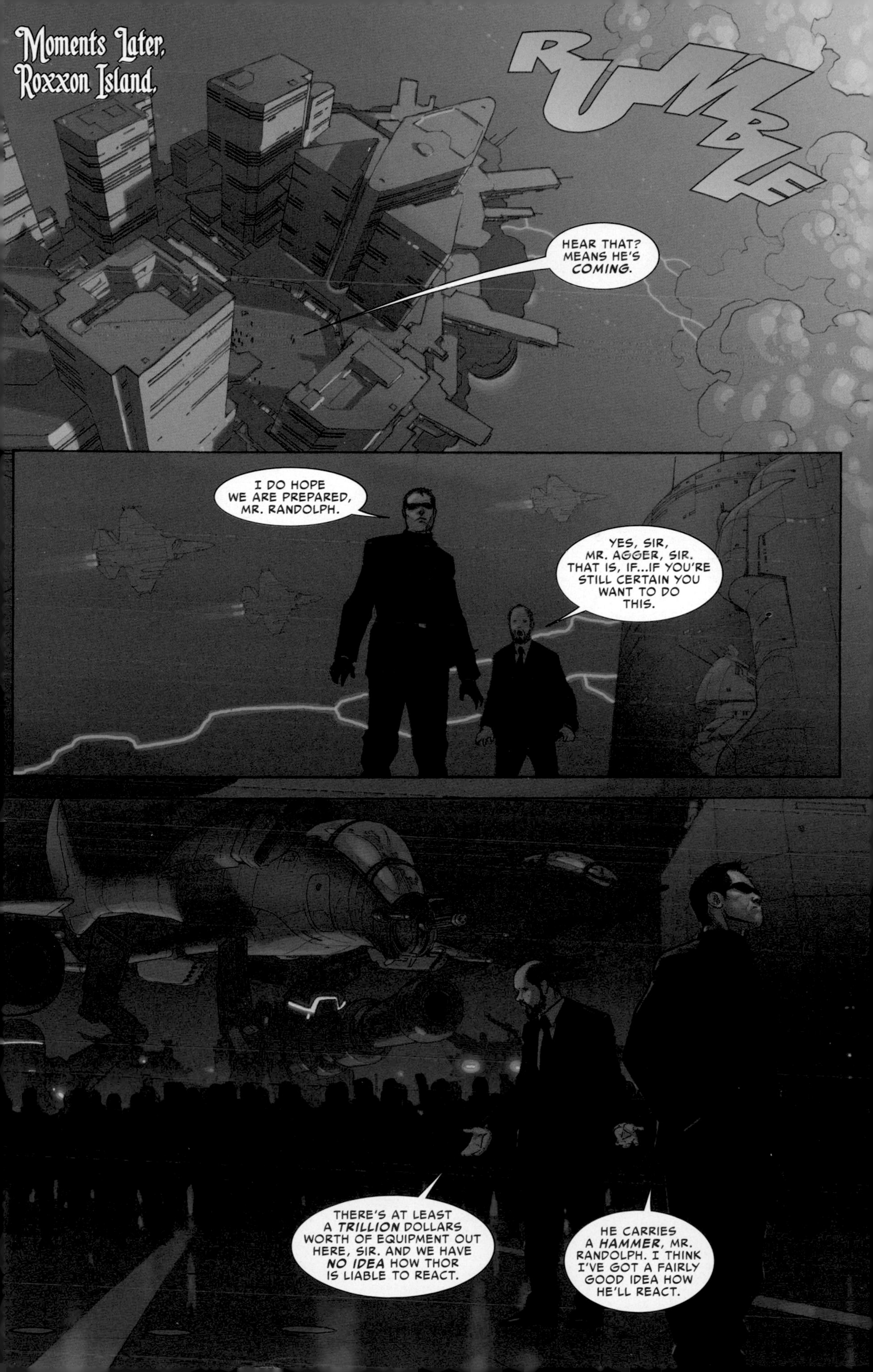
Moments Later, Roxxon Island.
RUMBLE
HEAR THAT? MEANS HE'S COMING.
I DO HOPE WE ARE PREPARED, MR. RANDOLPH.
YES, SIR, MR. AGGER, SIR. THAT IS, IF...IF YOU'RE STILL CERTAIN YOU WANT TO DO THIS.
THERE'S AT LEAST A TRILLION DOLLARS WORTH OF EQUIPMENT OUT HERE, SIR. AND WE HAVE NO IDEA HOW THOR IS LIABLE TO REACT.
HE CARRIES A HAMMER, MR. RANDOLPH. I THINK I'VE GOT A FAIRLY GOOD IDEA HOW HE'LL REACT.

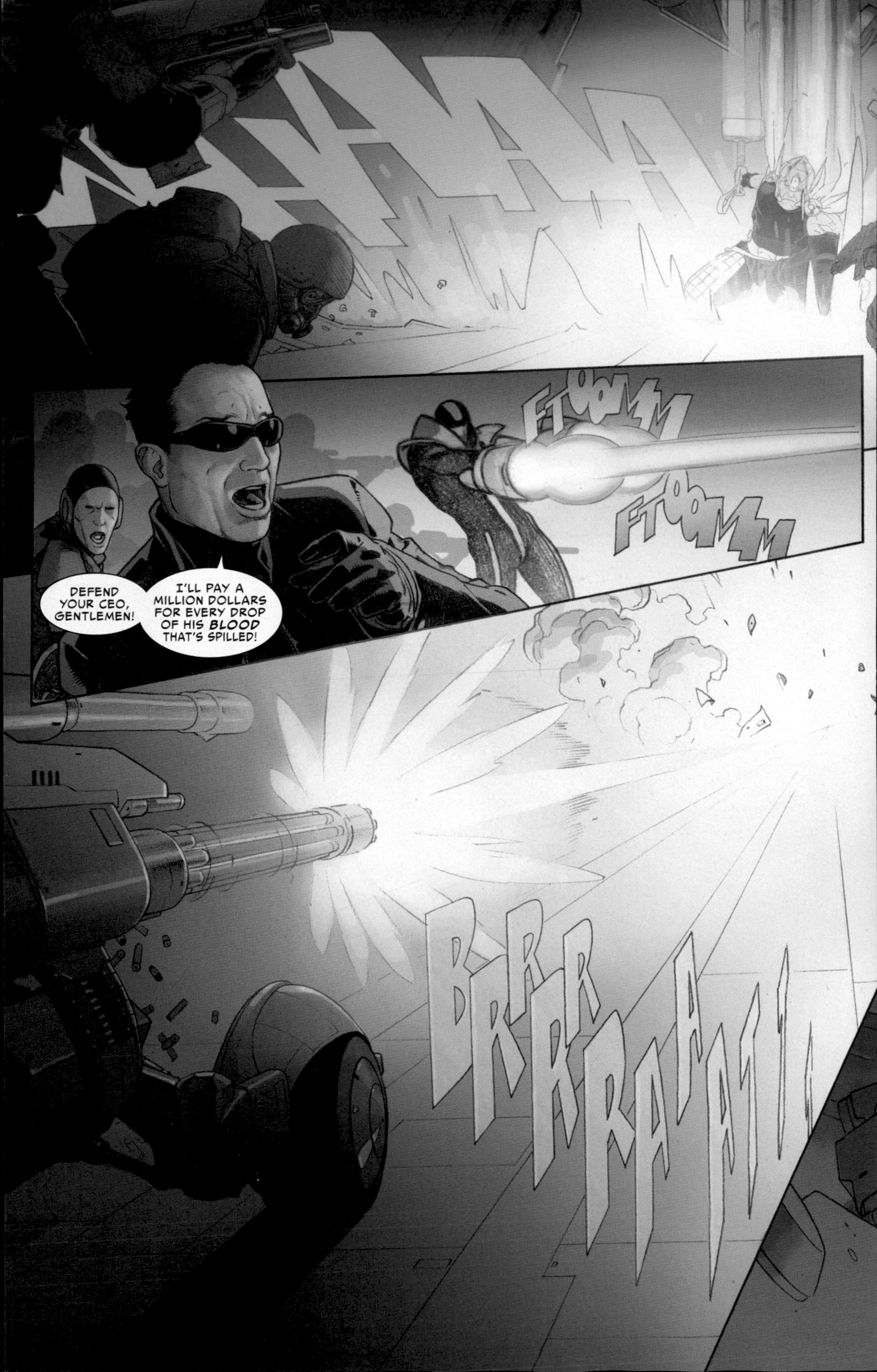
FTOOMM
FTOOMM
DEFEND YOUR CEO, GENTLEMEN!
I'LL PAY A MILLION DOLLARS FOR EVERY DROP OF HIS BLOOD THAT'S SPILLED!
BRRRRAAAT

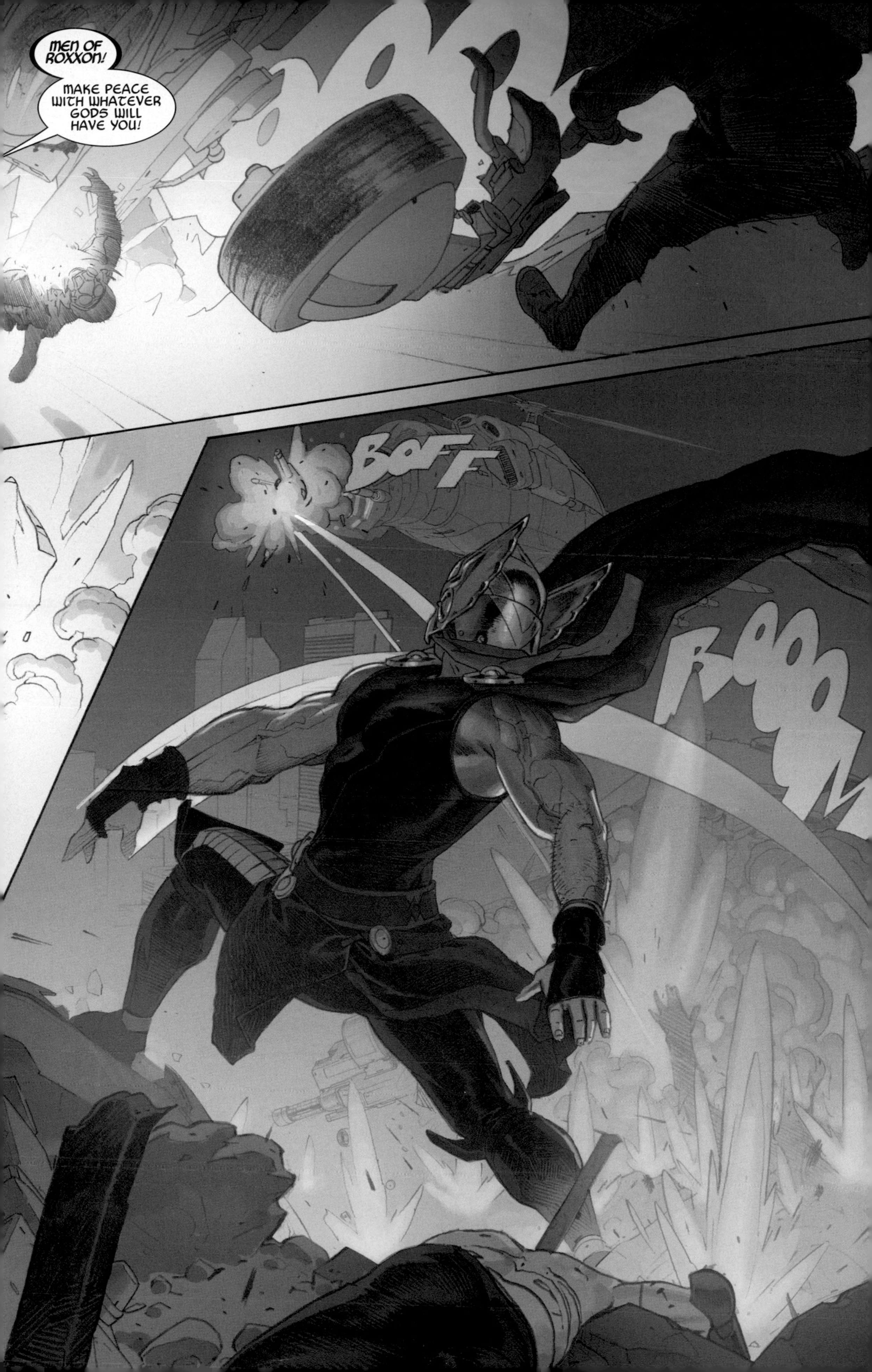
MEN OF ROXXON!
MAKE PEACE WITH WHATEVER GODS WILL HAVE YOU!
BOFF
BOOOM

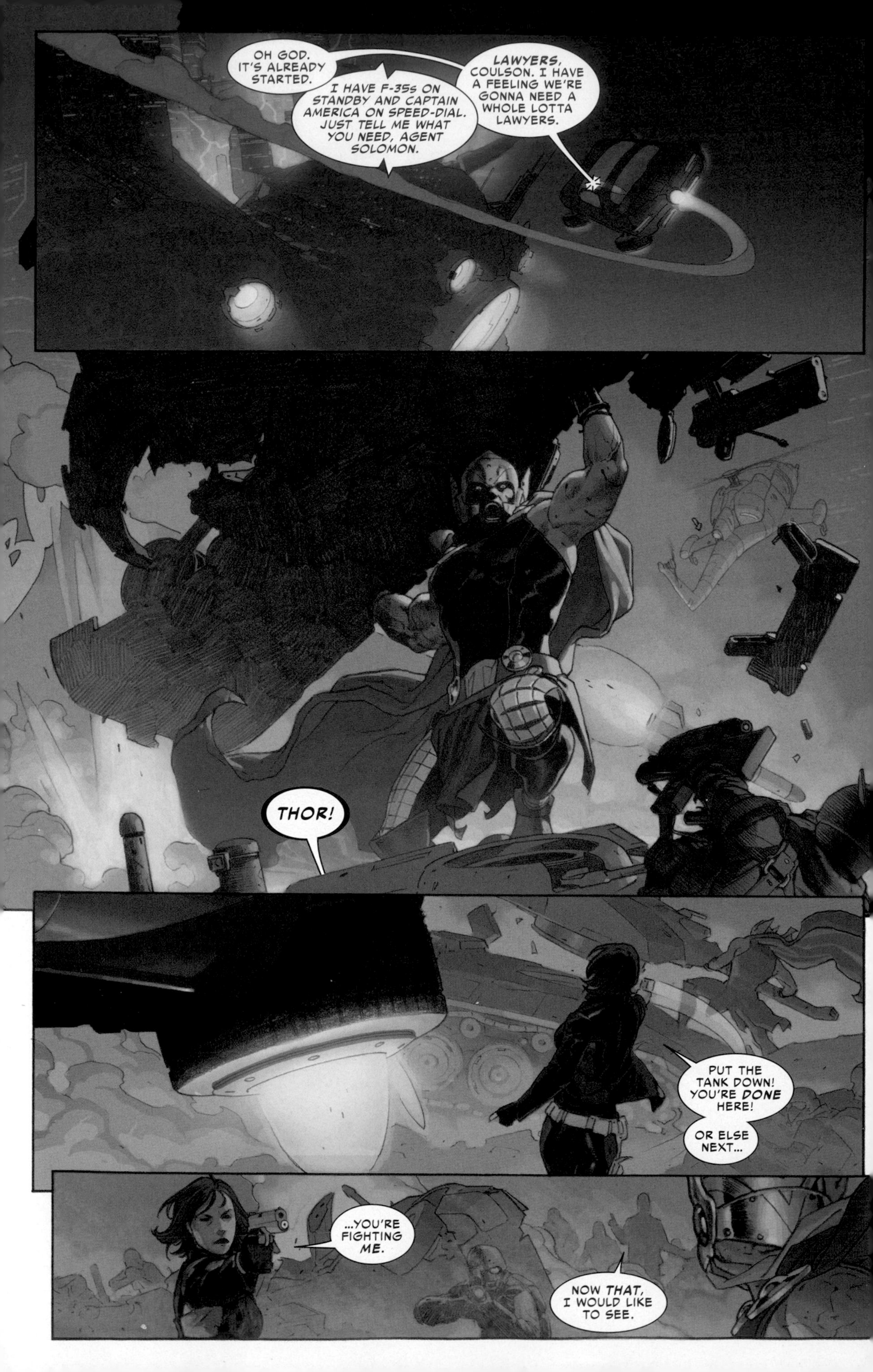
OH GOD. IT'S ALREADY STARTED.
I HAVE F-35s ON STANDBY AND CAPTAIN AMERICA ON SPEED-DIAL. JUST TELL ME WHAT YOU NEED, AGENT SOLOMON.
LAWYERS, COULSON. I HAVE A FEELING WE'RE GONNA NEED A WHOLE LOTTA LAWYERS.
THOR!
PUT THE TANK DOWN! YOU'RE DONE HERE!
OR ELSE NEXT...
...YOU'RE FIGHTING ME.
NOW THAT, I WOULD LIKE TO SEE.

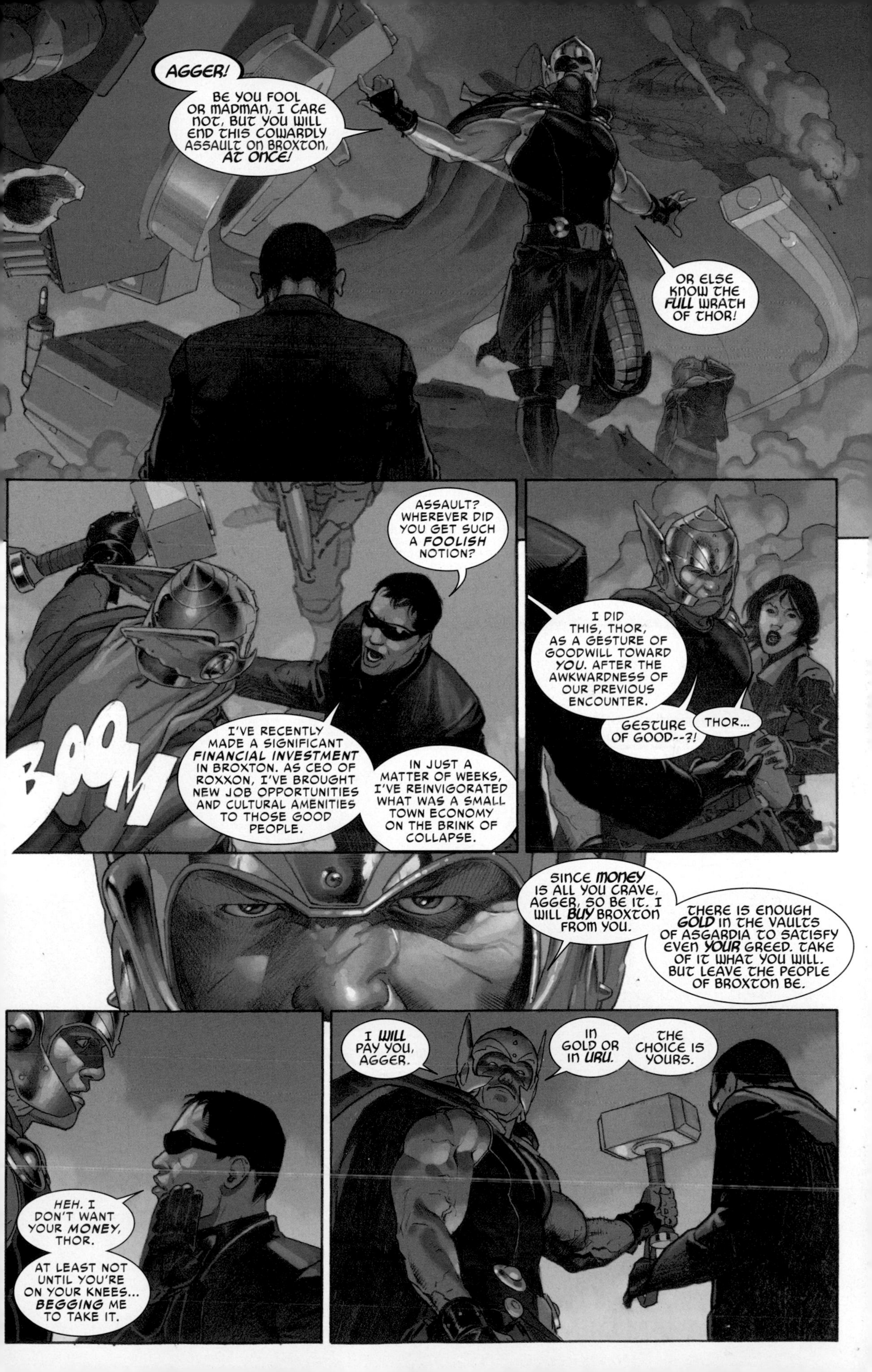

AGGER!
BE YOU FOOL OR MADMAN, I CARE NOT, BUT YOU WILL END THIS COWARDLY ASSAULT ON BROXTON, AT ONCE!
OR ELSE KNOW THE FULL WRATH OF THOR!
ASSAULT? WHEREVER DID YOU GET SUCH A FOOLISH NOTION?
I'VE RECENTLY MADE A SIGNIFICANT FINANCIAL INVESTMENT IN BROXTON. AS CEO OF ROXXON, I'VE BROUGHT NEW JOB OPPORTUNITIES AND CULTURAL AMENITIES TO THOSE GOOD PEOPLE.
IN JUST A MATTER OF WEEKS, I'VE REINVIGORATED WHAT WAS A SMALL TOWN ECONOMY ON THE BRINK OF COLLAPSE.
BOOM
I DID THIS, THOR, AS A GESTURE OF GOODWILL TOWARD YOU. AFTER THE AWKWARDNESS OF OUR PREVIOUS ENCOUNTER.
GESTURE OF GOOD--?!
THOR...
SINCE MONEY IS ALL YOU CRAVE, AGGER, SO BE IT. I WILL BUY BROXTON FROM YOU.
THERE IS ENOUGH GOLD IN THE VAULTS OF ASGARDIA TO SATISFY EVEN YOUR GREED. TAKE OF IT WHAT YOU WILL. BUT LEAVE THE PEOPLE OF BROXTON BE.
HEH. I DON'T WANT YOUR MONEY, THOR.
AT LEAST NOT UNTIL YOU'RE ON YOUR KNEES... BEGGING ME TO TAKE IT.
I WILL PAY YOU, AGGER.
IN GOLD OR IN URU.
THE CHOICE IS YOURS.

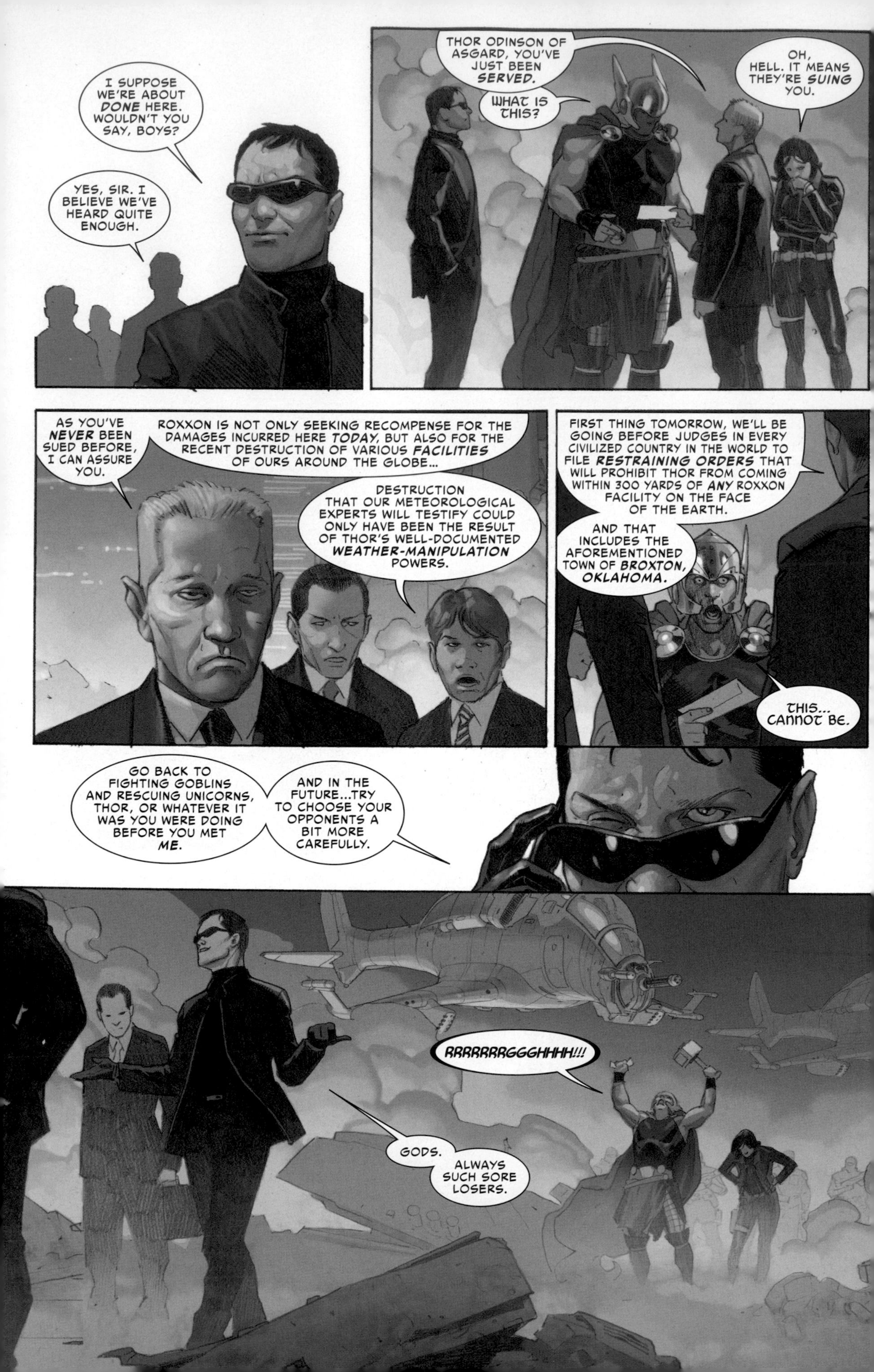

I SUPPOSE WE'RE ABOUT DONE HERE. WOULDN'T YOU SAY, BOYS?
YES, SIR. I BELIEVE WE'VE HEARD QUITE ENOUGH.
THOR ODINSON OF ASGARD, YOU'VE JUST BEEN SERVED.
WHAT IS THIS?
OH, HELL. IT MEANS THEY'RE SUING YOU.
AS YOU'VE NEVER BEEN SUED BEFORE, I CAN ASSURE YOU.
ROXXON IS NOT ONLY SEEKING RECOMPENSE FOR THE DAMAGES INCURRED HERE TODAY, BUT ALSO FOR THE RECENT DESTRUCTION OF VARIOUS FACILITIES OF OURS AROUND THE GLOBE...
DESTRUCTION THAT OUR METEOROLOGICAL EXPERTS WILL TESTIFY COULD ONLY HAVE BEEN THE RESULT OF THOR'S WELL-DOCUMENTED WEATHER-MANIPULATION POWERS.
FIRST THING TOMORROW, WE'LL BE GOING BEFORE JUDGES IN EVERY CIVILIZED COUNTRY IN THE WORLD TO FILE RESTRAINING ORDERS THAT WILL PROHIBIT THOR FROM COMING WITHIN 300 YARDS OF ANY ROXXON FACILITY ON THE FACE OF THE EARTH.
AND THAT INCLUDES THE AFOREMENTIONED TOWN OF BROXTON, OKLAHOMA.
THIS... CANNOT BE.
GO BACK TO FIGHTING GOBLINS AND RESCUING UNICORNS, THOR, OR WHATEVER IT WAS YOU WERE DOING BEFORE YOU MET ME.
AND IN THE FUTURE...TRY TO CHOOSE YOUR OPPONENTS A BIT MORE CAREFULLY.
RRRRRRRRGGGHHHH!!!
GODS.
ALWAYS SUCH SORE LOSERS.

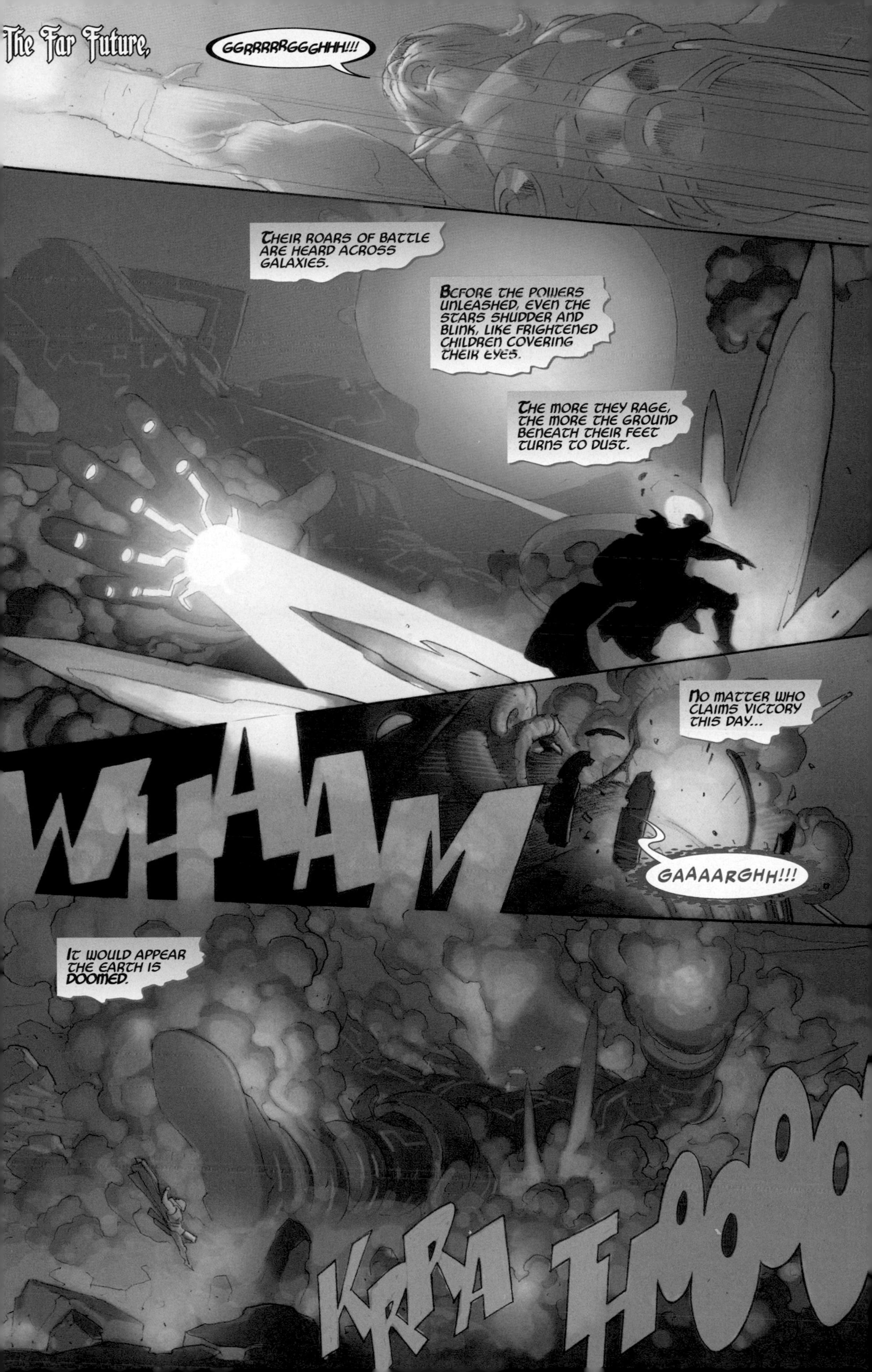
The Far Future,
GGRRRRRGGGHHH!!!
THEIR ROARS OF BATTLE ARE HEARD ACROSS GALAXIES.
BEFORE THE POWERS UNLEASHED, EVEN THE STARS SHUDDER AND BLINK, LIKE FRIGHTENED CHILDREN COVERING THEIR EYES.
THE MORE THEY RAGE, THE MORE THE GROUND BENEATH THEIR FEET TURNS TO DUST.
NO MATTER WHO CLAIMS VICTORY THIS DAY...
WHAAM
GAAAARGHH!!!
IT WOULD APPEAR THE EARTH IS DOOMED.
KRRA THOOOO

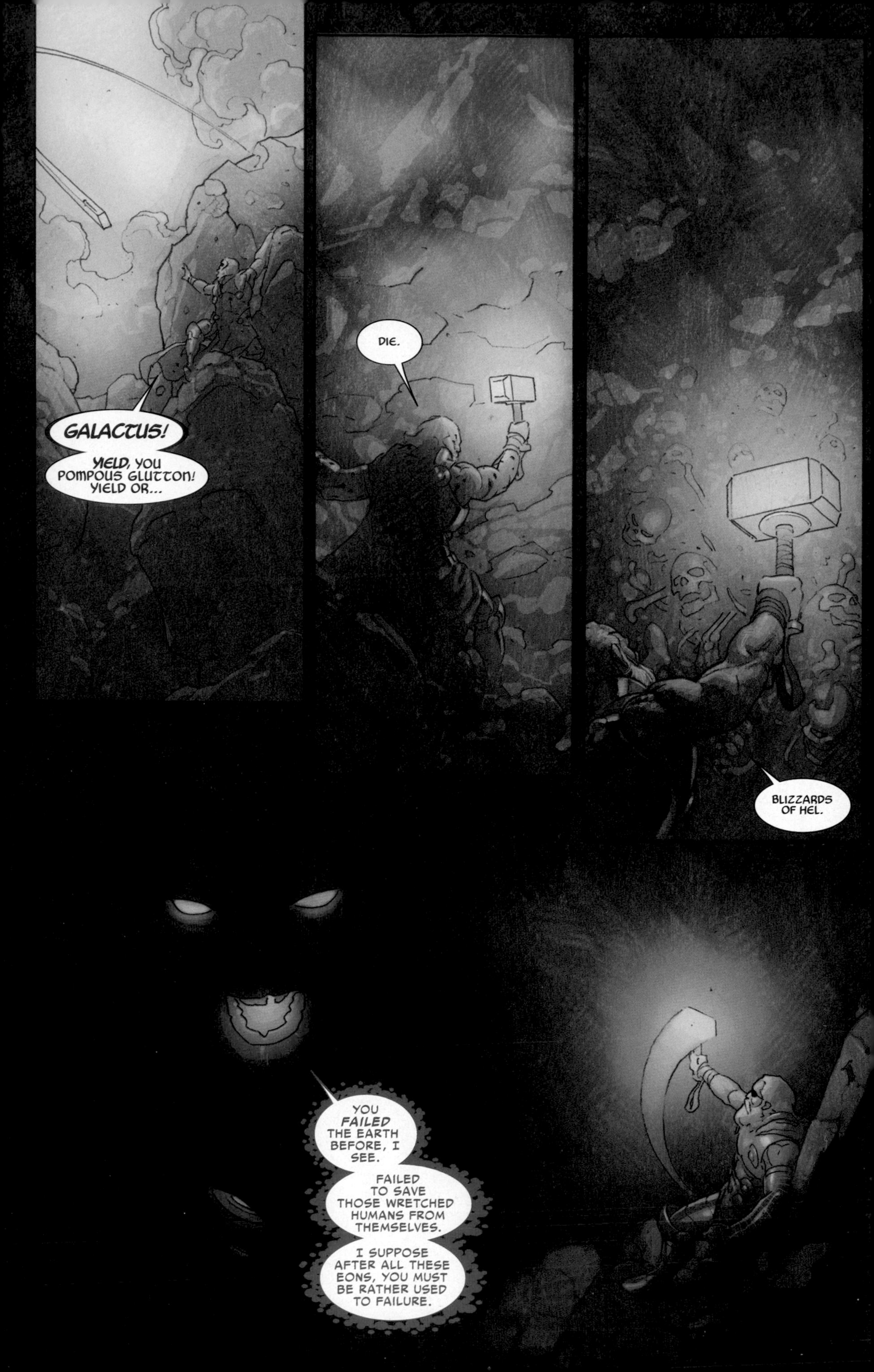
GALACTUS!
YIELD, YOU POMPOUS GLUTTON! YIELD OR...
DIE.
BLIZZARDS OF HEL.
YOU FAILED THE EARTH BEFORE, I SEE.
FAILED TO SAVE THOSE WRETCHED HUMANS FROM THEMSELVES.
I SUPPOSE AFTER ALL THESE EONS, YOU MUST BE RATHER USED TO FAILURE.

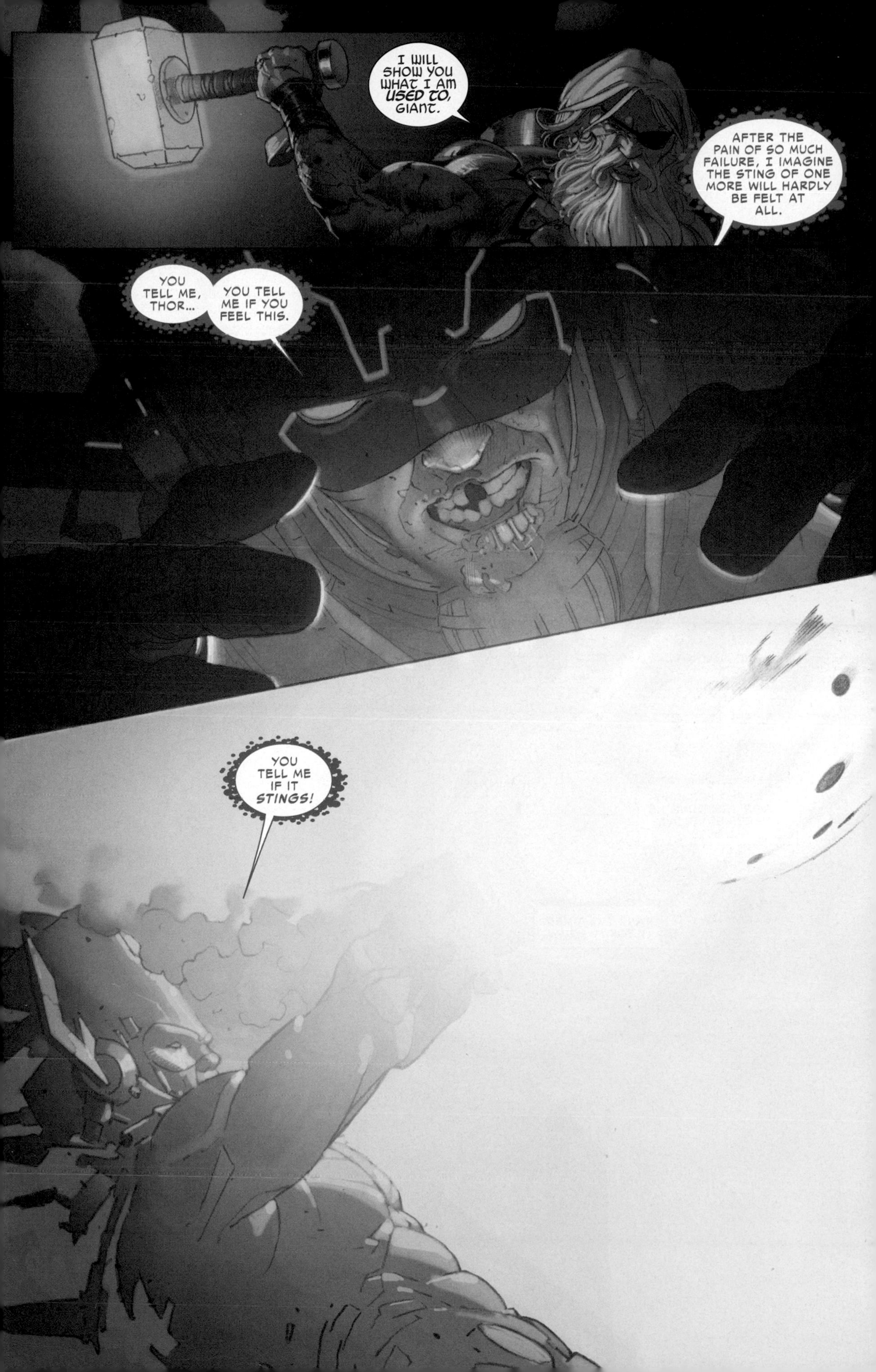
I WILL SHOW YOU WHAT I AM USED TO, GIANT.
AFTER THE PAIN OF SO MUCH FAILURE, I IMAGINE THE STING OF ONE MORE WILL HARDLY BE FELT AT ALL.
YOU TELL ME, THOR...
YOU TELL ME IF YOU FEEL THIS.
YOU TELL ME IF IT STINGS!

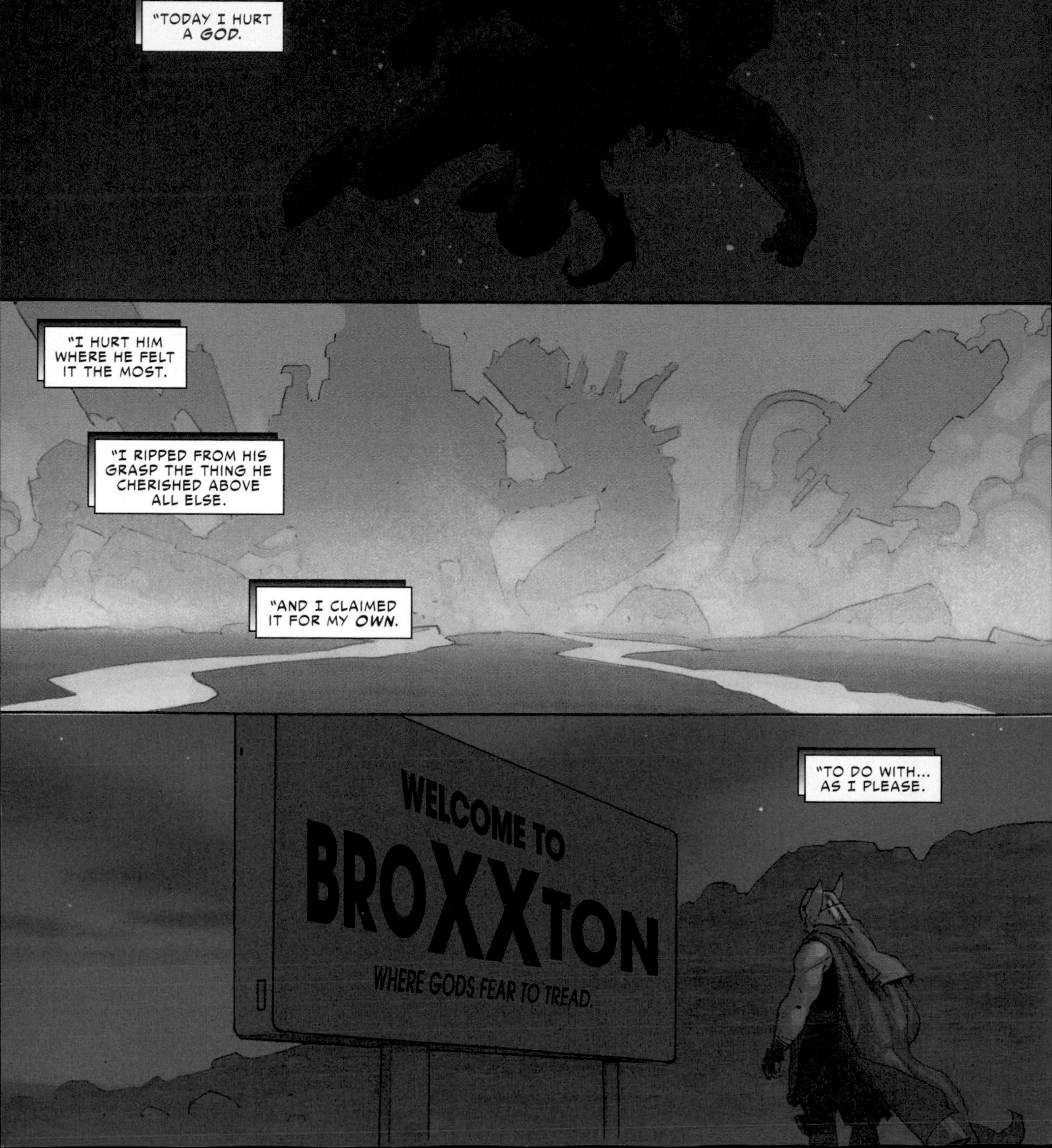
"TODAY I HURT A GOD.
"I HURT HIM WHERE HE FELT IT THE MOST.
"I RIPPED FROM HIS GRASP THE THING HE CHERISHED ABOVE ALL ELSE.
"AND I CLAIMED IT FOR MY OWN.
WELCOME TO BROXXTON
WHERE GODS FEAR TO TREAD.
"TO DO WITH... AS I PLEASE.

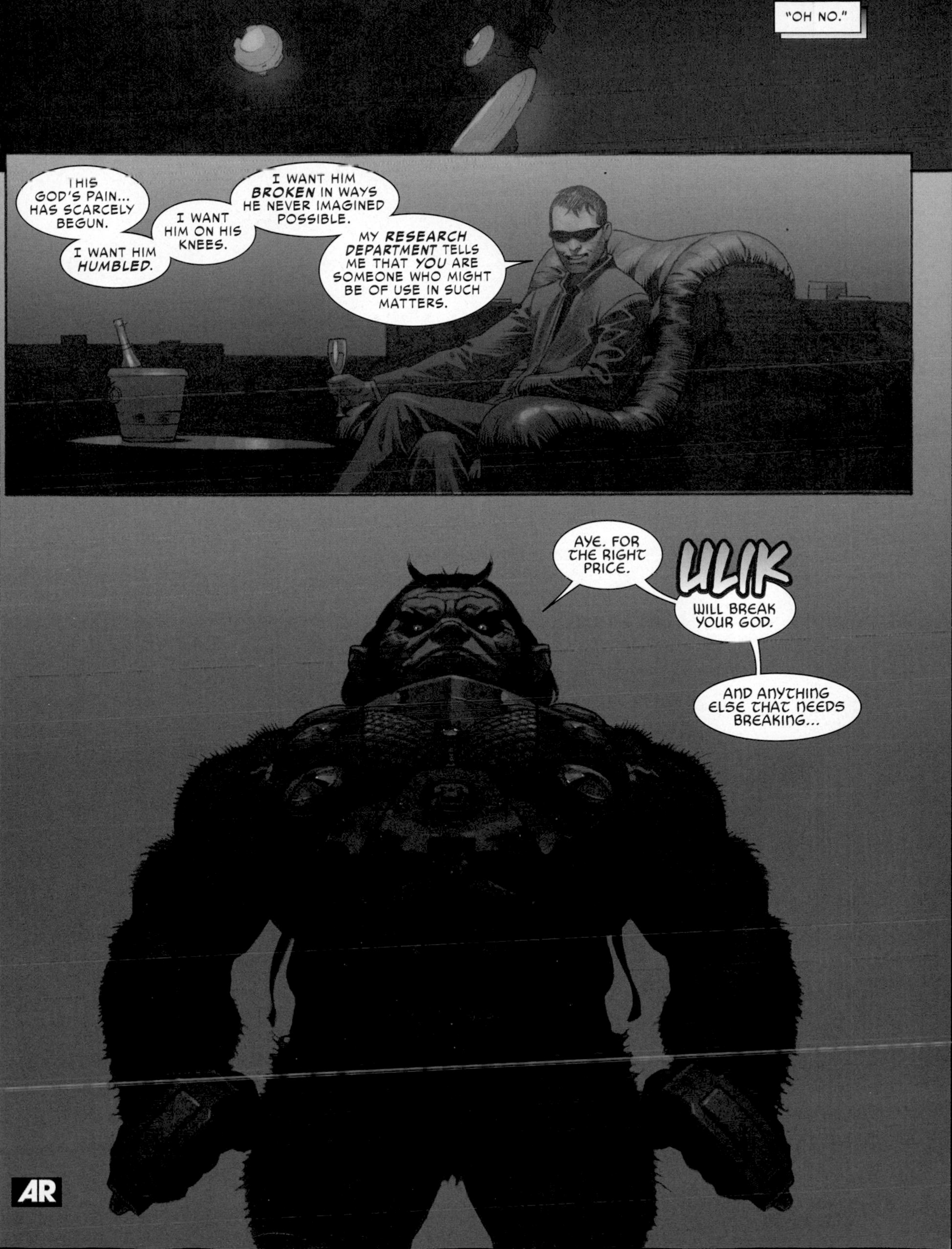
"OH NO."
THIS GOD'S PAIN... HAS SCARCELY BEGUN.
I WANT HIM HUMBLED.
I WANT HIM ON HIS KNEES.
I WANT HIM BROKEN IN WAYS HE NEVER IMAGINED POSSIBLE.
MY RESEARCH DEPARTMENT TELLS ME THAT YOU ARE SOMEONE WHO MIGHT BE OF USE IN SUCH MATTERS.
AYE. FOR THE RIGHT PRICE.
ULIK WILL BREAK YOUR GOD.
AND ANYTHING ELSE THAT NEEDS BREAKING...
AR

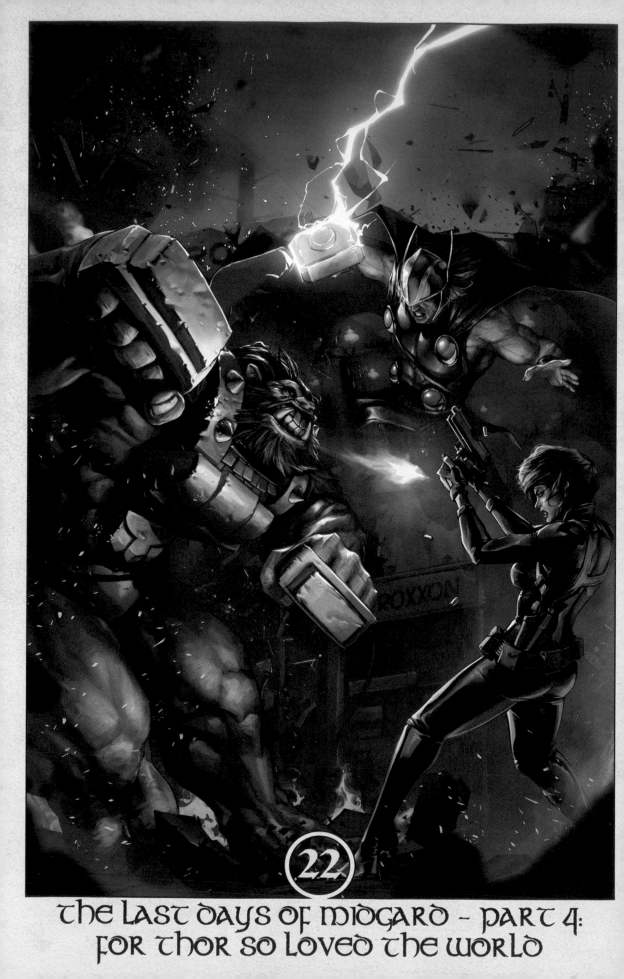

THE LAST DAYS OF MIDGARD – PART 4:
FOR THOR SO LOVED THE WORLD

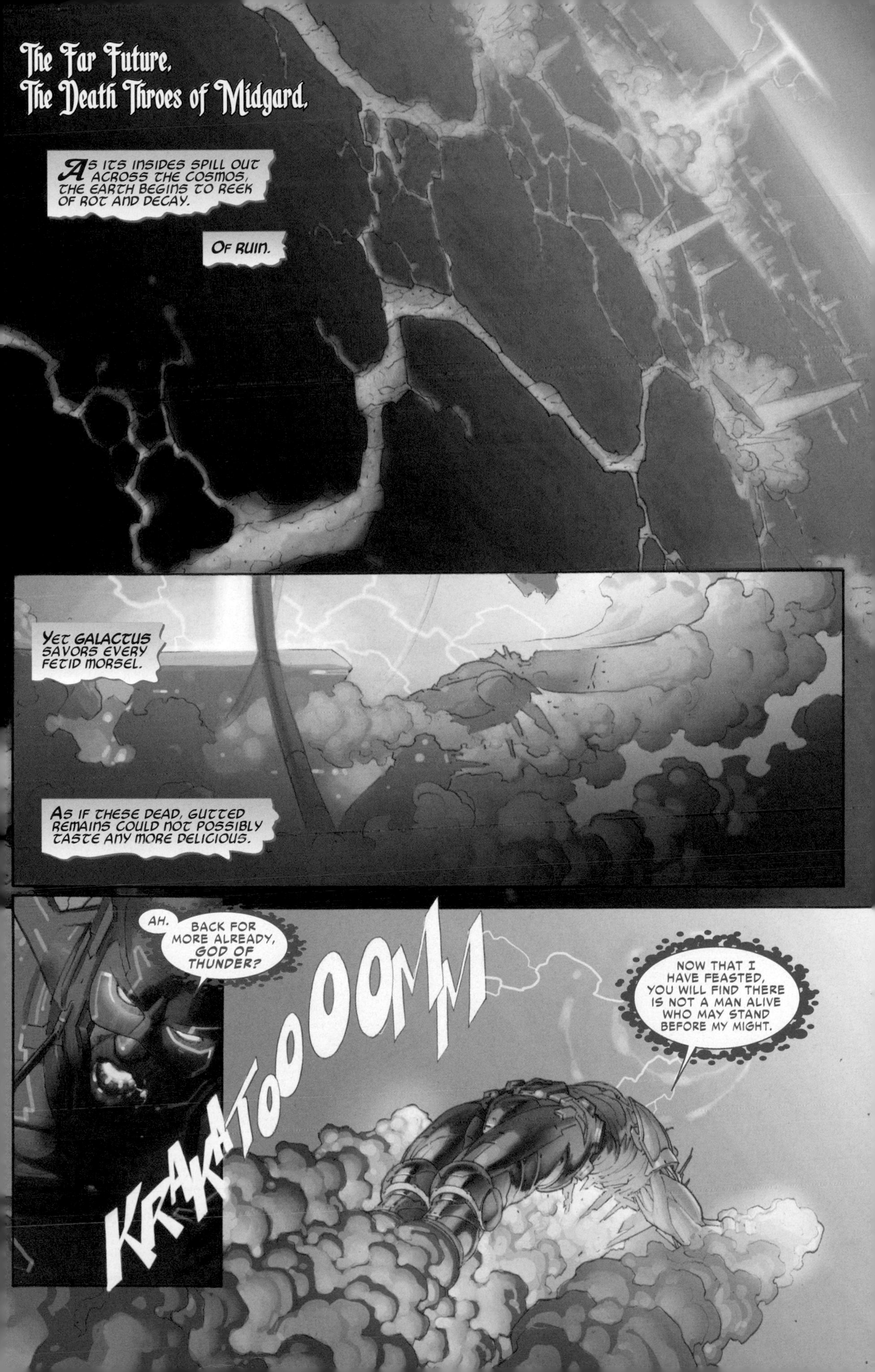
The Far Future.
The Death Throes of Midgard.
As its insides spill out across the cosmos, the earth begins to reek of rot and decay.
Of ruin.
Yet Galactus savors every fetid morsel.
As if these dead, gutted remains could not possibly taste any more delicious.
AH.
BACK FOR MORE ALREADY, GOD OF THUNDER?
KRAKATOOOOOMM
NOW THAT I HAVE FEASTED, YOU WILL FIND THERE IS NOT A MAN ALIVE WHO MAY STAND BEFORE MY MIGHT.

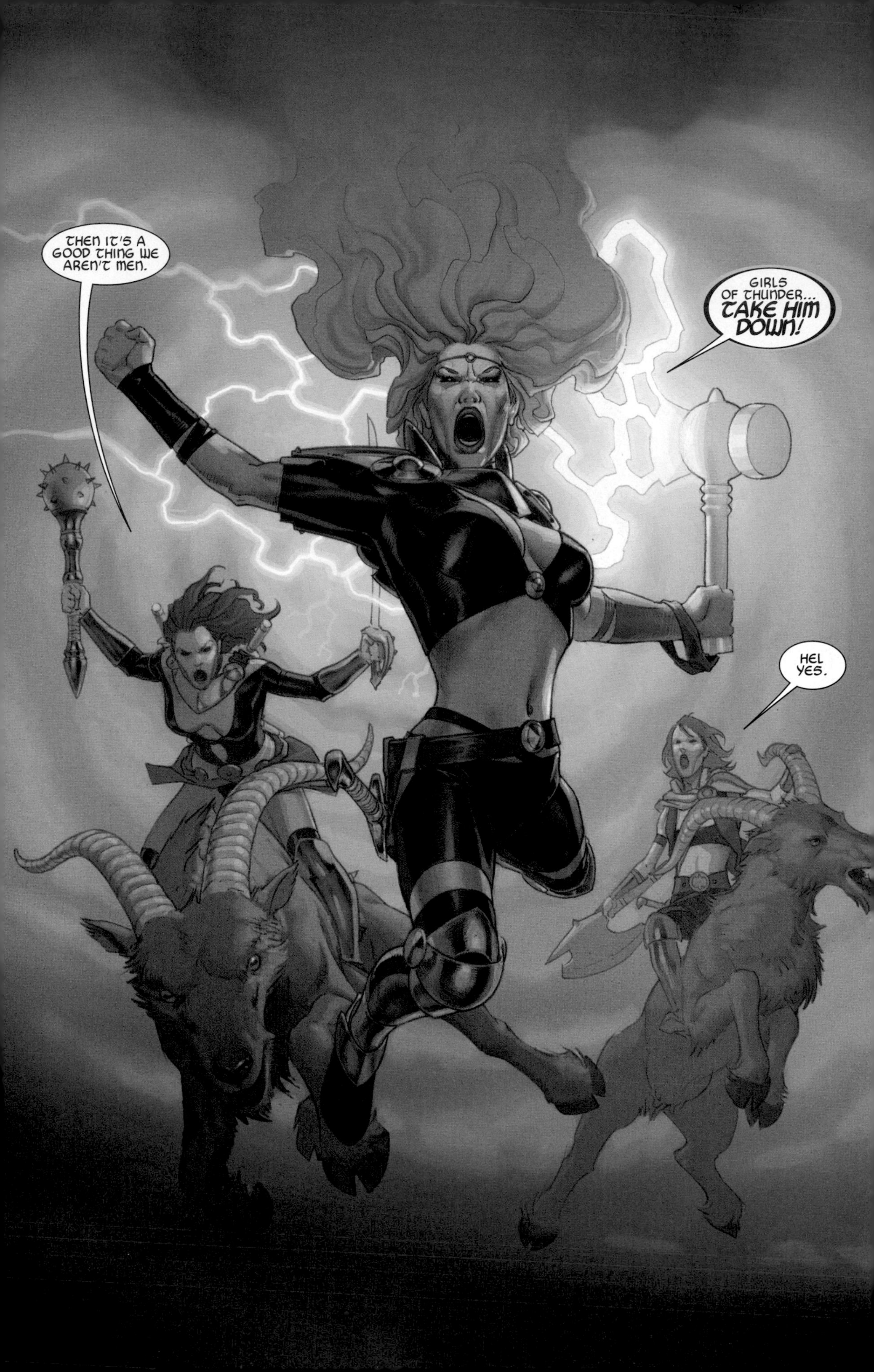
THEN IT'S A GOOD THING WE AREN'T MEN.
GIRLS OF THUNDER... TAKE HIM DOWN!
HEL YES.

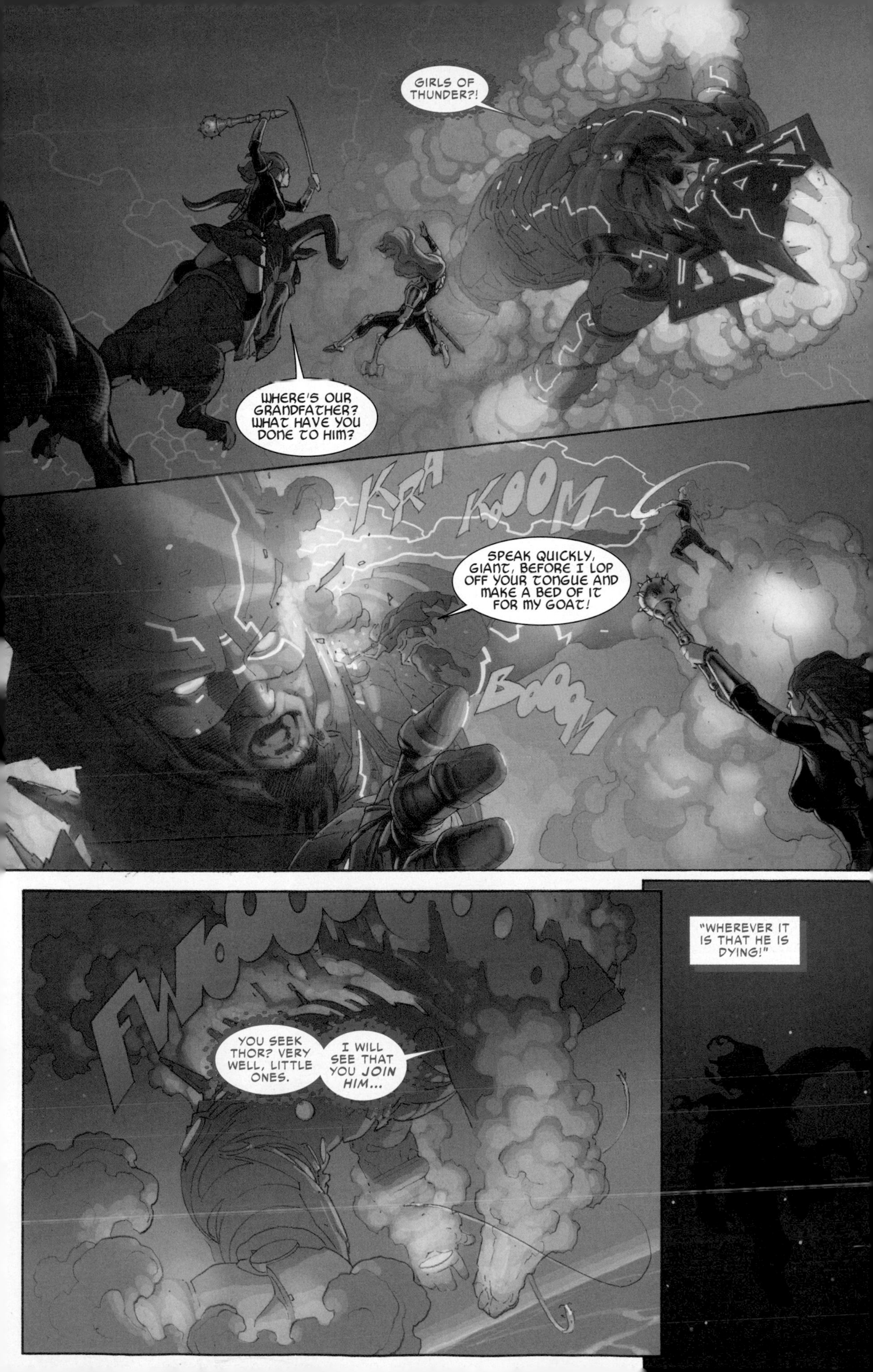
GIRLS OF THUNDER?!
WHERE'S OUR GRANDFATHER? WHAT HAVE YOU DONE TO HIM?
KRA KOOOM
SPEAK QUICKLY, GIANT, BEFORE I LOP OFF YOUR TONGUE AND MAKE A BED OF IT FOR MY GOAT!
BOOOM
YOU SEEK THOR? VERY WELL, LITTLE ONES.
I WILL SEE THAT YOU JOIN HIM...
"WHEREVER IT IS THAT HE IS DYING!"

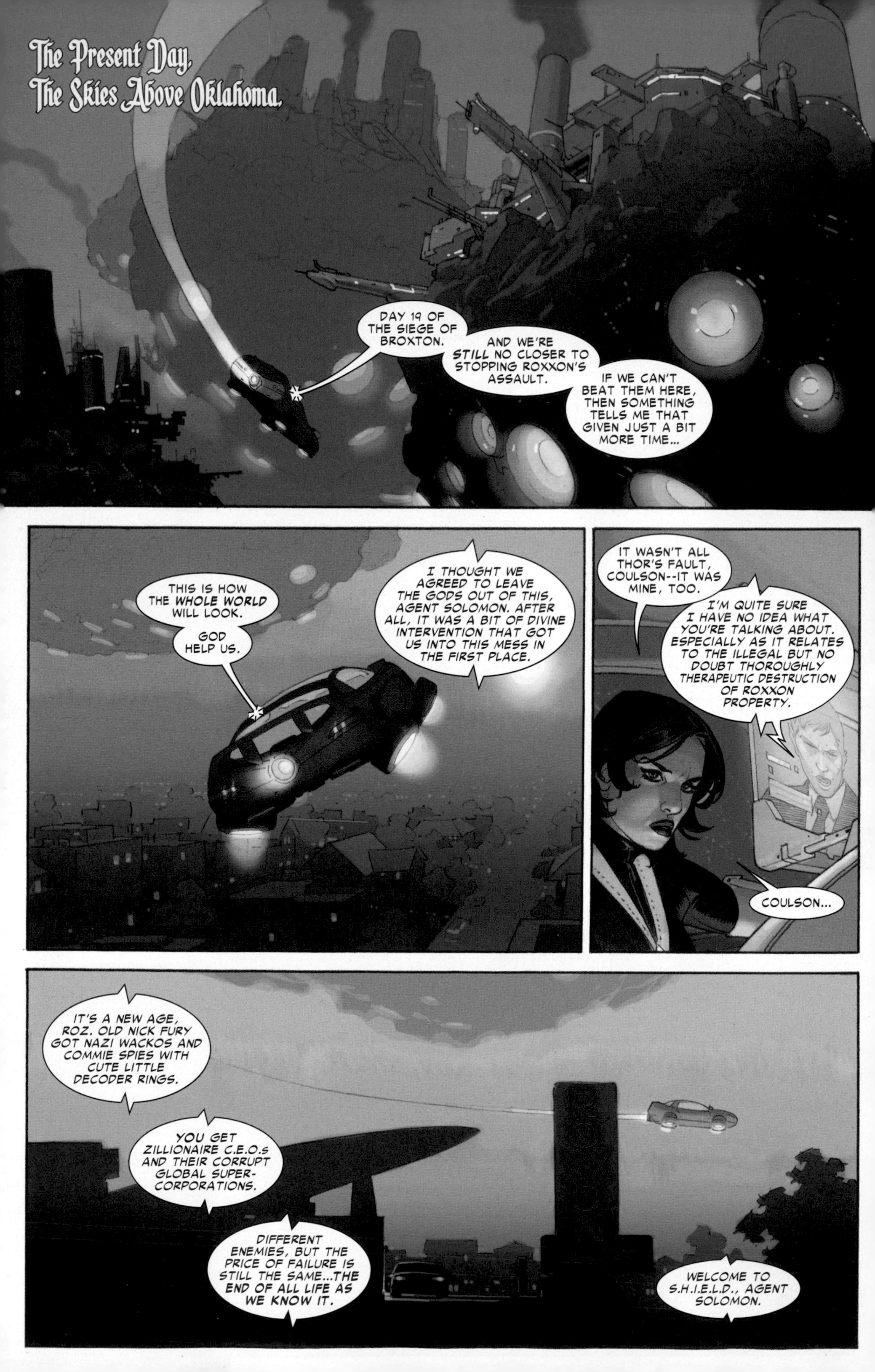
The Present Day,
The Skies Above Oklahoma.
DAY 19 OF THE SIEGE OF BROXTON.
AND WE'RE STILL NO CLOSER TO STOPPING ROXXON'S ASSAULT.
IF WE CAN'T BEAT THEM HERE, THEN SOMETHING TELLS ME THAT GIVEN JUST A BIT MORE TIME...
THIS IS HOW THE WHOLE WORLD WILL LOOK.
GOD HELP US.
I THOUGHT WE AGREED TO LEAVE THE GODS OUT OF THIS, AGENT SOLOMON. AFTER ALL, IT WAS A BIT OF DIVINE INTERVENTION THAT GOT US INTO THIS MESS IN THE FIRST PLACE.
IT WASN'T ALL THOR'S FAULT, COULSON--IT WAS MINE, TOO.
I'M QUITE SURE I HAVE NO IDEA WHAT YOU'RE TALKING ABOUT. ESPECIALLY AS IT RELATES TO THE ILLEGAL BUT NO DOUBT THOROUGHLY THERAPEUTIC DESTRUCTION OF ROXXON PROPERTY.
COULSON...
IT'S A NEW AGE, ROZ. OLD NICK FURY GOT NAZI WACKOS AND COMMIE SPIES WITH CUTE LITTLE DECODER RINGS.
YOU GET ZILLIONAIRE C.E.O.s AND THEIR CORRUPT GLOBAL SUPER-CORPORATIONS.
DIFFERENT ENEMIES, BUT THE PRICE OF FAILURE IS STILL THE SAME...THE END OF ALL LIFE AS WE KNOW IT.
WELCOME TO S.H.I.E.L.D., AGENT SOLOMON.

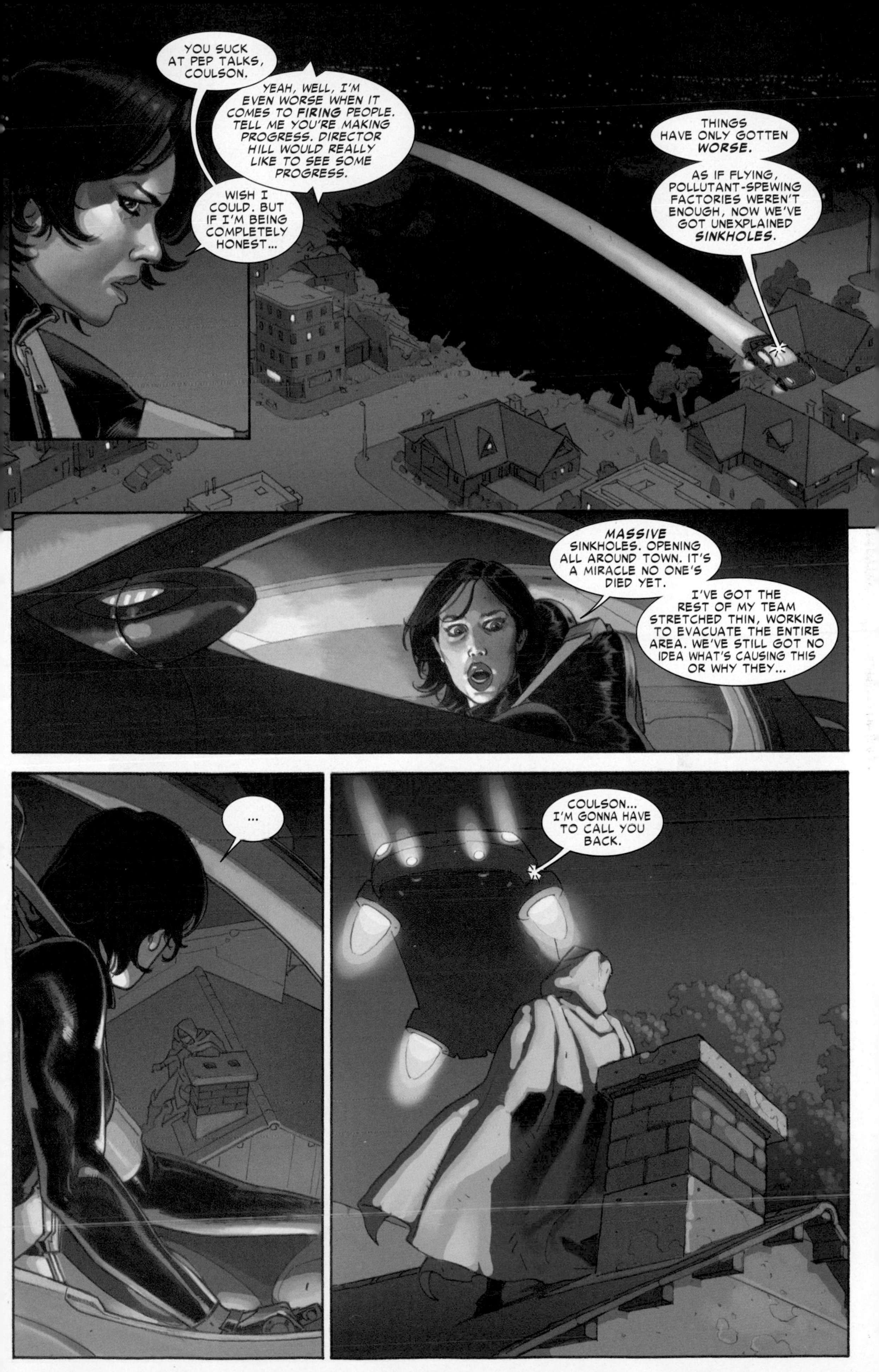
YOU SUCK AT PEP TALKS, COULSON.
YEAH, WELL, I'M EVEN WORSE WHEN IT COMES TO FIRING PEOPLE. TELL ME YOU'RE MAKING PROGRESS. DIRECTOR HILL WOULD REALLY LIKE TO SEE SOME PROGRESS.
WISH I COULD. BUT IF I'M BEING COMPLETELY HONEST...
THINGS HAVE ONLY GOTTEN WORSE.
AS IF FLYING, POLLUTANT-SPEWING FACTORIES WEREN'T ENOUGH, NOW WE'VE GOT UNEXPLAINED SINKHOLES.
MASSIVE SINKHOLES. OPENING ALL AROUND TOWN. IT'S A MIRACLE NO ONE'S DIED YET.
I'VE GOT THE REST OF MY TEAM STRETCHED THIN, WORKING TO EVACUATE THE ENTIRE AREA. WE'VE STILL GOT NO IDEA WHAT'S CAUSING THIS OR WHY THEY...
...
COULSON... I'M GONNA HAVE TO CALL YOU BACK.

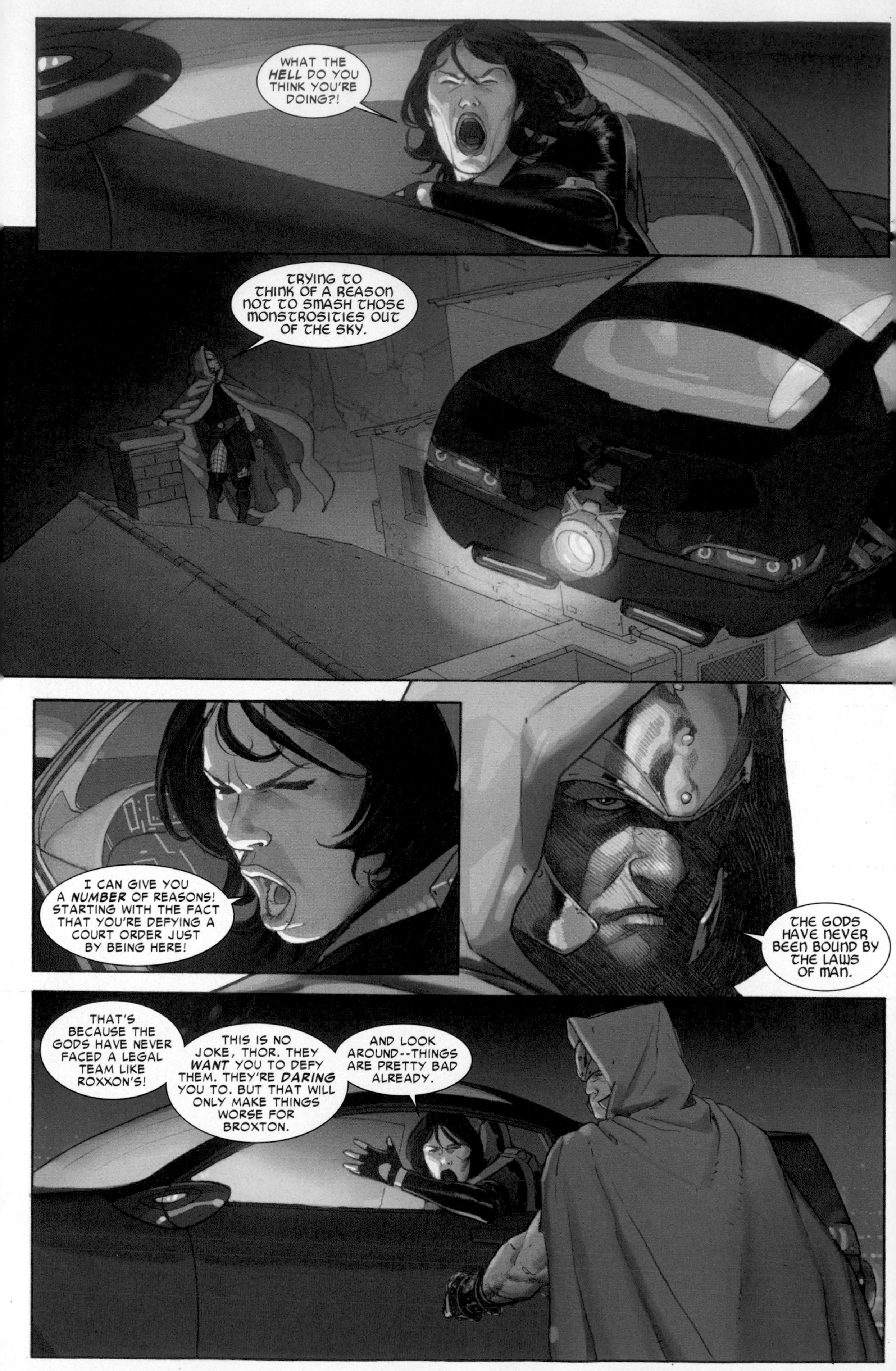

WHAT THE HELL DO YOU THINK YOU'RE DOING?!
TRYING TO THINK OF A REASON NOT TO SMASH THOSE MONSTROSITIES OUT OF THE SKY.
I CAN GIVE YOU A NUMBER OF REASONS! STARTING WITH THE FACT THAT YOU'RE DEFYING A COURT ORDER JUST BY BEING HERE!
THE GODS HAVE NEVER BEEN BOUND BY THE LAWS OF MAN.
THAT'S BECAUSE THE GODS HAVE NEVER FACED A LEGAL TEAM LIKE ROXXON'S!
THIS IS NO JOKE, THOR. THEY WANT YOU TO DEFY THEM. THEY'RE DARING YOU TO. BUT THAT WILL ONLY MAKE THINGS WORSE FOR BROXTON.
AND LOOK AROUND--THINGS ARE PRETTY BAD ALREADY.

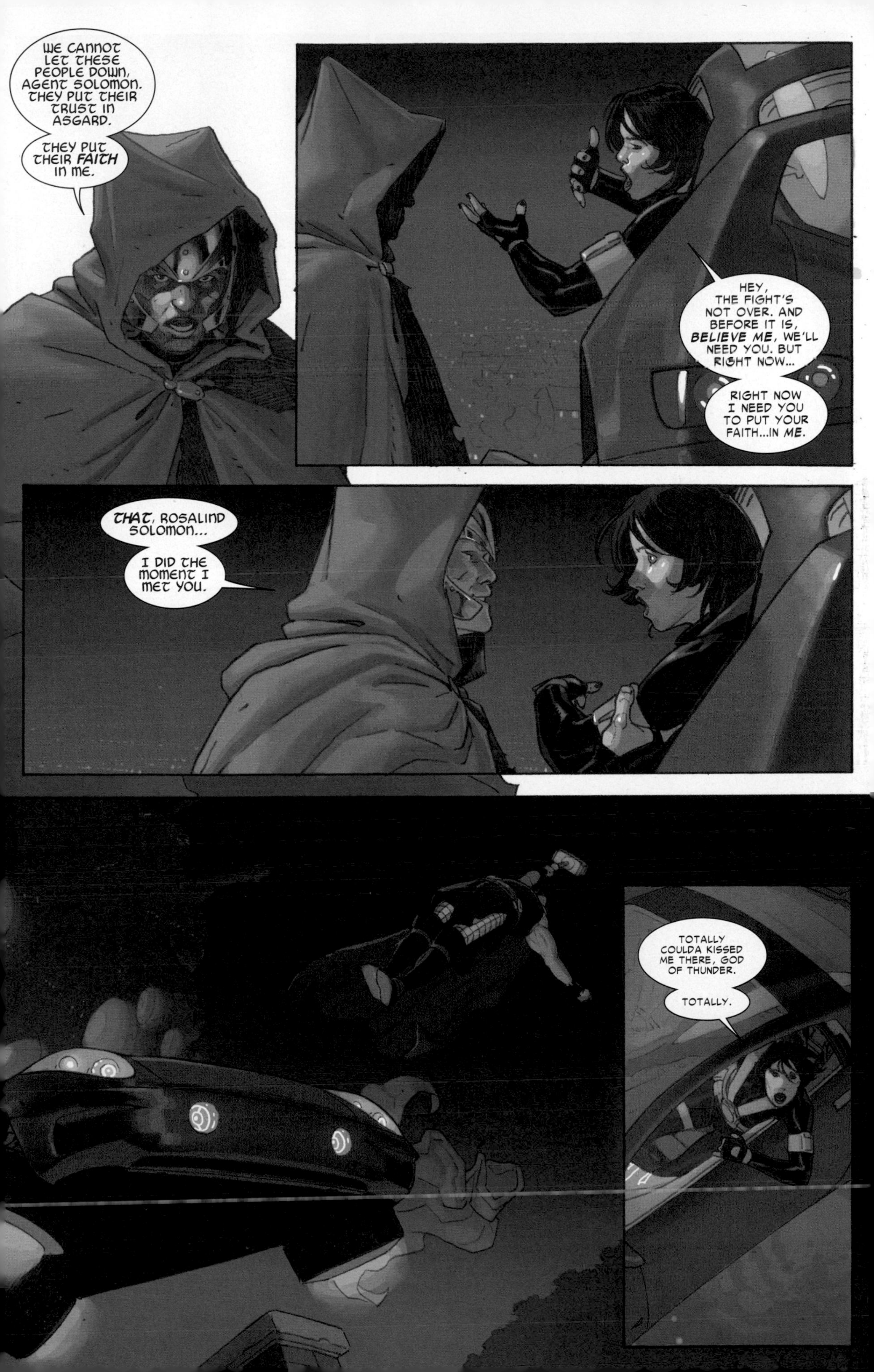

WE CANNOT LET THESE PEOPLE DOWN, AGENT SOLOMON. THEY PUT THEIR TRUST IN ASGARD.
THEY PUT THEIR FAITH IN ME.
HEY, THE FIGHT'S NOT OVER. AND BEFORE IT IS, BELIEVE ME, WE'LL NEED YOU. BUT RIGHT NOW...
RIGHT NOW I NEED YOU TO PUT YOUR FAITH...IN ME.
THAT, ROSALIND SOLOMON...
I DID THE MOMENT I MET YOU.
TOTALLY COULDA KISSED ME THERE, GOD OF THUNDER.
TOTALLY.

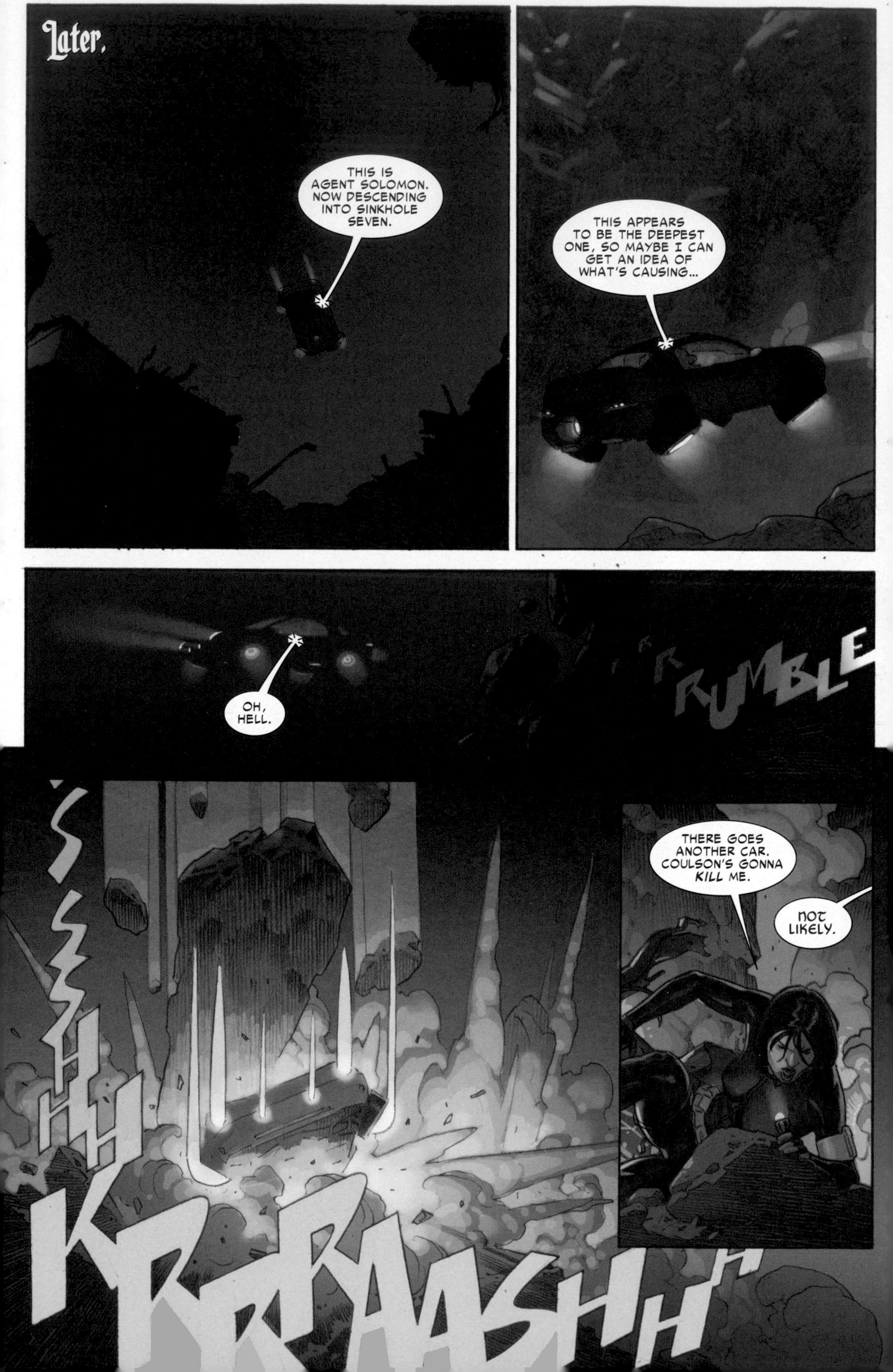
Later.
THIS IS AGENT SOLOMON. NOW DESCENDING INTO SINKHOLE SEVEN.
THIS APPEARS TO BE THE DEEPEST ONE, SO MAYBE I CAN GET AN IDEA OF WHAT'S CAUSING...
OH, HELL.
RRRUMBLE
THERE GOES ANOTHER CAR. COULSON'S GONNA KILL ME.
NOT LIKELY.
KRRAASHH

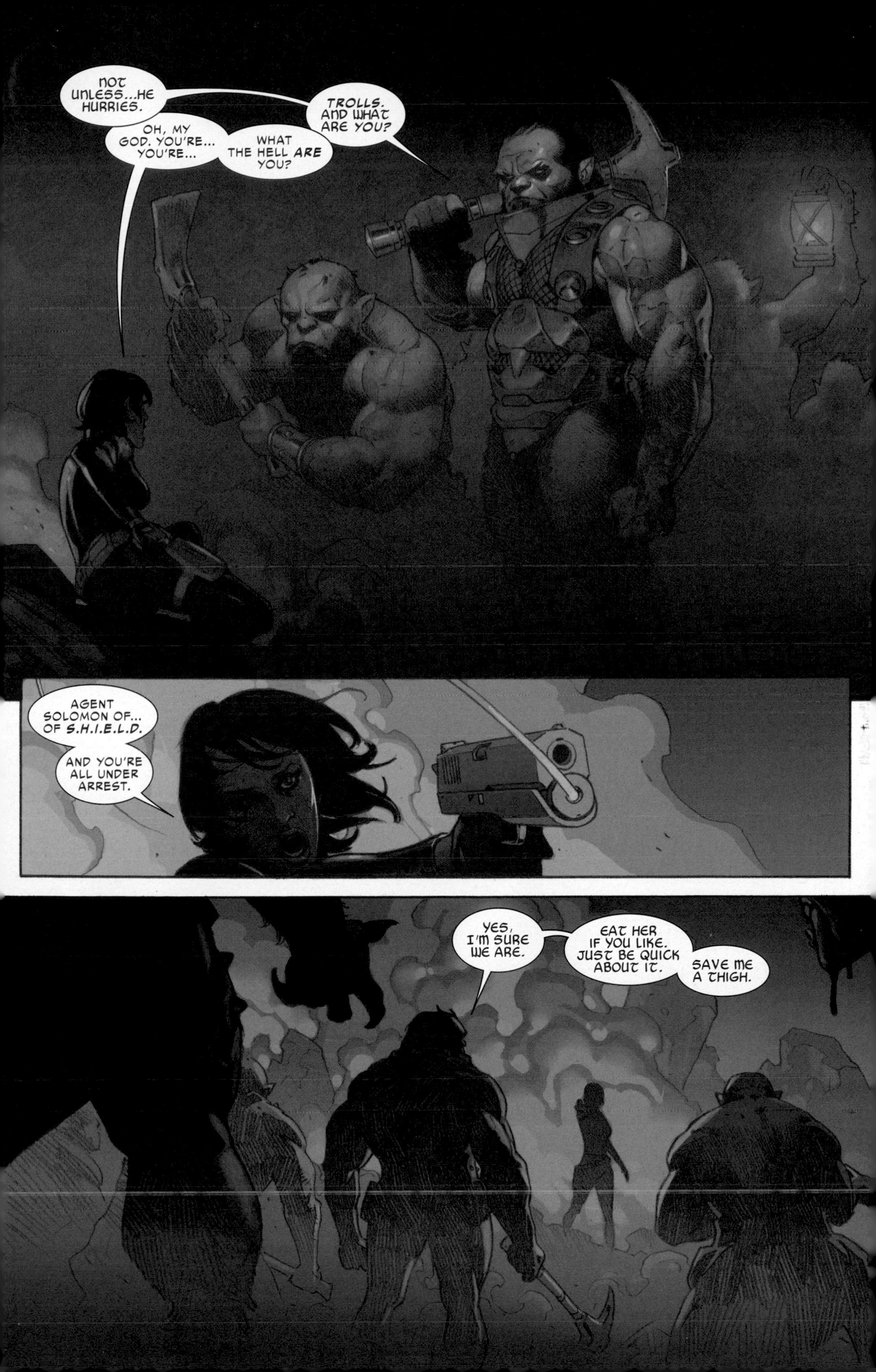
NOT UNLESS...HE HURRIES.
TROLLS. AND WHAT ARE YOU?
OH, MY GOD. YOU'RE... YOU'RE...
WHAT THE HELL ARE YOU?
AGENT SOLOMON OF... OF S.H.I.E.L.D.
AND YOU'RE ALL UNDER ARREST.
YES, I'M SURE WE ARE.
EAT HER IF YOU LIKE. JUST BE QUICK ABOUT IT.
SAVE ME A THIGH.

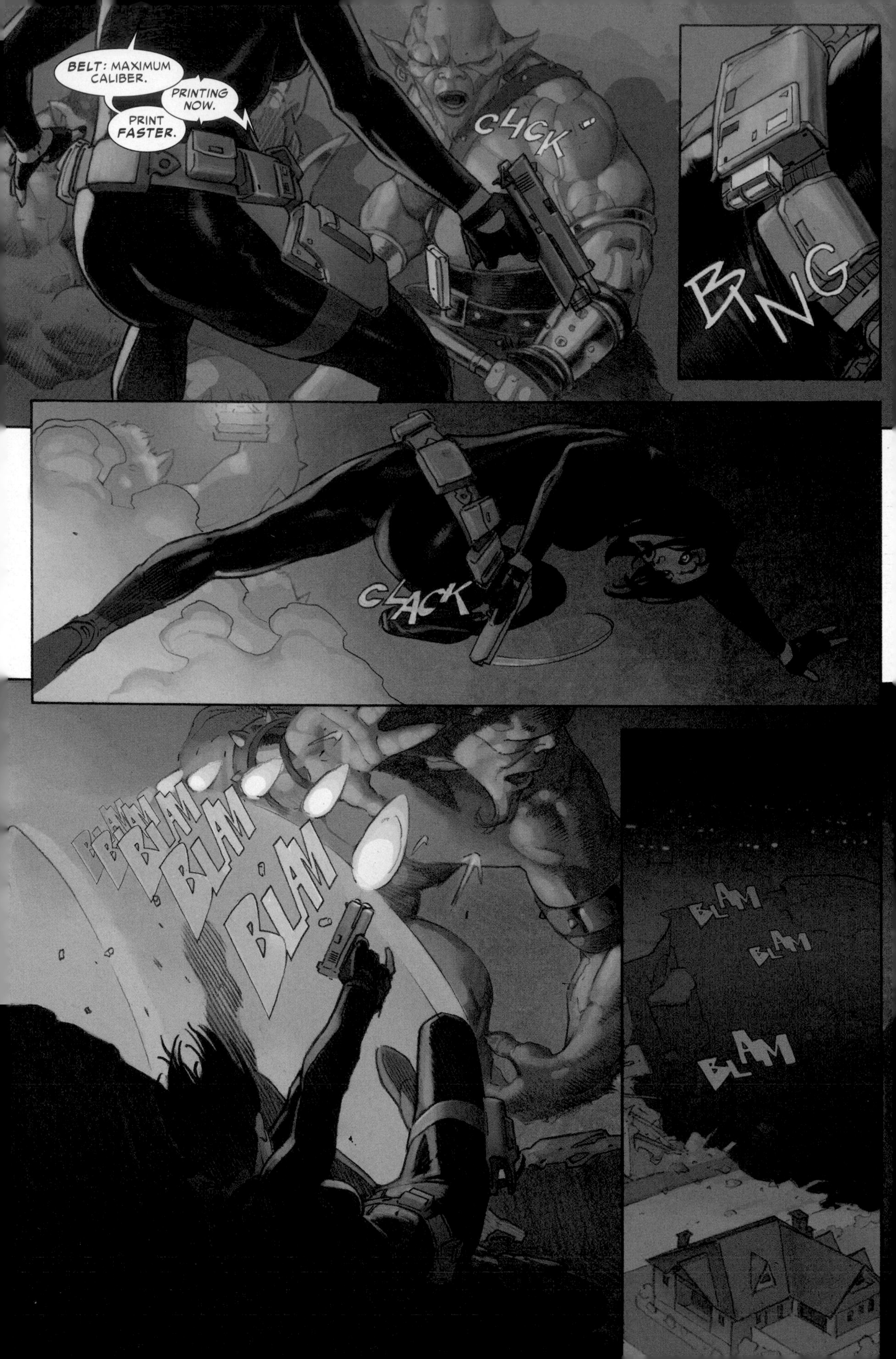
BELT: MAXIMUM CALIBER.
PRINTING NOW.
PRINT FASTER.
CLICK
BRING
CLACK
BLAM
BLAM
BLAM
BLAM
BLAM
BLAM
BLAM

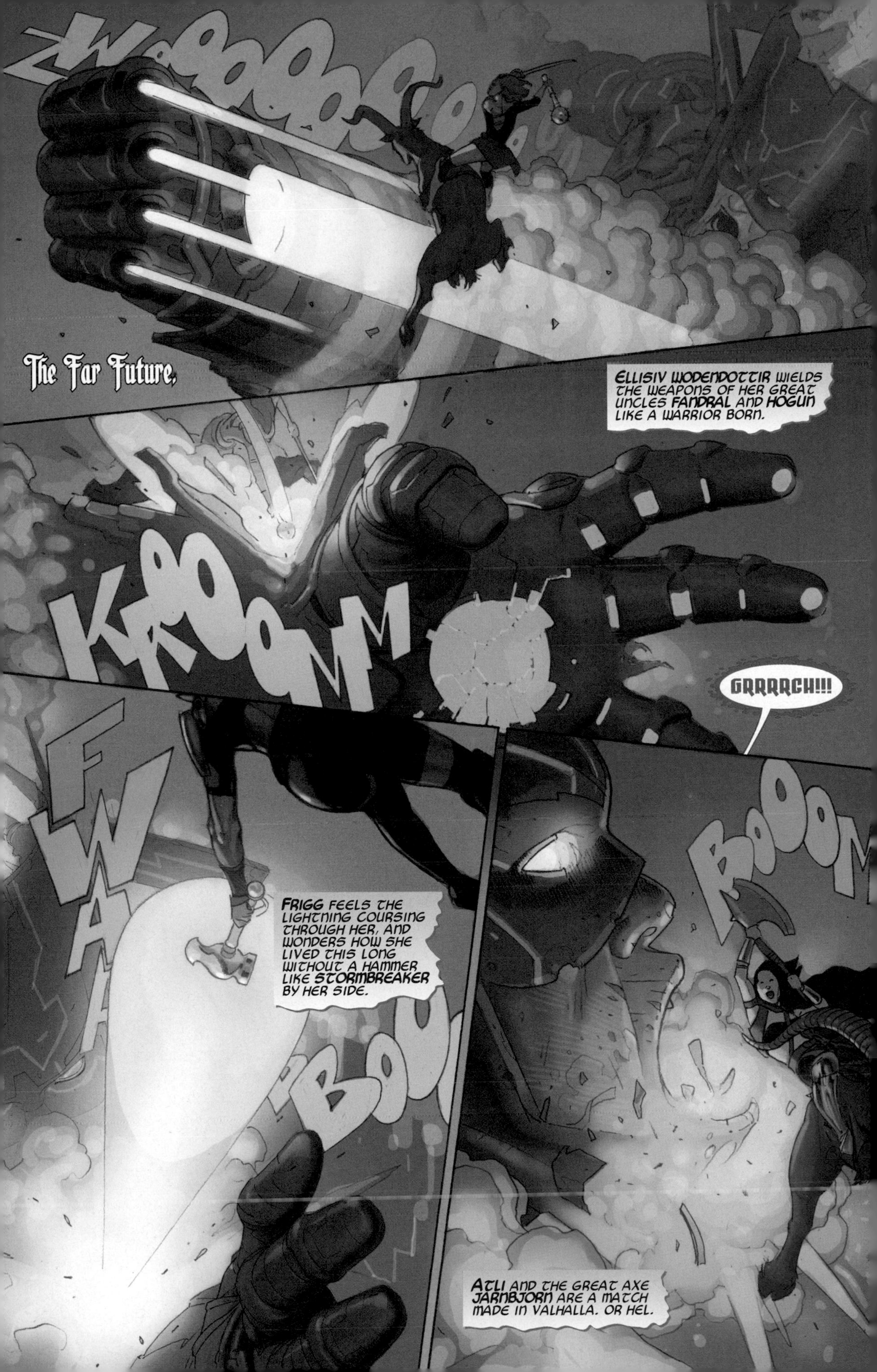
WOOOOOOOOOOOM
The Far Future.
ELLISIV WODENDOTTIR WIELDS THE WEAPONS OF HER GREAT UNCLES FANDRAL AND HOGUN LIKE A WARRIOR BORN.
KRAOOOM
GRRRRCH!!!
FWAAA
FRIGG FEELS THE LIGHTNING COURSING THROUGH HER, AND WONDERS HOW SHE LIVED THIS LONG WITHOUT A HAMMER LIKE STORMBREAKER BY HER SIDE.
BOOOM
ATLI AND THE GREAT AXE JARNBJORN ARE A MATCH MADE IN VALHALLA. OR HEL.

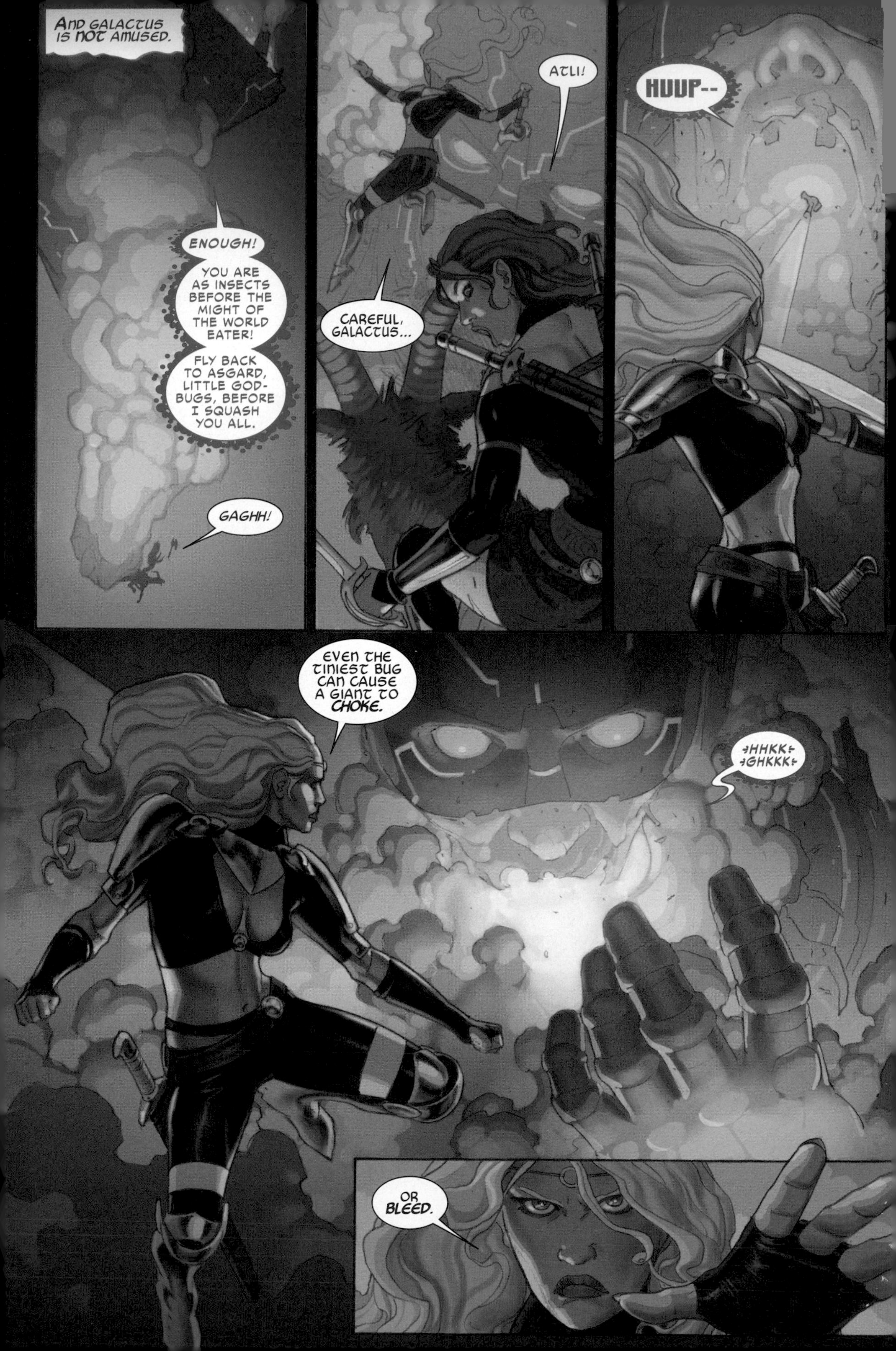

AND GALACTUS IS NOT AMUSED.
ENOUGH!
YOU ARE AS INSECTS BEFORE THE MIGHT OF THE WORLD EATER!
FLY BACK TO ASGARD, LITTLE GOD-BUGS, BEFORE I SQUASH YOU ALL.
GAGHH!
ATLI!
CAREFUL, GALACTUS...
HUUP--
EVEN THE TINIEST BUG CAN CAUSE A GIANT TO CHOKE.
HHKK GHKKK
OR BLEED.

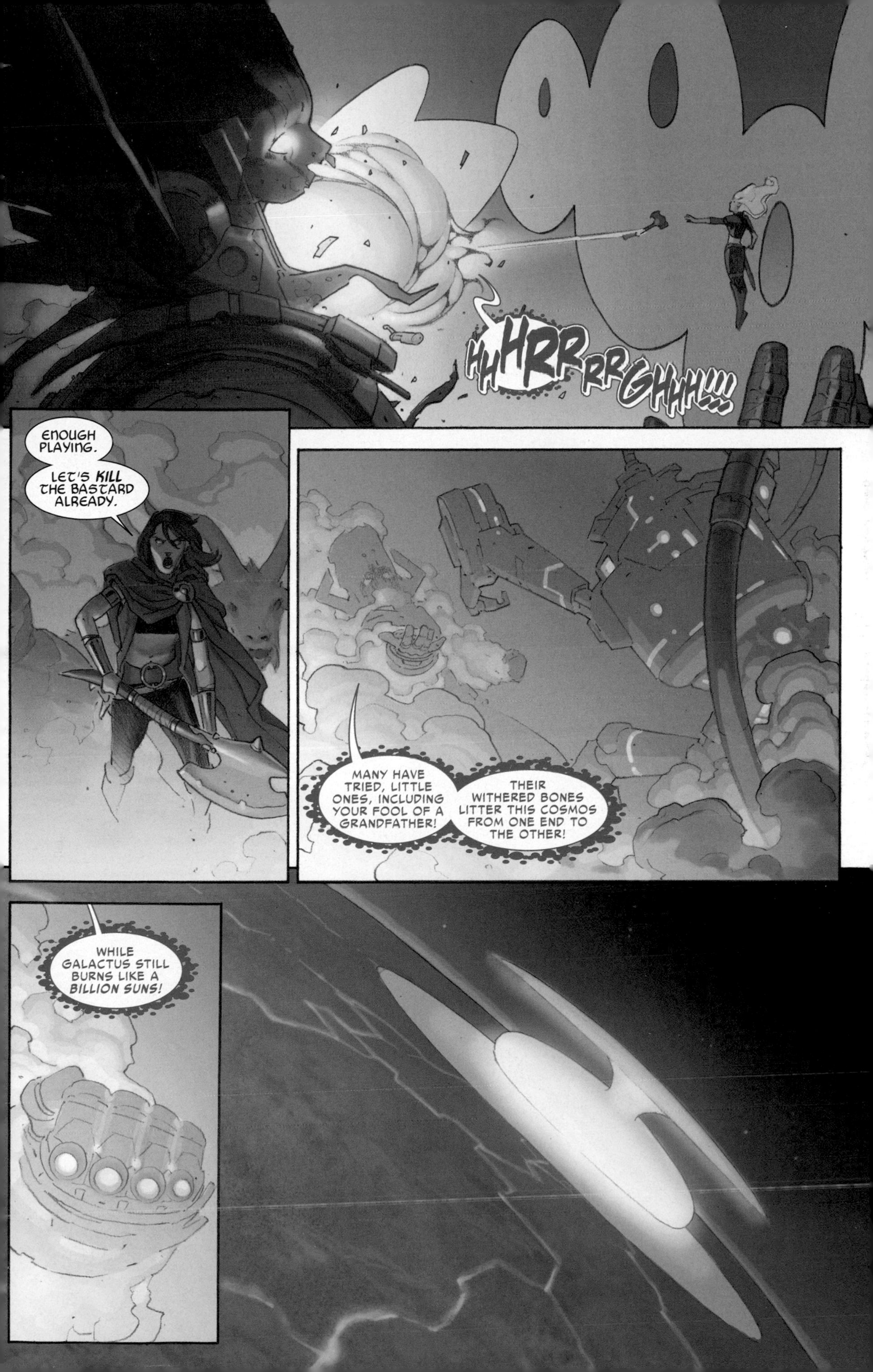
HHHRRRRRGHHH!!!
ENOUGH PLAYING.
LET'S KILL THE BASTARD ALREADY.
MANY HAVE TRIED, LITTLE ONES, INCLUDING YOUR FOOL OF A GRANDFATHER!
THEIR WITHERED BONES LITTER THIS COSMOS FROM ONE END TO THE OTHER!
WHILE GALACTUS STILL BURNS LIKE A BILLION SUNS!

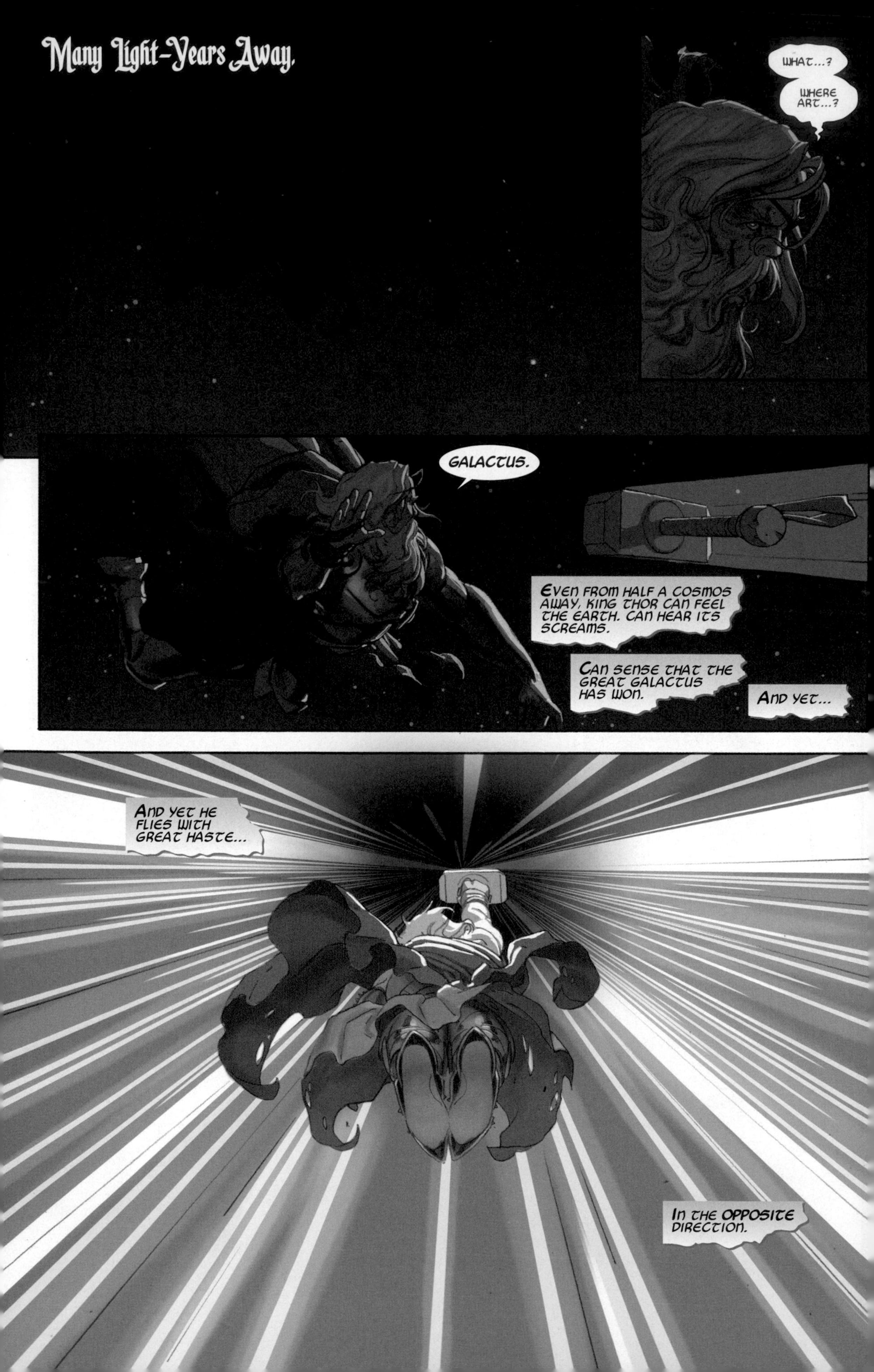
Many Light-Years Away.
WHAT...?
WHERE ART...?
GALACTUS.
EVEN FROM HALF A COSMOS AWAY, KING THOR CAN FEEL THE EARTH. CAN HEAR ITS SCREAMS.
CAN SENSE THAT THE GREAT GALACTUS HAS WON.
AND YET...
AND YET HE FLIES WITH GREAT HASTE...
IN THE OPPOSITE DIRECTION.

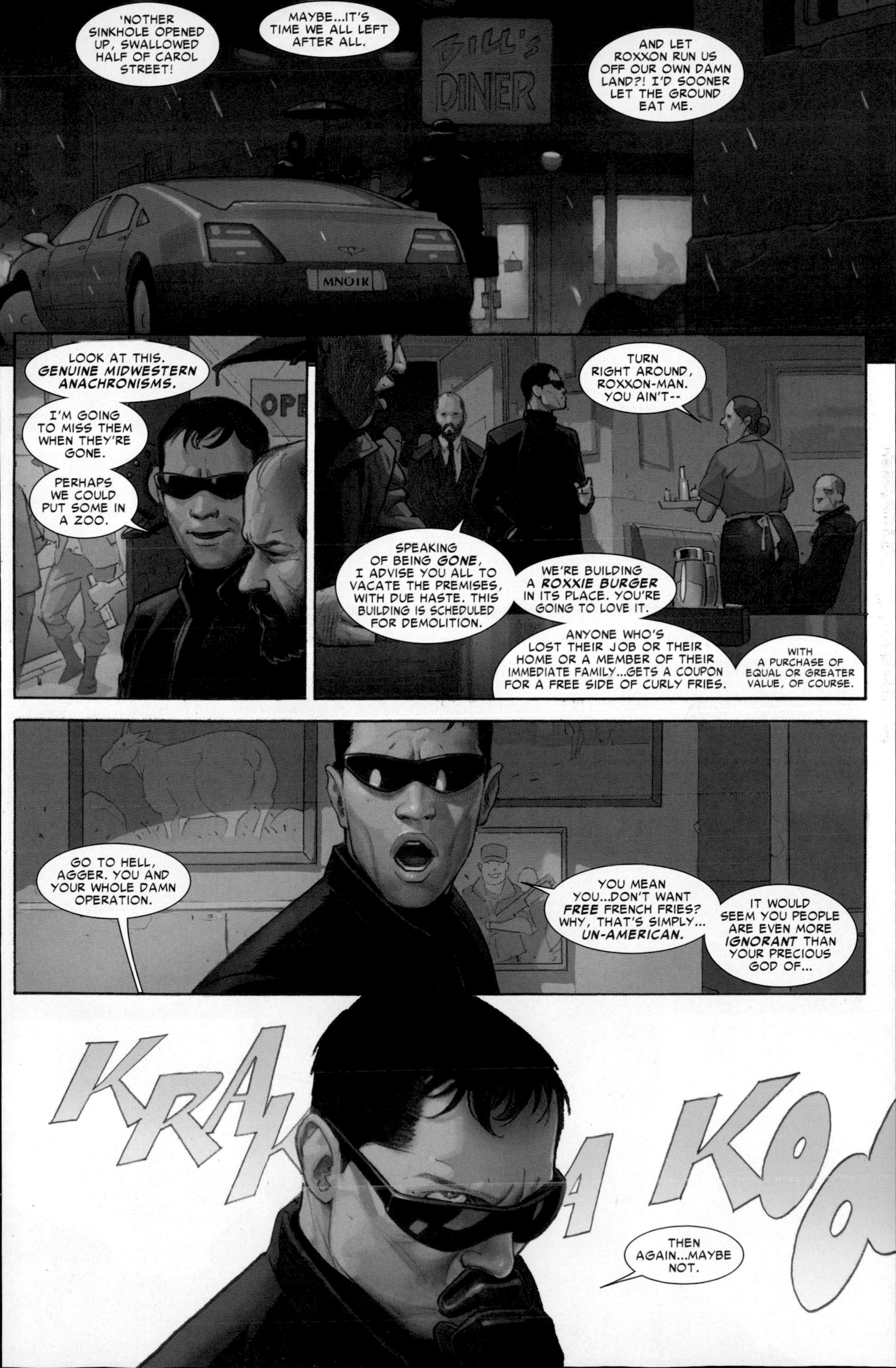
'NOTHER SINKHOLE OPENED UP, SWALLOWED HALF OF CAROL STREET!
MAYBE...IT'S TIME WE ALL LEFT AFTER ALL.
BILL'S DINER
AND LET ROXXON RUN US OFF OUR OWN DAMN LAND?! I'D SOONER LET THE GROUND EAT ME.
MNOIK
LOOK AT THIS. *GENUINE MIDWESTERN ANACHRONISMS.*
I'M GOING TO MISS THEM WHEN THEY'RE GONE.
PERHAPS WE COULD PUT SOME IN A ZOO.
TURN RIGHT AROUND, ROXXON-MAN. YOU AIN'T--
SPEAKING OF BEING *GONE*, I ADVISE YOU ALL TO VACATE THE PREMISES, WITH DUE HASTE. THIS BUILDING IS SCHEDULED FOR DEMOLITION.
WE'RE BUILDING A *ROXXIE BURGER* IN ITS PLACE. YOU'RE GOING TO LOVE IT.
ANYONE WHO'S LOST THEIR JOB OR THEIR HOME OR A MEMBER OF THEIR IMMEDIATE FAMILY...GETS A COUPON FOR A FREE SIDE OF CURLY FRIES.
WITH A PURCHASE OF EQUAL OR GREATER VALUE, OF COURSE.
GO TO HELL, AGGER. YOU AND YOUR WHOLE DAMN OPERATION.
YOU MEAN YOU...DON'T WANT *FREE* FRENCH FRIES? WHY, THAT'S SIMPLY... *UN-AMERICAN.*
IT WOULD SEEM YOU PEOPLE ARE EVEN MORE *IGNORANT* THAN YOUR PRECIOUS GOD OF...
KRAKA KOO
THEN AGAIN...MAYBE NOT.

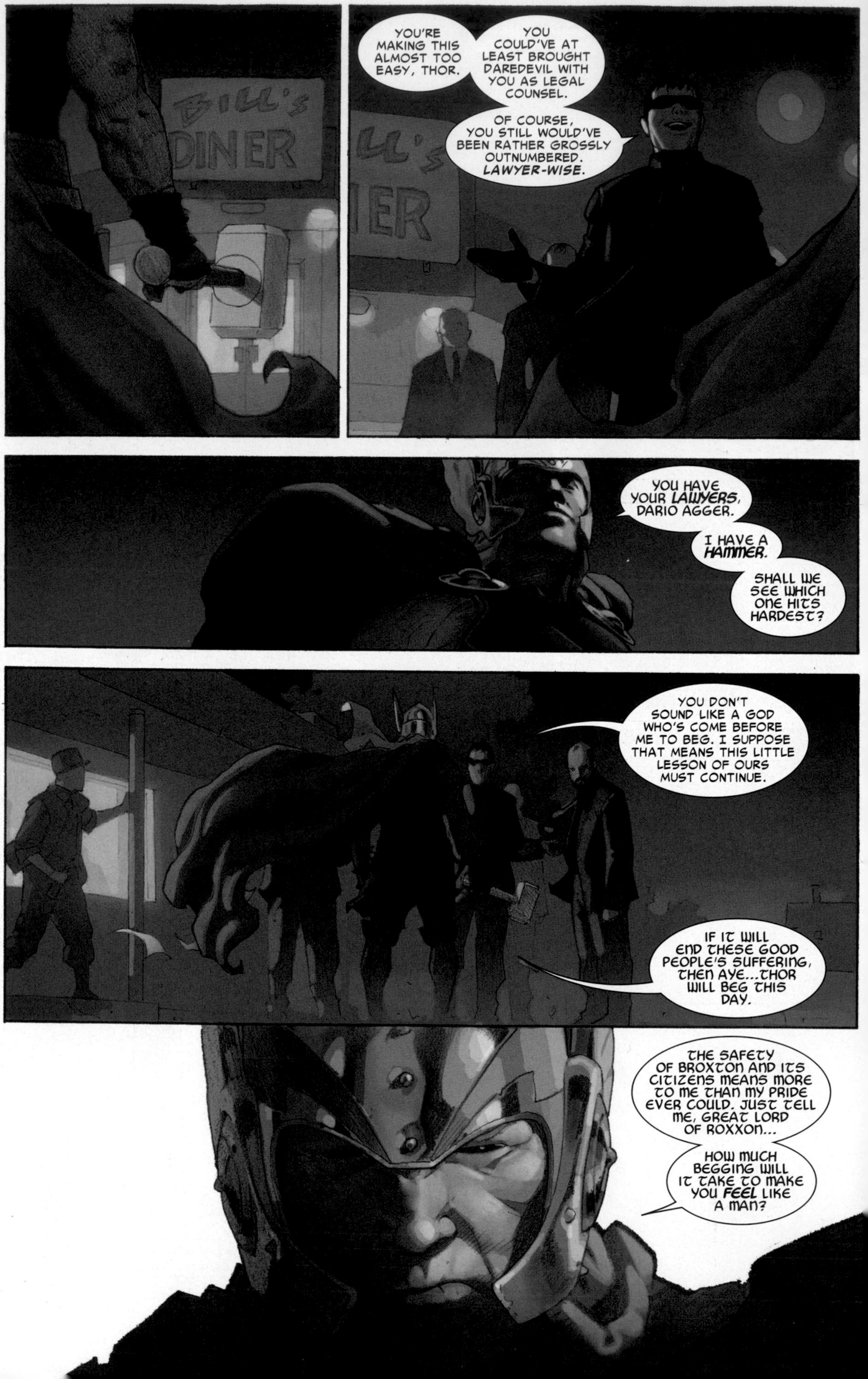
BILL'S DINER
YOU'RE MAKING THIS ALMOST TOO EASY, THOR.
YOU COULD'VE AT LEAST BROUGHT DAREDEVIL WITH YOU AS LEGAL COUNSEL.
OF COURSE, YOU STILL WOULD'VE BEEN RATHER GROSSLY OUTNUMBERED. LAWYER-WISE.
YOU HAVE YOUR LAWYERS, DARIO AGGER.
I HAVE A HAMMER.
SHALL WE SEE WHICH ONE HITS HARDEST?
YOU DON'T SOUND LIKE A GOD WHO'S COME BEFORE ME TO BEG. I SUPPOSE THAT MEANS THIS LITTLE LESSON OF OURS MUST CONTINUE.
IF IT WILL END THESE GOOD PEOPLE'S SUFFERING, THEN AYE...THOR WILL BEG THIS DAY.
THE SAFETY OF BROXTON AND ITS CITIZENS MEANS MORE TO ME THAN MY PRIDE EVER COULD. JUST TELL ME, GREAT LORD OF ROXXON...
HOW MUCH BEGGING WILL IT TAKE TO MAKE YOU FEEL LIKE A MAN?

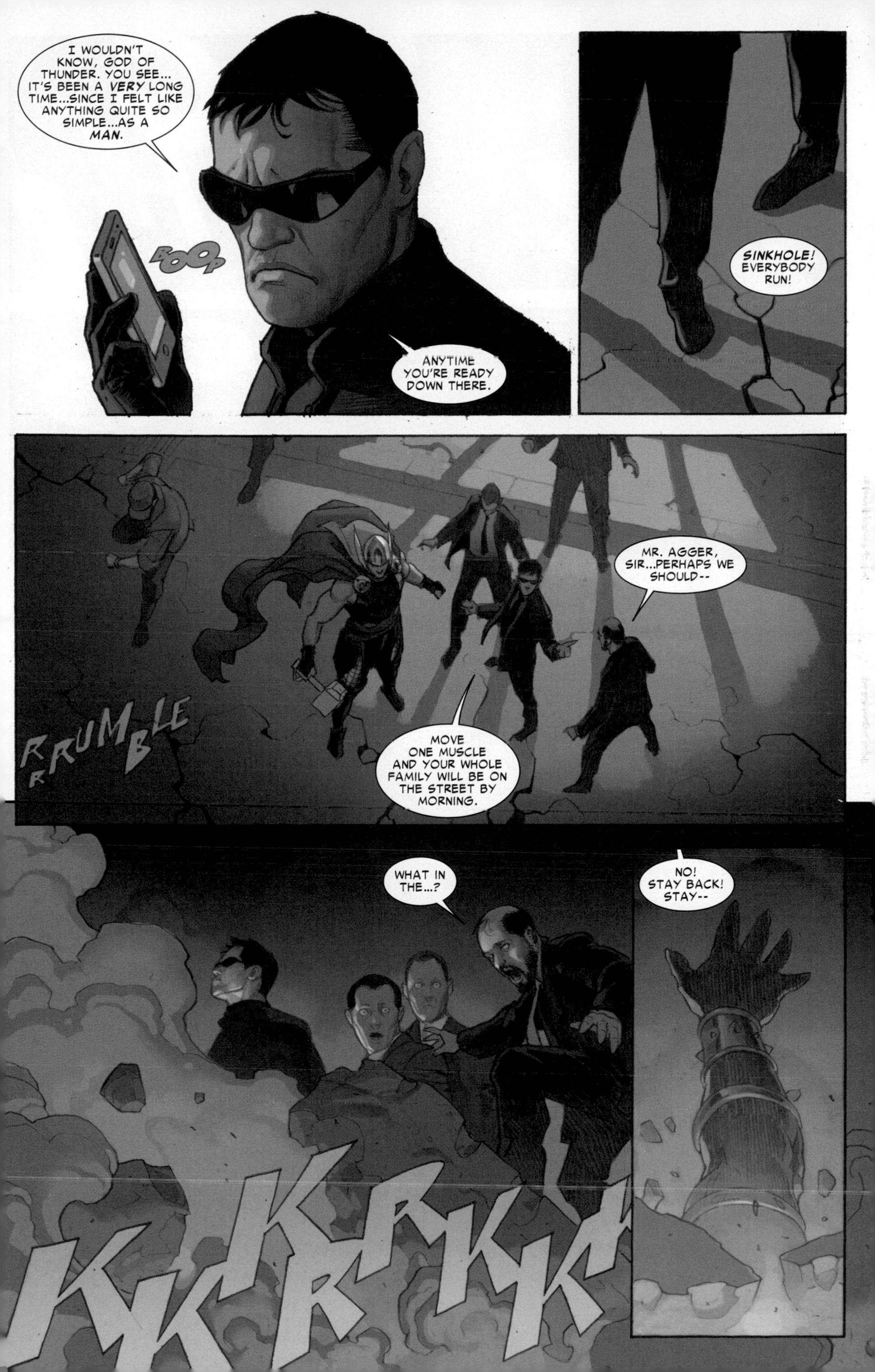
I WOULDN'T KNOW, GOD OF THUNDER. YOU SEE... IT'S BEEN A VERY LONG TIME...SINCE I FELT LIKE ANYTHING QUITE SO SIMPLE...AS A MAN.
BOOP
ANYTIME YOU'RE READY DOWN THERE.
SINKHOLE! EVERYBODY RUN!
MR. AGGER, SIR...PERHAPS WE SHOULD--
RRRUMBLE
MOVE ONE MUSCLE AND YOUR WHOLE FAMILY WILL BE ON THE STREET BY MORNING.
WHAT IN THE...?
NO! STAY BACK! STAY--
KKRRKK

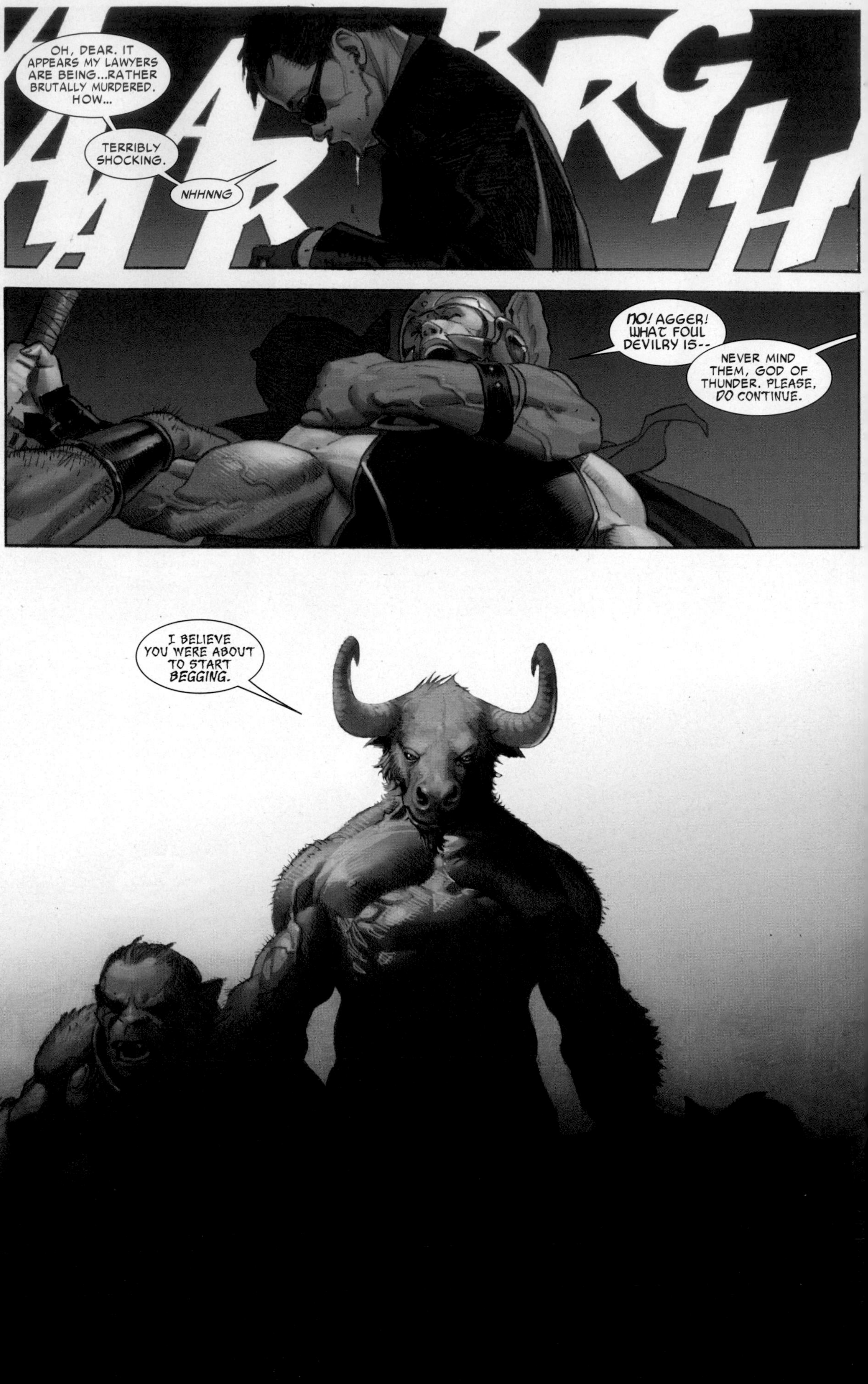
AARRGH
OH, DEAR. IT APPEARS MY LAWYERS ARE BEING...RATHER BRUTALLY MURDERED. HOW...
TERRIBLY SHOCKING.
NHHNNG
NO! AGGER! WHAT FOUL DEVILRY IS--
NEVER MIND THEM, GOD OF THUNDER. PLEASE, DO CONTINUE.
I BELIEVE YOU WERE ABOUT TO START BEGGING.

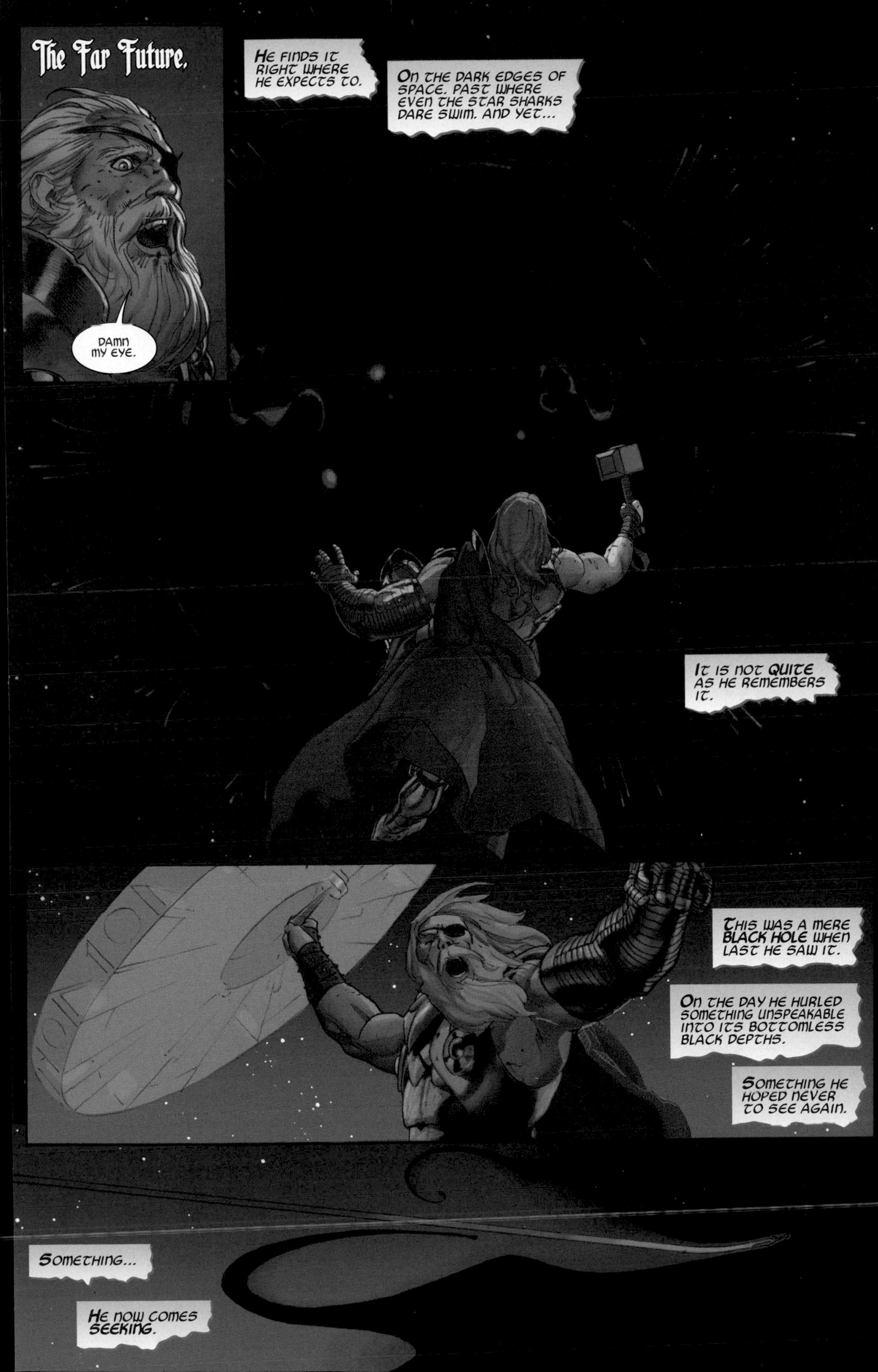
The Far Future.
Damn my eye.
He finds it right where he expects to.
On the dark edges of space. Past where even the star sharks dare swim. And yet...
It is not QUITE as he remembers it.
This was a mere BLACK HOLE when last he saw it.
On the day he hurled something unspeakable into its bottomless black depths.
Something he hoped never to see again.
Something...
He now comes SEEKING.

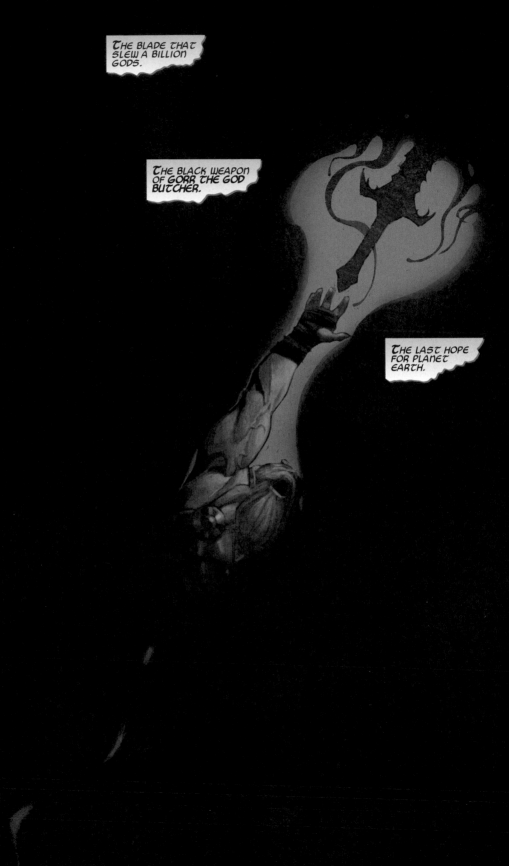

ALL-BLACK THE NECROSWORD.

THE BLADE THAT SLEW A BILLION GODS.

THE BLACK WEAPON OF GORR THE GOD BUTCHER.

THE LAST HOPE FOR PLANET EARTH.

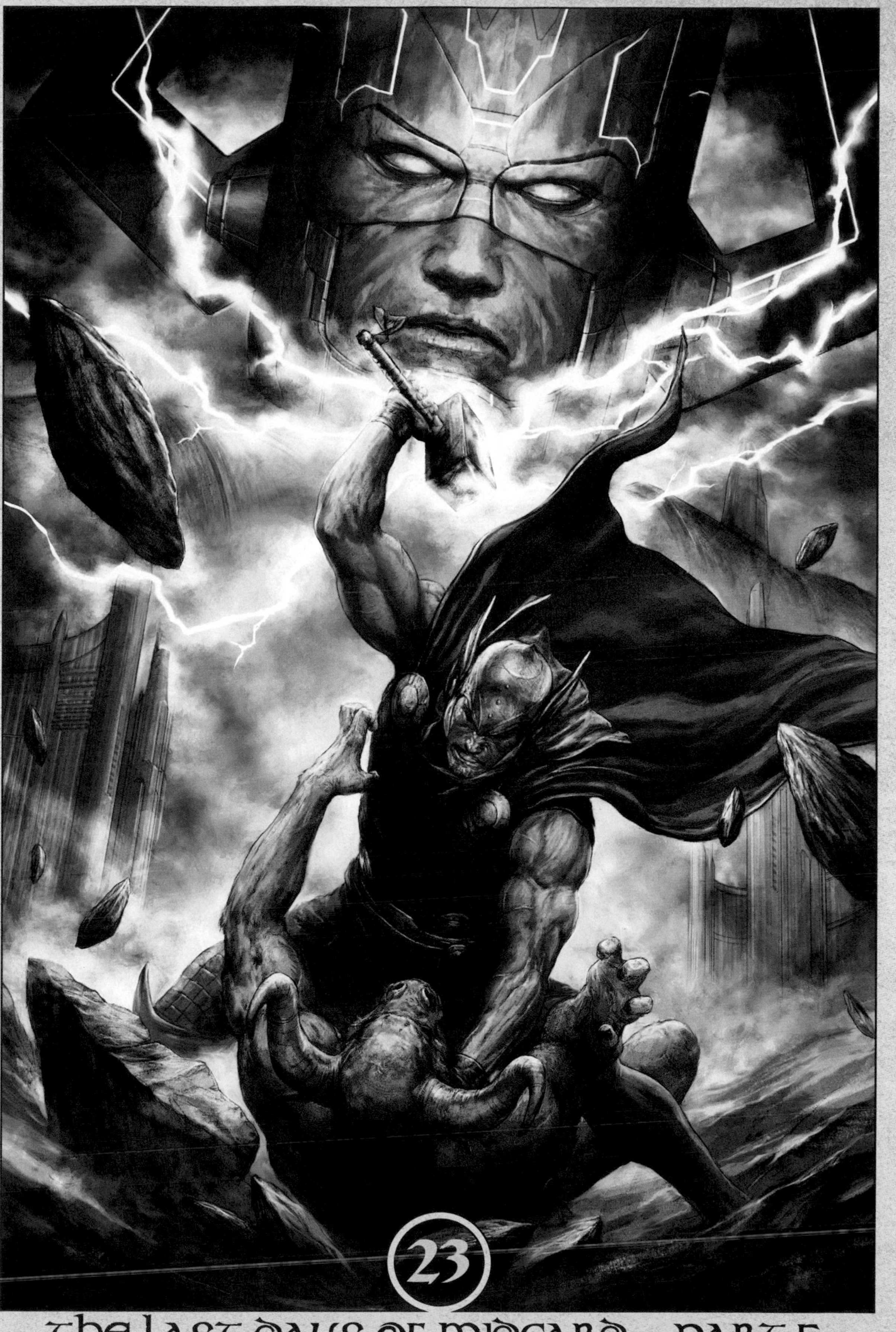
23

THE LAST DAYS OF MIDGARD - PART 5:
BLOOD OF THE EARTH

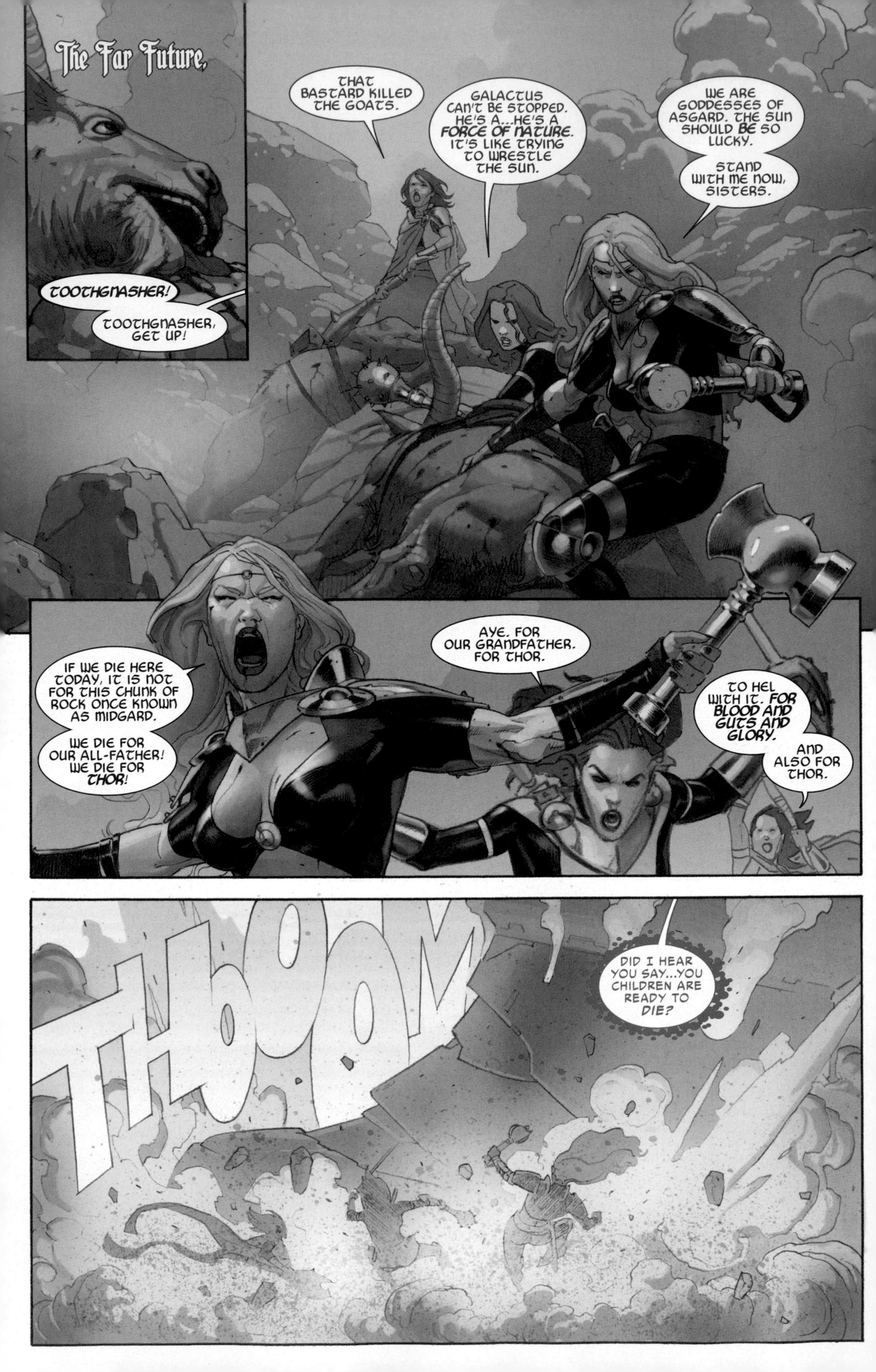
The Far Future,
TOOTHGNASHER!
TOOTHGNASHER, GET UP!
THAT BASTARD KILLED THE GOATS.
GALACTUS CAN'T BE STOPPED. HE'S A...HE'S A FORCE OF NATURE. IT'S LIKE TRYING TO WRESTLE THE SUN.
WE ARE GODDESSES OF ASGARD. THE SUN SHOULD BE SO LUCKY.
STAND WITH ME NOW, SISTERS.
IF WE DIE HERE TODAY, IT IS NOT FOR THIS CHUNK OF ROCK ONCE KNOWN AS MIDGARD.
WE DIE FOR OUR ALL-FATHER! WE DIE FOR THOR!
AYE. FOR OUR GRANDFATHER. FOR THOR.
TO HEL WITH IT. FOR BLOOD AND GUTS AND GLORY.
AND ALSO FOR THOR.
THOOOM
DID I HEAR YOU SAY...YOU CHILDREN ARE READY TO DIE?

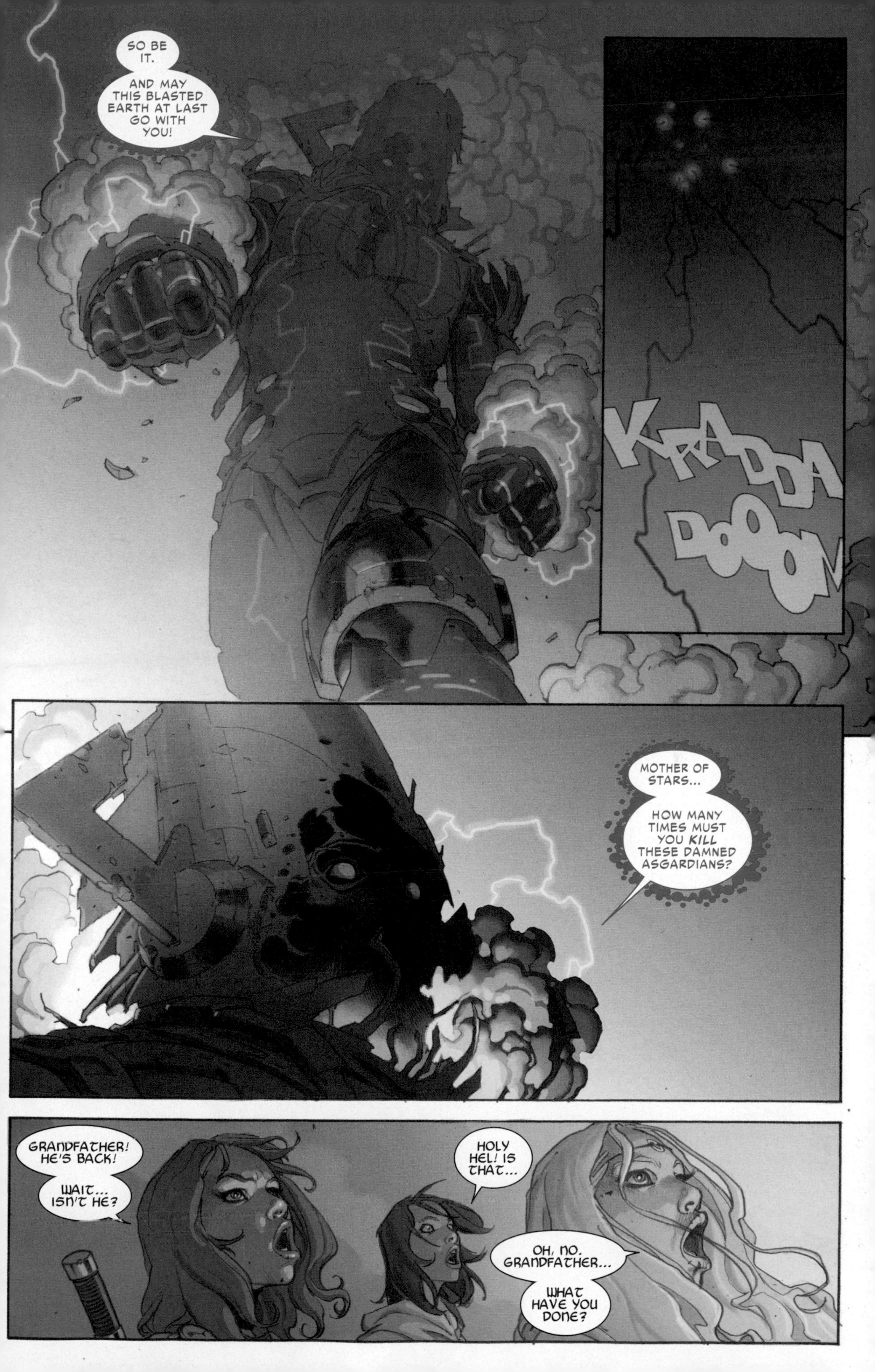
SO BE IT.
AND MAY THIS BLASTED EARTH AT LAST GO WITH YOU!
KRADDA DOOOOM
MOTHER OF STARS...
HOW MANY TIMES MUST YOU KILL THESE DAMNED ASGARDIANS?
GRANDFATHER! HE'S BACK!
WAIT... ISN'T HE?
HOLY HEL! IS THAT...
OH, NO. GRANDFATHER...
WHAT HAVE YOU DONE?

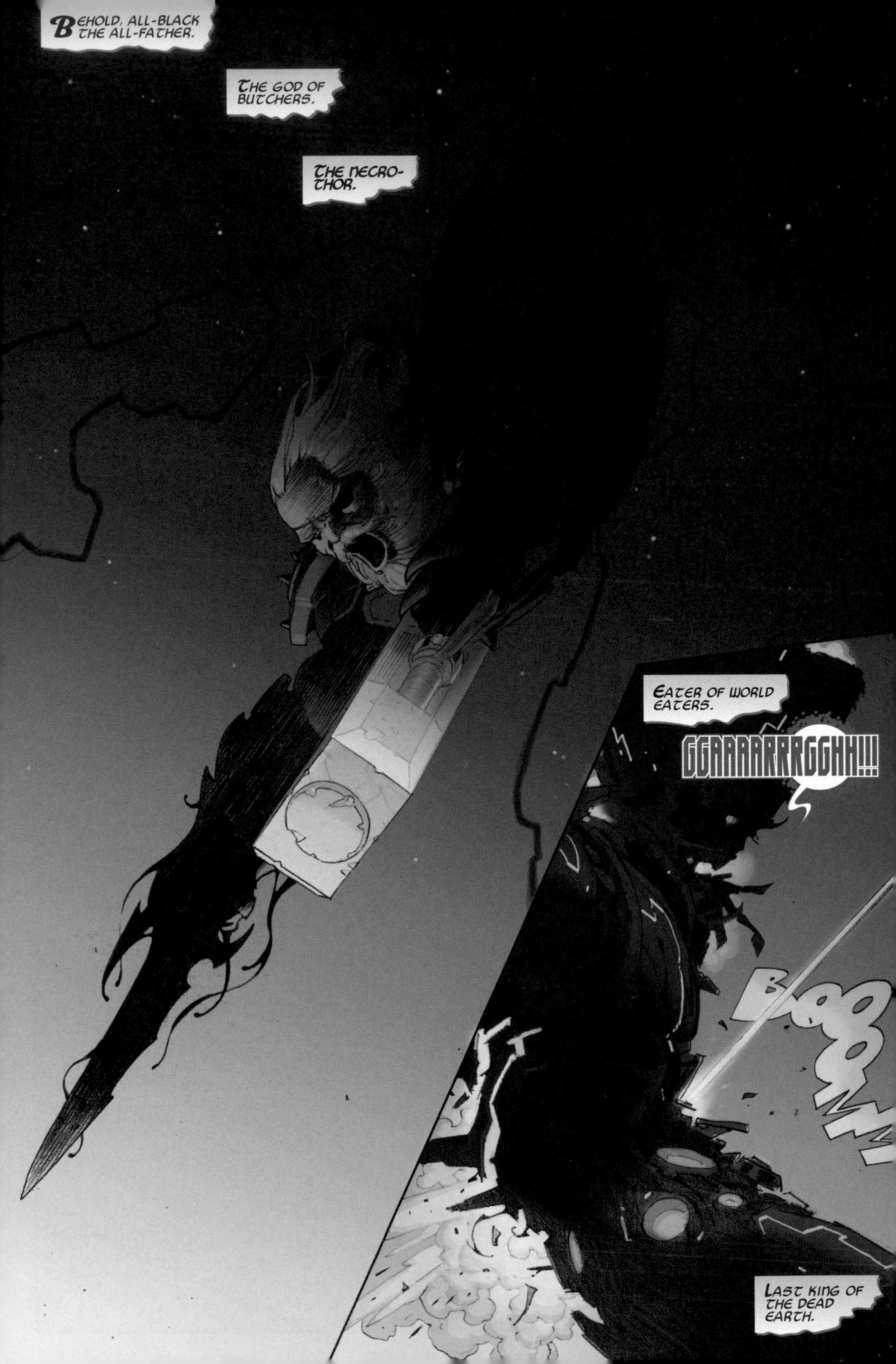

BEHOLD, ALL-BLACK THE ALL-FATHER.
THE GOD OF BUTCHERS.
THE NECRO-THOR.
EATER OF WORLD EATERS.
GGAAAARRRGGHH!!!
BOOOM!!
LAST KING OF THE DEAD EARTH.

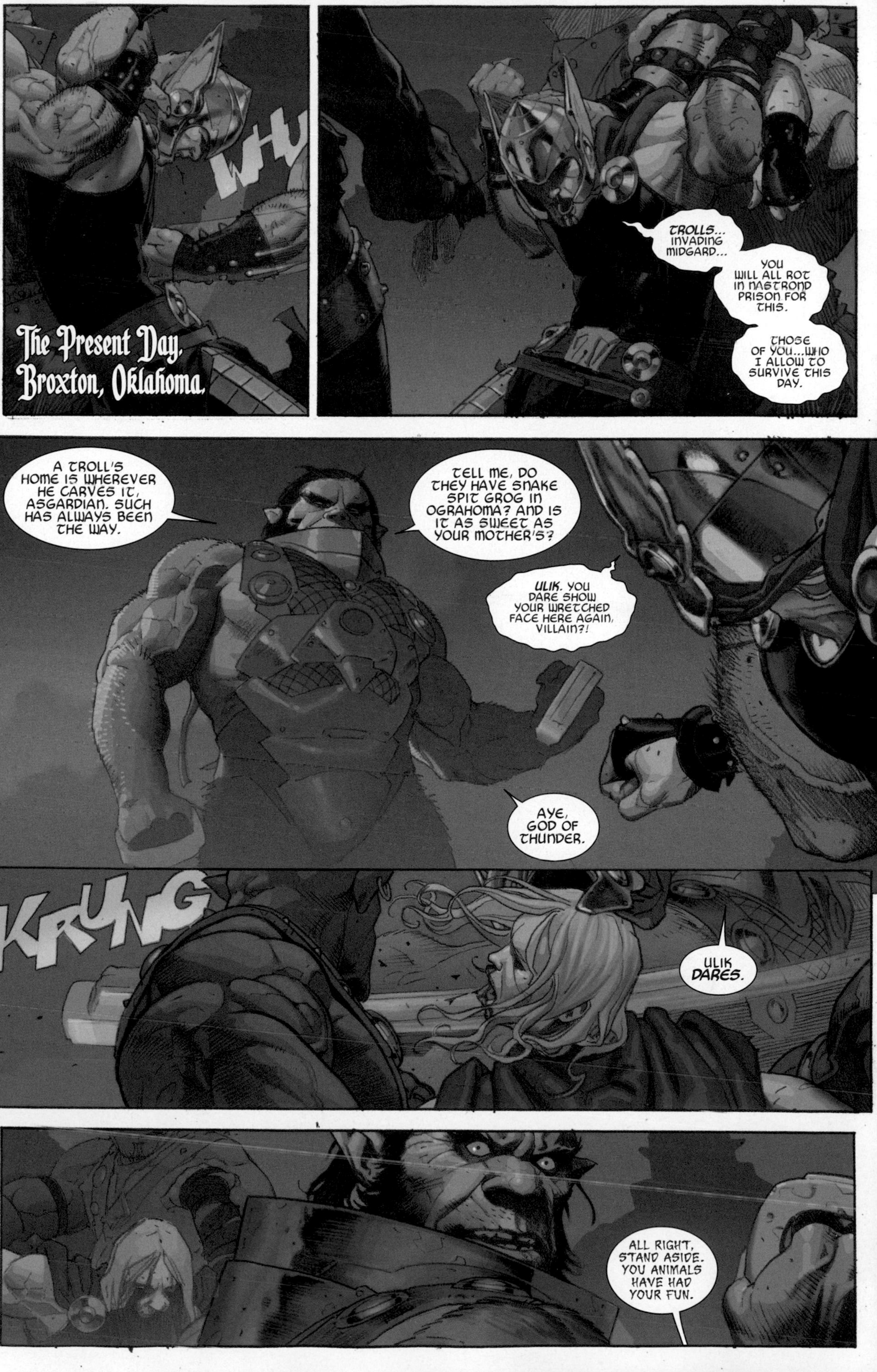
WHU
The Present Day, Broxton, Oklahoma.
TROLLS... INVADING MIDGARD...
YOU WILL ALL ROT IN NASTROND PRISON FOR THIS.
THOSE OF YOU...WHO I ALLOW TO SURVIVE THIS DAY.
A TROLL'S HOME IS WHEREVER HE CARVES IT, ASGARDIAN. SUCH HAS ALWAYS BEEN THE WAY.
TELL ME, DO THEY HAVE SNAKE SPIT GROG IN OGRAHOMA? AND IS IT AS SWEET AS YOUR MOTHER'S?
ULIK. YOU DARE SHOW YOUR WRETCHED FACE HERE AGAIN, VILLAIN?!
AYE, GOD OF THUNDER.
KRUNG
ULIK DARES.
ALL RIGHT, STAND ASIDE. YOU ANIMALS HAVE HAD YOUR FUN.

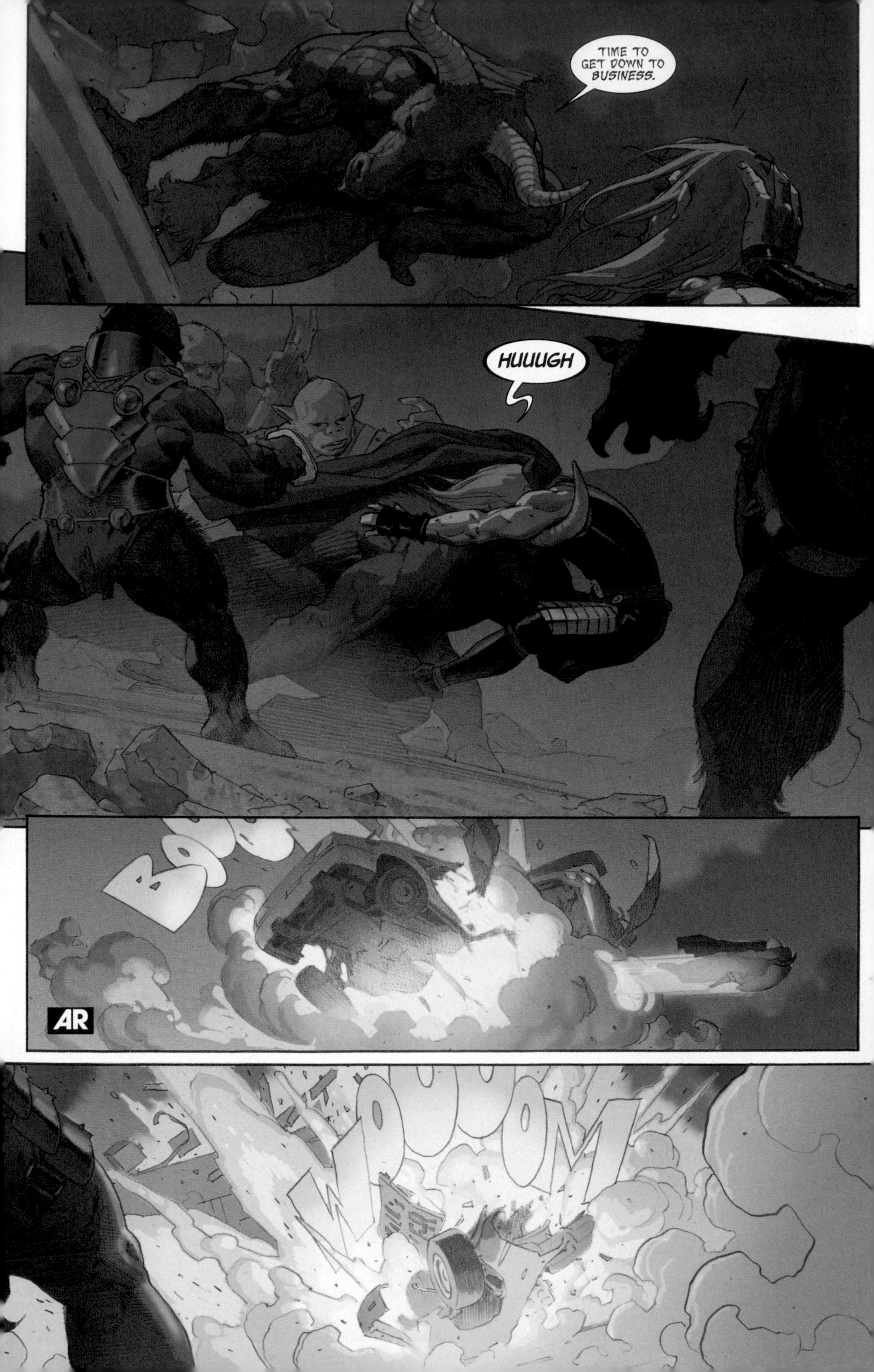
TIME TO GET DOWN TO BUSINESS.
HUUUGH

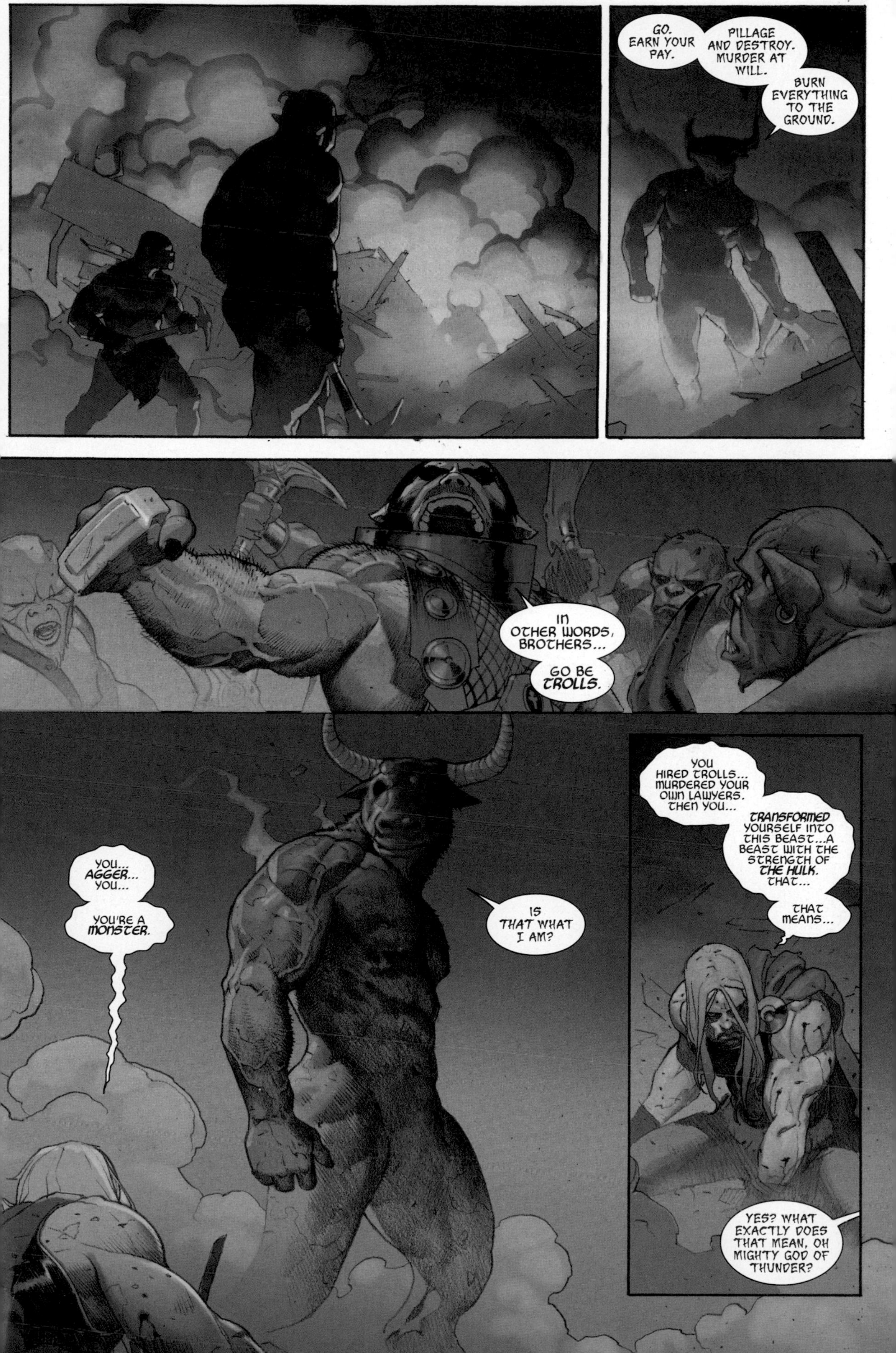
GO. EARN YOUR PAY.
PILLAGE AND DESTROY. MURDER AT WILL.
BURN EVERYTHING TO THE GROUND.
IN OTHER WORDS, BROTHERS...
GO BE TROLLS.
YOU... AGGER... YOU...
YOU'RE A MONSTER.
IS THAT WHAT I AM?
YOU HIRED TROLLS... MURDERED YOUR OWN LAWYERS. THEN YOU...
TRANSFORMED YOURSELF INTO THIS BEAST...A BEAST WITH THE STRENGTH OF THE HULK. THAT...
THAT MEANS...
YES? WHAT EXACTLY DOES THAT MEAN, OH MIGHTY GOD OF THUNDER?

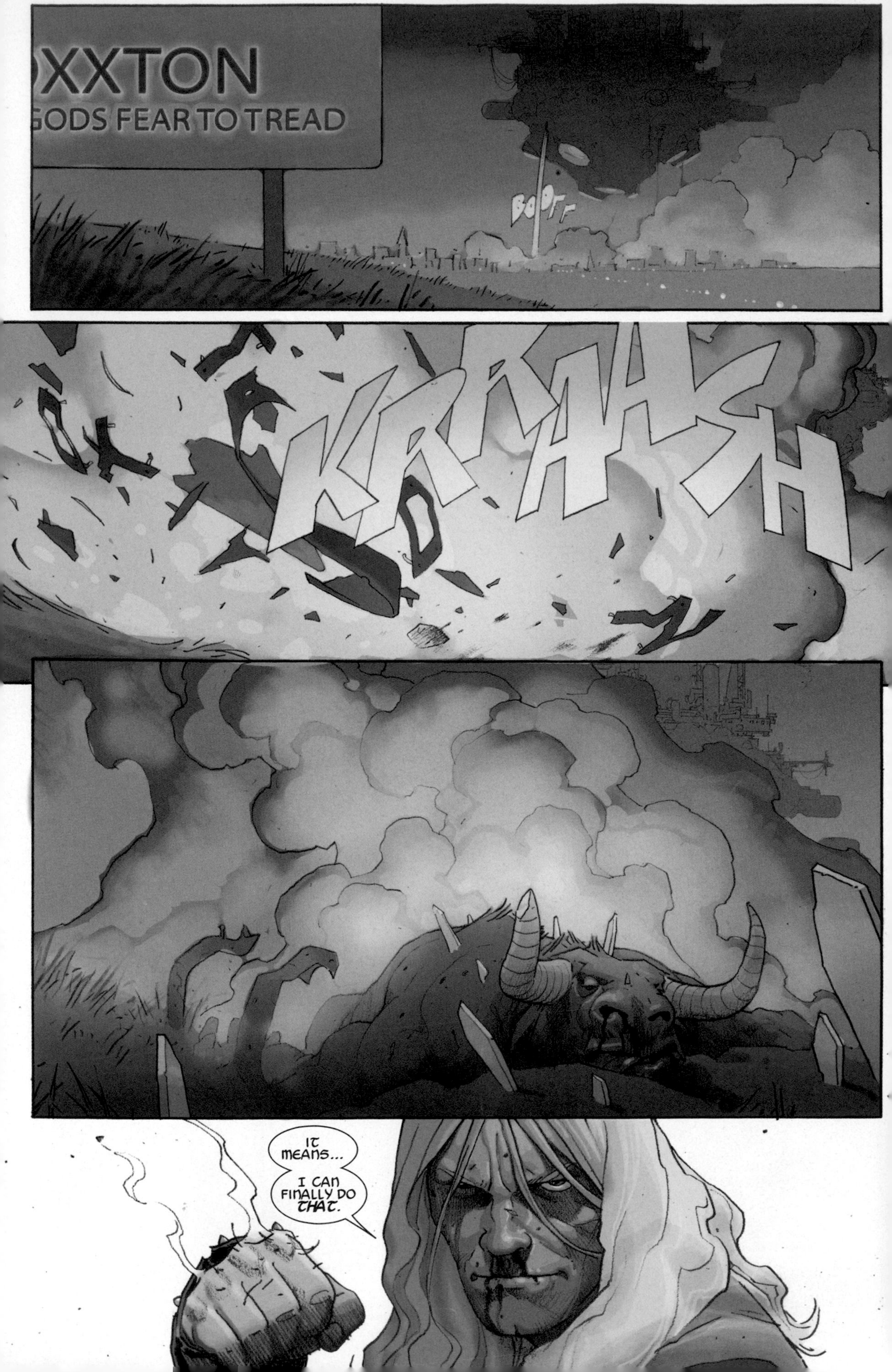

OXXTON
GODS FEAR TO TREAD
BOOFF
KRAASH
IT MEANS...
I CAN FINALLY DO THAT.

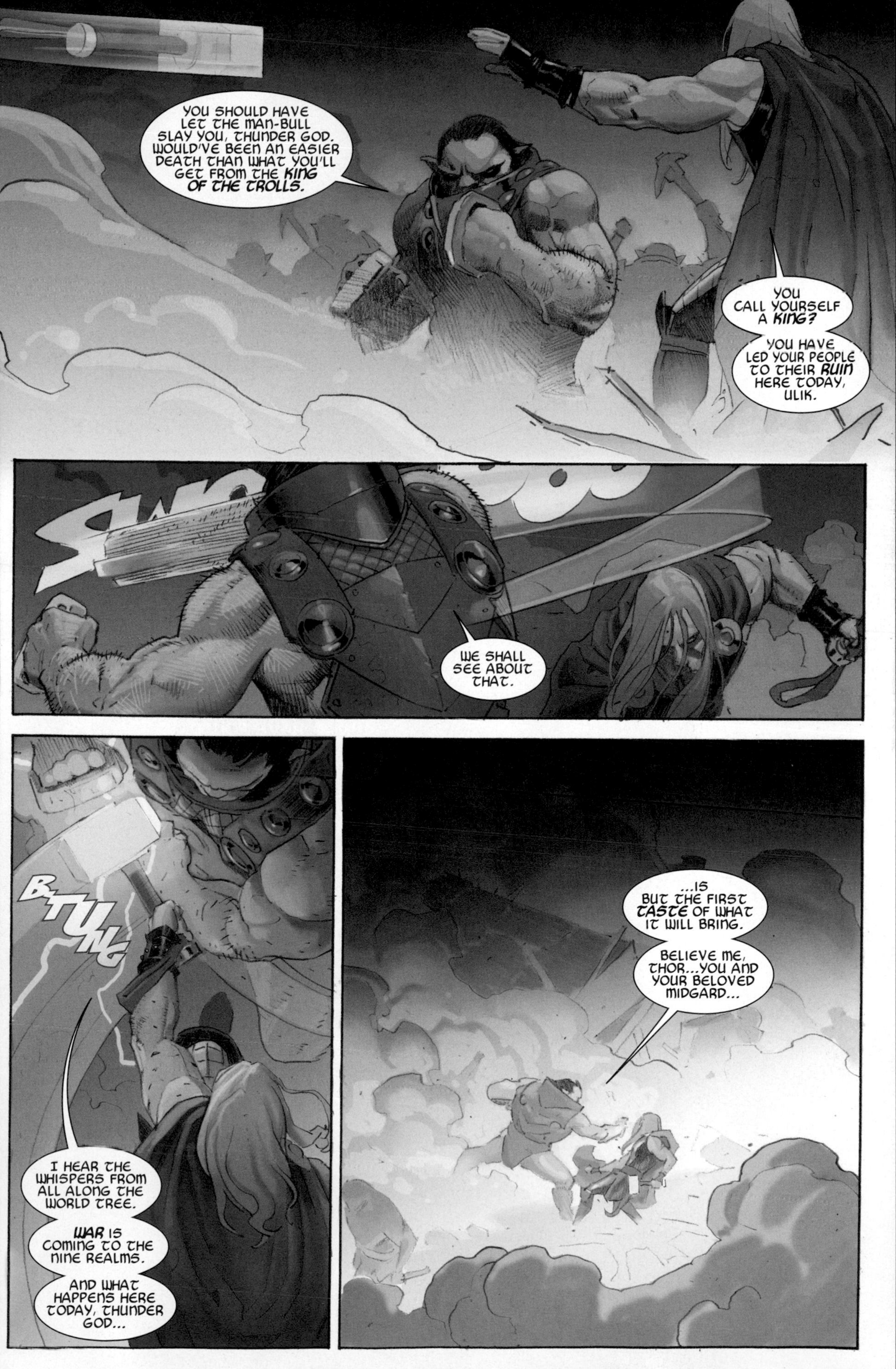
YOU SHOULD HAVE LET THE MAN-BULL SLAY YOU, THUNDER GOD. WOULD'VE BEEN AN EASIER DEATH THAN WHAT YOU'LL GET FROM THE KING OF THE TROLLS.
YOU CALL YOURSELF A KING?
YOU HAVE LED YOUR PEOPLE TO THEIR RUIN HERE TODAY, ULIK.
WE SHALL SEE ABOUT THAT.
B-TUNG
I HEAR THE WHISPERS FROM ALL ALONG THE WORLD TREE.
WAR IS COMING TO THE NINE REALMS.
AND WHAT HAPPENS HERE TODAY, THUNDER GOD...
...IS BUT THE FIRST TASTE OF WHAT IT WILL BRING.
BELIEVE ME, THOR...YOU AND YOUR BELOVED MIDGARD...

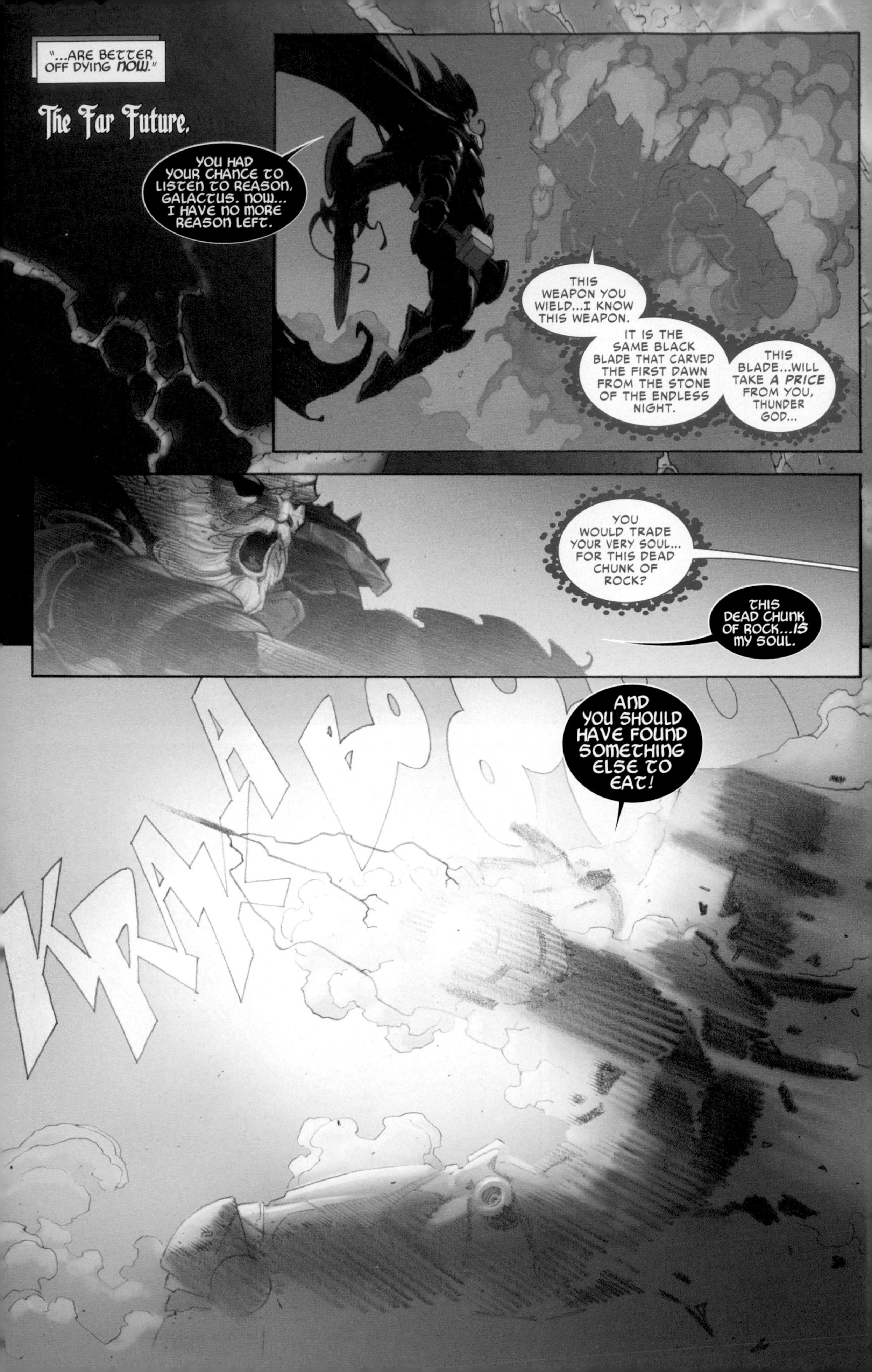
"...ARE BETTER OFF DYING NOW."
The Far Future.
YOU HAD YOUR CHANCE TO LISTEN TO REASON, GALACTUS. NOW... I HAVE NO MORE REASON LEFT.
THIS WEAPON YOU WIELD...I KNOW THIS WEAPON.
IT IS THE SAME BLACK BLADE THAT CARVED THE FIRST DAWN FROM THE STONE OF THE ENDLESS NIGHT.
THIS BLADE...WILL TAKE A PRICE FROM YOU, THUNDER GOD...
YOU WOULD TRADE YOUR VERY SOUL... FOR THIS DEAD CHUNK OF ROCK?
THIS DEAD CHUNK OF ROCK...IS MY SOUL.
AND YOU SHOULD HAVE FOUND SOMETHING ELSE TO EAT!
KRAKABOOM

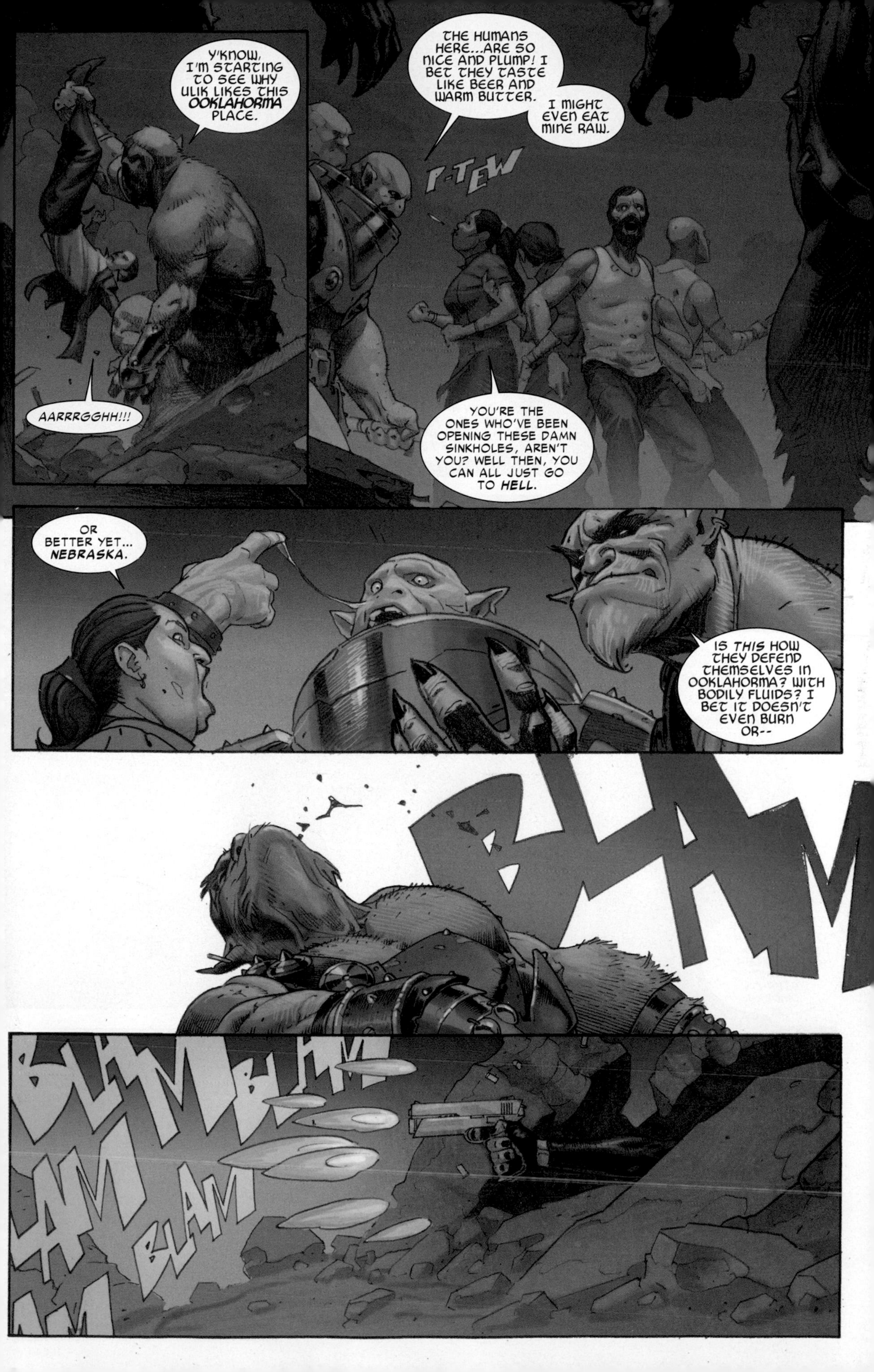

Y'KNOW, I'M STARTING TO SEE WHY ULIK LIKES THIS OOKLAHORMA PLACE.
AARRRGGHH!!!
THE HUMANS HERE...ARE SO NICE AND PLUMP! I BET THEY TASTE LIKE BEER AND WARM BUTTER.
I MIGHT EVEN EAT MINE RAW.
P-TEW
YOU'RE THE ONES WHO'VE BEEN OPENING THESE DAMN SINKHOLES, AREN'T YOU? WELL THEN, YOU CAN ALL JUST GO TO HELL.
OR BETTER YET... NEBRASKA.
IS THIS HOW THEY DEFEND THEMSELVES IN OOKLAHORMA? WITH BODILY FLUIDS? I BET IT DOESN'T EVEN BURN OR--
BLAM
BLAM BLAM
BLAM
BLAM

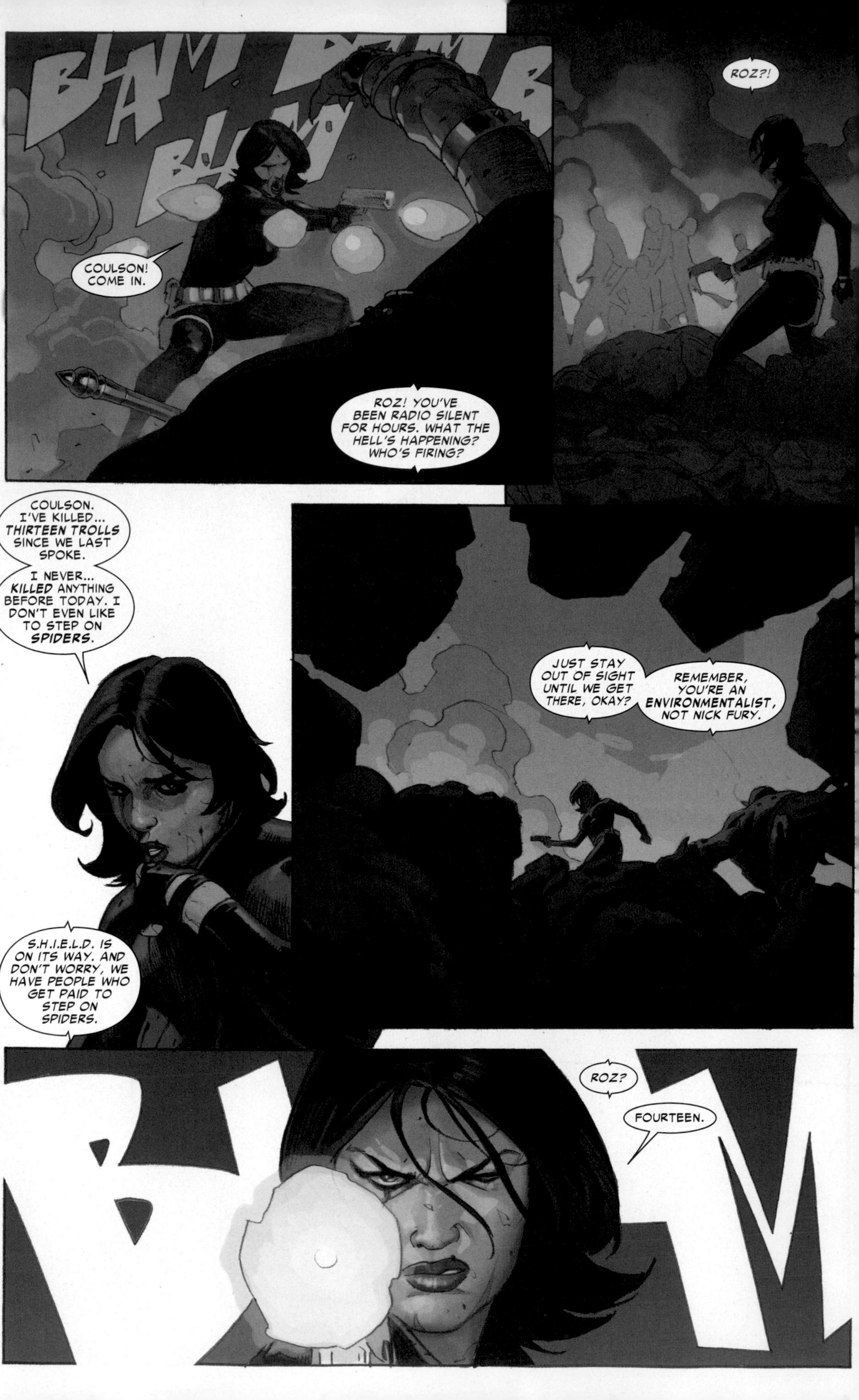
BLAM BLAM BLAM
COULSON! COME IN.
ROZ?!
ROZ! YOU'VE BEEN RADIO SILENT FOR HOURS. WHAT THE HELL'S HAPPENING? WHO'S FIRING?
COULSON. I'VE KILLED... THIRTEEN TROLLS SINCE WE LAST SPOKE.
I NEVER... KILLED ANYTHING BEFORE TODAY. I DON'T EVEN LIKE TO STEP ON SPIDERS.
JUST STAY OUT OF SIGHT UNTIL WE GET THERE, OKAY?
REMEMBER, YOU'RE AN ENVIRONMENTALIST, NOT NICK FURY.
S.H.I.E.L.D. IS ON ITS WAY. AND DON'T WORRY, WE HAVE PEOPLE WHO GET PAID TO STEP ON SPIDERS.
ROZ?
FOURTEEN.

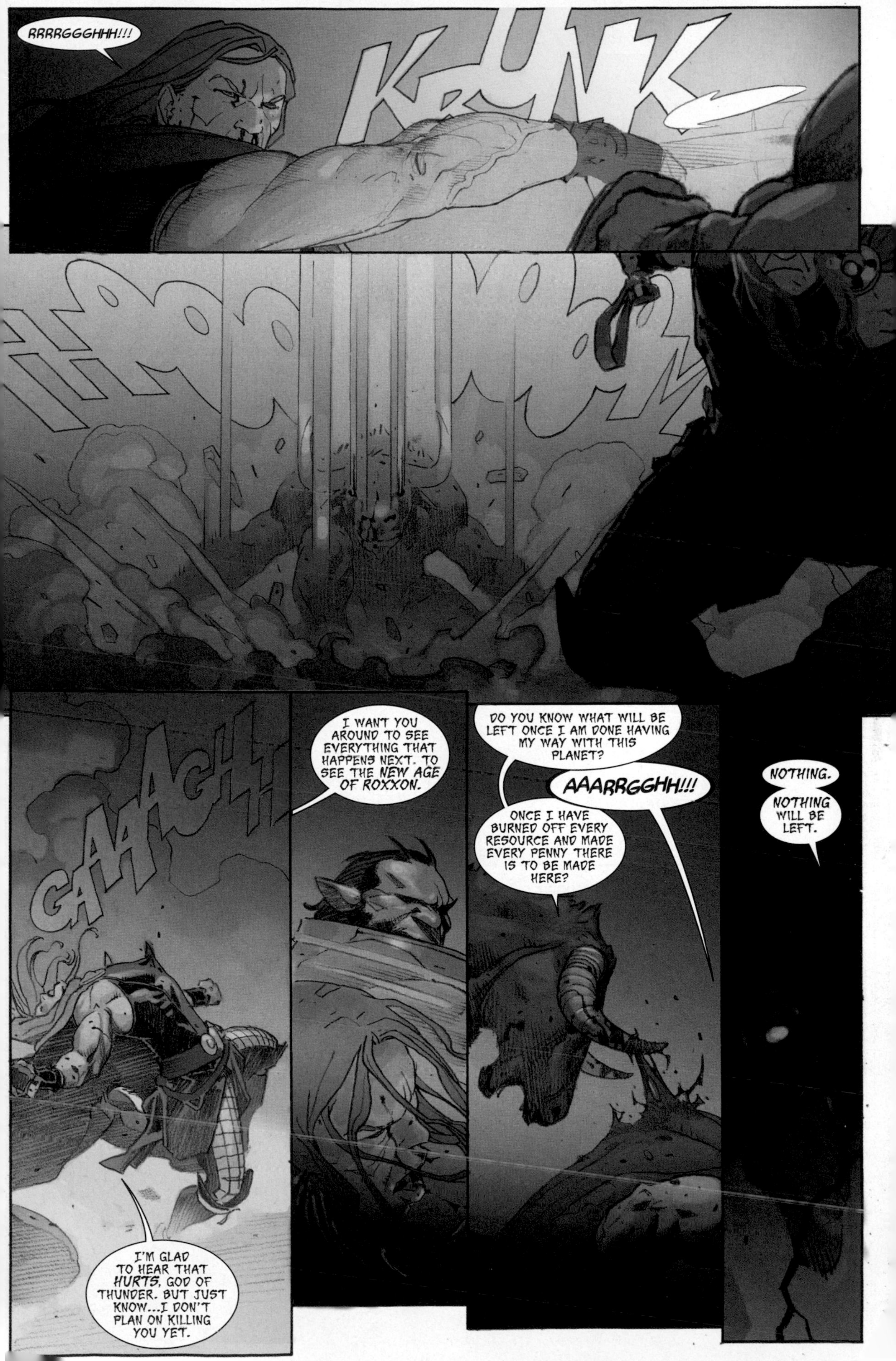
RRRRGGGHHH!!!
KRUNK
THOOOOOOM
GAAAGH!!
I'M GLAD TO HEAR THAT HURTS, GOD OF THUNDER. BUT JUST KNOW...I DON'T PLAN ON KILLING YOU YET.
I WANT YOU AROUND TO SEE EVERYTHING THAT HAPPENS NEXT. TO SEE THE NEW AGE OF ROXXON.
DO YOU KNOW WHAT WILL BE LEFT ONCE I AM DONE HAVING MY WAY WITH THIS PLANET?
ONCE I HAVE BURNED OFF EVERY RESOURCE AND MADE EVERY PENNY THERE IS TO BE MADE HERE?
AAARRGGHH!!!
NOTHING.
NOTHING WILL BE LEFT.

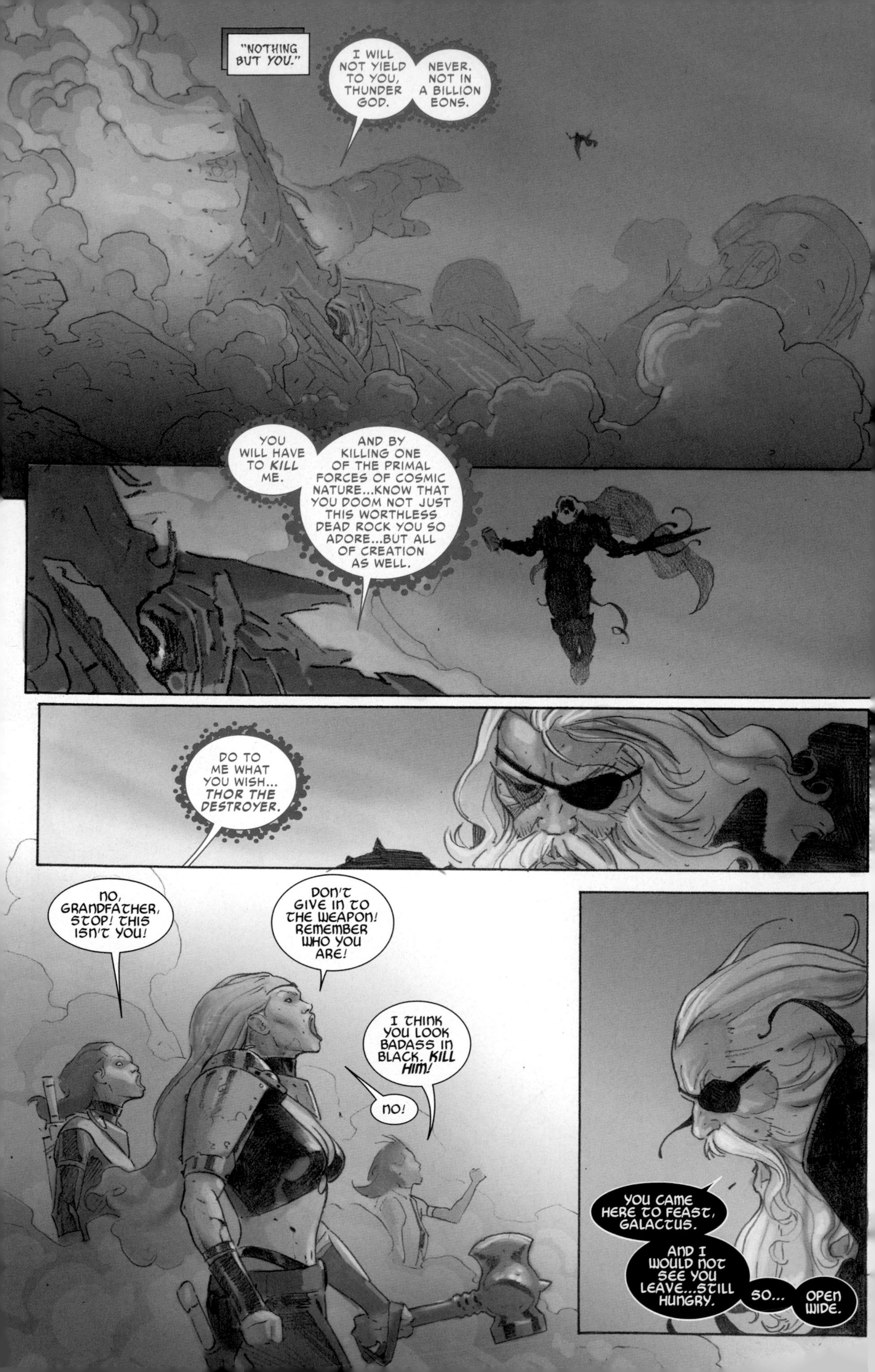
"NOTHING BUT YOU."
I WILL NOT YIELD TO YOU, THUNDER GOD.
NEVER. NOT IN A BILLION EONS.
YOU WILL HAVE TO KILL ME.
AND BY KILLING ONE OF THE PRIMAL FORCES OF COSMIC NATURE...KNOW THAT YOU DOOM NOT JUST THIS WORTHLESS DEAD ROCK YOU SO ADORE...BUT ALL OF CREATION AS WELL.
DO TO ME WHAT YOU WISH... THOR THE DESTROYER.
NO, GRANDFATHER, STOP! THIS ISN'T YOU!
DON'T GIVE IN TO THE WEAPON! REMEMBER WHO YOU ARE!
I THINK YOU LOOK BADASS IN BLACK. KILL HIM!
NO!
YOU CAME HERE TO FEAST, GALACTUS.
AND I WOULD NOT SEE YOU LEAVE...STILL HUNGRY.
SO...
OPEN WIDE.

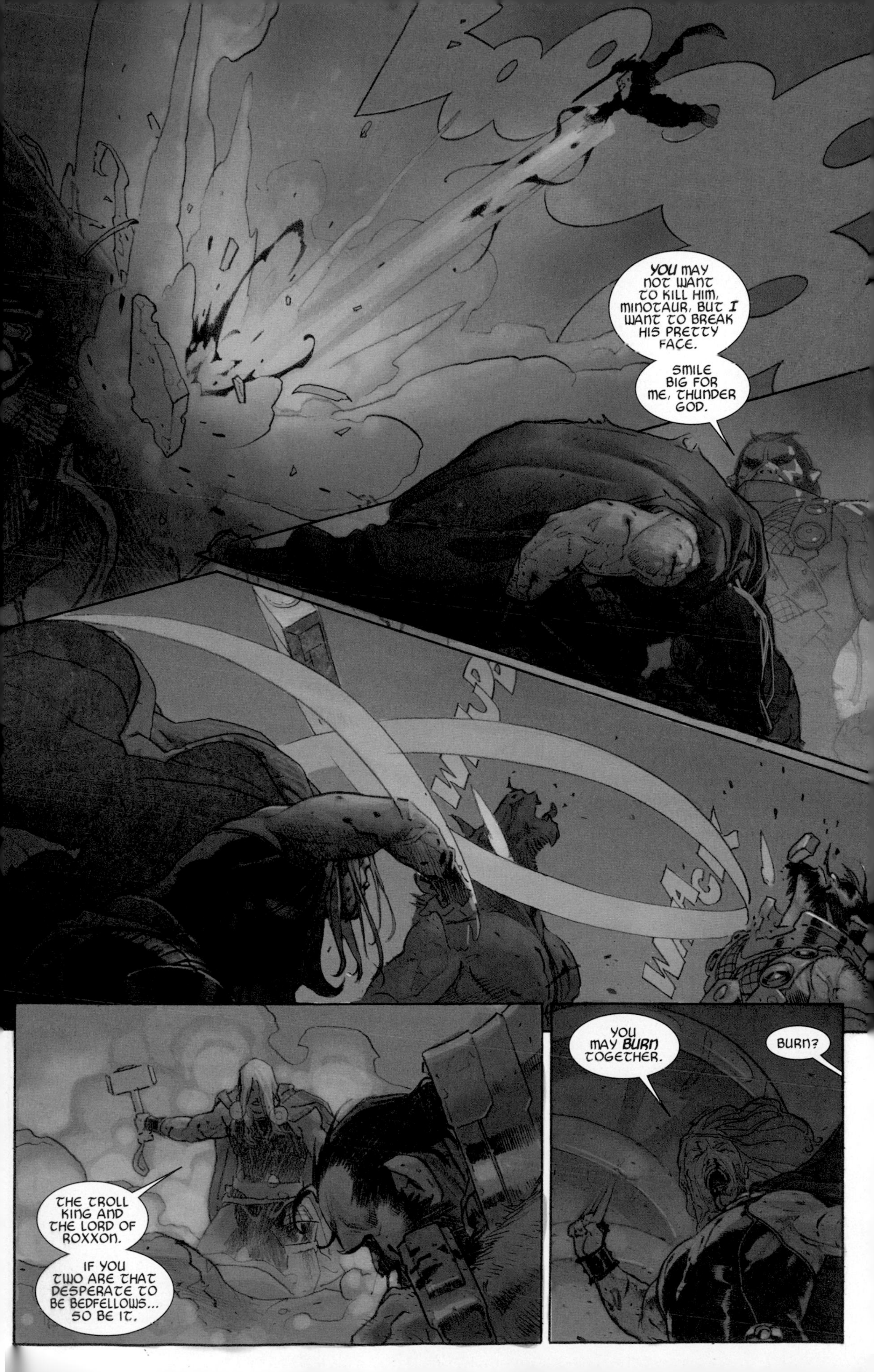
BOOOM
YOU MAY NOT WANT TO KILL HIM, MINOTAUR, BUT I WANT TO BREAK HIS PRETTY FACE.
SMILE BIG FOR ME, THUNDER GOD.
WHUP
WHACK
THE TROLL KING AND THE LORD OF ROXXON.
IF YOU TWO ARE THAT DESPERATE TO BE BEDFELLOWS... SO BE IT.
YOU MAY BURN TOGETHER.
BURN?

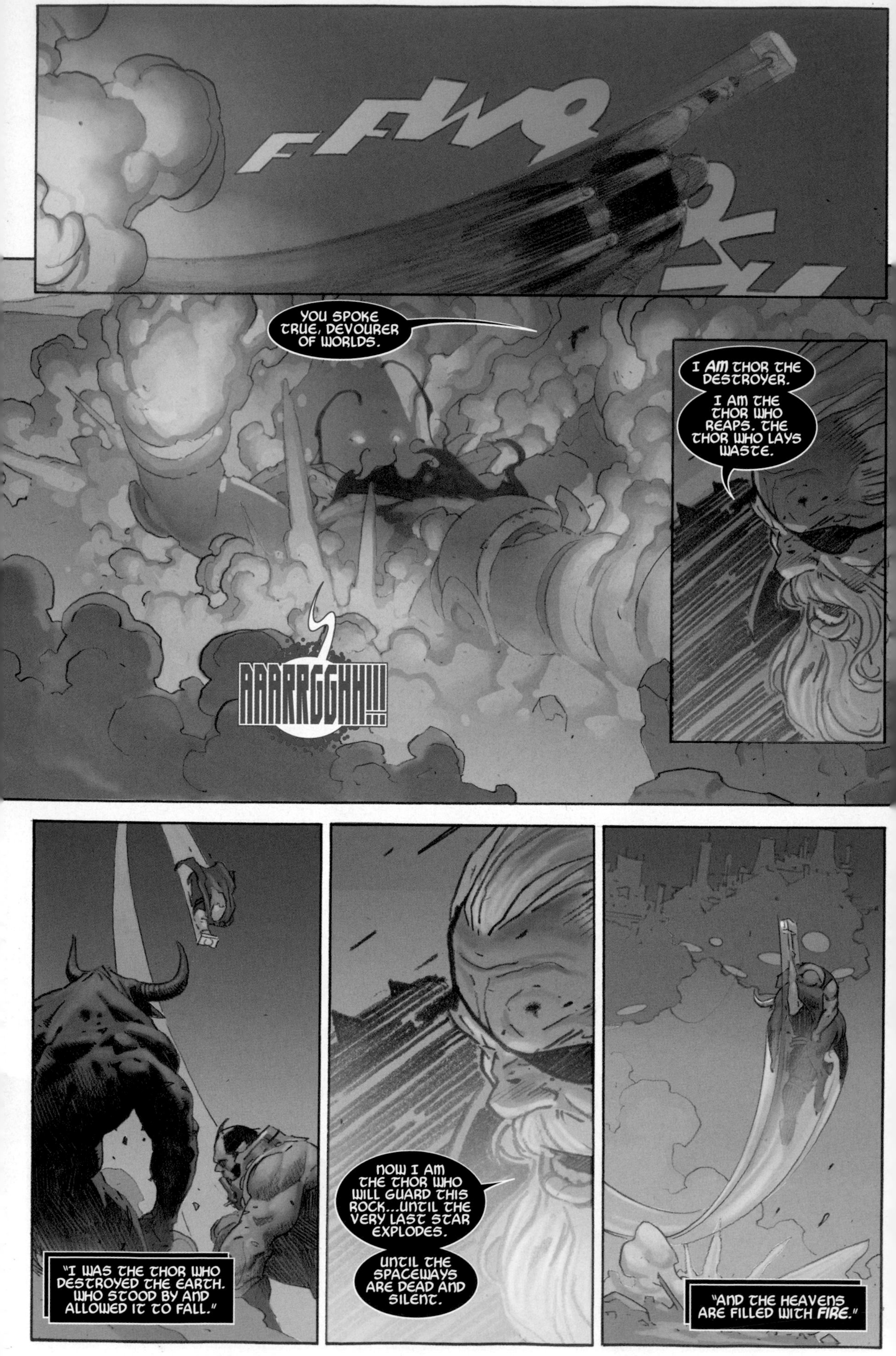
FFWOOKK
YOU SPOKE TRUE, DEVOURER OF WORLDS.
AAARRGGHH!!!
I AM THOR THE DESTROYER.
I AM THE THOR WHO REAPS. THE THOR WHO LAYS WASTE.
"I WAS THE THOR WHO DESTROYED THE EARTH. WHO STOOD BY AND ALLOWED IT TO FALL."
NOW I AM THE THOR WHO WILL GUARD THIS ROCK...UNTIL THE VERY LAST STAR EXPLODES.
UNTIL THE SPACEWAYS ARE DEAD AND SILENT.
"AND THE HEAVENS ARE FILLED WITH FIRE."

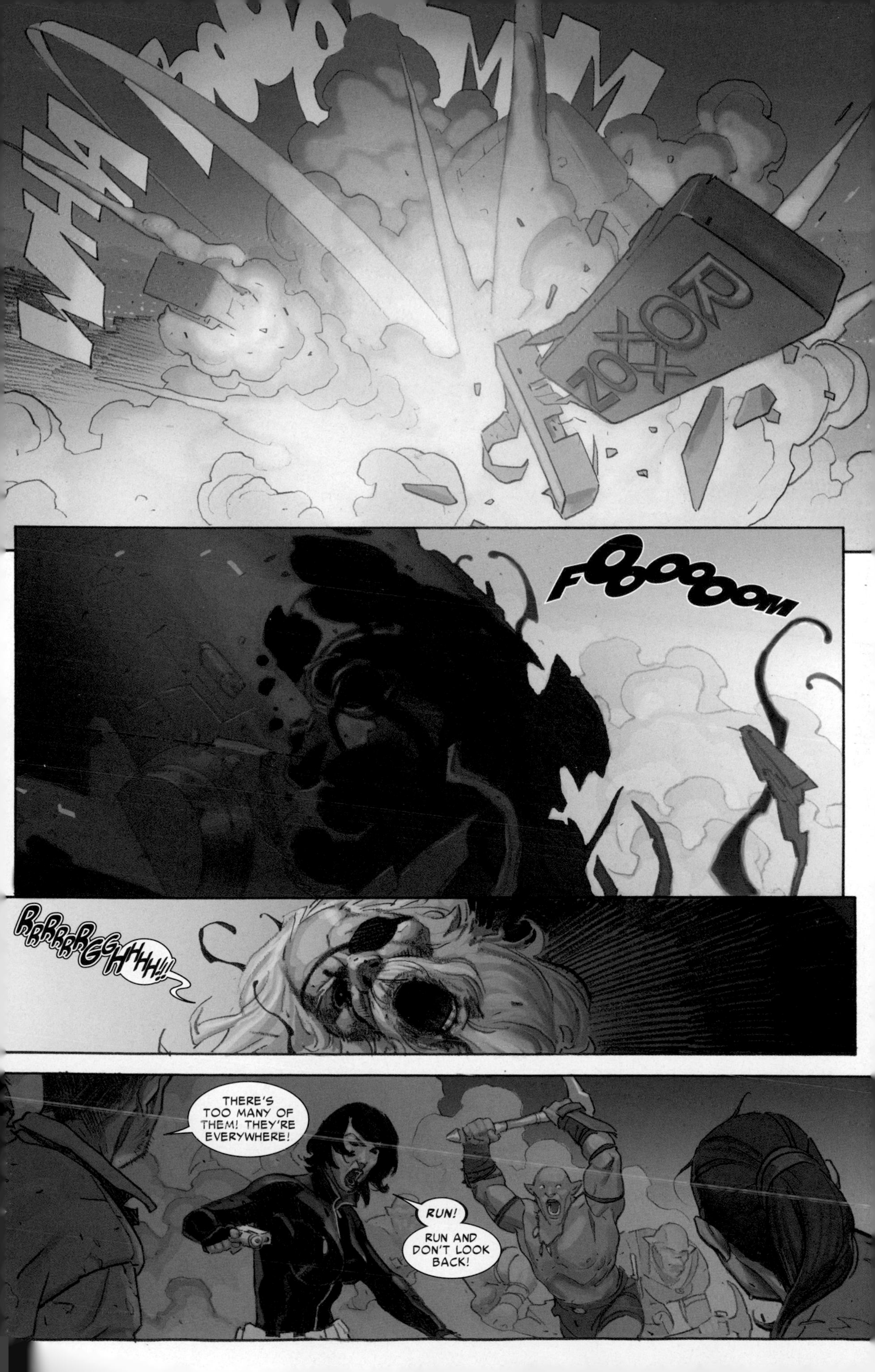
FOOOOOOM
RRRRRRGGHHHH!!!
THERE'S TOO MANY OF THEM! THEY'RE EVERYWHERE!
RUN!
RUN AND DON'T LOOK BACK!

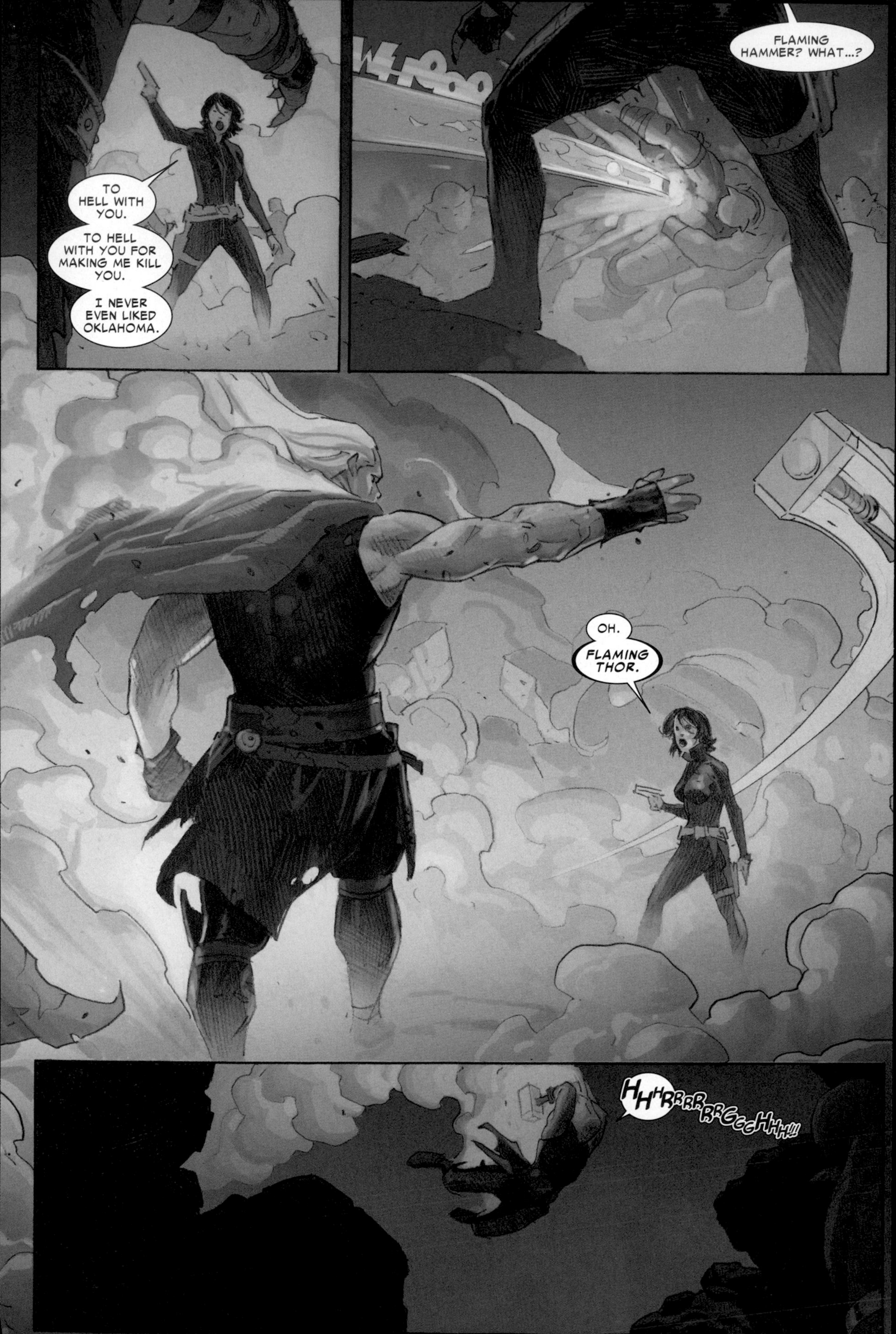
TO HELL WITH YOU.
TO HELL WITH YOU FOR MAKING ME KILL YOU.
I NEVER EVEN LIKED OKLAHOMA.
FLAMING HAMMER? WHAT...?
OH.
FLAMING THOR.
HHHRRRRRRRGGGHHHH!!!

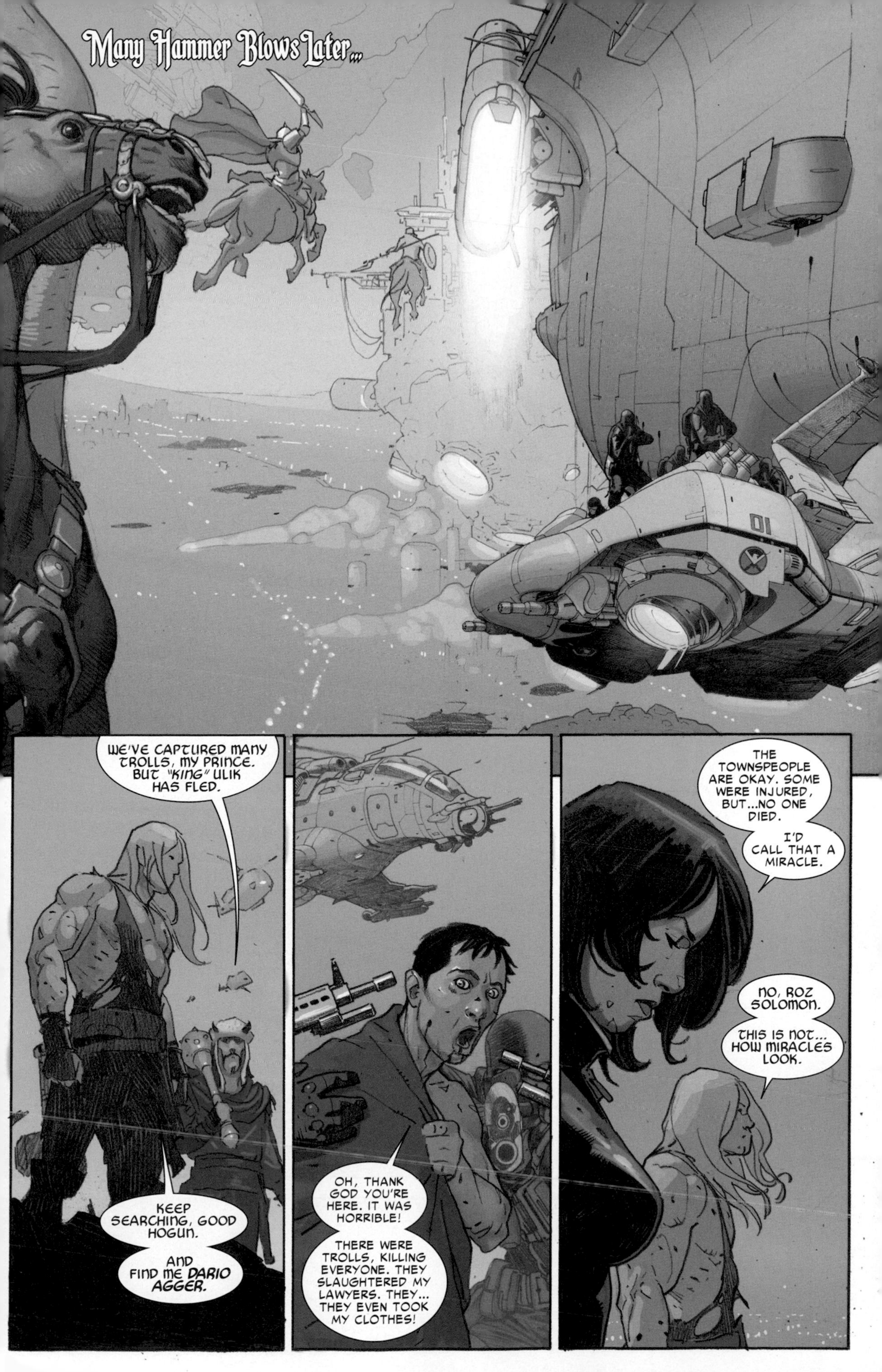
Many Hammer Blows Later...
WE'VE CAPTURED MANY TROLLS, MY PRINCE. BUT "KING" ULIK HAS FLED.
KEEP SEARCHING, GOOD HOGUN.
AND FIND ME DARIO AGGER.
OH, THANK GOD YOU'RE HERE. IT WAS HORRIBLE!
THERE WERE TROLLS, KILLING EVERYONE. THEY SLAUGHTERED MY LAWYERS. THEY... THEY EVEN TOOK MY CLOTHES!
THE TOWNSPEOPLE ARE OKAY. SOME WERE INJURED, BUT...NO ONE DIED.
I'D CALL THAT A MIRACLE.
NO, ROZ SOLOMON.
THIS IS NOT... HOW MIRACLES LOOK.

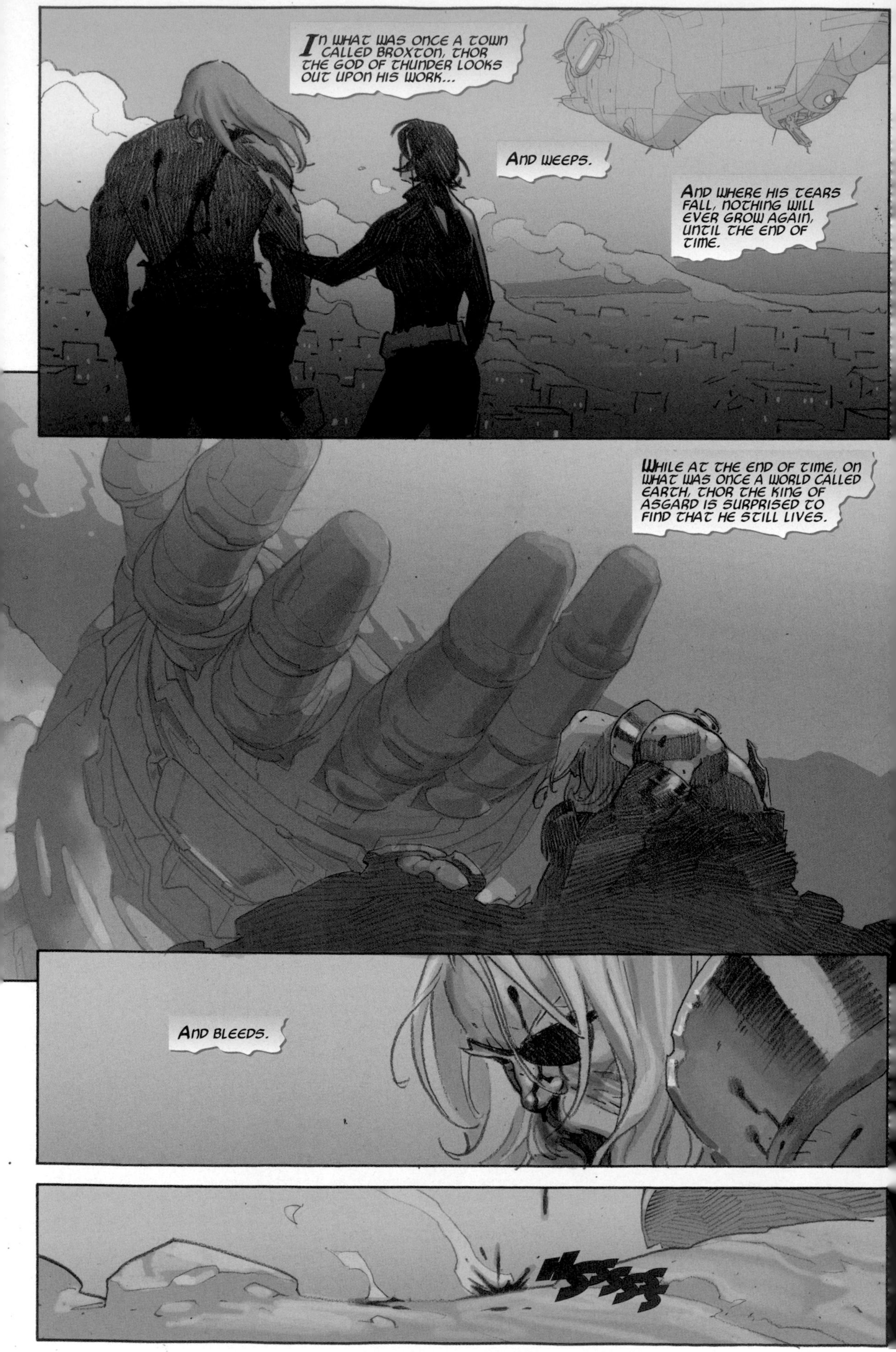
In what was once a town called Broxton, Thor the God of Thunder looks out upon his work...
And weeps.
And where his tears fall, nothing will ever grow again, until the end of time.
While at the end of time, on what was once a world called Earth, Thor the King of Asgard is surprised to find that he still lives.
And bleeds.
HSSSSS

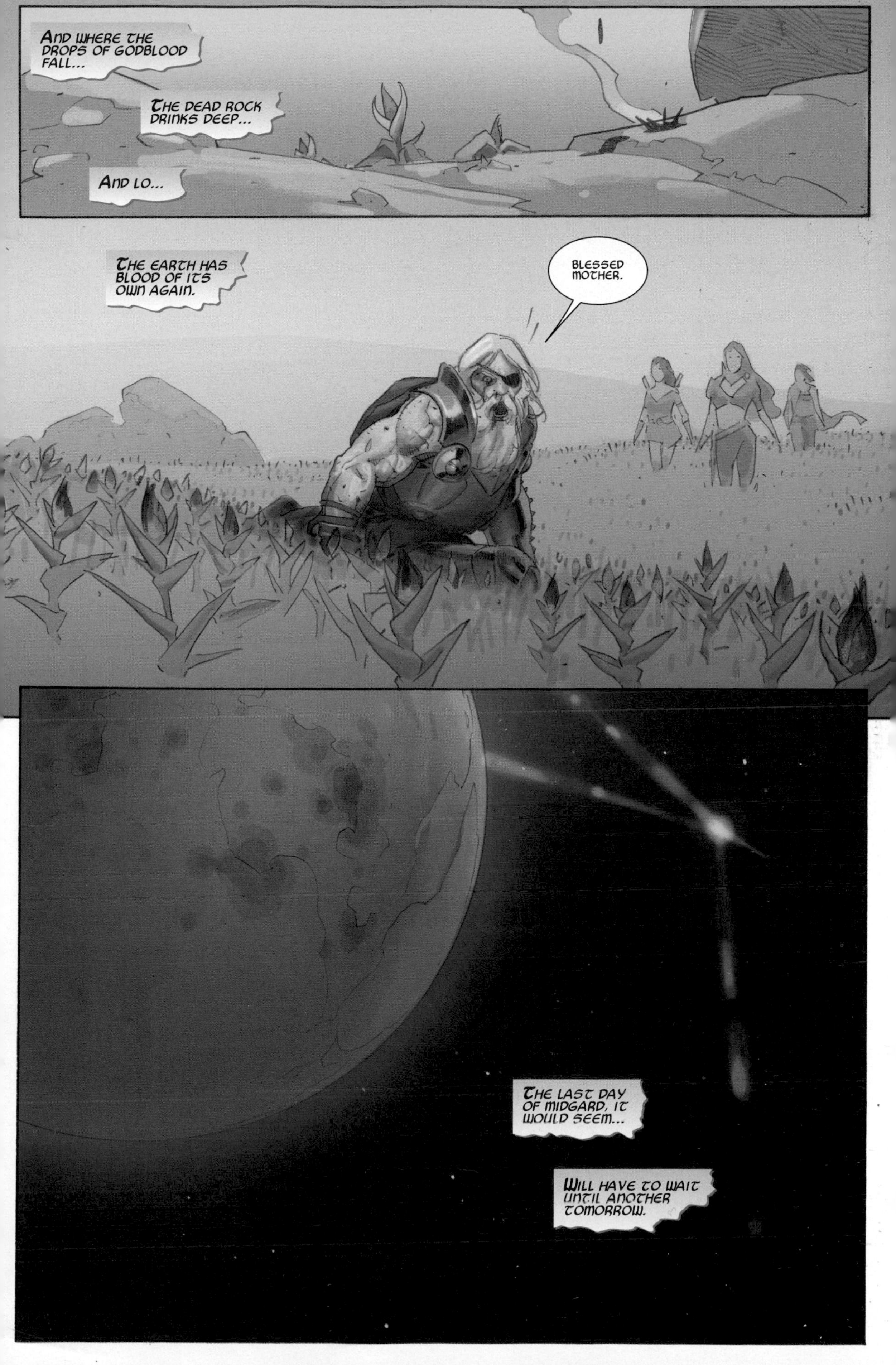
AND WHERE THE DROPS OF GODBLOOD FALL...
THE DEAD ROCK DRINKS DEEP...
AND LO...
THE EARTH HAS BLOOD OF ITS OWN AGAIN.
BLESSED MOTHER.
THE LAST DAY OF MIDGARD, IT WOULD SEEM...
WILL HAVE TO WAIT UNTIL ANOTHER TOMORROW.

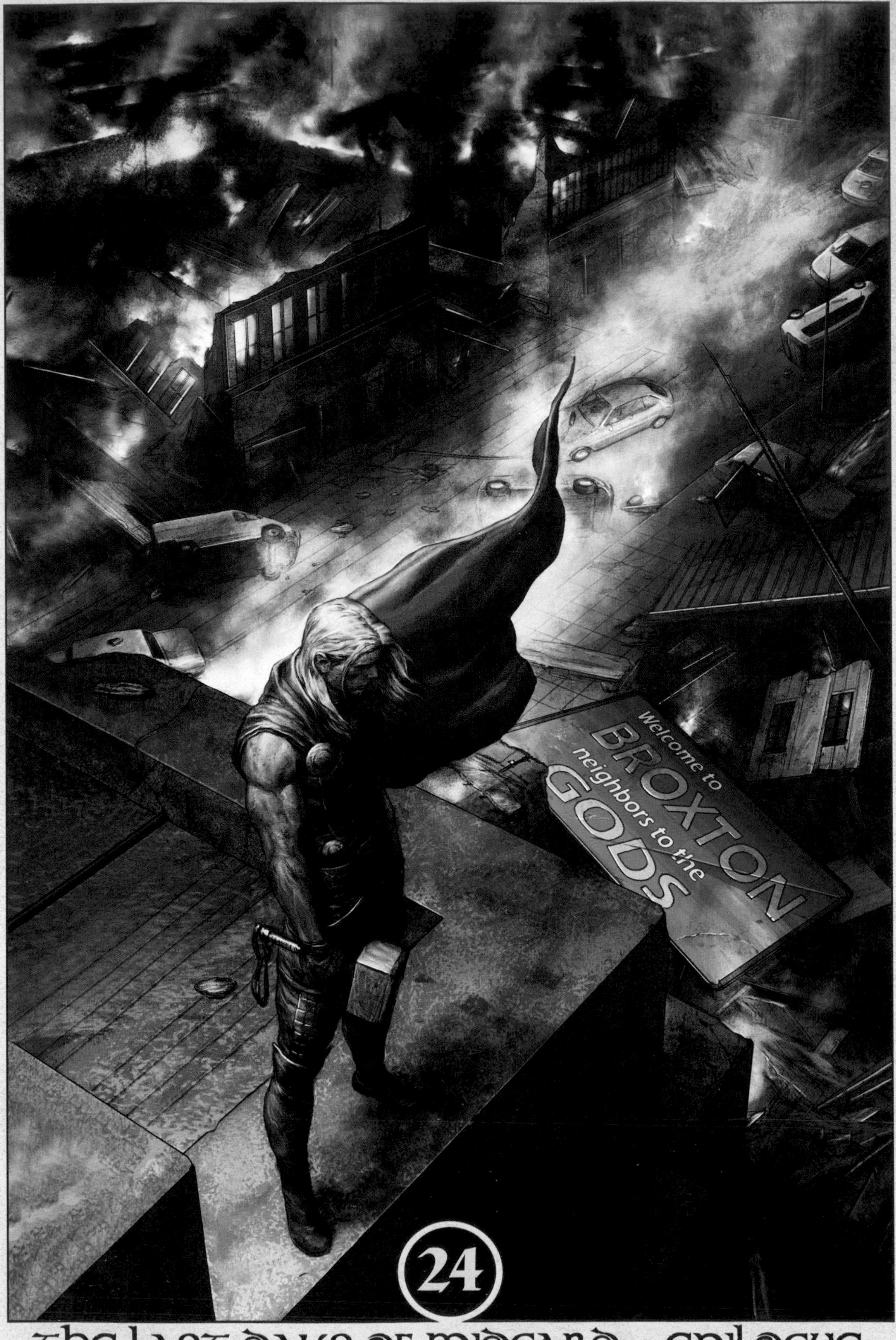
Welcome to
BROXTON
neighbors to the
GODS
24

THE LAST DAYS OF MIDGARD - EPILOGUE:
ADIEU, MIDGARD, ADIEU

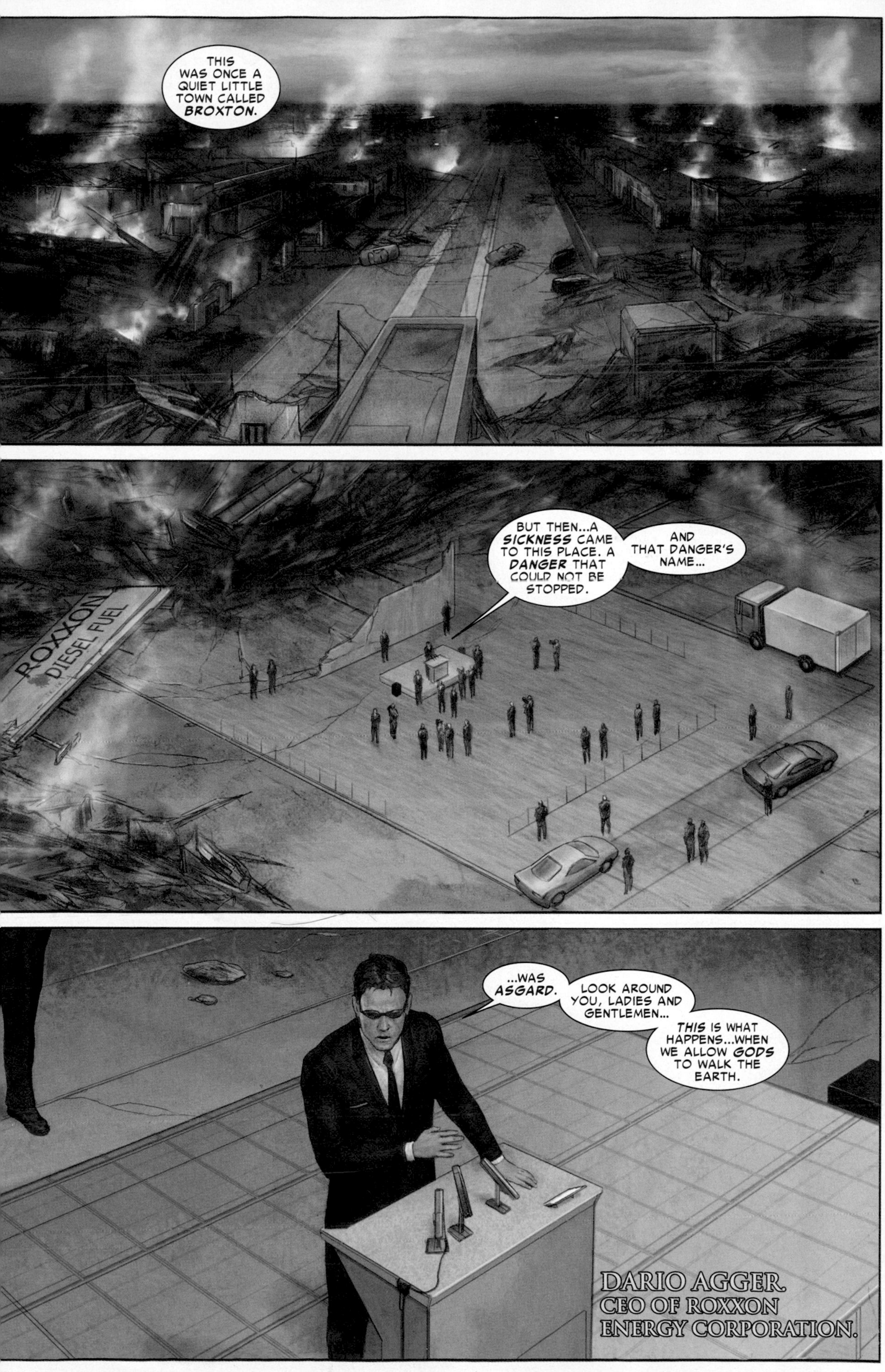
THIS WAS ONCE A QUIET LITTLE TOWN CALLED BROXTON.
ROXXON DIESEL FUEL
BUT THEN...A SICKNESS CAME TO THIS PLACE. A DANGER THAT COULD NOT BE STOPPED.
AND THAT DANGER'S NAME...
...WAS ASGARD.
LOOK AROUND YOU, LADIES AND GENTLEMEN...
THIS IS WHAT HAPPENS...WHEN WE ALLOW GODS TO WALK THE EARTH.
DARIO AGGER. CEO OF ROXXON ENERGY CORPORATION.

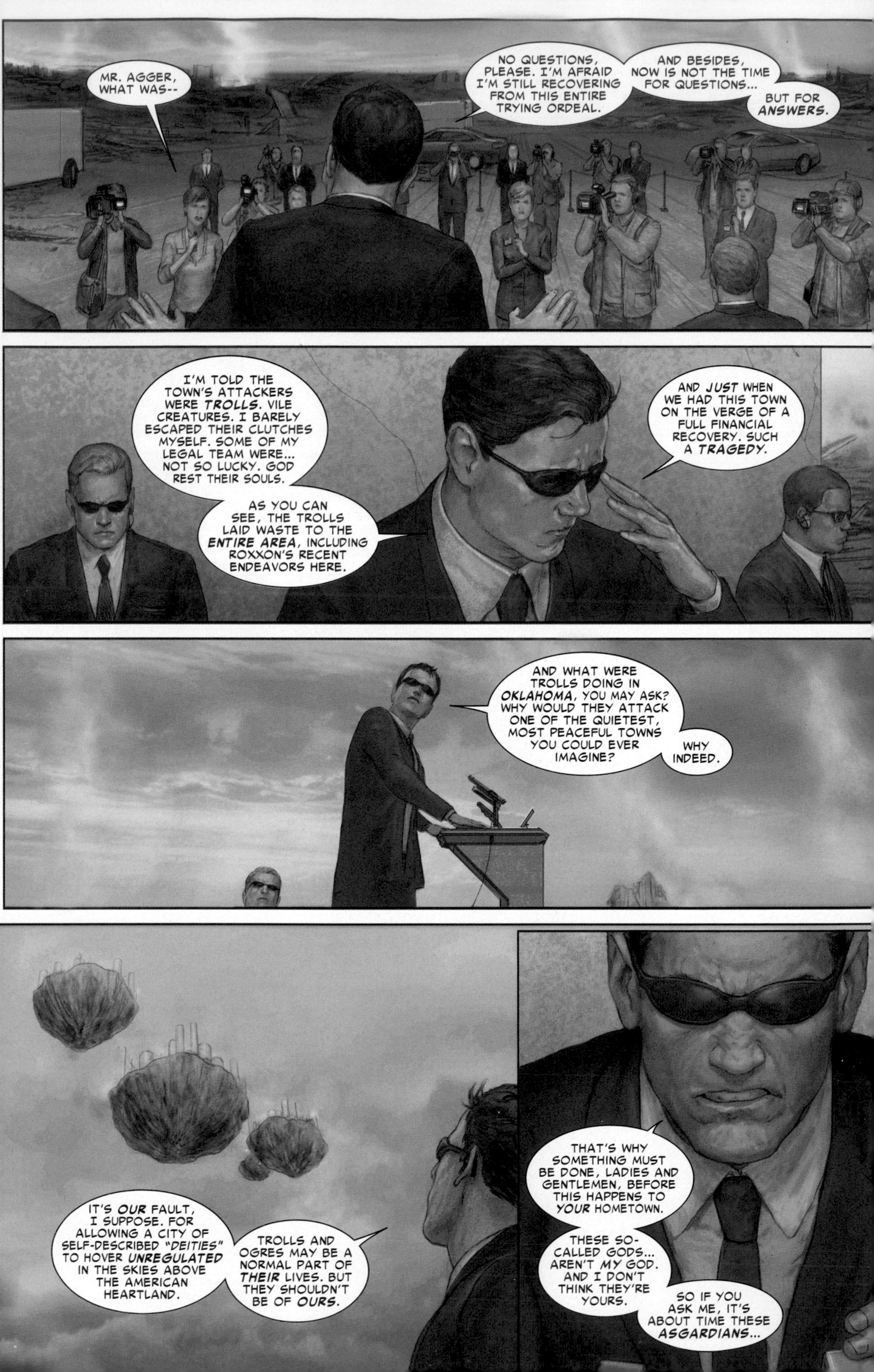
MR. AGGER, WHAT WAS--
NO QUESTIONS, PLEASE. I'M AFRAID I'M STILL RECOVERING FROM THIS ENTIRE TRYING ORDEAL.
AND BESIDES, NOW IS NOT THE TIME FOR QUESTIONS...
BUT FOR ANSWERS.
I'M TOLD THE TOWN'S ATTACKERS WERE TROLLS. VILE CREATURES. I BARELY ESCAPED THEIR CLUTCHES MYSELF. SOME OF MY LEGAL TEAM WERE... NOT SO LUCKY. GOD REST THEIR SOULS.
AS YOU CAN SEE, THE TROLLS LAID WASTE TO THE ENTIRE AREA, INCLUDING ROXXON'S RECENT ENDEAVORS HERE.
AND JUST WHEN WE HAD THIS TOWN ON THE VERGE OF A FULL FINANCIAL RECOVERY. SUCH A TRAGEDY.
AND WHAT WERE TROLLS DOING IN OKLAHOMA, YOU MAY ASK? WHY WOULD THEY ATTACK ONE OF THE QUIETEST, MOST PEACEFUL TOWNS YOU COULD EVER IMAGINE?
WHY INDEED.
IT'S OUR FAULT, I SUPPOSE. FOR ALLOWING A CITY OF SELF-DESCRIBED "DEITIES" TO HOVER UNREGULATED IN THE SKIES ABOVE THE AMERICAN HEARTLAND.
TROLLS AND OGRES MAY BE A NORMAL PART OF THEIR LIVES. BUT THEY SHOULDN'T BE OF OURS.
THAT'S WHY SOMETHING MUST BE DONE, LADIES AND GENTLEMEN, BEFORE THIS HAPPENS TO YOUR HOMETOWN.
THESE SO-CALLED GODS... AREN'T MY GOD. AND I DON'T THINK THEY'RE YOURS.
SO IF YOU ASK ME, IT'S ABOUT TIME THESE ASGARDIANS...

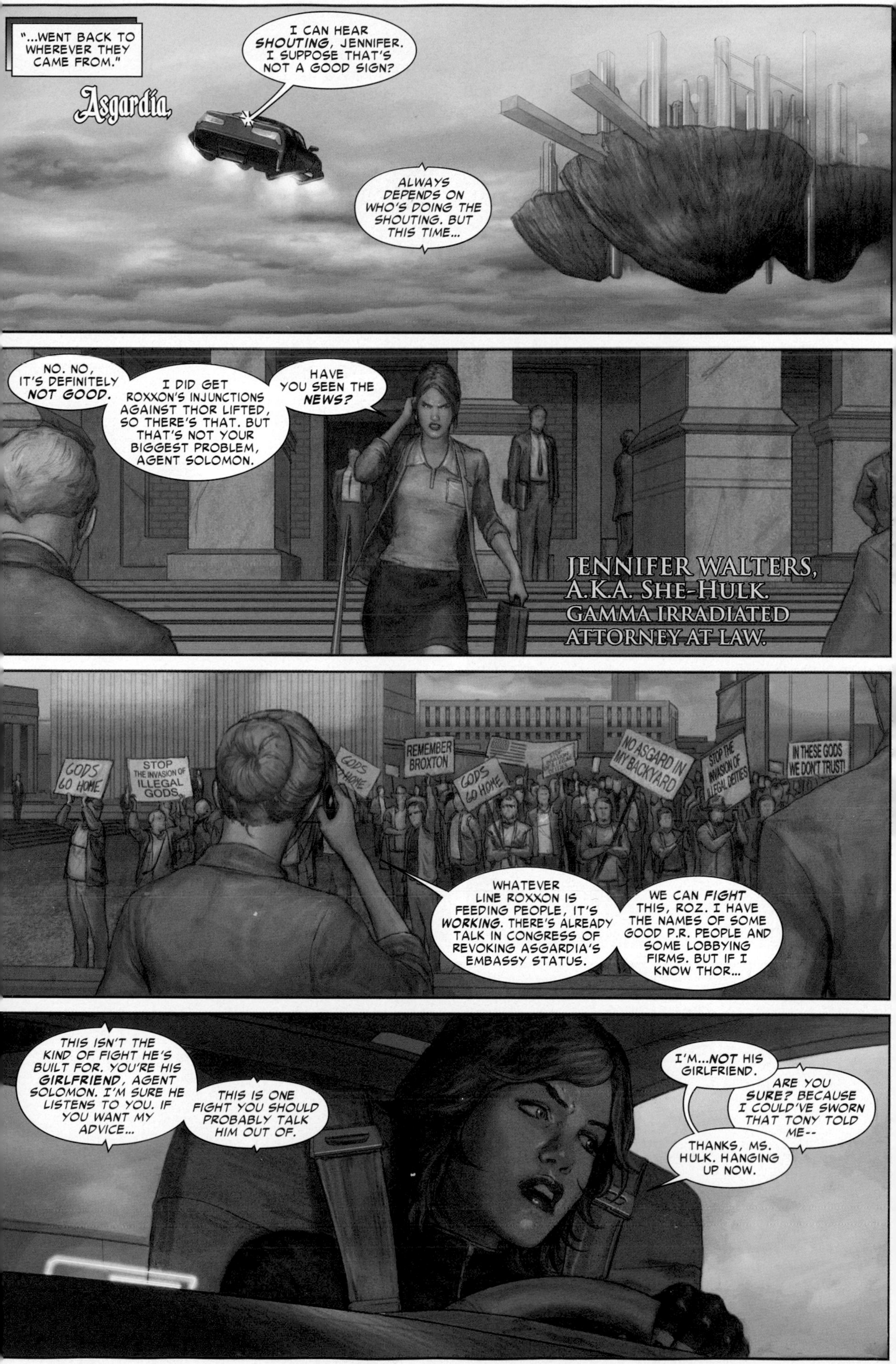
"...WENT BACK TO WHEREVER THEY CAME FROM."
Asgardia
I CAN HEAR SHOUTING, JENNIFER. I SUPPOSE THAT'S NOT A GOOD SIGN?
ALWAYS DEPENDS ON WHO'S DOING THE SHOUTING. BUT THIS TIME...
NO. NO, IT'S DEFINITELY NOT GOOD.
I DID GET ROXXON'S INJUNCTIONS AGAINST THOR LIFTED, SO THERE'S THAT. BUT THAT'S NOT YOUR BIGGEST PROBLEM, AGENT SOLOMON.
HAVE YOU SEEN THE NEWS?
JENNIFER WALTERS, A.K.A. SHE-HULK. GAMMA IRRADIATED ATTORNEY AT LAW.
GODS GO HOME
STOP THE INVASION OF ILLEGAL GODS
REMEMBER BROXTON
GODS GO HOME
NO ASGARD IN MY BACKYARD
STOP THE INVASION OF ILLEGAL DEITIES
IN THESE GODS WE DON'T TRUST!
WHATEVER LINE ROXXON IS FEEDING PEOPLE, IT'S WORKING. THERE'S ALREADY TALK IN CONGRESS OF REVOKING ASGARDIA'S EMBASSY STATUS.
WE CAN FIGHT THIS, ROZ. I HAVE THE NAMES OF SOME GOOD P.R. PEOPLE AND SOME LOBBYING FIRMS. BUT IF I KNOW THOR...
THIS ISN'T THE KIND OF FIGHT HE'S BUILT FOR. YOU'RE HIS GIRLFRIEND, AGENT SOLOMON. I'M SURE HE LISTENS TO YOU. IF YOU WANT MY ADVICE...
THIS IS ONE FIGHT YOU SHOULD PROBABLY TALK HIM OUT OF.
I'M...NOT HIS GIRLFRIEND.
ARE YOU SURE? BECAUSE I COULD'VE SWORN THAT TONY TOLD ME--
THANKS, MS. HULK. HANGING UP NOW.

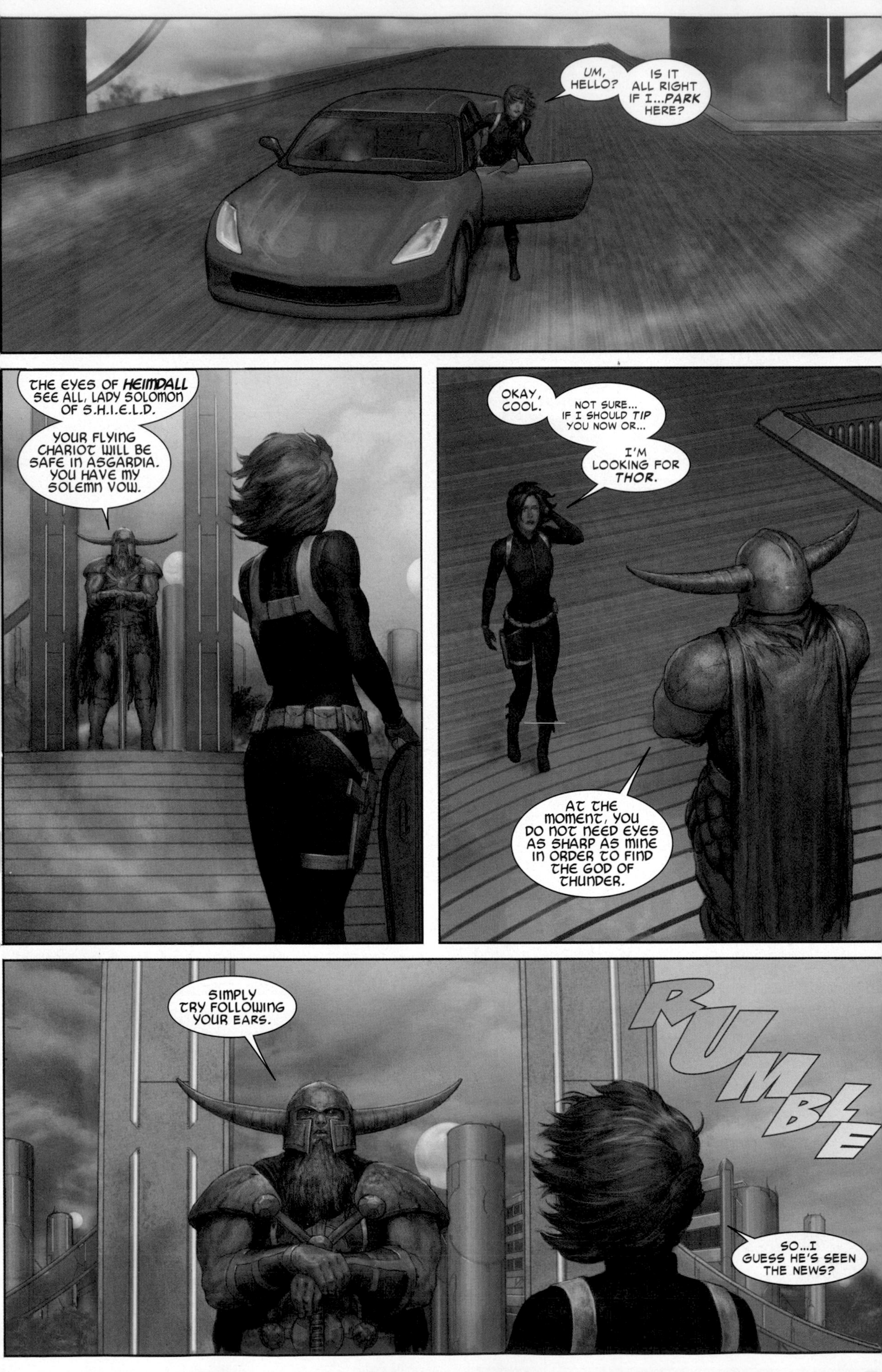
UM, HELLO?
IS IT ALL RIGHT IF I...PARK HERE?
THE EYES OF HEIMDALL SEE ALL, LADY SOLOMON OF S.H.I.E.L.D.
YOUR FLYING CHARIOT WILL BE SAFE IN ASGARDIA. YOU HAVE MY SOLEMN VOW.
OKAY, COOL.
NOT SURE... IF I SHOULD TIP YOU NOW OR...
I'M LOOKING FOR THOR.
AT THE MOMENT, YOU DO NOT NEED EYES AS SHARP AS MINE IN ORDER TO FIND THE GOD OF THUNDER.
SIMPLY TRY FOLLOWING YOUR EARS.
RUMBLE
SO...I GUESS HE'S SEEN THE NEWS?

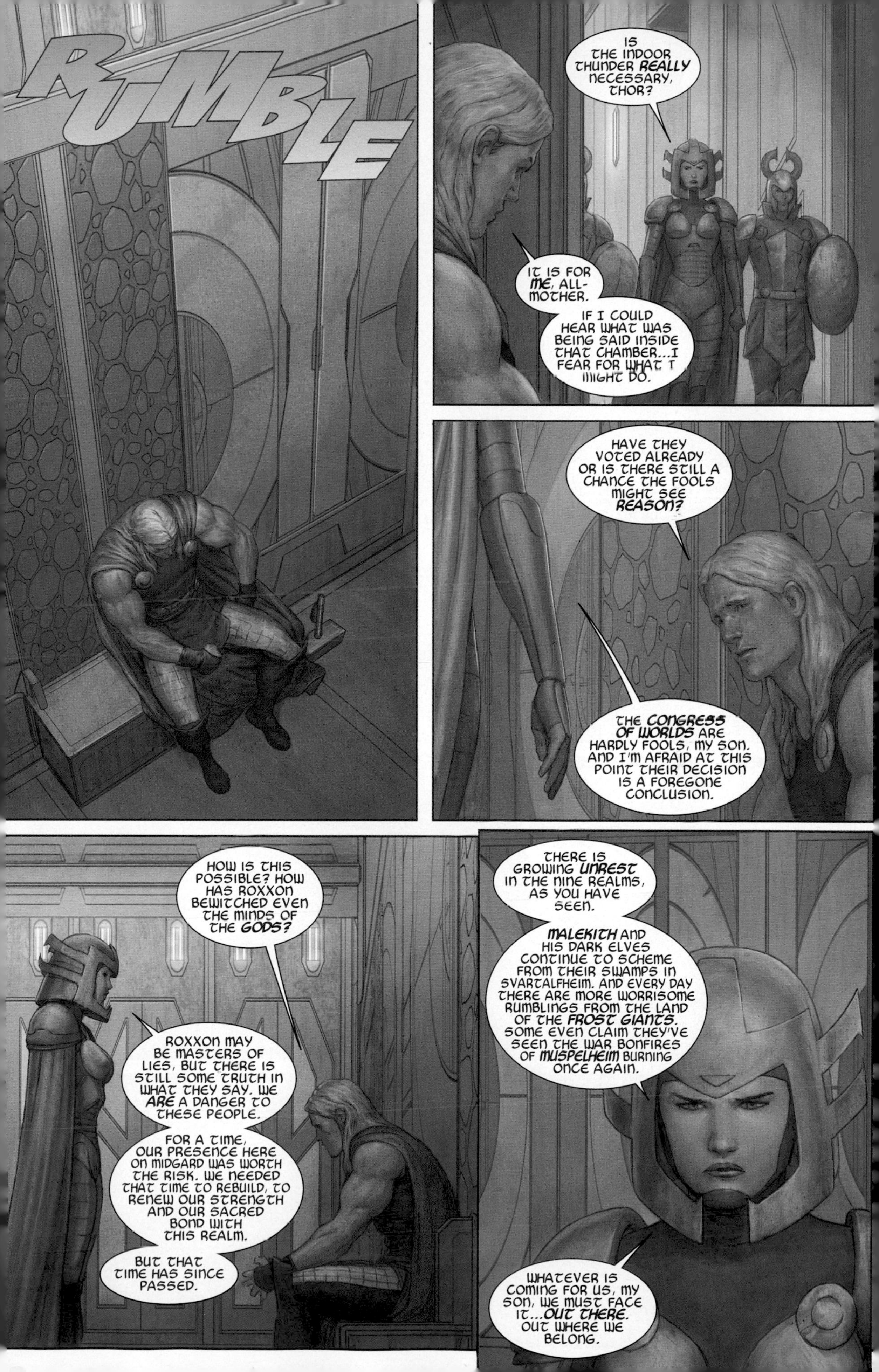
RUMBLE
IS THE INDOOR THUNDER REALLY NECESSARY, THOR?
IT IS FOR ME, ALL-MOTHER.
IF I COULD HEAR WHAT WAS BEING SAID INSIDE THAT CHAMBER...I FEAR FOR WHAT I MIGHT DO.
HAVE THEY VOTED ALREADY OR IS THERE STILL A CHANCE THE FOOLS MIGHT SEE REASON?
THE CONGRESS OF WORLDS ARE HARDLY FOOLS, MY SON. AND I'M AFRAID AT THIS POINT THEIR DECISION IS A FOREGONE CONCLUSION.
HOW IS THIS POSSIBLE? HOW HAS ROXXON BEWITCHED EVEN THE MINDS OF THE GODS?
ROXXON MAY BE MASTERS OF LIES, BUT THERE IS STILL SOME TRUTH IN WHAT THEY SAY. WE ARE A DANGER TO THESE PEOPLE.
FOR A TIME, OUR PRESENCE HERE ON MIDGARD WAS WORTH THE RISK. WE NEEDED THAT TIME TO REBUILD, TO RENEW OUR STRENGTH AND OUR SACRED BOND WITH THIS REALM.
BUT THAT TIME HAS SINCE PASSED.
THERE IS GROWING UNREST IN THE NINE REALMS, AS YOU HAVE SEEN.
MALEKITH AND HIS DARK ELVES CONTINUE TO SCHEME FROM THEIR SWAMPS IN SVARTALFHEIM. AND EVERY DAY THERE ARE MORE WORRISOME RUMBLINGS FROM THE LAND OF THE FROST GIANTS. SOME EVEN CLAIM THEY'VE SEEN THE WAR BONFIRES OF MUSPELHEIM BURNING ONCE AGAIN.
WHATEVER IS COMING FOR US, MY SON, WE MUST FACE IT...OUT THERE. OUT WHERE WE BELONG.

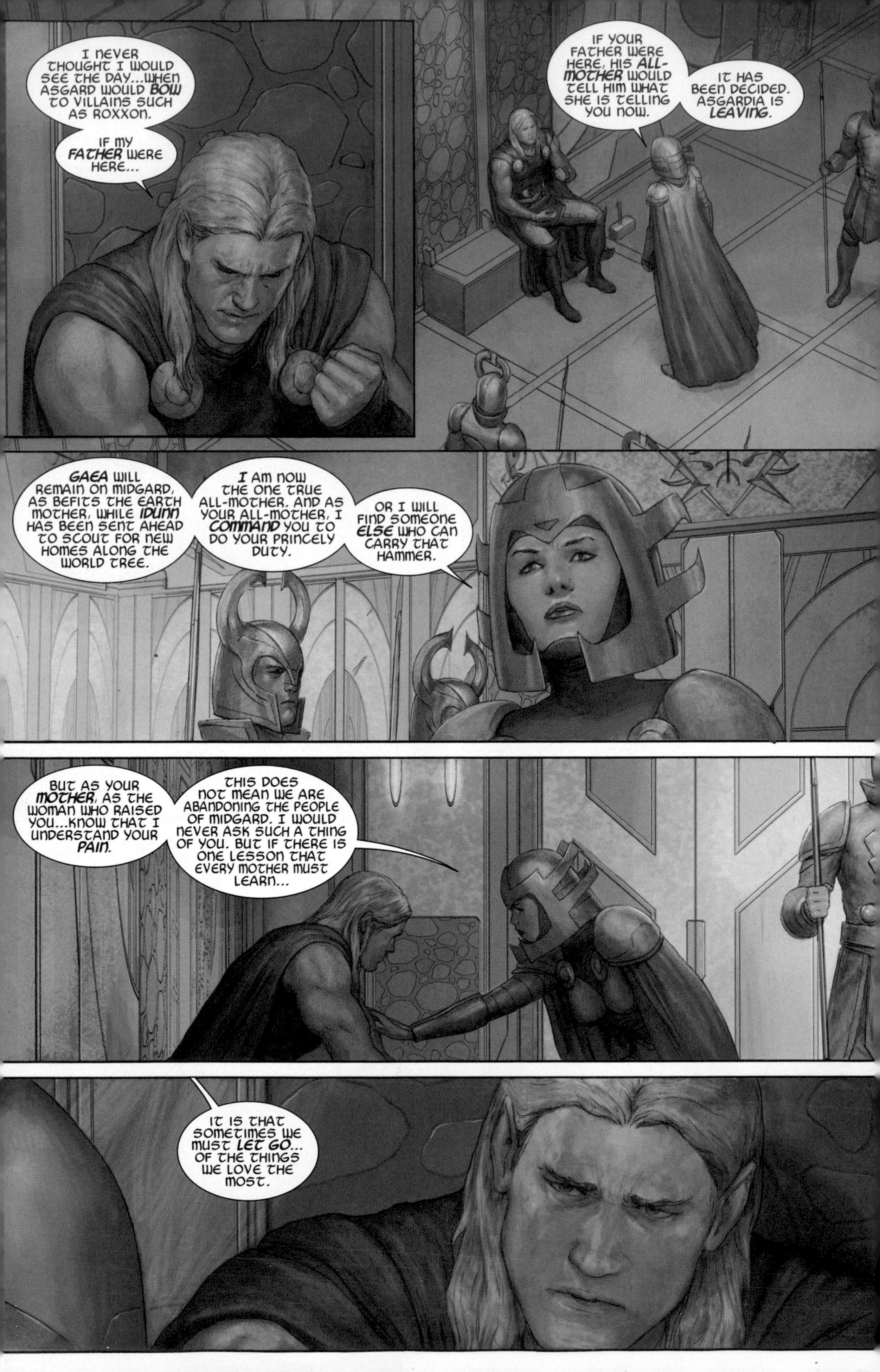
I NEVER THOUGHT I WOULD SEE THE DAY...WHEN ASGARD WOULD BOW TO VILLAINS SUCH AS ROXXON.
IF MY FATHER WERE HERE...
IF YOUR FATHER WERE HERE, HIS ALL-MOTHER WOULD TELL HIM WHAT SHE IS TELLING YOU NOW.
IT HAS BEEN DECIDED. ASGARDIA IS LEAVING.
GAEA WILL REMAIN ON MIDGARD, AS BEFITS THE EARTH MOTHER, WHILE IDUNN HAS BEEN SENT AHEAD TO SCOUT FOR NEW HOMES ALONG THE WORLD TREE.
I AM NOW THE ONE TRUE ALL-MOTHER. AND AS YOUR ALL-MOTHER, I COMMAND YOU TO DO YOUR PRINCELY DUTY.
OR I WILL FIND SOMEONE ELSE WHO CAN CARRY THAT HAMMER.
BUT AS YOUR MOTHER, AS THE WOMAN WHO RAISED YOU...KNOW THAT I UNDERSTAND YOUR PAIN.
THIS DOES NOT MEAN WE ARE ABANDONING THE PEOPLE OF MIDGARD. I WOULD NEVER ASK SUCH A THING OF YOU. BUT IF THERE IS ONE LESSON THAT EVERY MOTHER MUST LEARN...
IT IS THAT SOMETIMES WE MUST LET GO... OF THE THINGS WE LOVE THE MOST.

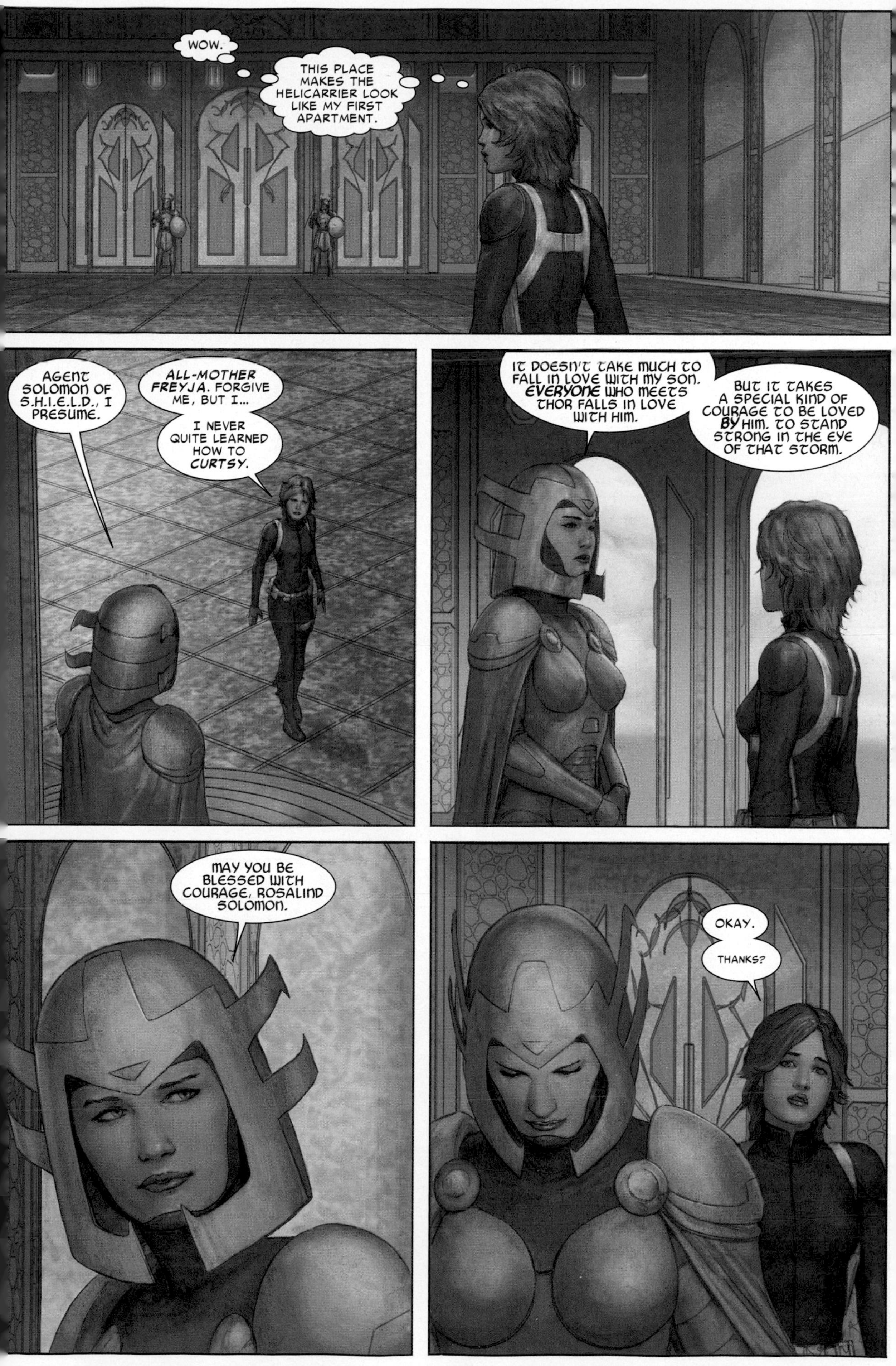
WOW.
THIS PLACE MAKES THE HELICARRIER LOOK LIKE MY FIRST APARTMENT.
AGENT SOLOMON OF S.H.I.E.L.D., I PRESUME.
ALL-MOTHER FREYJA. FORGIVE ME, BUT I...
I NEVER QUITE LEARNED HOW TO CURTSY.
IT DOESN'T TAKE MUCH TO FALL IN LOVE WITH MY SON. EVERYONE WHO MEETS THOR FALLS IN LOVE WITH HIM.
BUT IT TAKES A SPECIAL KIND OF COURAGE TO BE LOVED BY HIM. TO STAND STRONG IN THE EYE OF THAT STORM.
MAY YOU BE BLESSED WITH COURAGE, ROSALIND SOLOMON.
OKAY.
THANKS?

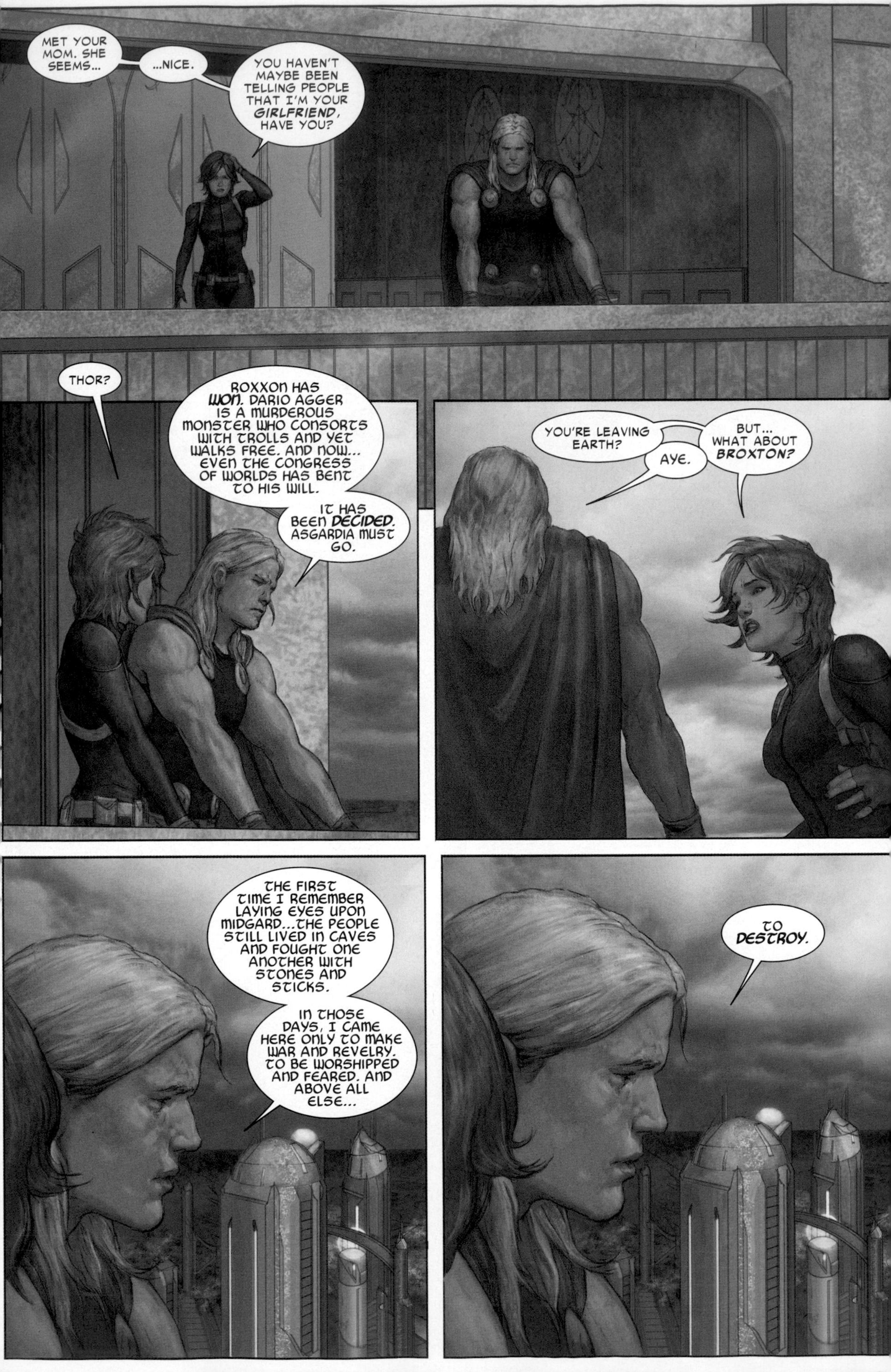
MET YOUR MOM. SHE SEEMS...
...NICE.
YOU HAVEN'T MAYBE BEEN TELLING PEOPLE THAT I'M YOUR GIRLFRIEND, HAVE YOU?
THOR?
ROXXON HAS WON. DARIO AGGER IS A MURDEROUS MONSTER WHO CONSORTS WITH TROLLS AND YET WALKS FREE. AND NOW... EVEN THE CONGRESS OF WORLDS HAS BENT TO HIS WILL.
IT HAS BEEN DECIDED. ASGARDIA MUST GO.
YOU'RE LEAVING EARTH?
AYE.
BUT... WHAT ABOUT BROXTON?
THE FIRST TIME I REMEMBER LAYING EYES UPON MIDGARD...THE PEOPLE STILL LIVED IN CAVES AND FOUGHT ONE ANOTHER WITH STONES AND STICKS.
IN THOSE DAYS, I CAME HERE ONLY TO MAKE WAR AND REVELRY. TO BE WORSHIPPED AND FEARED. AND ABOVE ALL ELSE...
TO DESTROY.

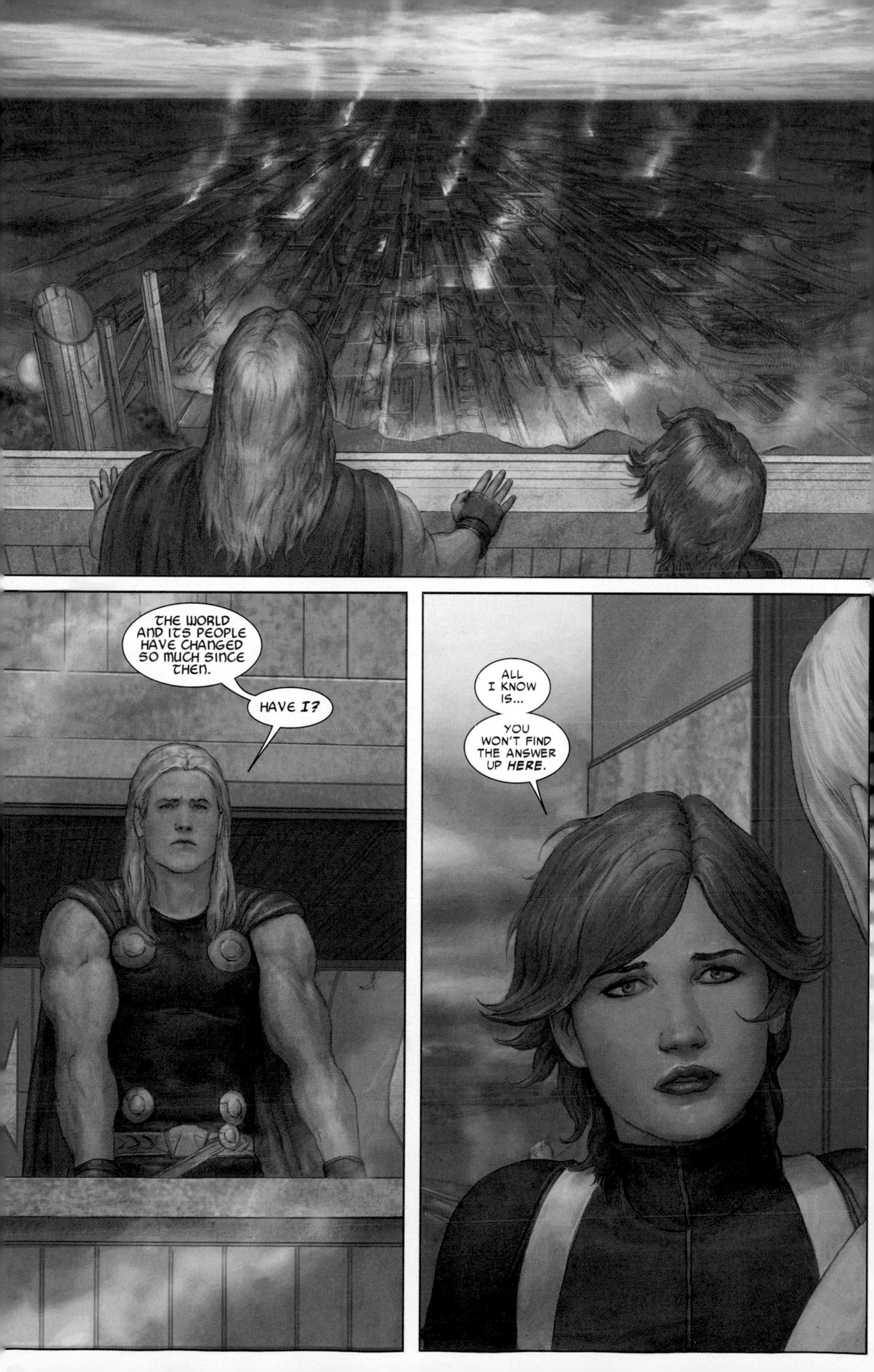
THE WORLD AND ITS PEOPLE HAVE CHANGED SO MUCH SINCE THEN.
HAVE I?
ALL I KNOW IS...
YOU WON'T FIND THE ANSWER UP HERE.

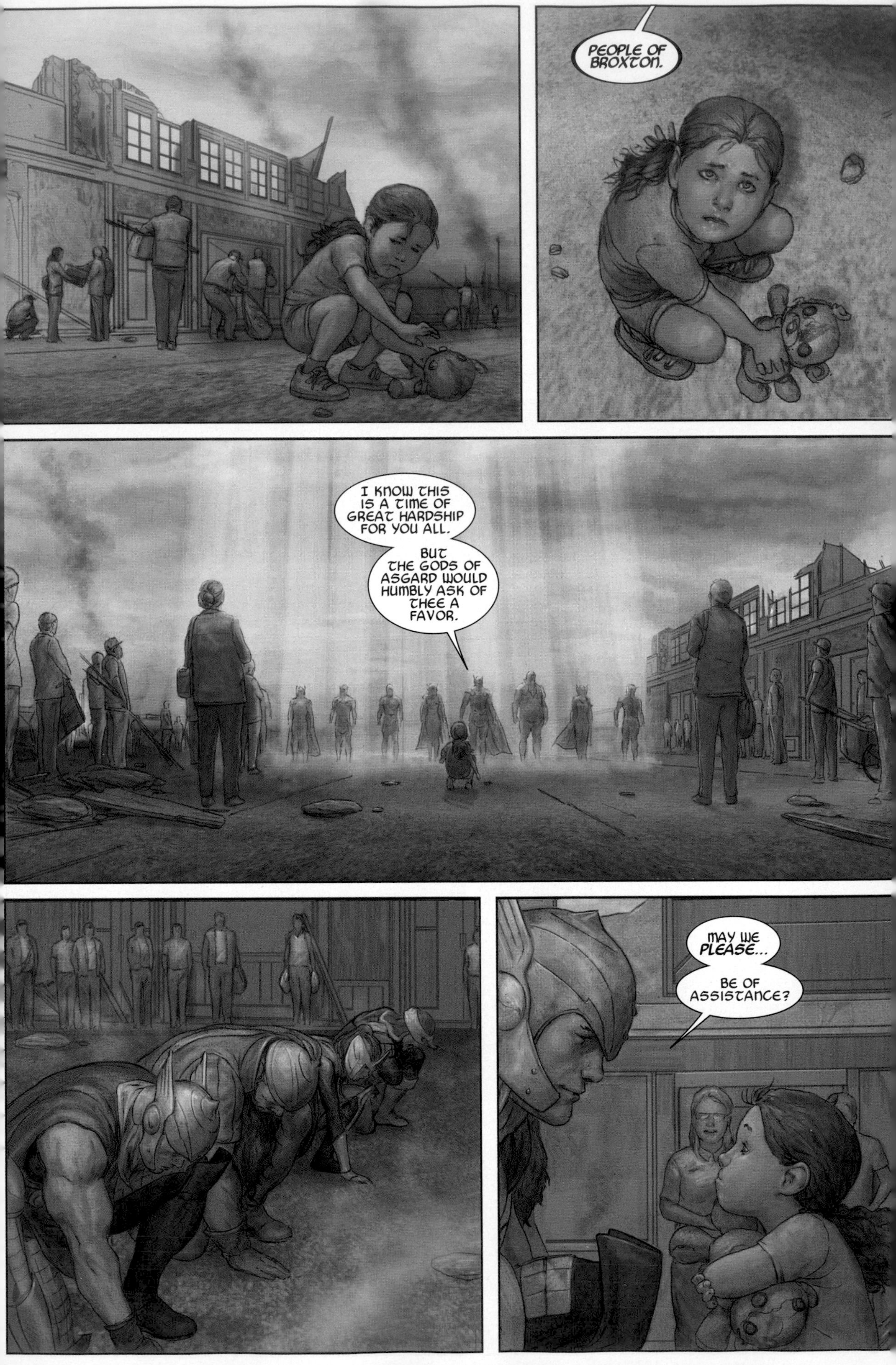
PEOPLE OF BROXTON.
I KNOW THIS IS A TIME OF GREAT HARDSHIP FOR YOU ALL.
BUT THE GODS OF ASGARD WOULD HUMBLY ASK OF THEE A FAVOR.
MAY WE PLEASE...
BE OF ASSISTANCE?

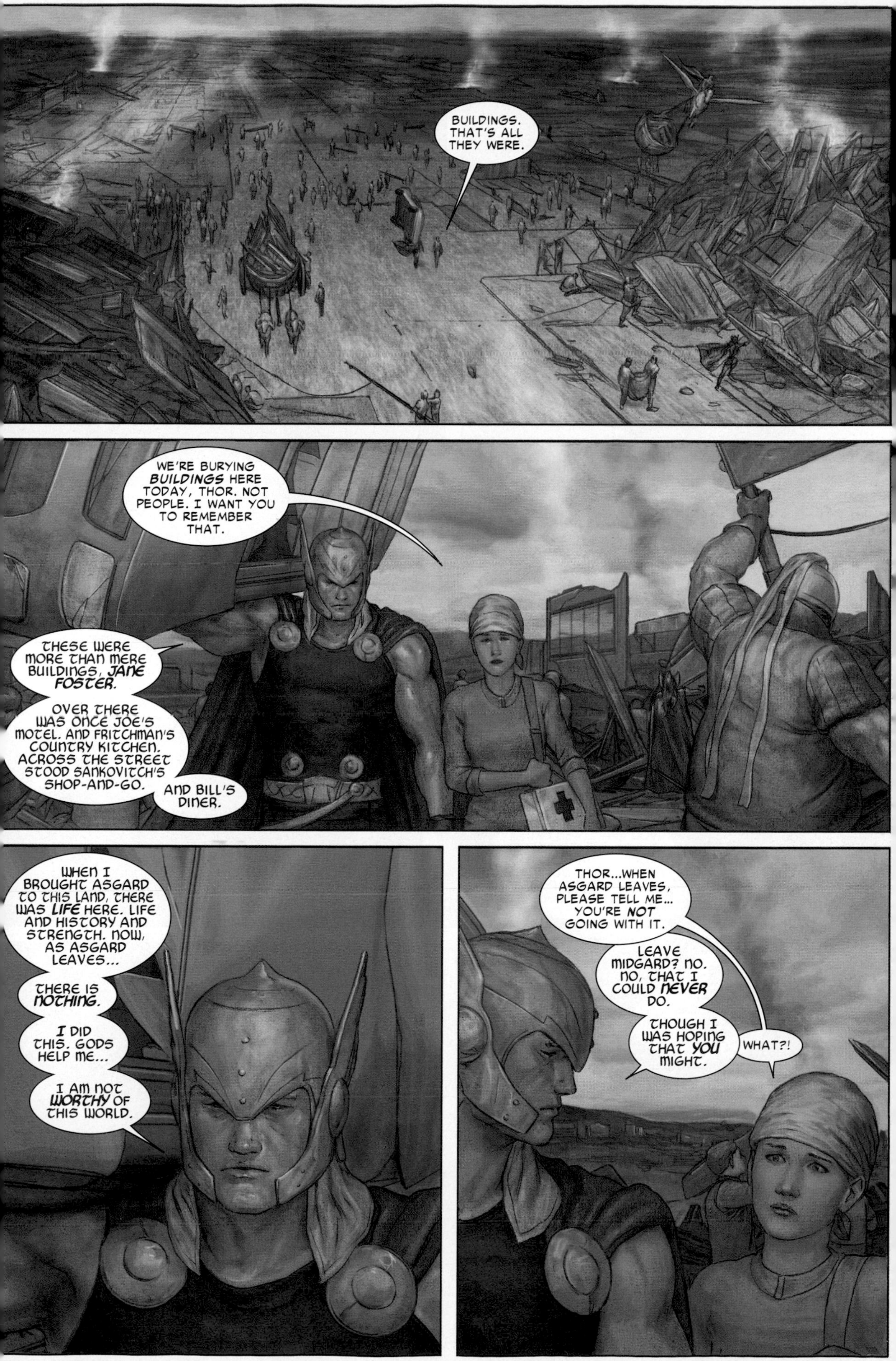
BUILDINGS. THAT'S ALL THEY WERE.
WE'RE BURYING BUILDINGS HERE TODAY, THOR. NOT PEOPLE. I WANT YOU TO REMEMBER THAT.
THESE WERE MORE THAN MERE BUILDINGS, JANE FOSTER.
OVER THERE WAS ONCE JOE'S MOTEL. AND FRITCHMAN'S COUNTRY KITCHEN. ACROSS THE STREET STOOD SANKOVITCH'S SHOP-AND-GO.
AND BILL'S DINER.
WHEN I BROUGHT ASGARD TO THIS LAND, THERE WAS LIFE HERE. LIFE AND HISTORY AND STRENGTH. NOW, AS ASGARD LEAVES...
THERE IS NOTHING.
I DID THIS. GODS HELP ME...
I AM NOT WORTHY OF THIS WORLD.
THOR...WHEN ASGARD LEAVES, PLEASE TELL ME... YOU'RE NOT GOING WITH IT.
LEAVE MIDGARD? NO. NO, THAT I COULD NEVER DO.
THOUGH I WAS HOPING THAT YOU MIGHT.
WHAT?!

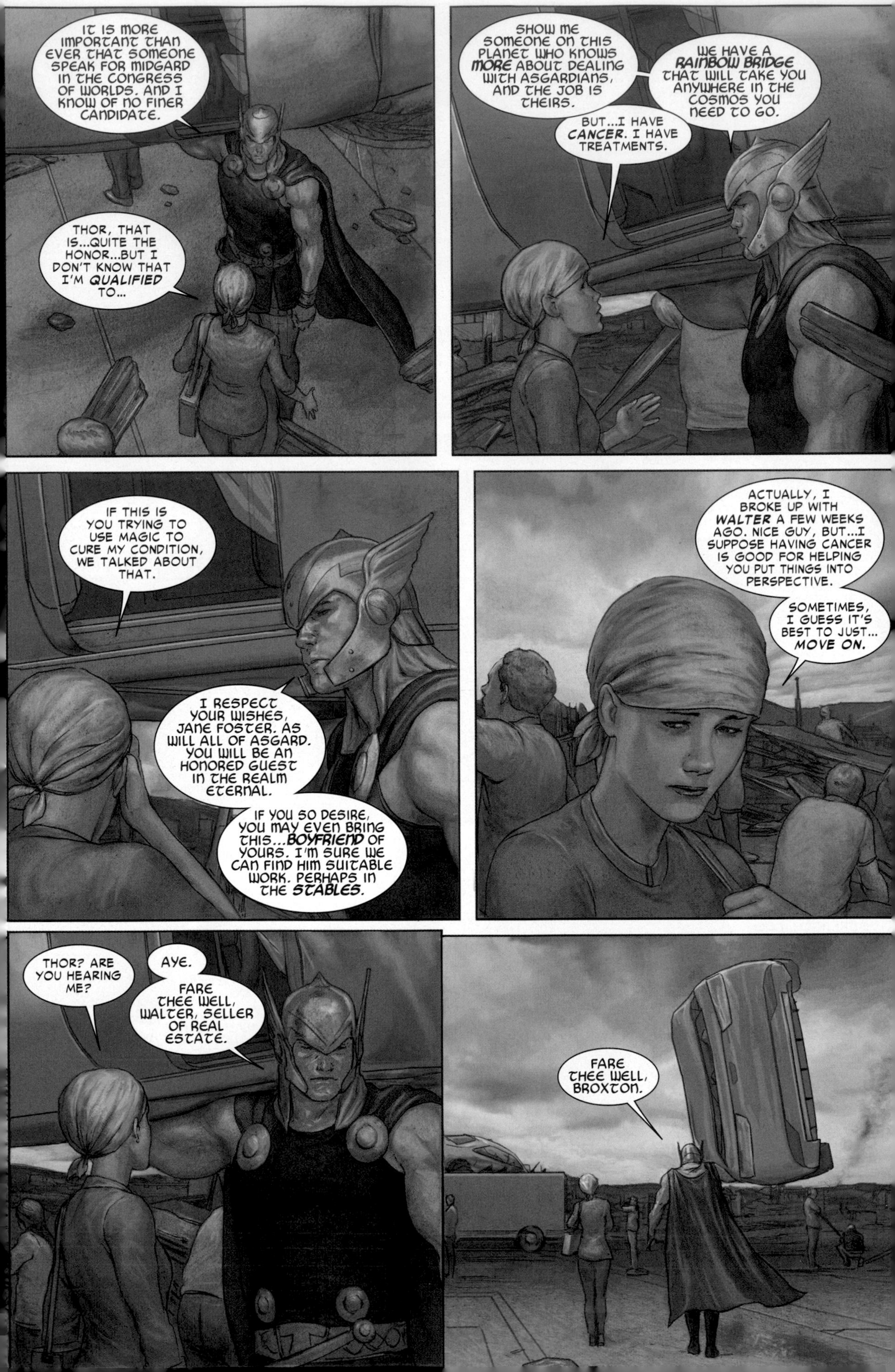
IT IS MORE IMPORTANT THAN EVER THAT SOMEONE SPEAK FOR MIDGARD IN THE CONGRESS OF WORLDS. AND I KNOW OF NO FINER CANDIDATE.
THOR, THAT IS...QUITE THE HONOR...BUT I DON'T KNOW THAT I'M QUALIFIED TO...
SHOW ME SOMEONE ON THIS PLANET WHO KNOWS MORE ABOUT DEALING WITH ASGARDIANS, AND THE JOB IS THEIRS.
WE HAVE A RAINBOW BRIDGE THAT WILL TAKE YOU ANYWHERE IN THE COSMOS YOU NEED TO GO.
BUT...I HAVE CANCER. I HAVE TREATMENTS.
IF THIS IS YOU TRYING TO USE MAGIC TO CURE MY CONDITION, WE TALKED ABOUT THAT.
I RESPECT YOUR WISHES, JANE FOSTER. AS WILL ALL OF ASGARD. YOU WILL BE AN HONORED GUEST IN THE REALM ETERNAL.
IF YOU SO DESIRE, YOU MAY EVEN BRING THIS...BOYFRIEND OF YOURS. I'M SURE WE CAN FIND HIM SUITABLE WORK. PERHAPS IN THE STABLES.
ACTUALLY, I BROKE UP WITH WALTER A FEW WEEKS AGO. NICE GUY, BUT...I SUPPOSE HAVING CANCER IS GOOD FOR HELPING YOU PUT THINGS INTO PERSPECTIVE.
SOMETIMES, I GUESS IT'S BEST TO JUST... MOVE ON.
THOR? ARE YOU HEARING ME?
AYE.
FARE THEE WELL, WALTER, SELLER OF REAL ESTATE.
FARE THEE WELL, BROXTON.

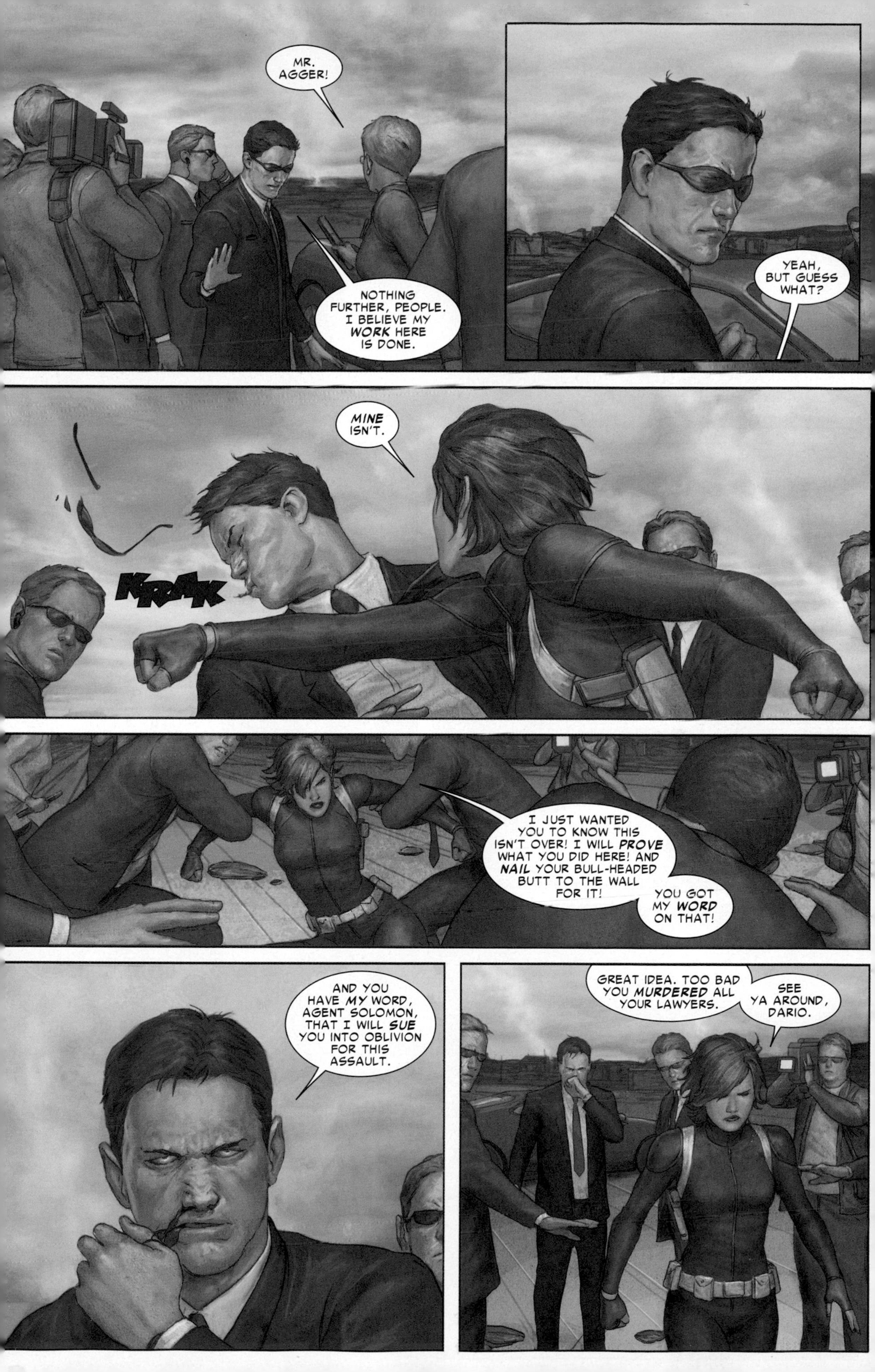
MR. AGGER!
NOTHING FURTHER, PEOPLE. I BELIEVE MY WORK HERE IS DONE.
YEAH, BUT GUESS WHAT?
MINE ISN'T.
KRAAK
I JUST WANTED YOU TO KNOW THIS ISN'T OVER! I WILL PROVE WHAT YOU DID HERE! AND NAIL YOUR BULL-HEADED BUTT TO THE WALL FOR IT!
YOU GOT MY WORD ON THAT!
AND YOU HAVE MY WORD, AGENT SOLOMON, THAT I WILL SUE YOU INTO OBLIVION FOR THIS ASSAULT.
GREAT IDEA. TOO BAD YOU MURDERED ALL YOUR LAWYERS.
SEE YA AROUND, DARIO.

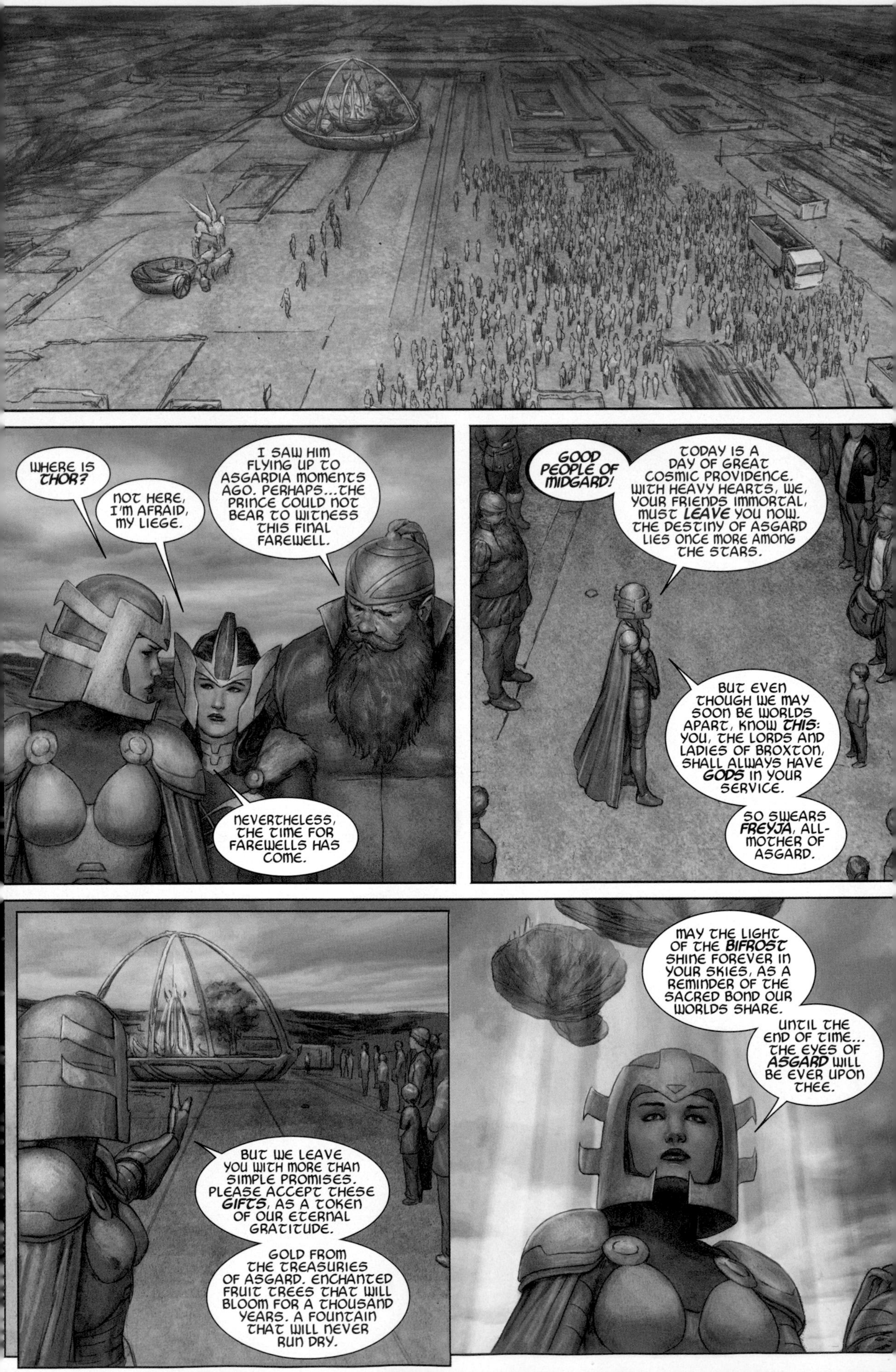
WHERE IS THOR?
NOT HERE, I'M AFRAID, MY LIEGE.
I SAW HIM FLYING UP TO ASGARDIA MOMENTS AGO. PERHAPS...THE PRINCE COULD NOT BEAR TO WITNESS THIS FINAL FAREWELL.
NEVERTHELESS, THE TIME FOR FAREWELLS HAS COME.
GOOD PEOPLE OF MIDGARD!
TODAY IS A DAY OF GREAT COSMIC PROVIDENCE. WITH HEAVY HEARTS, WE, YOUR FRIENDS IMMORTAL, MUST LEAVE YOU NOW. THE DESTINY OF ASGARD LIES ONCE MORE AMONG THE STARS.
BUT EVEN THOUGH WE MAY SOON BE WORLDS APART, KNOW THIS: YOU, THE LORDS AND LADIES OF BROXTON, SHALL ALWAYS HAVE GODS IN YOUR SERVICE.
SO SWEARS FREYJA, ALL-MOTHER OF ASGARD.
BUT WE LEAVE YOU WITH MORE THAN SIMPLE PROMISES. PLEASE ACCEPT THESE GIFTS, AS A TOKEN OF OUR ETERNAL GRATITUDE.
GOLD FROM THE TREASURIES OF ASGARD. ENCHANTED FRUIT TREES THAT WILL BLOOM FOR A THOUSAND YEARS. A FOUNTAIN THAT WILL NEVER RUN DRY.
MAY THE LIGHT OF THE BIFROST SHINE FOREVER IN YOUR SKIES, AS A REMINDER OF THE SACRED BOND OUR WORLDS SHARE.
UNTIL THE END OF TIME... THE EYES OF ASGARD WILL BE EVER UPON THEE.

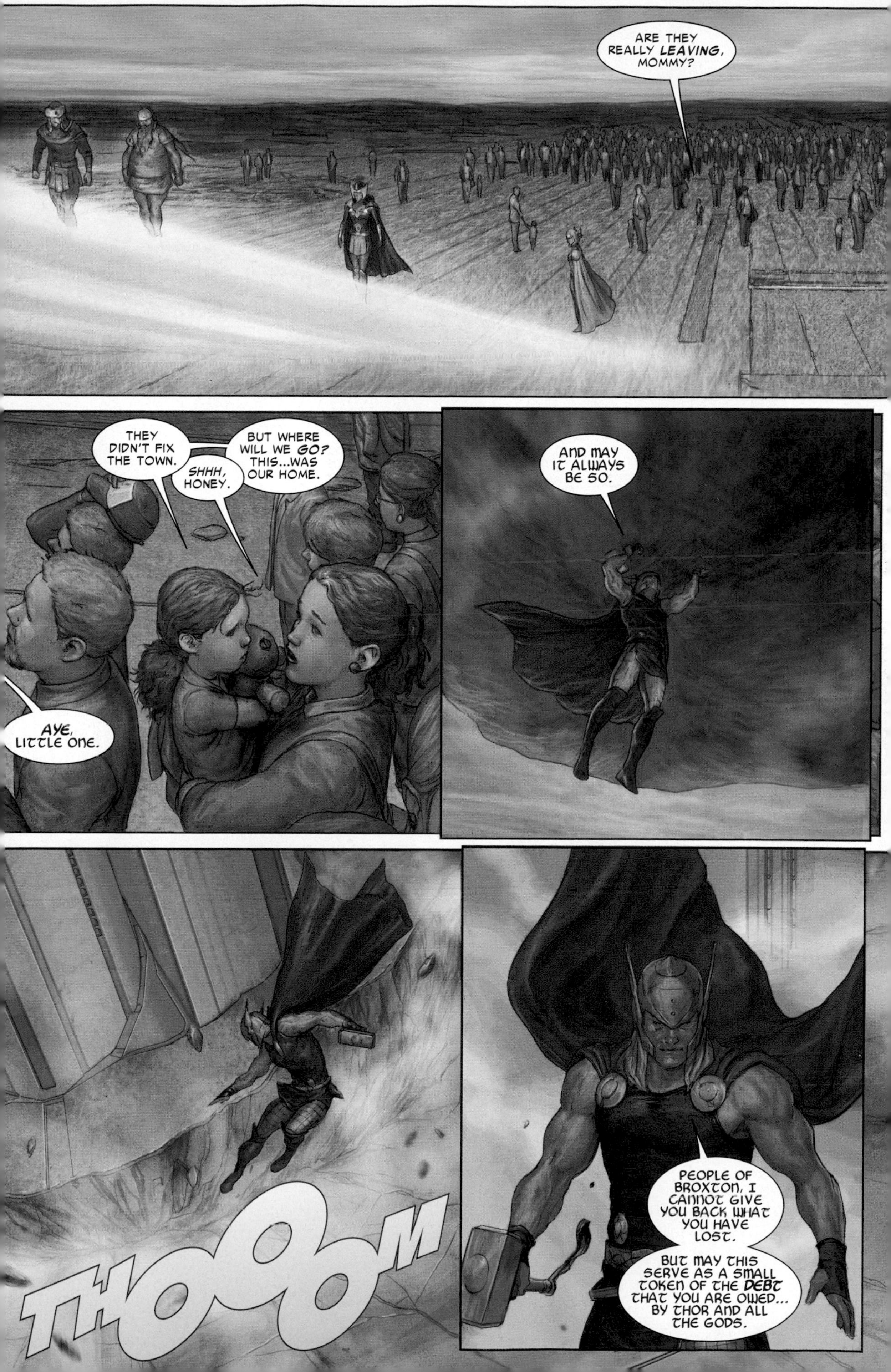

ARE THEY REALLY LEAVING, MOMMY?
THEY DIDN'T FIX THE TOWN.
BUT WHERE WILL WE GO? THIS...WAS OUR HOME.
SHHH, HONEY.
AYE, LITTLE ONE.
AND MAY IT ALWAYS BE SO.
THOOOM
PEOPLE OF BROXTON, I CANNOT GIVE YOU BACK WHAT YOU HAVE LOST.
BUT MAY THIS SERVE AS A SMALL TOKEN OF THE DEBT THAT YOU ARE OWED... BY THOR AND ALL THE GODS.

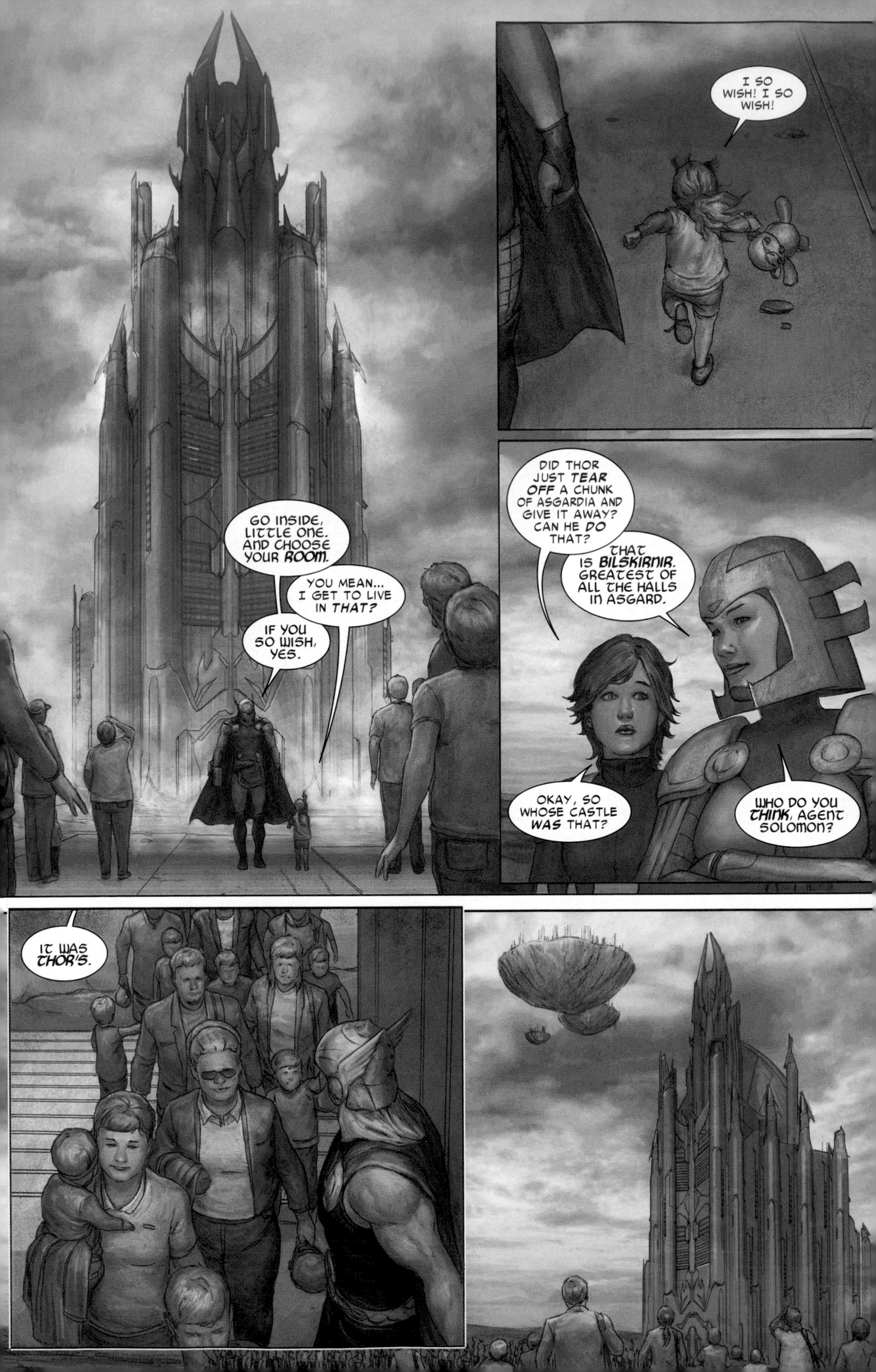
GO INSIDE, LITTLE ONE. AND CHOOSE YOUR **ROOM**.
YOU MEAN... I GET TO LIVE IN *THAT?*
IF YOU SO WISH, YES.
I SO WISH! I SO WISH!
DID THOR JUST **TEAR OFF** A CHUNK OF ASGARDIA AND GIVE IT AWAY? CAN HE *DO* THAT?
THAT IS **BILSKIRNIR**. GREATEST OF ALL THE HALLS IN ASGARD.
OKAY, SO WHOSE CASTLE **WAS** THAT?
WHO DO YOU *THINK*, AGENT SOLOMON?
IT WAS **THOR'S**.

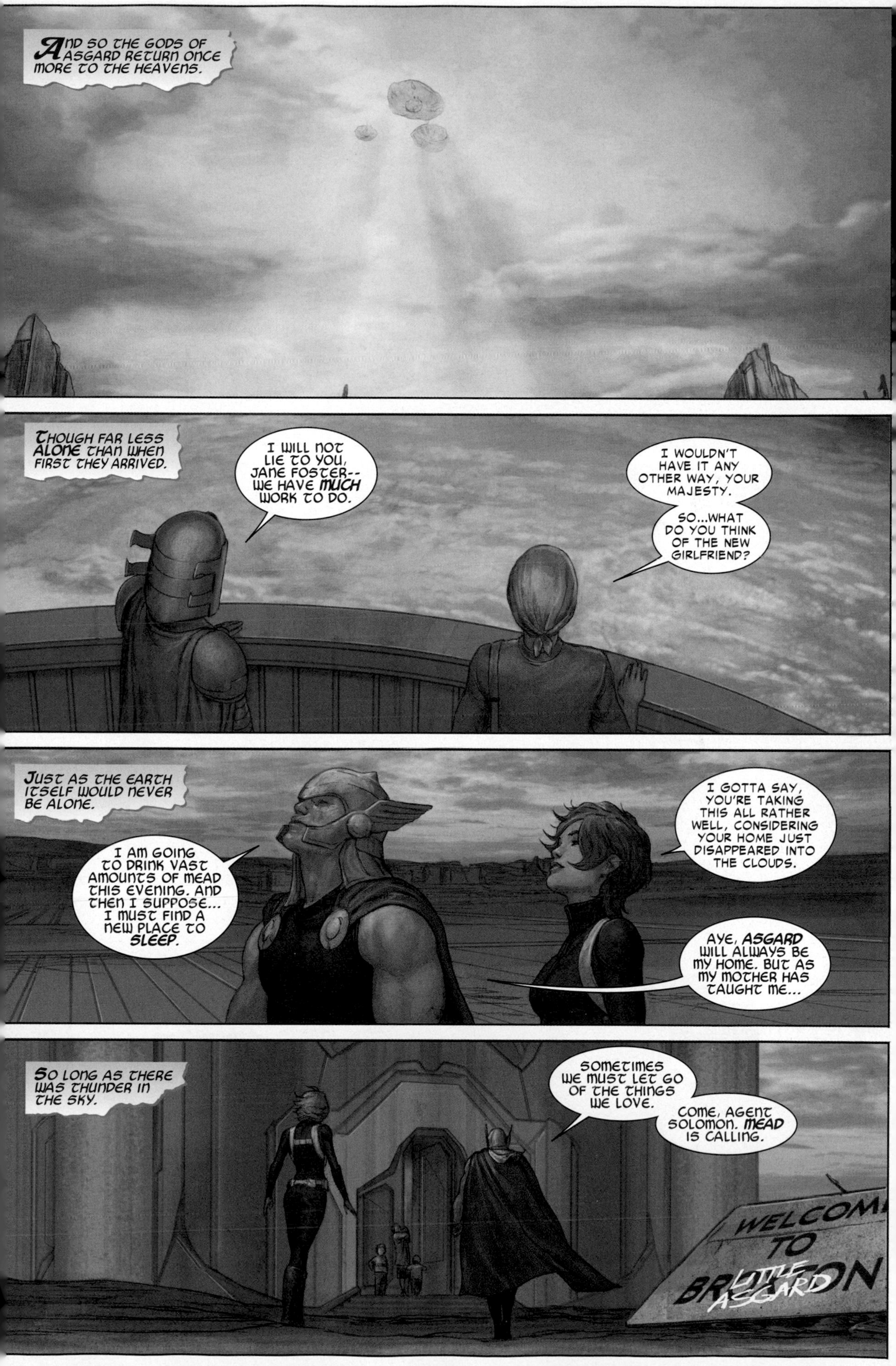
And so the gods of Asgard return once more to the heavens.
Though far less ALONE than when first they arrived.
I will not lie to you, Jane Foster-- we have MUCH work to do.
I wouldn't have it any other way, your majesty.
So...what do you think of the new girlfriend?
Just as the earth itself would never be alone.
I am going to drink vast amounts of mead this evening. And then I suppose... I must find a new place to SLEEP.
I gotta say, you're taking this all rather well, considering your home just disappeared into the clouds.
Aye, ASGARD will always be my home. But as my mother has taught me...
So long as there was thunder in the sky.
Sometimes we must let go of the things we love.
Come, Agent Solomon. MEAD is calling.
WELCOM
TO
LITTLE ASGARD

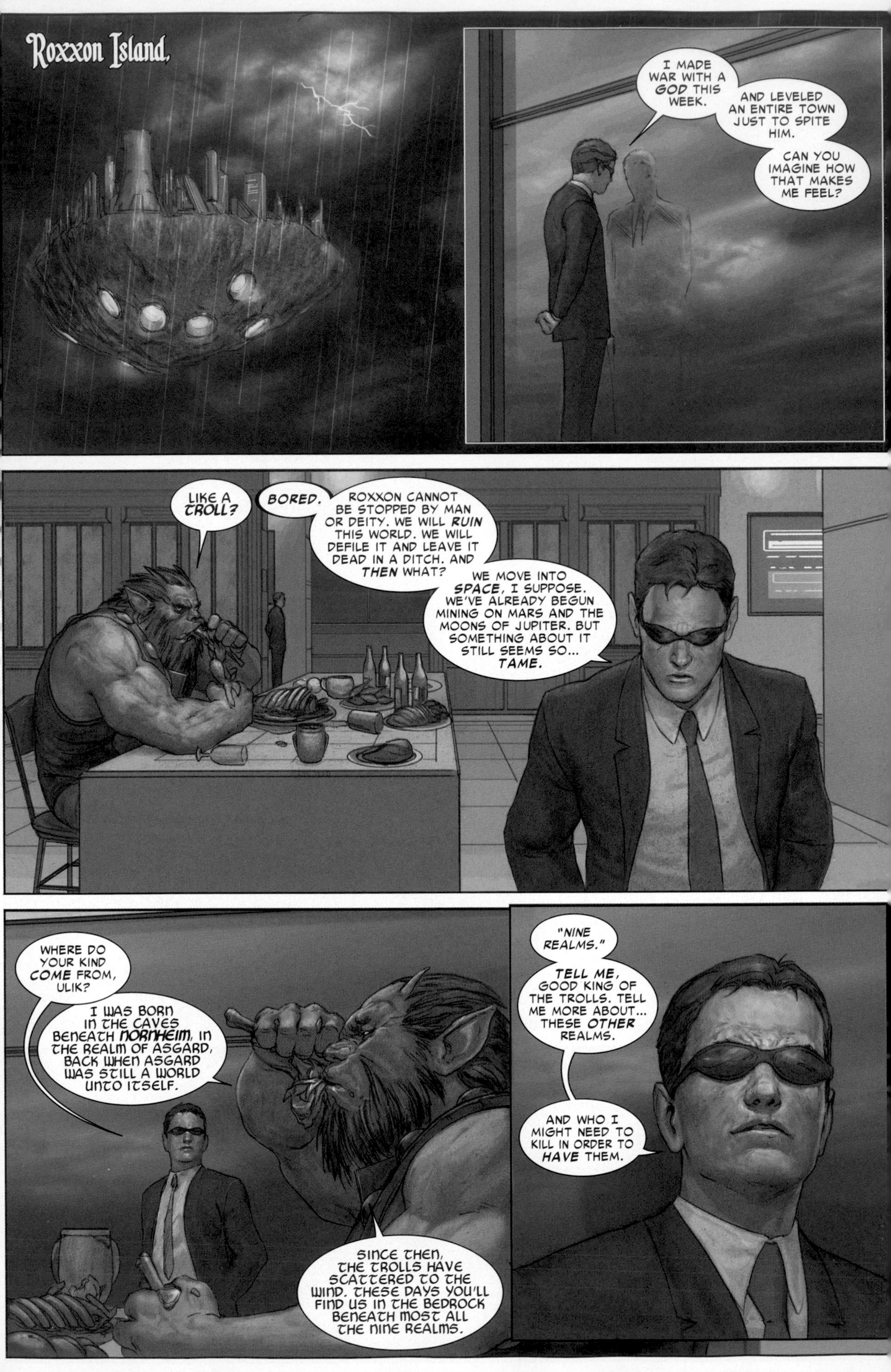

Roxxon Island.
I MADE WAR WITH A GOD THIS WEEK.
AND LEVELED AN ENTIRE TOWN JUST TO SPITE HIM.
CAN YOU IMAGINE HOW THAT MAKES ME FEEL?
LIKE A TROLL?
BORED.
ROXXON CANNOT BE STOPPED BY MAN OR DEITY. WE WILL RUIN THIS WORLD. WE WILL DEFILE IT AND LEAVE IT DEAD IN A DITCH. AND THEN WHAT?
WE MOVE INTO SPACE, I SUPPOSE. WE'VE ALREADY BEGUN MINING ON MARS AND THE MOONS OF JUPITER. BUT SOMETHING ABOUT IT STILL SEEMS SO... TAME.
WHERE DO YOUR KIND COME FROM, ULIK?
I WAS BORN IN THE CAVES BENEATH NORNHEIM, IN THE REALM OF ASGARD, BACK WHEN ASGARD WAS STILL A WORLD UNTO ITSELF.
SINCE THEN, THE TROLLS HAVE SCATTERED TO THE WIND. THESE DAYS YOU'LL FIND US IN THE BEDROCK BENEATH MOST ALL THE NINE REALMS.
"NINE REALMS."
TELL ME, GOOD KING OF THE TROLLS. TELL ME MORE ABOUT... THESE OTHER REALMS.
AND WHO I MIGHT NEED TO KILL IN ORDER TO HAVE THEM.

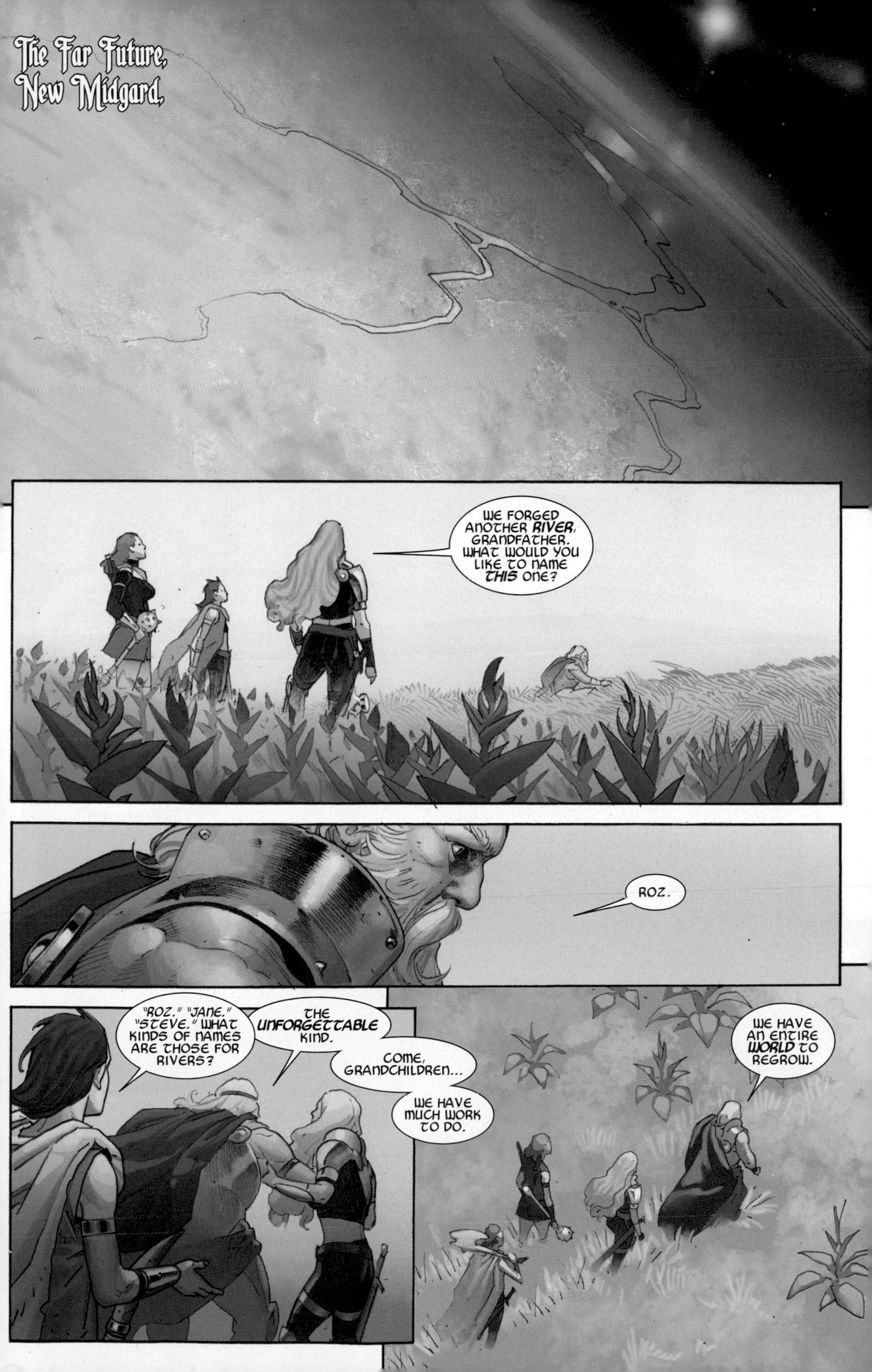
The Far Future, New Midgard,
WE FORGED ANOTHER RIVER, GRANDFATHER. WHAT WOULD YOU LIKE TO NAME THIS ONE?
ROZ.
"ROZ." "JANE." "STEVE." WHAT KINDS OF NAMES ARE THOSE FOR RIVERS?
THE UNFORGETTABLE KIND.
COME, GRANDCHILDREN...
WE HAVE MUCH WORK TO DO.
WE HAVE AN ENTIRE WORLD TO REGROW.

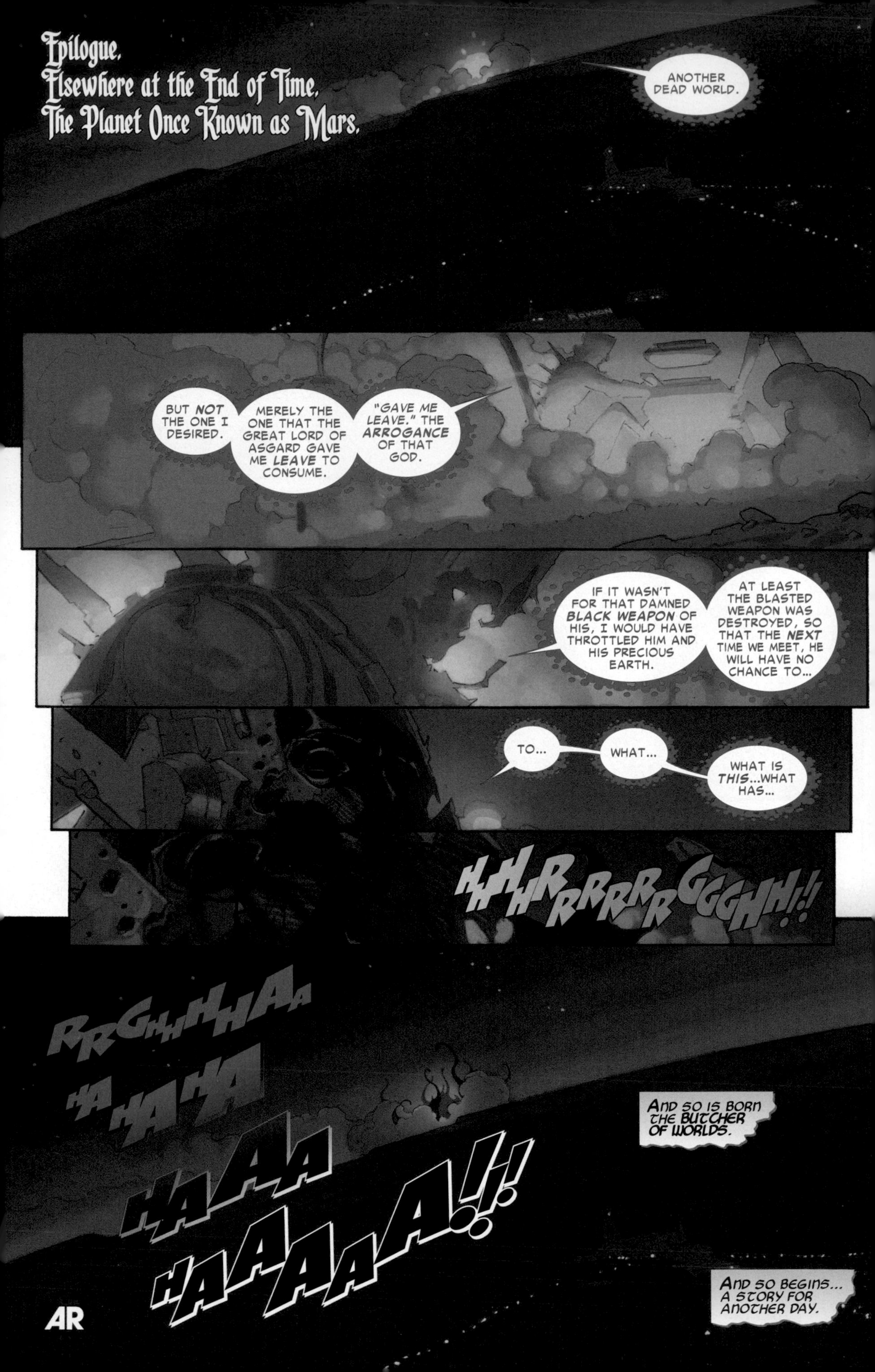
Epilogue,
Elsewhere at the End of Time,
The Planet Once Known as Mars.
ANOTHER DEAD WORLD.
BUT NOT THE ONE I DESIRED.
MERELY THE ONE THAT THE GREAT LORD OF ASGARD GAVE ME LEAVE TO CONSUME.
"GAVE ME LEAVE." THE ARROGANCE OF THAT GOD.
IF IT WASN'T FOR THAT DAMNED BLACK WEAPON OF HIS, I WOULD HAVE THROTTLED HIM AND HIS PRECIOUS EARTH.
AT LEAST THE BLASTED WEAPON WAS DESTROYED, SO THAT THE NEXT TIME WE MEET, HE WILL HAVE NO CHANCE TO...
TO...
WHAT...
WHAT IS THIS...WHAT HAS...
HHHHRRRRRRGGGHH!!!
RRGHHHHAA
HAHAHA
HAAA
HAAAAA!!!
AND SO IS BORN THE BUTCHER OF WORLDS.
AND SO BEGINS... A STORY FOR ANOTHER DAY.
AR

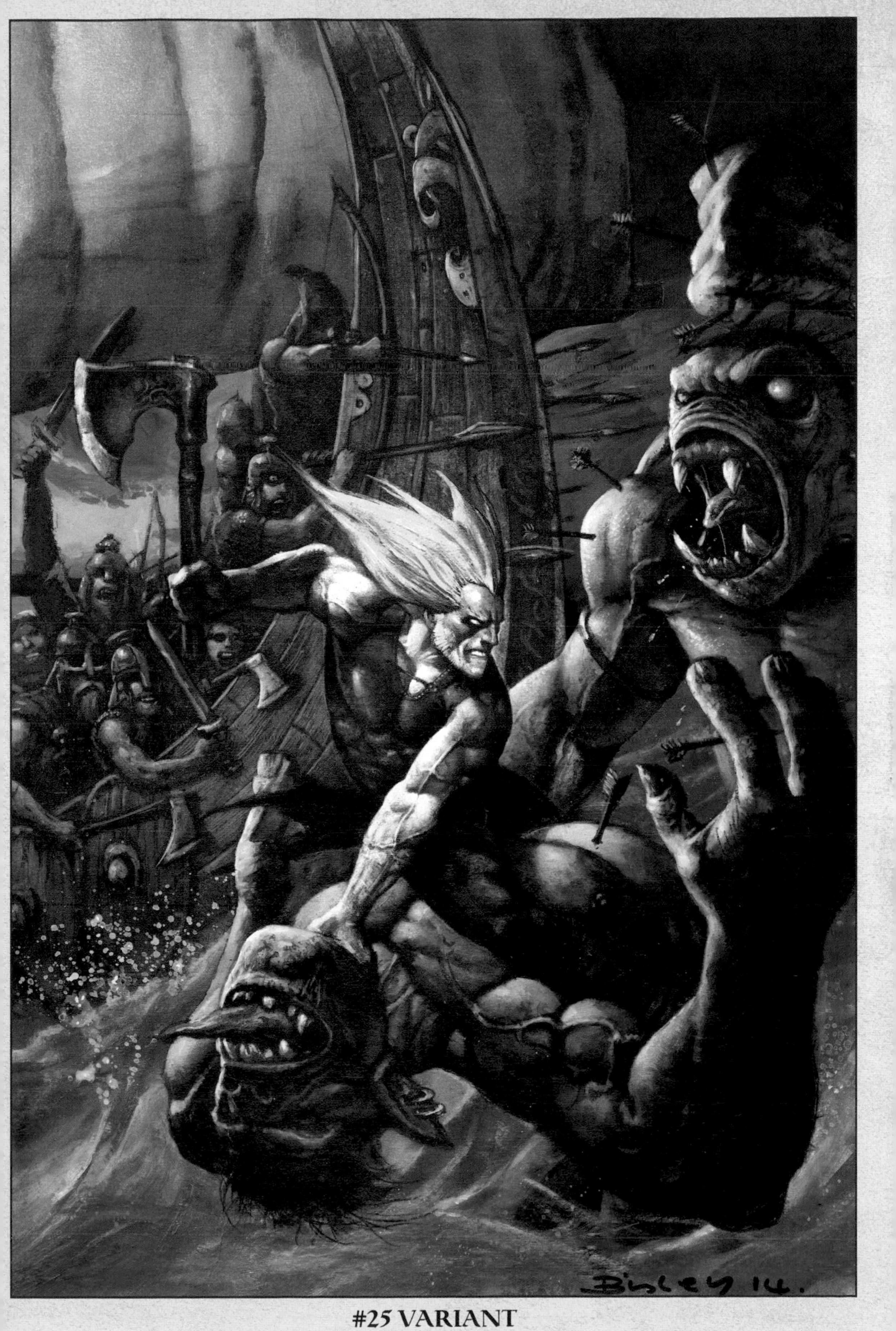
BISLEY 14.

#25 VARIANT
BY SIMON BISLEY

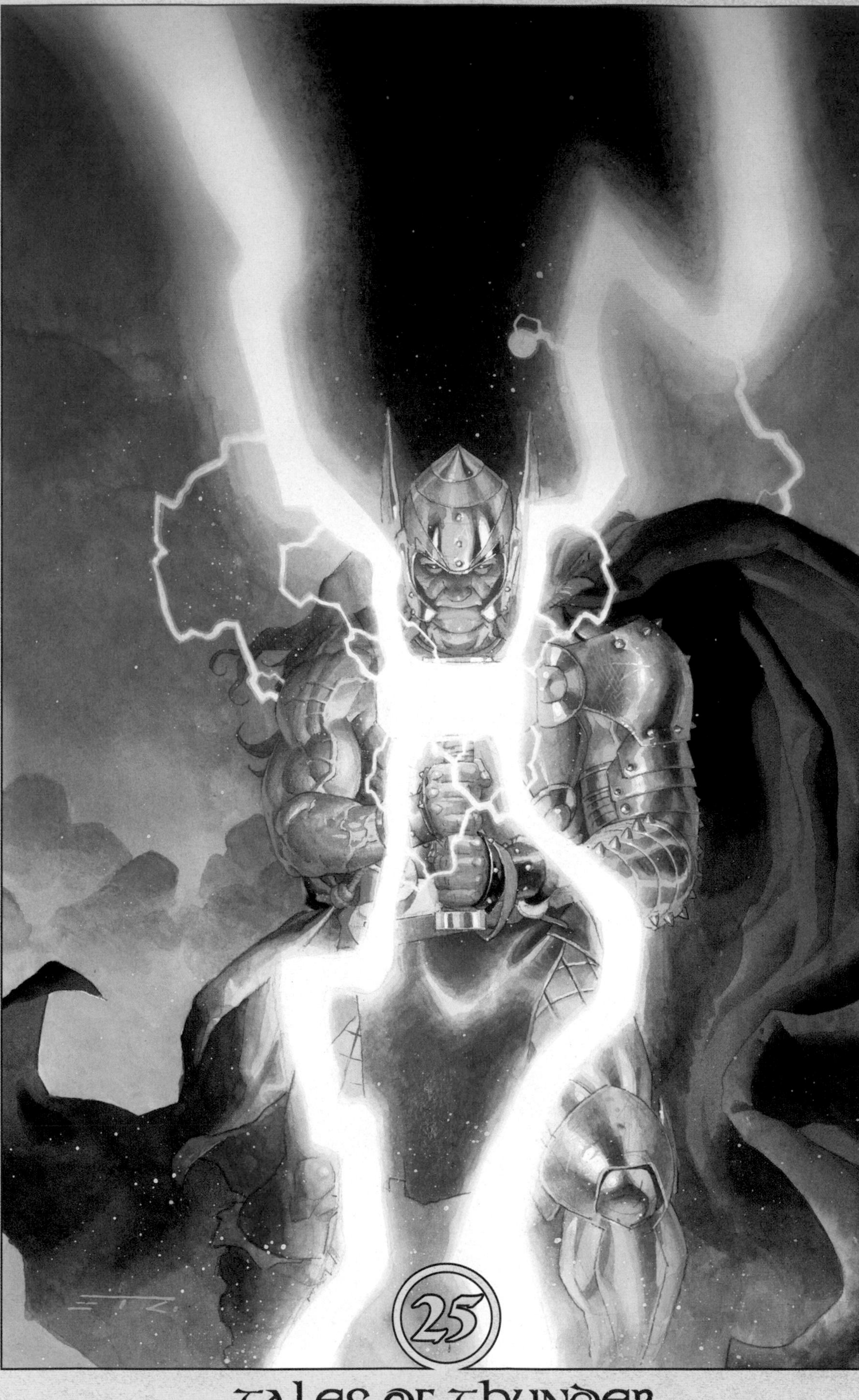
25

TALES OF THUNDER

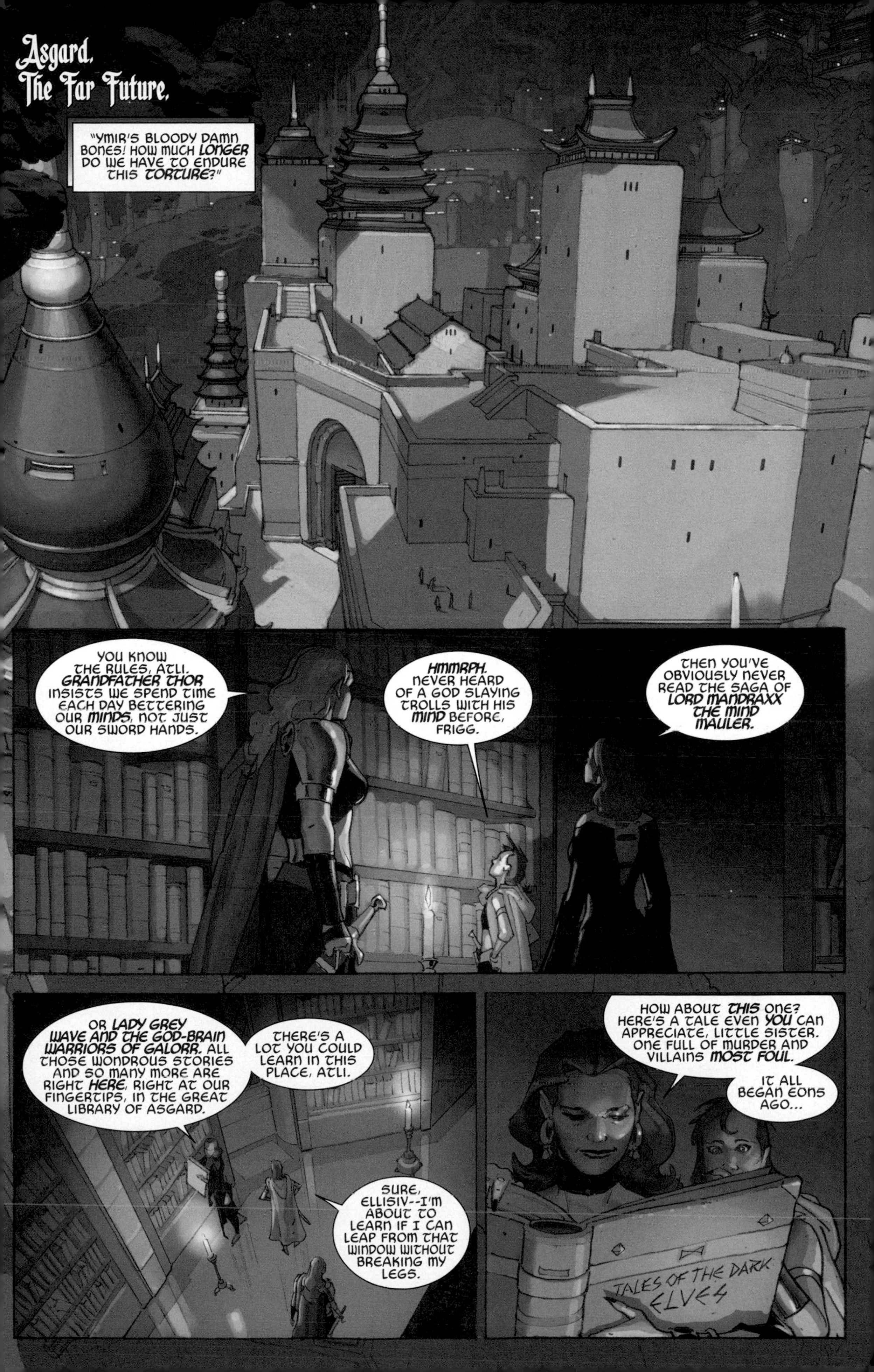
Asgard.
The Far Future.
"YMIR'S BLOODY DAMN BONES! HOW MUCH LONGER DO WE HAVE TO ENDURE THIS TORTURE?"
YOU KNOW THE RULES, ATLI. GRANDFATHER THOR INSISTS WE SPEND TIME EACH DAY BETTERING OUR MINDS, NOT JUST OUR SWORD HANDS.
HMMRPH. NEVER HEARD OF A GOD SLAYING TROLLS WITH HIS MIND BEFORE, FRIGG.
THEN YOU'VE OBVIOUSLY NEVER READ THE SAGA OF LORD MANDRAXX THE MIND MAULER.
OR LADY GREY WAVE AND THE GOD-BRAIN WARRIORS OF GALORR. ALL THOSE WONDROUS STORIES AND SO MANY MORE ARE RIGHT HERE, RIGHT AT OUR FINGERTIPS, IN THE GREAT LIBRARY OF ASGARD.
THERE'S A LOT YOU COULD LEARN IN THIS PLACE, ATLI.
SURE, ELLISIV--I'M ABOUT TO LEARN IF I CAN LEAP FROM THAT WINDOW WITHOUT BREAKING MY LEGS.
HOW ABOUT THIS ONE? HERE'S A TALE EVEN YOU CAN APPRECIATE, LITTLE SISTER. ONE FULL OF MURDER AND VILLAINS MOST FOUL.
IT ALL BEGAN EONS AGO...
TALES OF THE DARK ELVES

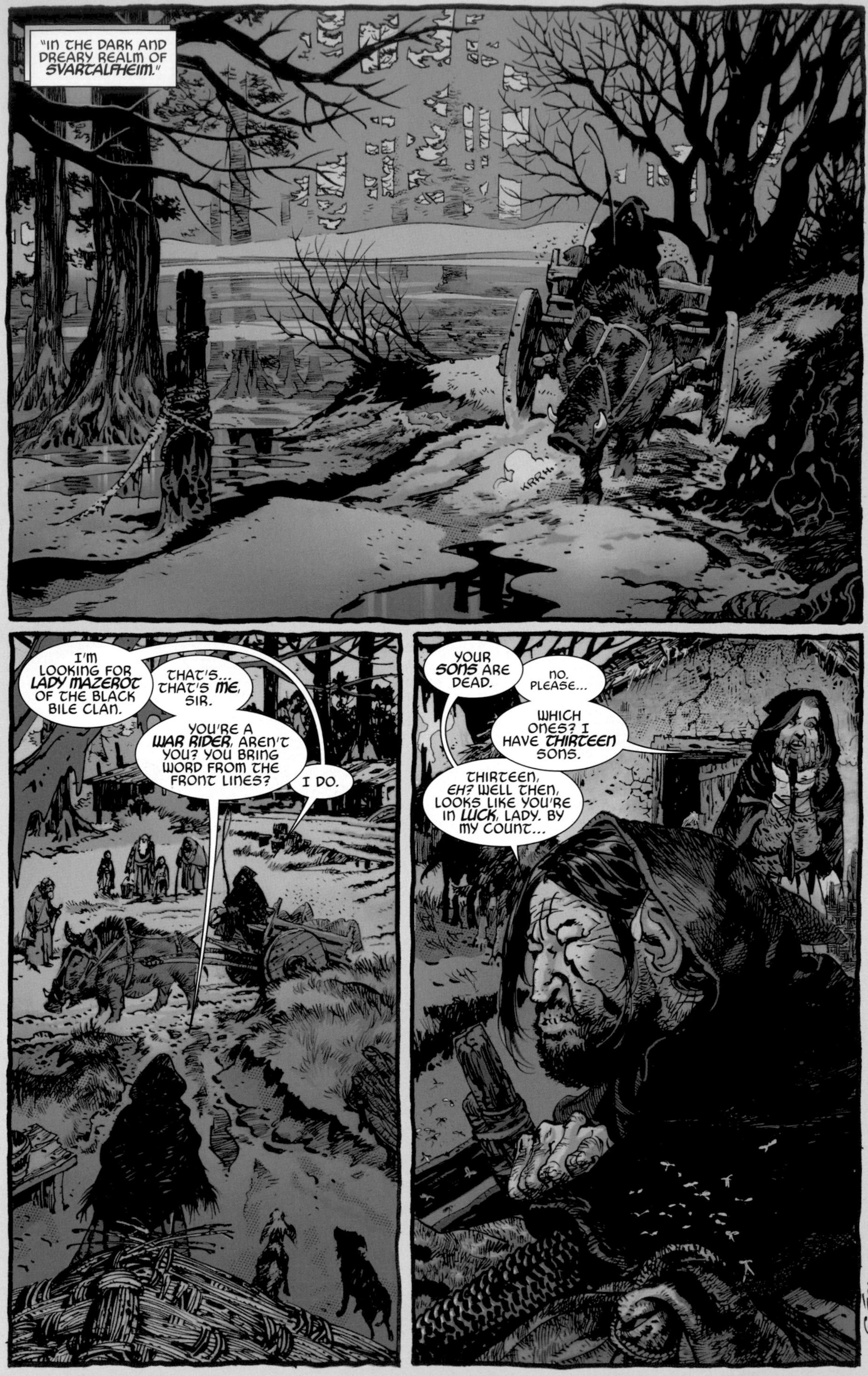
"IN THE DARK AND DREARY REALM OF SVARTALFHEIM."
KRRH..
I'M LOOKING FOR LADY MAZEROT OF THE BLACK BILE CLAN.
THAT'S... THAT'S ME, SIR.
YOU'RE A WAR RIDER, AREN'T YOU? YOU BRING WORD FROM THE FRONT LINES?
I DO.
YOUR SONS ARE DEAD.
NO. PLEASE...
WHICH ONES? I HAVE THIRTEEN SONS.
THIRTEEN, EH? WELL THEN, LOOKS LIKE YOU'RE IN LUCK, LADY. BY MY COUNT...

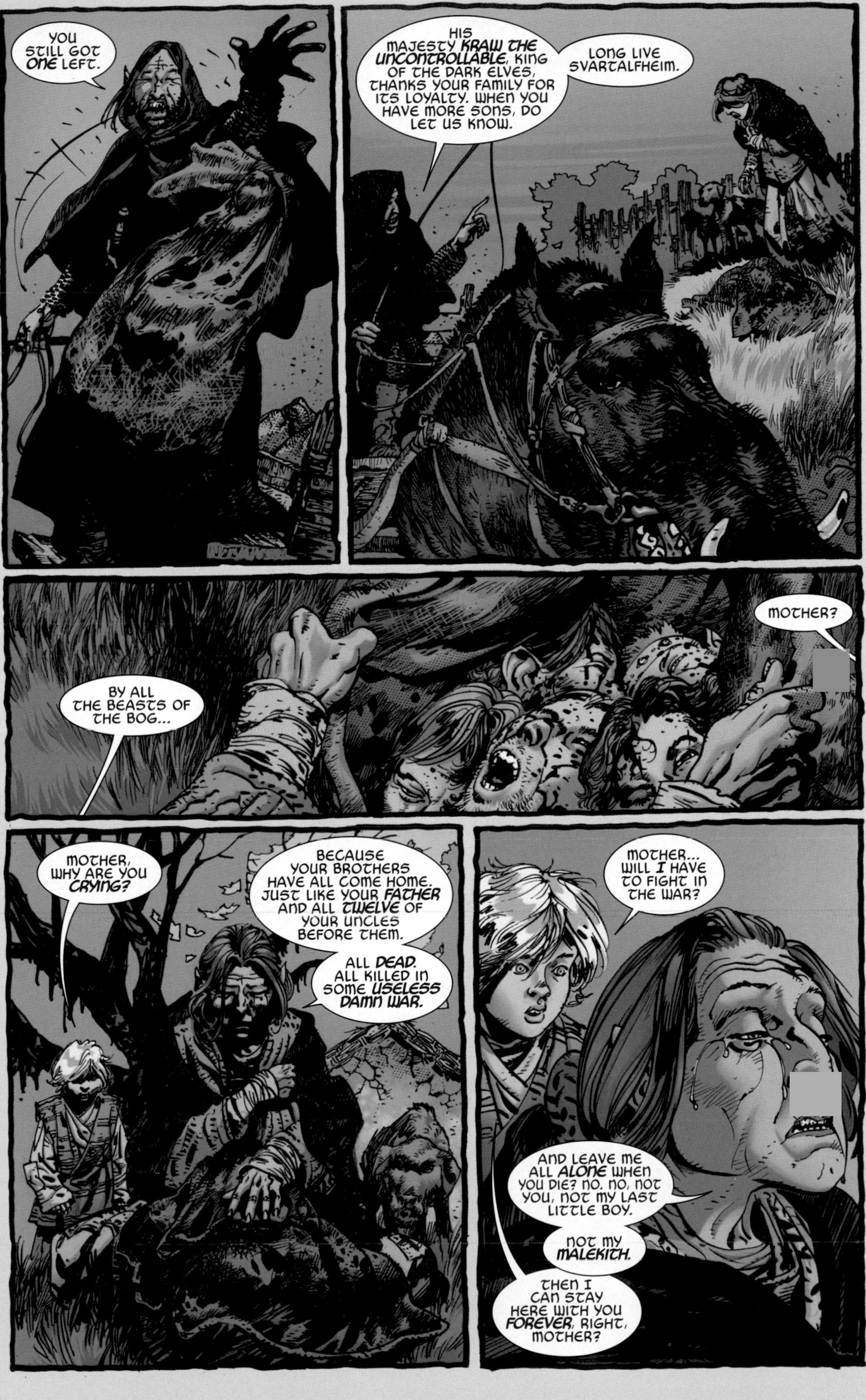
YOU STILL GOT ONE LEFT.
HIS MAJESTY KRAW THE UNCONTROLLABLE, KING OF THE DARK ELVES, THANKS YOUR FAMILY FOR ITS LOYALTY. WHEN YOU HAVE MORE SONS, DO LET US KNOW.
LONG LIVE SVARTALFHEIM.
MOTHER?
BY ALL THE BEASTS OF THE BOG...
MOTHER, WHY ARE YOU CRYING?
BECAUSE YOUR BROTHERS HAVE ALL COME HOME. JUST LIKE YOUR FATHER AND ALL TWELVE OF YOUR UNCLES BEFORE THEM.
ALL DEAD. ALL KILLED IN SOME USELESS DAMN WAR.
MOTHER... WILL I HAVE TO FIGHT IN THE WAR?
AND LEAVE ME ALL ALONE WHEN YOU DIE? NO. NO, NOT YOU, NOT MY LAST LITTLE BOY.
NOT MY MALEKITH.
THEN I CAN STAY HERE WITH YOU FOREVER, RIGHT, MOTHER?

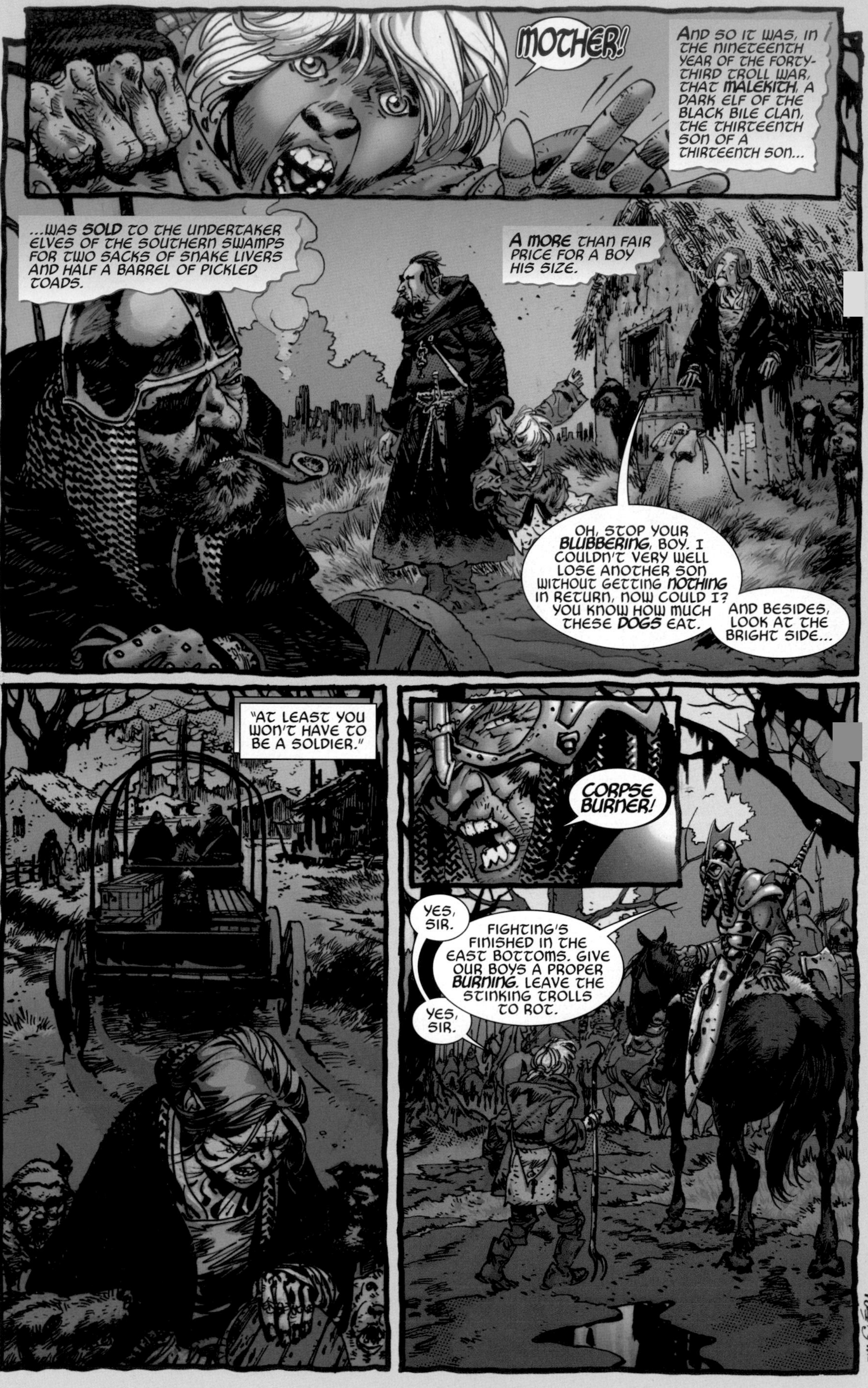
MOTHER!
AND SO IT WAS, IN THE NINETEENTH YEAR OF THE FORTY-THIRD TROLL WAR, THAT MALEKITH, A DARK ELF OF THE BLACK BILE CLAN, THE THIRTEENTH SON OF A THIRTEENTH SON...
...WAS SOLD TO THE UNDERTAKER ELVES OF THE SOUTHERN SWAMPS FOR TWO SACKS OF SNAKE LIVERS AND HALF A BARREL OF PICKLED TOADS.
A MORE THAN FAIR PRICE FOR A BOY HIS SIZE.
OH, STOP YOUR BLUBBERING, BOY. I COULDN'T VERY WELL LOSE ANOTHER SON WITHOUT GETTING NOTHING IN RETURN, NOW COULD I? YOU KNOW HOW MUCH THESE DOGS EAT.
AND BESIDES, LOOK AT THE BRIGHT SIDE...
"AT LEAST YOU WON'T HAVE TO BE A SOLDIER."
CORPSE BURNER!
YES, SIR.
FIGHTING'S FINISHED IN THE EAST BOTTOMS. GIVE OUR BOYS A PROPER BURNING. LEAVE THE STINKING TROLLS TO ROT.
YES, SIR.

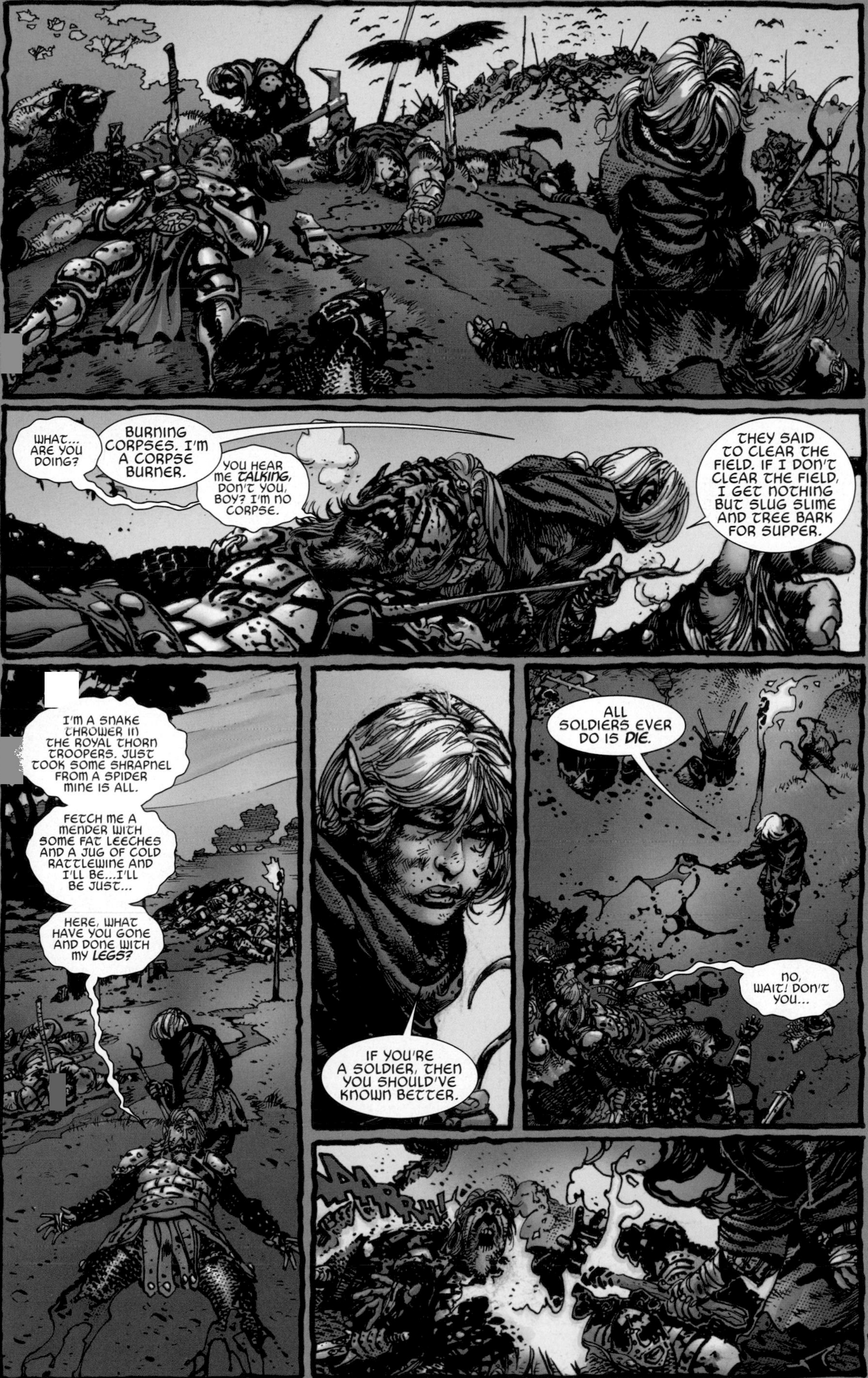
WHAT... ARE YOU DOING?
BURNING CORPSES. I'M A CORPSE BURNER.
YOU HEAR ME *TALKING*, DON'T YOU, BOY? I'M NO CORPSE.
THEY SAID TO CLEAR THE FIELD. IF I DON'T CLEAR THE FIELD, I GET NOTHING BUT SLUG SLIME AND TREE BARK FOR SUPPER.
I'M A SNAKE THROWER IN THE ROYAL THORN TROOPERS. JUST TOOK SOME SHRAPNEL FROM A SPIDER MINE IS ALL.
FETCH ME A MENDER WITH SOME FAT LEECHES AND A JUG OF COLD RATTLEWINE AND I'LL BE...I'LL BE JUST...
HERE, WHAT HAVE YOU GONE AND DONE WITH MY *LEGS?*
IF YOU'RE A SOLDIER, THEN YOU SHOULD'VE KNOWN BETTER.
ALL SOLDIERS EVER DO IS *DIE*.
NO, WAIT! DON'T YOU...

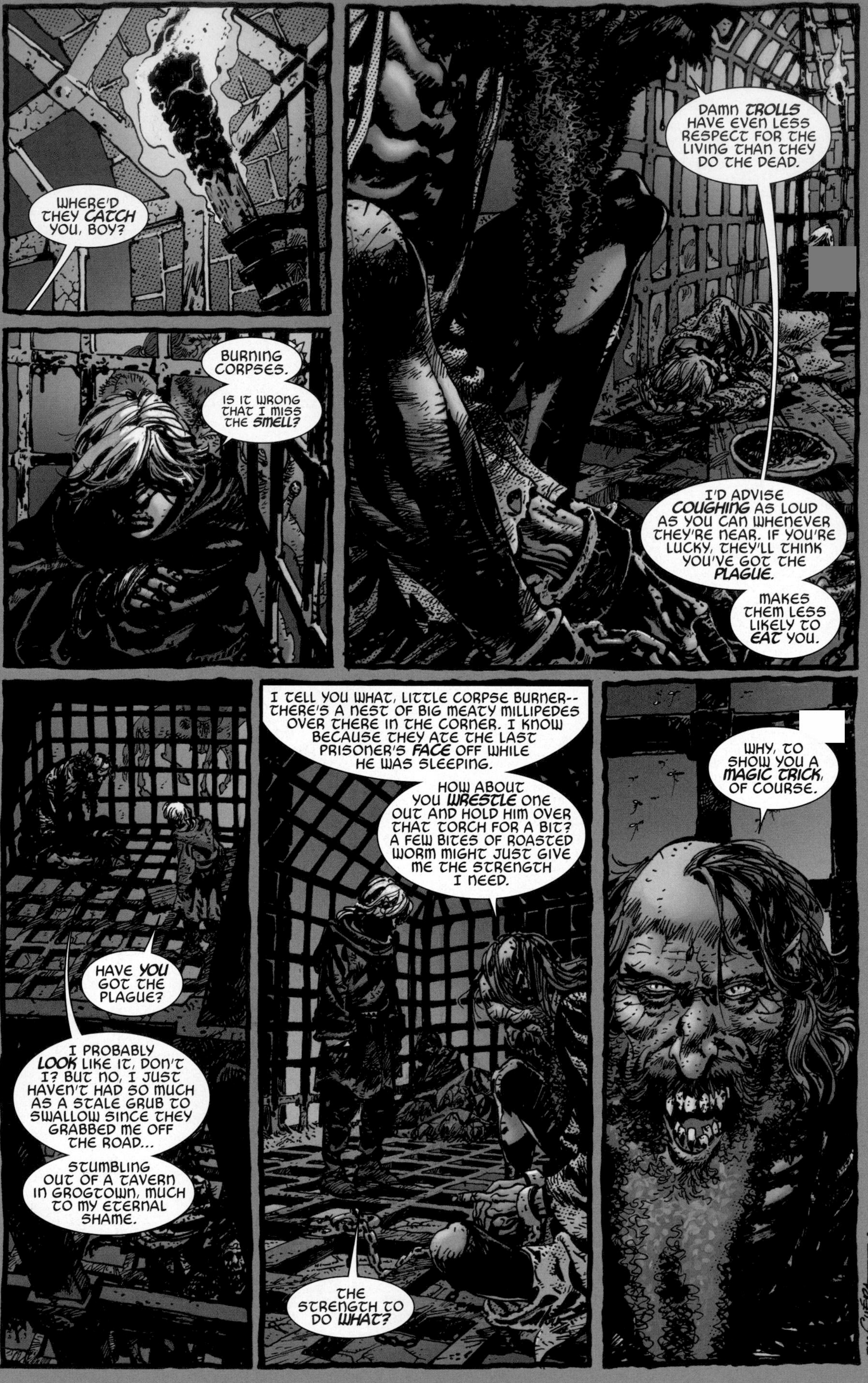
WHERE'D THEY CATCH YOU, BOY?
DAMN TROLLS HAVE EVEN LESS RESPECT FOR THE LIVING THAN THEY DO THE DEAD.
BURNING CORPSES.
IS IT WRONG THAT I MISS THE SMELL?
I'D ADVISE COUGHING AS LOUD AS YOU CAN WHENEVER THEY'RE NEAR. IF YOU'RE LUCKY, THEY'LL THINK YOU'VE GOT THE PLAGUE.
MAKES THEM LESS LIKELY TO EAT YOU.
HAVE YOU GOT THE PLAGUE?
I PROBABLY LOOK LIKE IT, DON'T I? BUT NO, I JUST HAVEN'T HAD SO MUCH AS A STALE GRUB TO SWALLOW SINCE THEY GRABBED ME OFF THE ROAD...
STUMBLING OUT OF A TAVERN IN GROGTOWN, MUCH TO MY ETERNAL SHAME.
I TELL YOU WHAT, LITTLE CORPSE BURNER--THERE'S A NEST OF BIG MEATY MILLIPEDES OVER THERE IN THE CORNER. I KNOW BECAUSE THEY ATE THE LAST PRISONER'S FACE OFF WHILE HE WAS SLEEPING.
HOW ABOUT YOU WRESTLE ONE OUT AND HOLD HIM OVER THAT TORCH FOR A BIT? A FEW BITES OF ROASTED WORM MIGHT JUST GIVE ME THE STRENGTH I NEED.
THE STRENGTH TO DO WHAT?
WHY, TO SHOW YOU A MAGIC TRICK, OF COURSE.

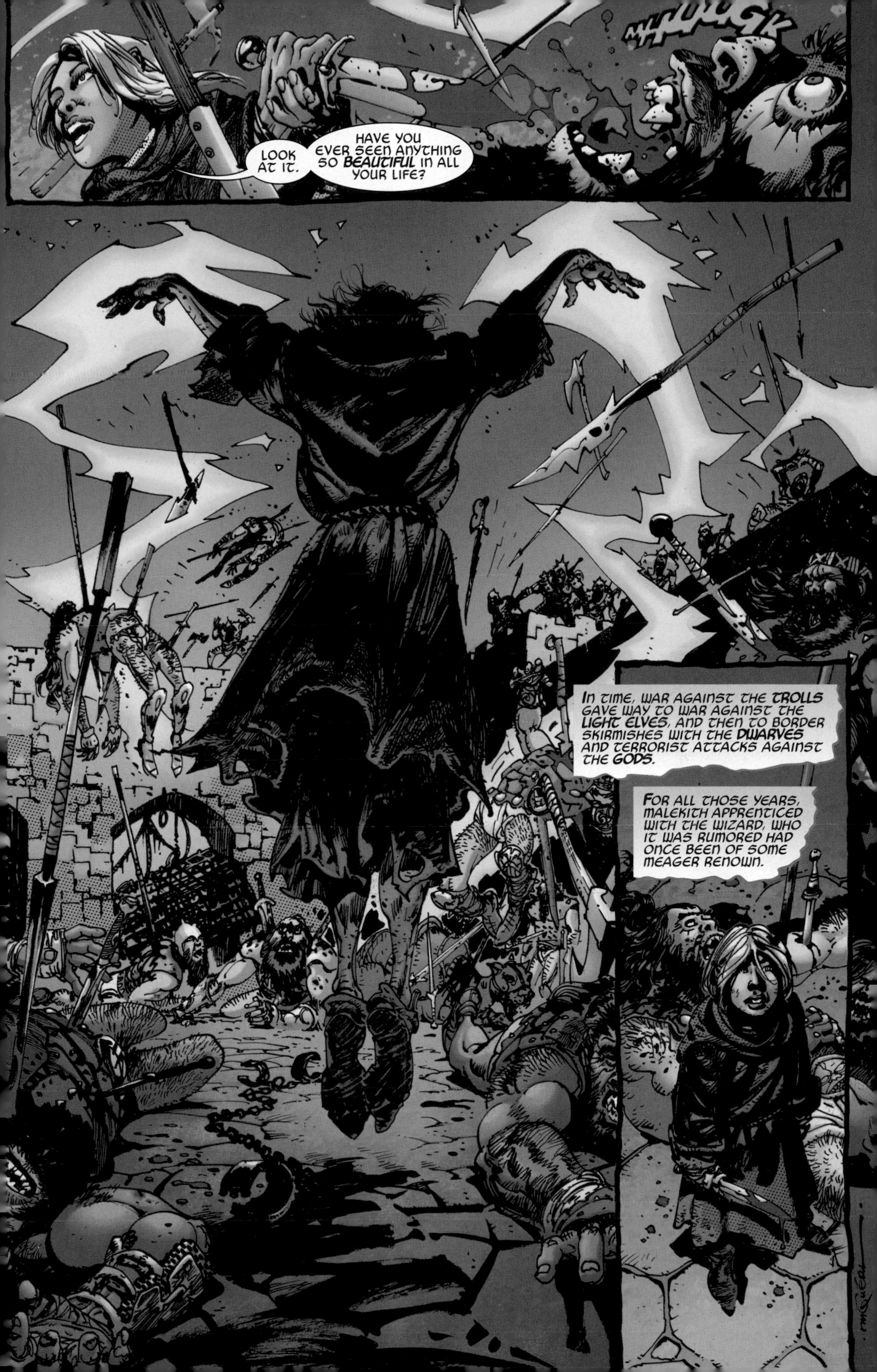
MMMUUGK
LOOK AT IT.
HAVE YOU EVER SEEN ANYTHING SO BEAUTIFUL IN ALL YOUR LIFE?
IN TIME, WAR AGAINST THE TROLLS GAVE WAY TO WAR AGAINST THE LIGHT ELVES, AND THEN TO BORDER SKIRMISHES WITH THE DWARVES AND TERRORIST ATTACKS AGAINST THE GODS.
FOR ALL THOSE YEARS, MALEKITH APPRENTICED WITH THE WIZARD, WHO IT WAS RUMORED HAD ONCE BEEN OF SOME MEAGER RENOWN.

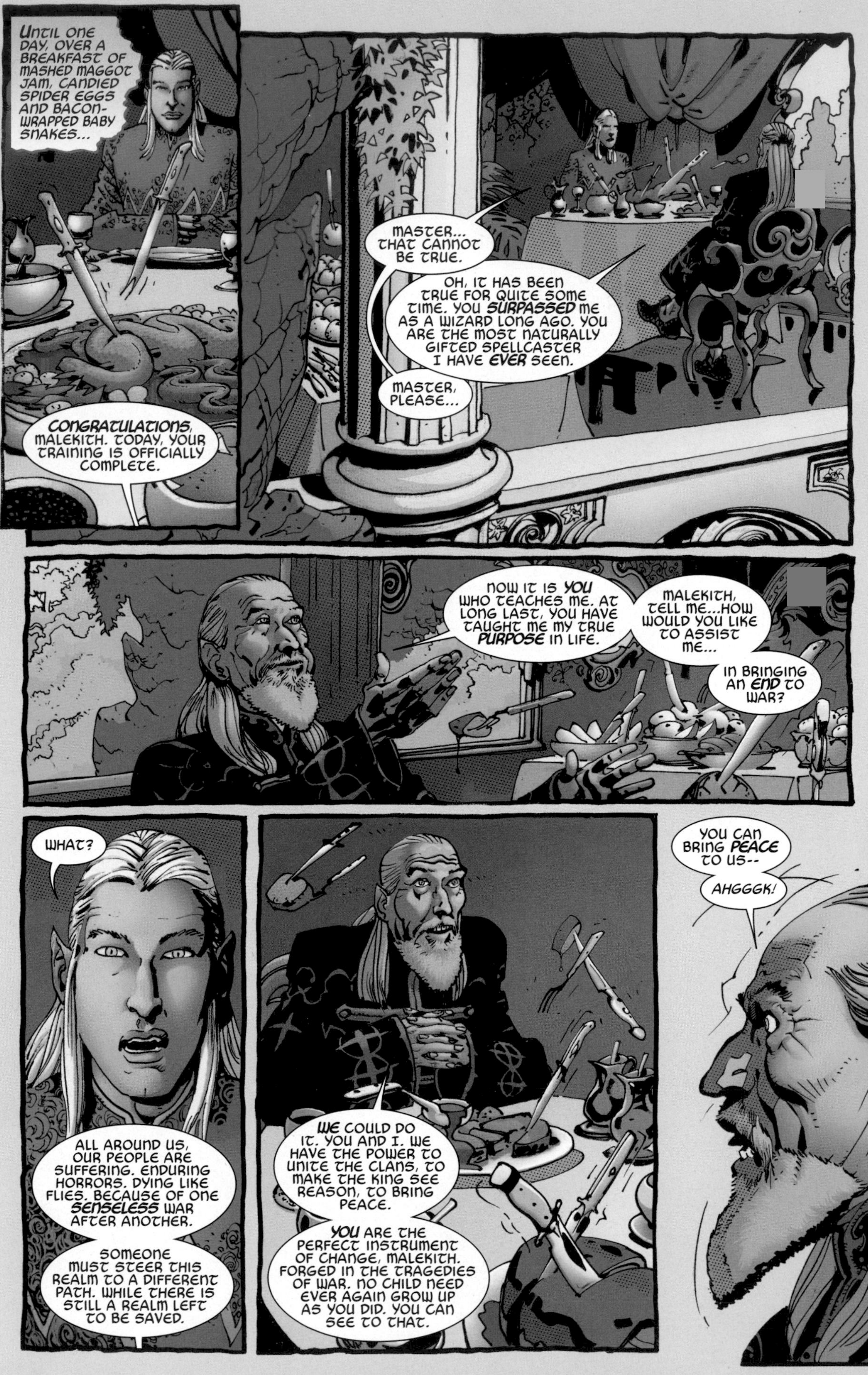
UNTIL ONE DAY, OVER A BREAKFAST OF MASHED MAGGOT JAM, CANDIED SPIDER EGGS AND BACON-WRAPPED BABY SNAKES...
CONGRATULATIONS, MALEKITH. TODAY, YOUR TRAINING IS OFFICIALLY COMPLETE.
MASTER... THAT CANNOT BE TRUE.
OH, IT HAS BEEN TRUE FOR QUITE SOME TIME. YOU SURPASSED ME AS A WIZARD LONG AGO. YOU ARE THE MOST NATURALLY GIFTED SPELLCASTER I HAVE EVER SEEN.
MASTER, PLEASE...
NOW IT IS YOU WHO TEACHES ME. AT LONG LAST, YOU HAVE TAUGHT ME MY TRUE PURPOSE IN LIFE.
MALEKITH, TELL ME...HOW WOULD YOU LIKE TO ASSIST ME...
IN BRINGING AN END TO WAR?
WHAT?
ALL AROUND US, OUR PEOPLE ARE SUFFERING. ENDURING HORRORS. DYING LIKE FLIES. BECAUSE OF ONE SENSELESS WAR AFTER ANOTHER.
SOMEONE MUST STEER THIS REALM TO A DIFFERENT PATH. WHILE THERE IS STILL A REALM LEFT TO BE SAVED.
WE COULD DO IT. YOU AND I. WE HAVE THE POWER TO UNITE THE CLANS, TO MAKE THE KING SEE REASON, TO BRING PEACE.
YOU ARE THE PERFECT INSTRUMENT OF CHANGE, MALEKITH. FORGED IN THE TRAGEDIES OF WAR. NO CHILD NEED EVER AGAIN GROW UP AS YOU DID. YOU CAN SEE TO THAT.
YOU CAN BRING PEACE TO US--
AHGGGK!

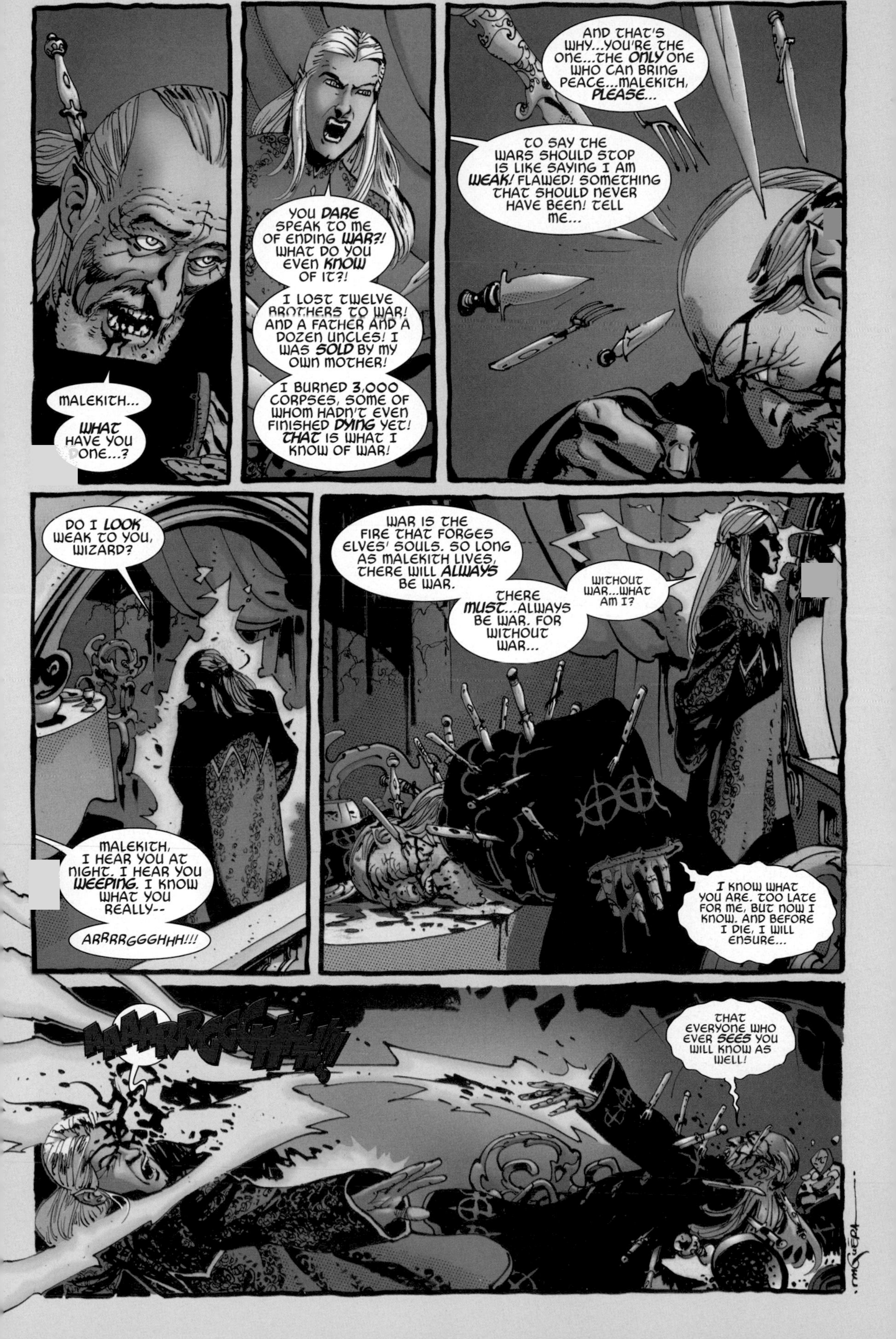

MALEKITH... WHAT HAVE YOU DONE...?
YOU DARE SPEAK TO ME OF ENDING WAR?! WHAT DO YOU EVEN KNOW OF IT?!
I LOST TWELVE BROTHERS TO WAR! AND A FATHER AND A DOZEN UNCLES! I WAS SOLD BY MY OWN MOTHER!
I BURNED 3,000 CORPSES, SOME OF WHOM HADN'T EVEN FINISHED DYING YET! THAT IS WHAT I KNOW OF WAR!
AND THAT'S WHY...YOU'RE THE ONE...THE ONLY ONE WHO CAN BRING PEACE...MALEKITH, PLEASE...
TO SAY THE WARS SHOULD STOP IS LIKE SAYING I AM WEAK! FLAWED! SOMETHING THAT SHOULD NEVER HAVE BEEN! TELL ME...
DO I LOOK WEAK TO YOU, WIZARD?
MALEKITH, I HEAR YOU AT NIGHT. I HEAR YOU WEEPING. I KNOW WHAT YOU REALLY--
ARRRRGGGHHH!!!
WAR IS THE FIRE THAT FORGES ELVES' SOULS. SO LONG AS MALEKITH LIVES, THERE WILL ALWAYS BE WAR.
THERE MUST...ALWAYS BE WAR. FOR WITHOUT WAR...
WITHOUT WAR...WHAT AM I?
I KNOW WHAT YOU ARE. TOO LATE FOR ME, BUT NOW I KNOW. AND BEFORE I DIE, I WILL ENSURE...
AAAARRGGGHH!!
THAT EVERYONE WHO EVER SEES YOU WILL KNOW AS WELL!

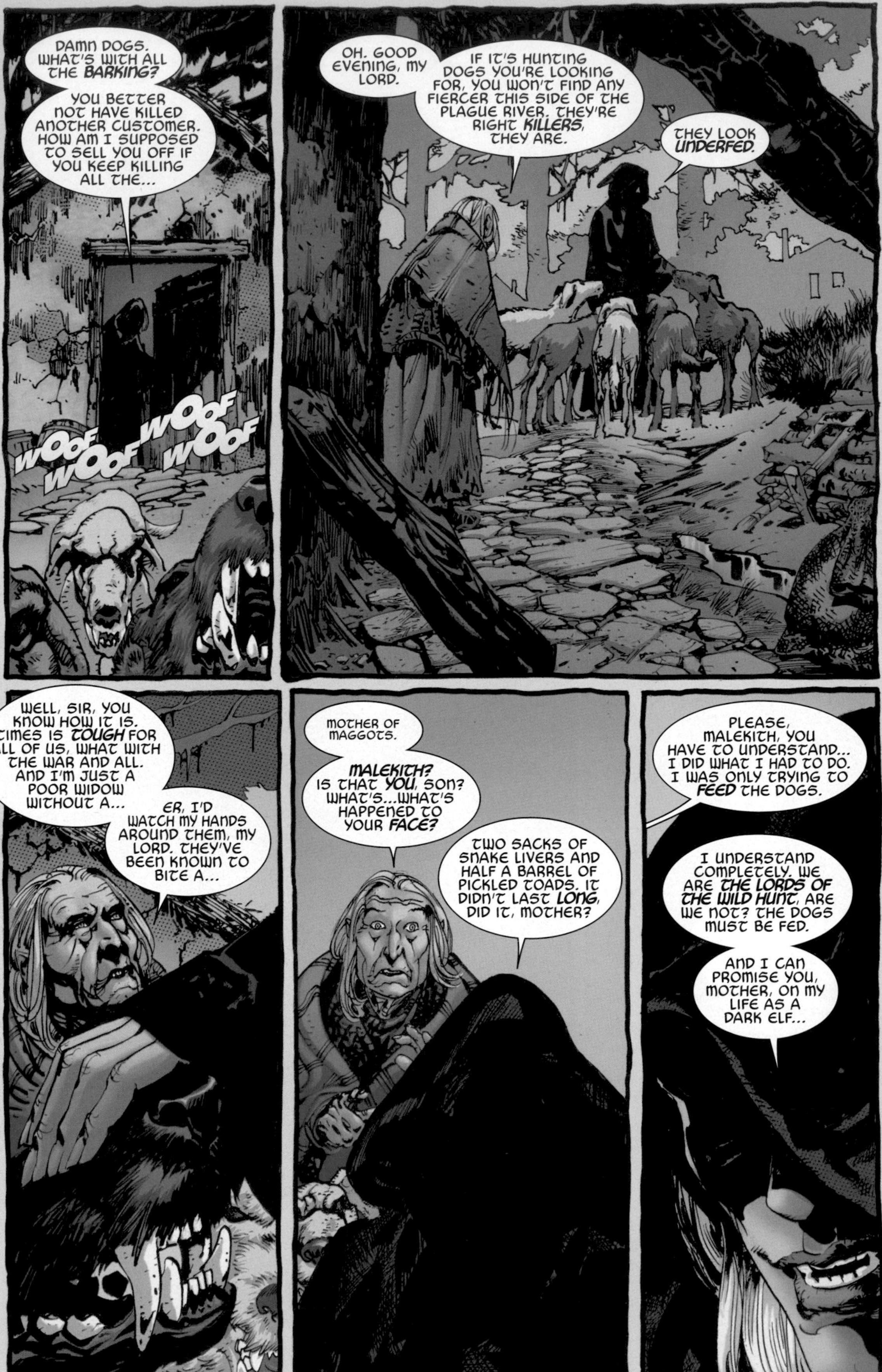
DAMN DOGS. WHAT'S WITH ALL THE BARKING?
YOU BETTER NOT HAVE KILLED ANOTHER CUSTOMER. HOW AM I SUPPOSED TO SELL YOU OFF IF YOU KEEP KILLING ALL THE...
WOOF WOOF WOOF WOOF
OH. GOOD EVENING, MY LORD.
IF IT'S HUNTING DOGS YOU'RE LOOKING FOR, YOU WON'T FIND ANY FIERCER THIS SIDE OF THE PLAGUE RIVER. THEY'RE RIGHT KILLERS, THEY ARE.
THEY LOOK UNDERFED.
WELL, SIR, YOU KNOW HOW IT IS. TIMES IS TOUGH FOR ALL OF US, WHAT WITH THE WAR AND ALL. AND I'M JUST A POOR WIDOW WITHOUT A...
ER, I'D WATCH MY HANDS AROUND THEM, MY LORD. THEY'VE BEEN KNOWN TO BITE A...
MOTHER OF MAGGOTS.
MALEKITH? IS THAT YOU, SON? WHAT'S...WHAT'S HAPPENED TO YOUR FACE?
TWO SACKS OF SNAKE LIVERS AND HALF A BARREL OF PICKLED TOADS. IT DIDN'T LAST LONG, DID IT, MOTHER?
PLEASE, MALEKITH, YOU HAVE TO UNDERSTAND... I DID WHAT I HAD TO DO. I WAS ONLY TRYING TO FEED THE DOGS.
I UNDERSTAND COMPLETELY. WE ARE THE LORDS OF THE WILD HUNT, ARE WE NOT? THE DOGS MUST BE FED.
AND I CAN PROMISE YOU, MOTHER, ON MY LIFE AS A DARK ELF...

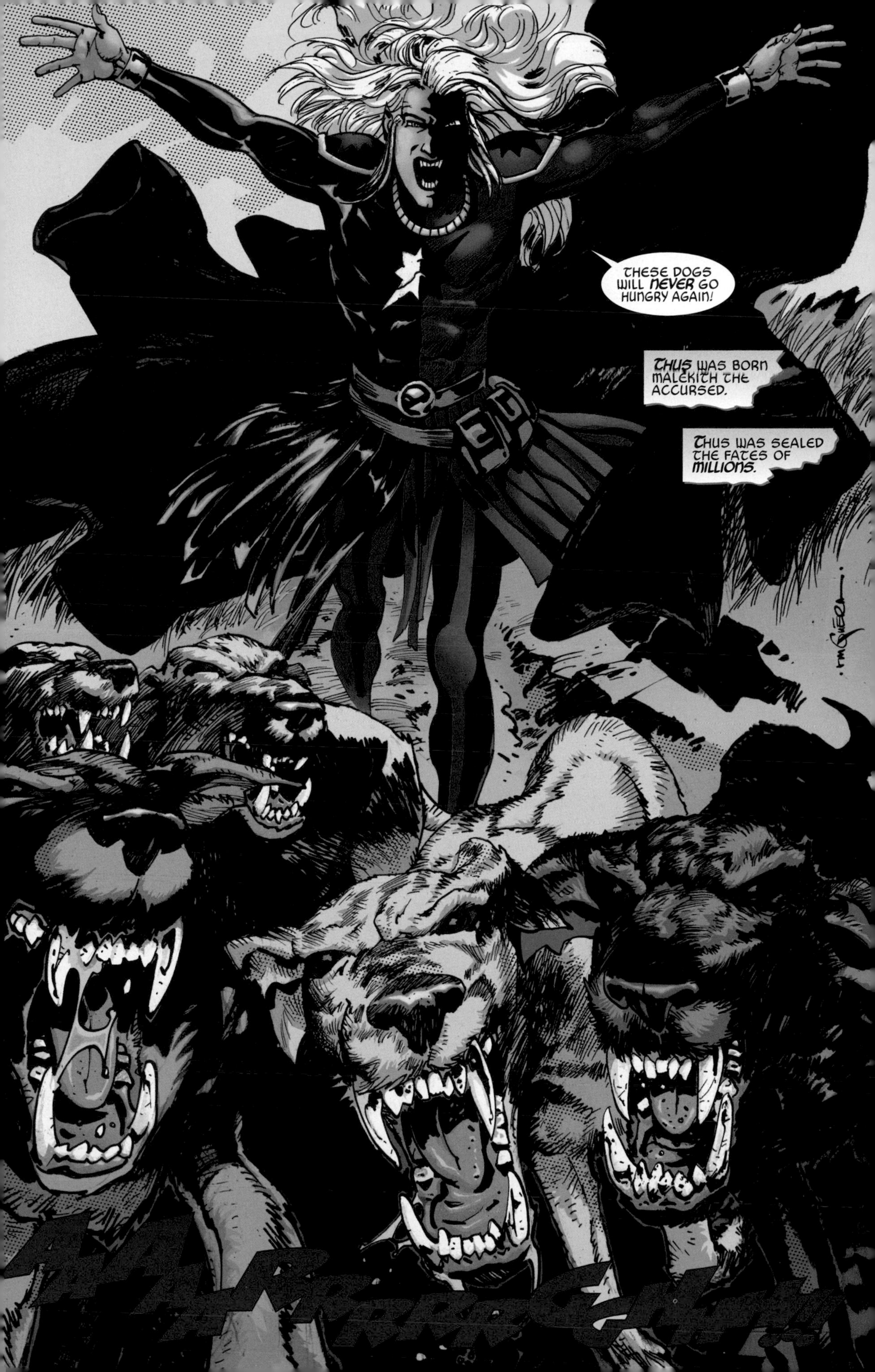
THESE DOGS WILL NEVER GO HUNGRY AGAIN!
THUS WAS BORN MALEKITH THE ACCURSED.
THUS WAS SEALED THE FATES OF MILLIONS.

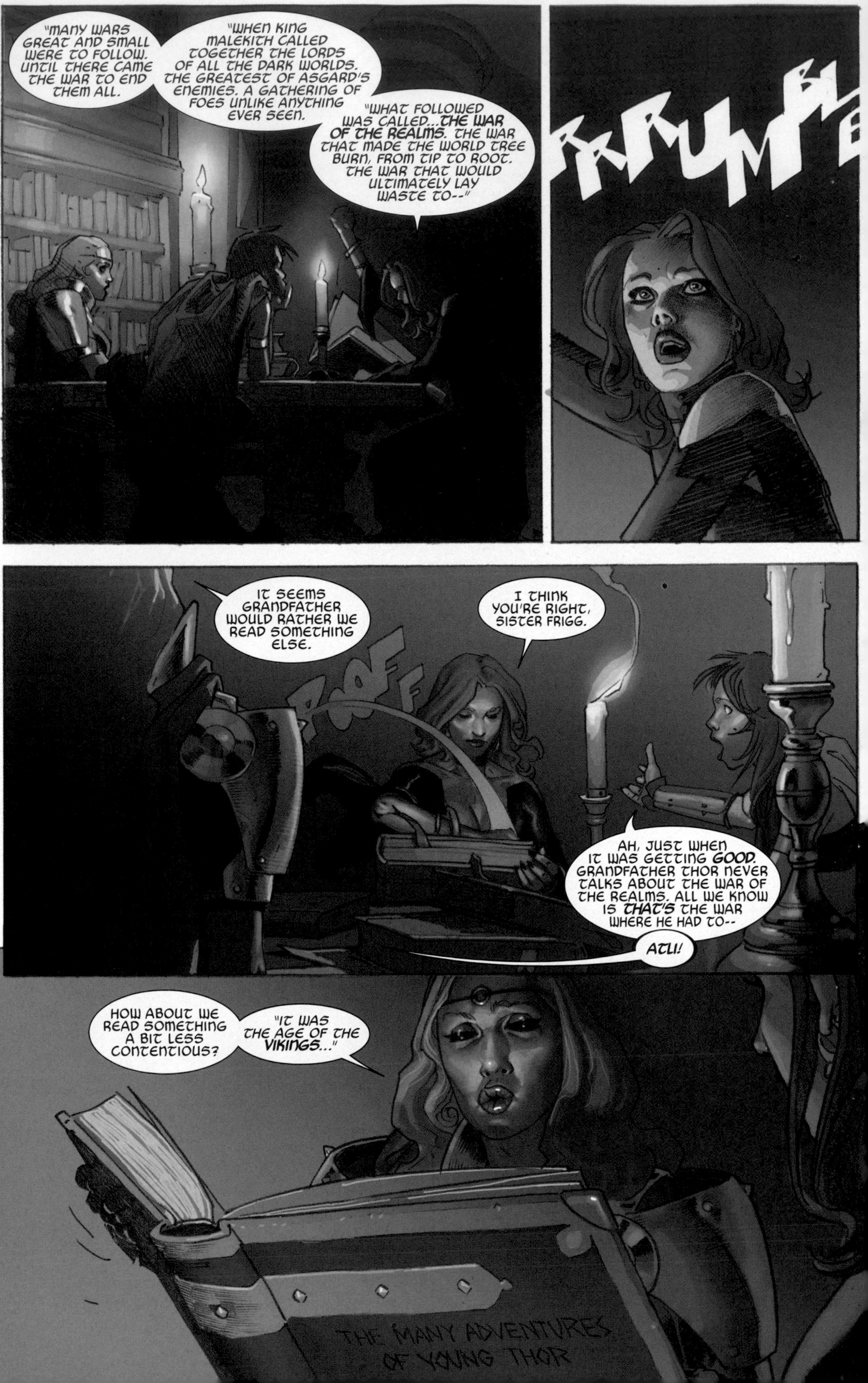
"MANY WARS GREAT AND SMALL WERE TO FOLLOW. UNTIL THERE CAME THE WAR TO END THEM ALL.
"WHEN KING MALEKITH CALLED TOGETHER THE LORDS OF ALL THE DARK WORLDS. THE GREATEST OF ASGARD'S ENEMIES. A GATHERING OF FOES UNLIKE ANYTHING EVER SEEN.
"WHAT FOLLOWED WAS CALLED...THE WAR OF THE REALMS. THE WAR THAT MADE THE WORLD TREE BURN, FROM TIP TO ROOT. THE WAR THAT WOULD ULTIMATELY LAY WASTE TO--"
KRRUMBLE
IT SEEMS GRANDFATHER WOULD RATHER WE READ SOMETHING ELSE.
I THINK YOU'RE RIGHT, SISTER FRIGG.
POOFF
AH, JUST WHEN IT WAS GETTING GOOD. GRANDFATHER THOR NEVER TALKS ABOUT THE WAR OF THE REALMS. ALL WE KNOW IS THAT'S THE WAR WHERE HE HAD TO--
ATLI!
HOW ABOUT WE READ SOMETHING A BIT LESS CONTENTIOUS?
"IT WAS THE AGE OF THE VIKINGS..."
THE MANY ADVENTURES OF YOUNG THOR

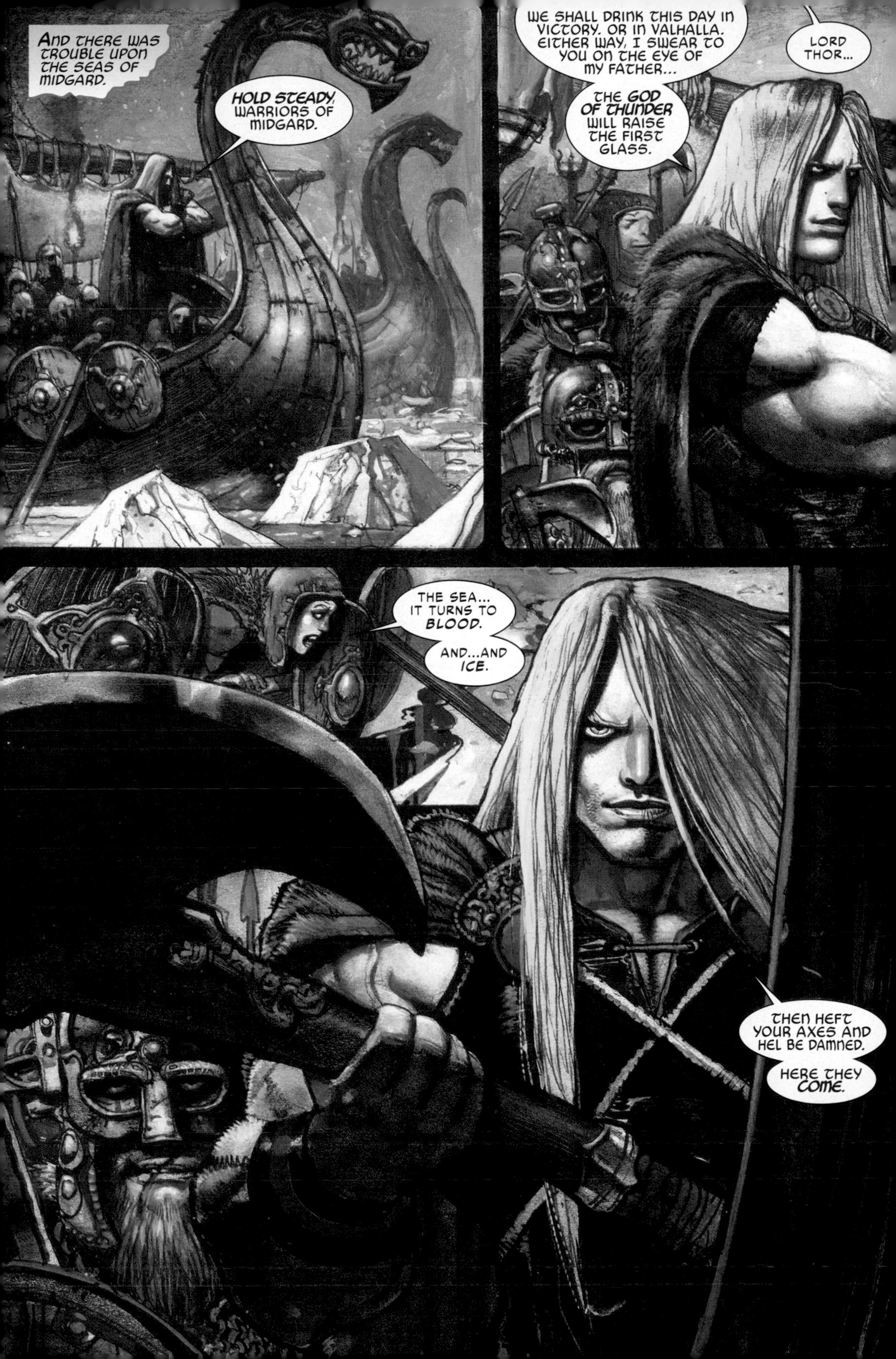
And there was trouble upon the seas of Midgard.
HOLD STEADY, WARRIORS OF MIDGARD.
WE SHALL DRINK THIS DAY IN VICTORY. OR IN VALHALLA. EITHER WAY, I SWEAR TO YOU ON THE EYE OF MY FATHER...
THE GOD OF THUNDER WILL RAISE THE FIRST GLASS.
LORD THOR...
THE SEA... IT TURNS TO BLOOD.
AND...AND ICE.
THEN HEFT YOUR AXES AND HEL BE DAMNED.
HERE THEY COME.

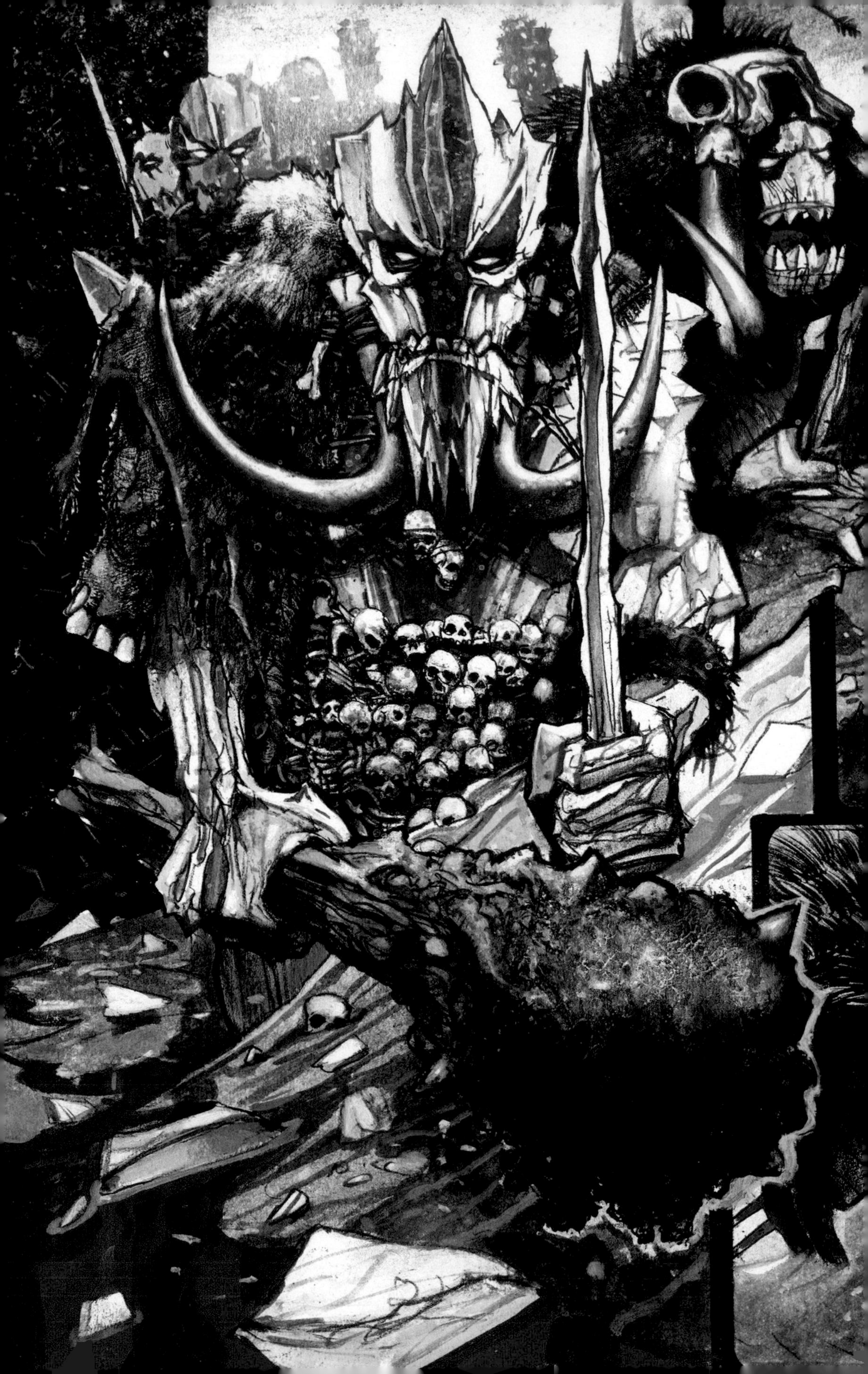

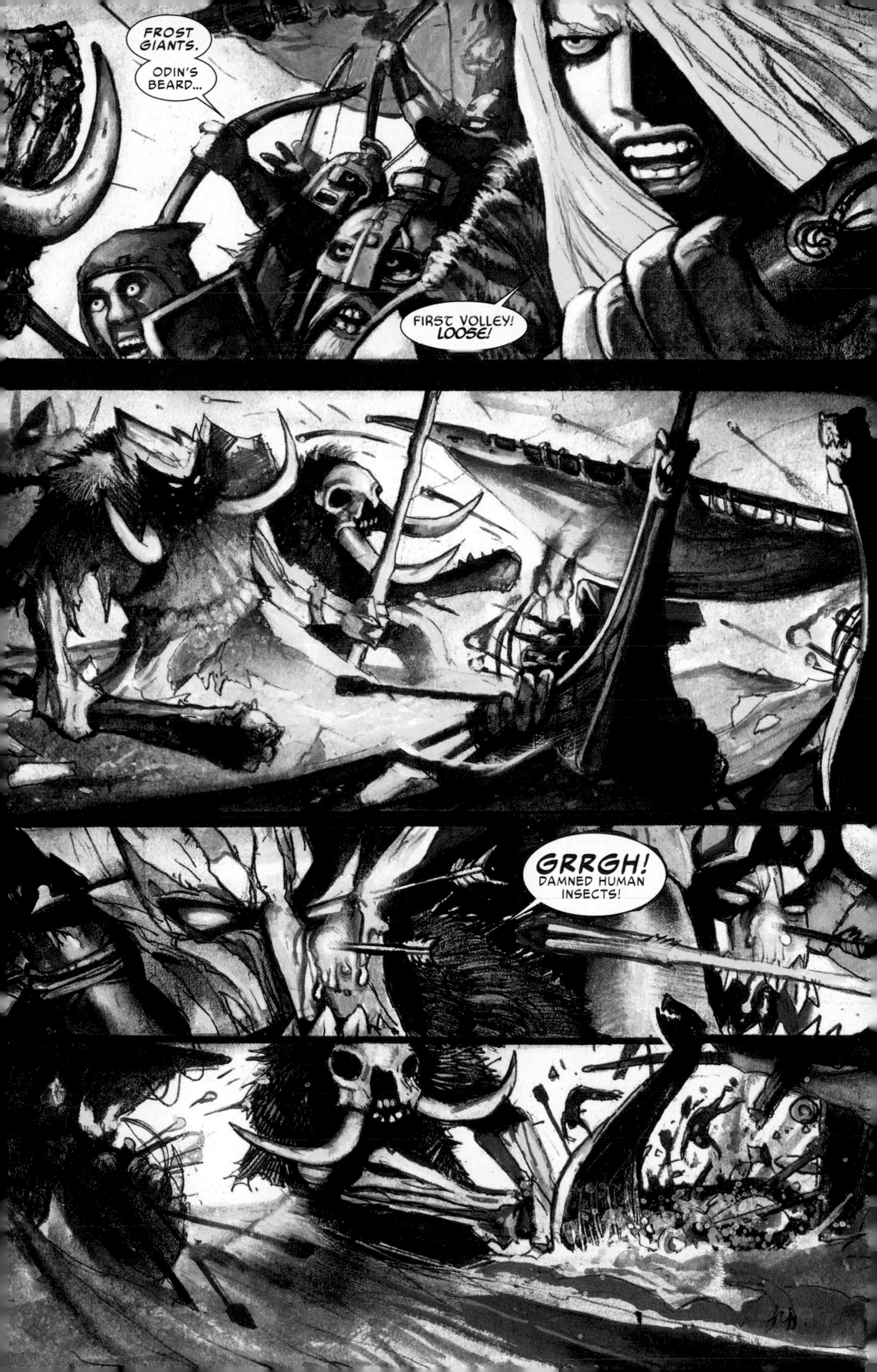
FROST GIANTS.
ODIN'S BEARD...
FIRST VOLLEY! LOOSE!
GRRGH! DAMNED HUMAN INSECTS!

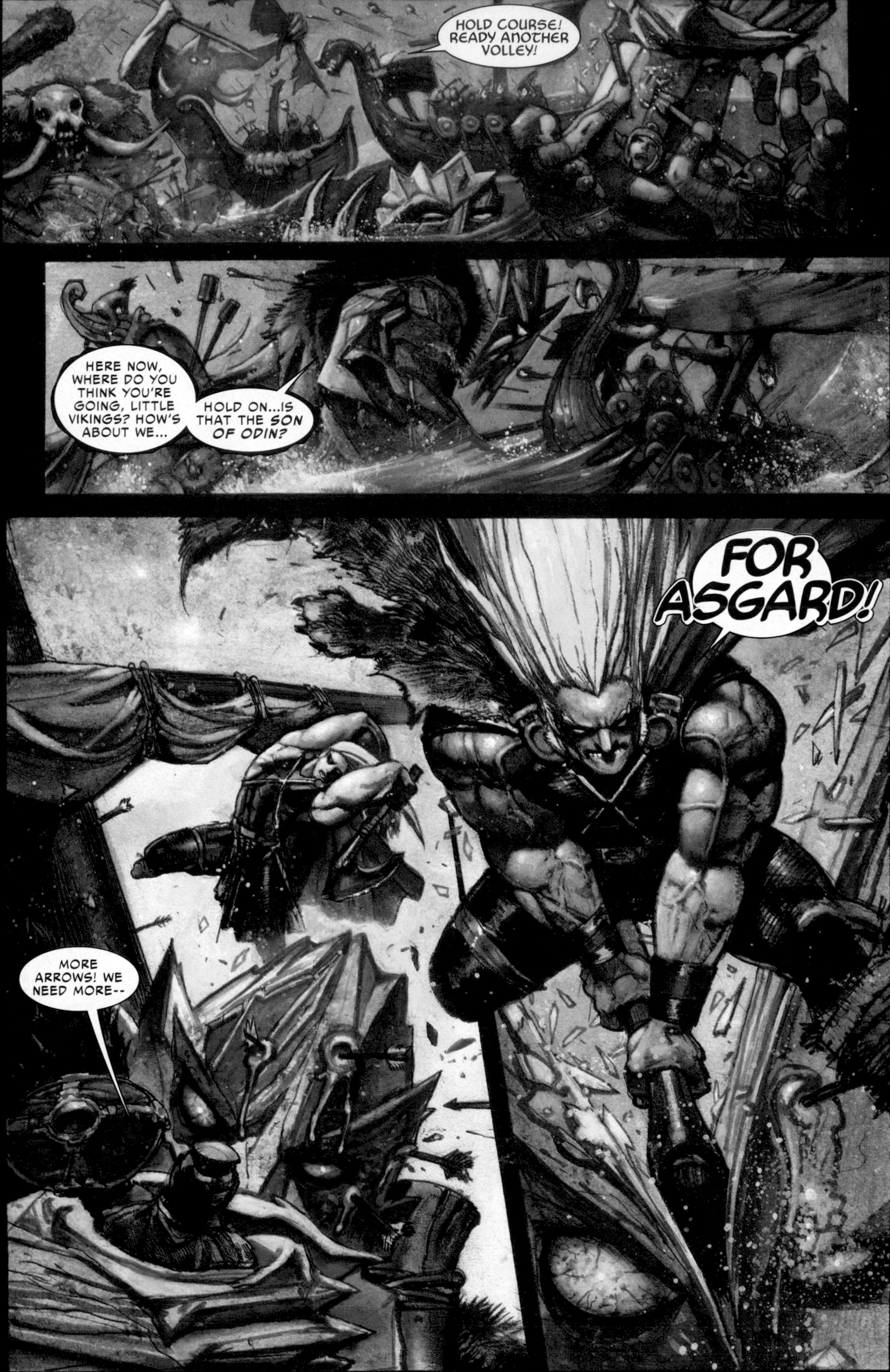
HOLD COURSE! READY ANOTHER VOLLEY!
HERE NOW, WHERE DO YOU THINK YOU'RE GOING, LITTLE VIKINGS? HOW'S ABOUT WE...
HOLD ON...IS THAT THE SON OF ODIN?
FOR ASGARD!
MORE ARROWS! WE NEED MORE--

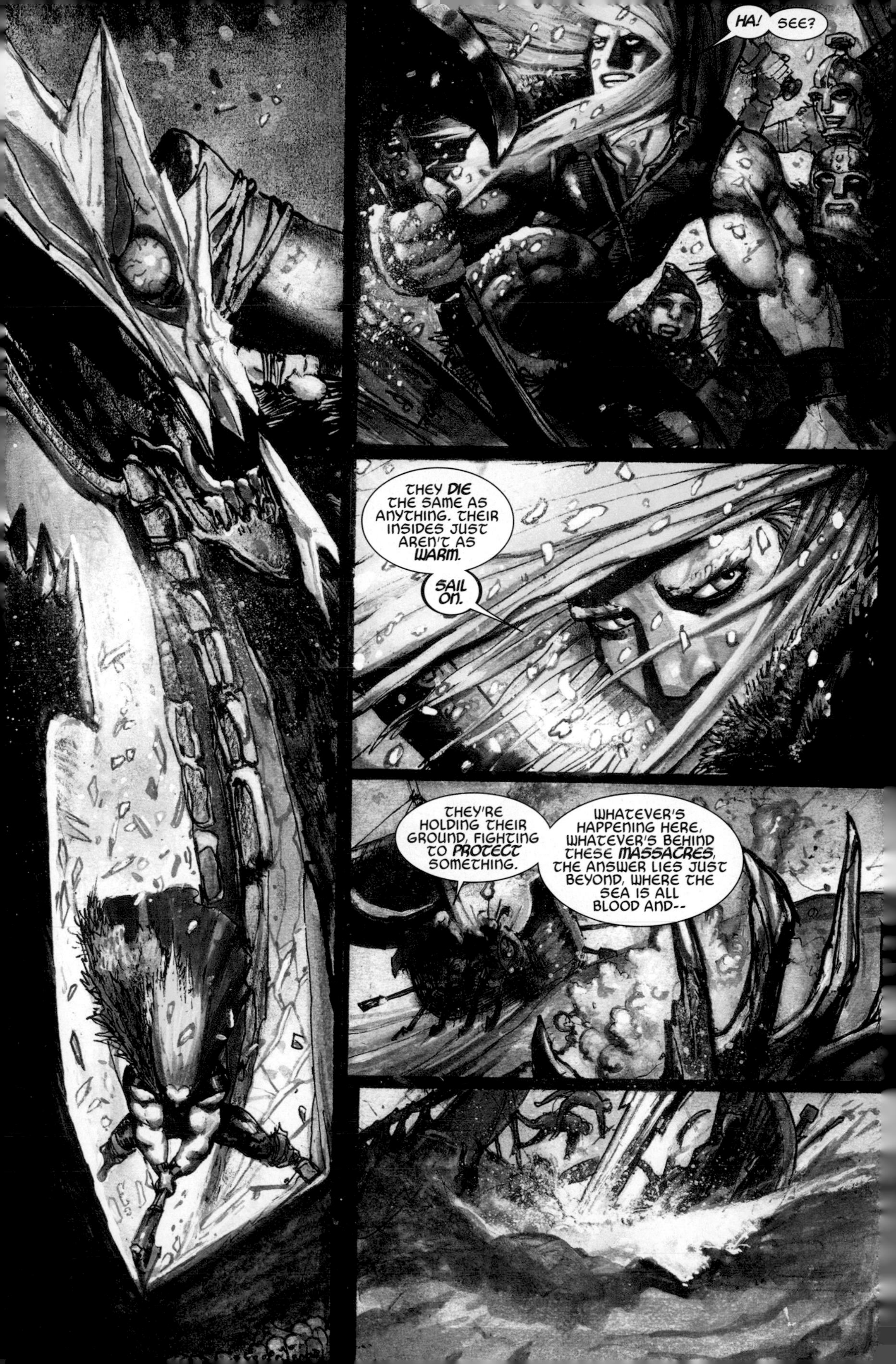
HA!
SEE?
THEY DIE THE SAME AS ANYTHING. THEIR INSIDES JUST AREN'T AS WARM.
SAIL ON.
THEY'RE HOLDING THEIR GROUND, FIGHTING TO PROTECT SOMETHING.
WHATEVER'S HAPPENING HERE, WHATEVER'S BEHIND THESE MASSACRES, THE ANSWER LIES JUST BEYOND, WHERE THE SEA IS ALL BLOOD AND--

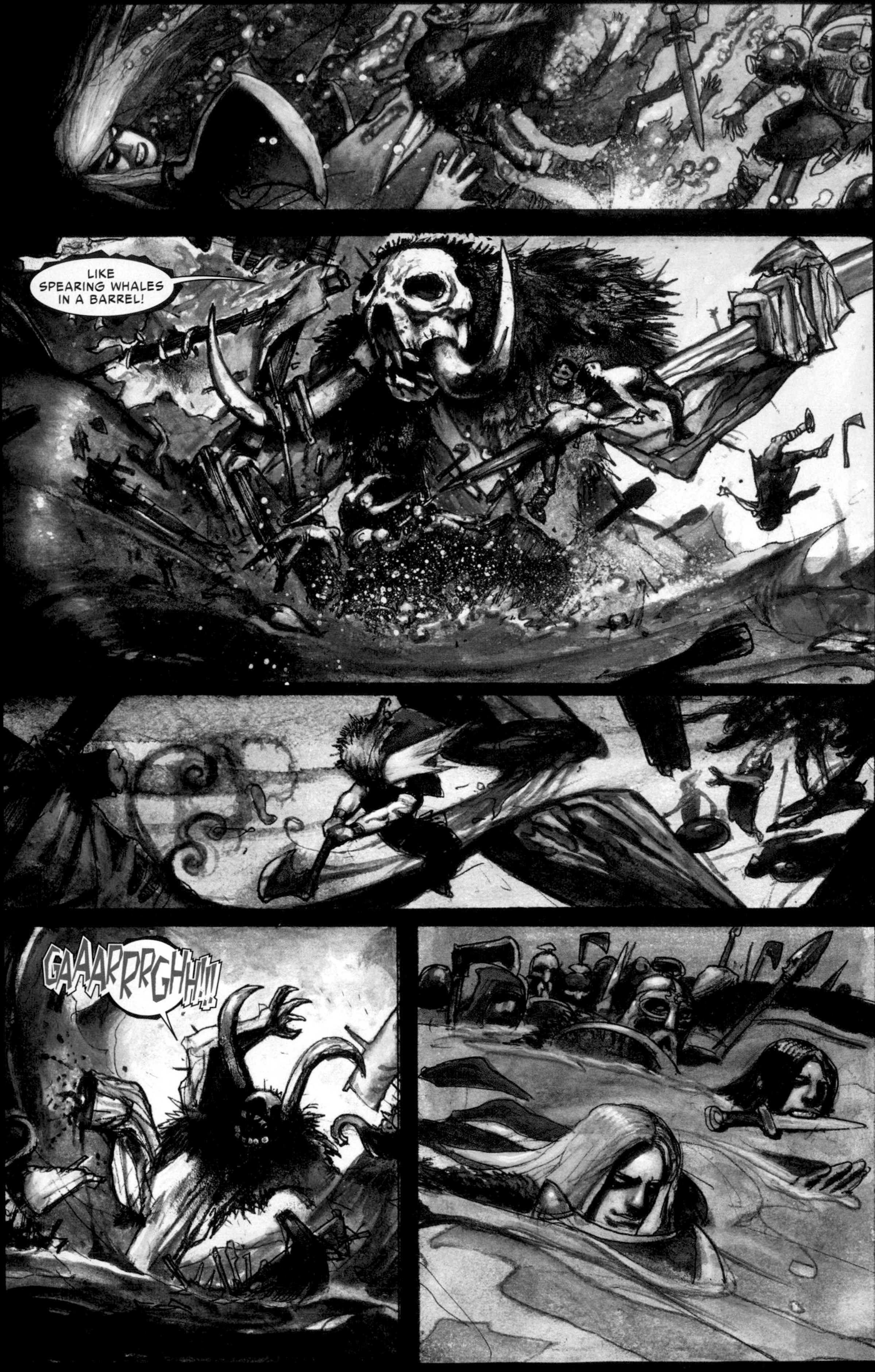
LIKE SPEARING WHALES IN A BARREL!
GAAARRRGHH!!!

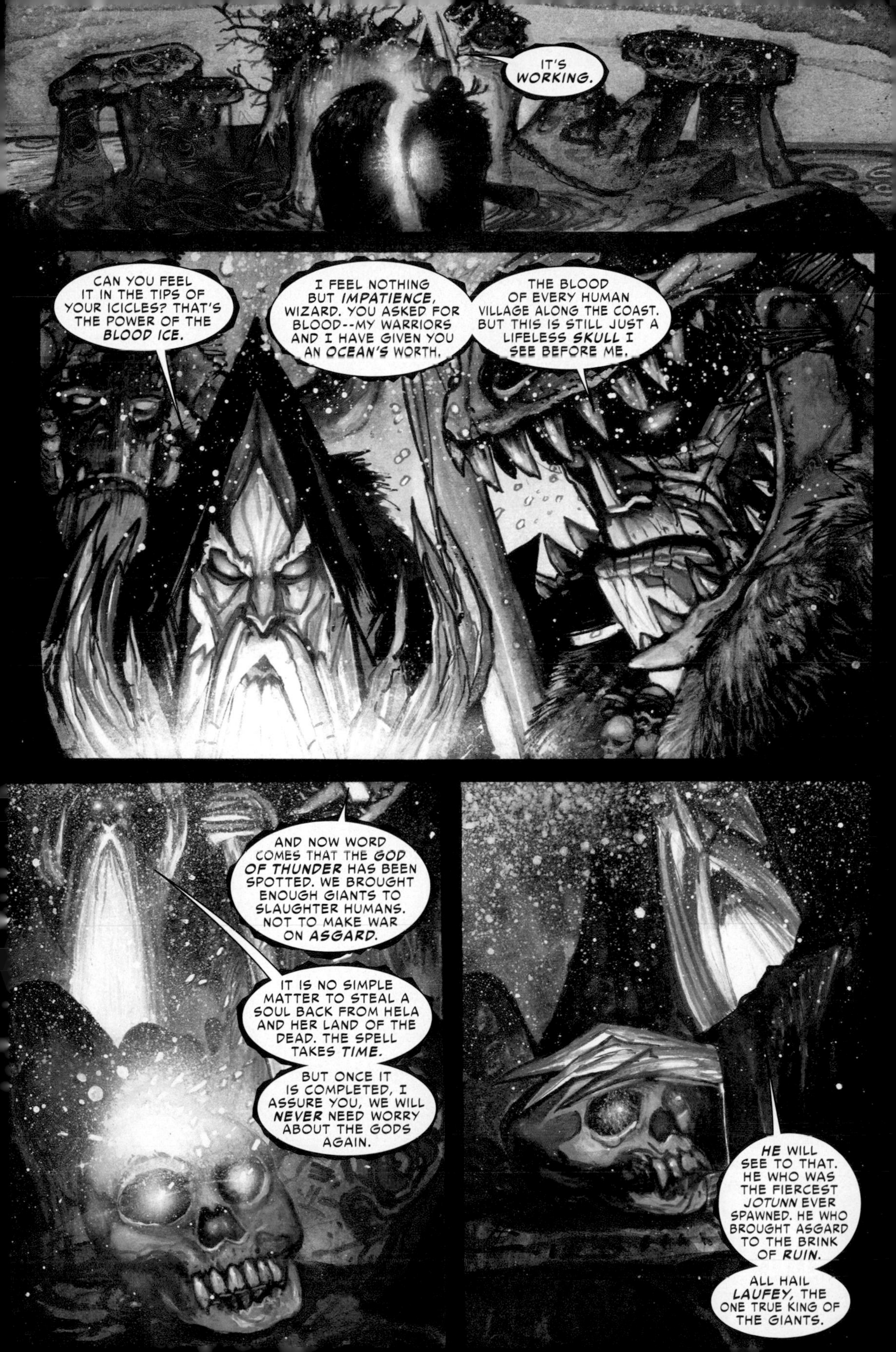

IT'S WORKING.
CAN YOU FEEL IT IN THE TIPS OF YOUR ICICLES? THAT'S THE POWER OF THE BLOOD ICE.
I FEEL NOTHING BUT IMPATIENCE, WIZARD. YOU ASKED FOR BLOOD--MY WARRIORS AND I HAVE GIVEN YOU AN OCEAN'S WORTH.
THE BLOOD OF EVERY HUMAN VILLAGE ALONG THE COAST. BUT THIS IS STILL JUST A LIFELESS SKULL I SEE BEFORE ME.
AND NOW WORD COMES THAT THE GOD OF THUNDER HAS BEEN SPOTTED. WE BROUGHT ENOUGH GIANTS TO SLAUGHTER HUMANS. NOT TO MAKE WAR ON ASGARD.
IT IS NO SIMPLE MATTER TO STEAL A SOUL BACK FROM HELA AND HER LAND OF THE DEAD. THE SPELL TAKES TIME.
BUT ONCE IT IS COMPLETED, I ASSURE YOU, WE WILL NEVER NEED WORRY ABOUT THE GODS AGAIN.
HE WILL SEE TO THAT. HE WHO WAS THE FIERCEST JOTUNN EVER SPAWNED. HE WHO BROUGHT ASGARD TO THE BRINK OF RUIN.
ALL HAIL LAUFEY, THE ONE TRUE KING OF THE GIANTS.

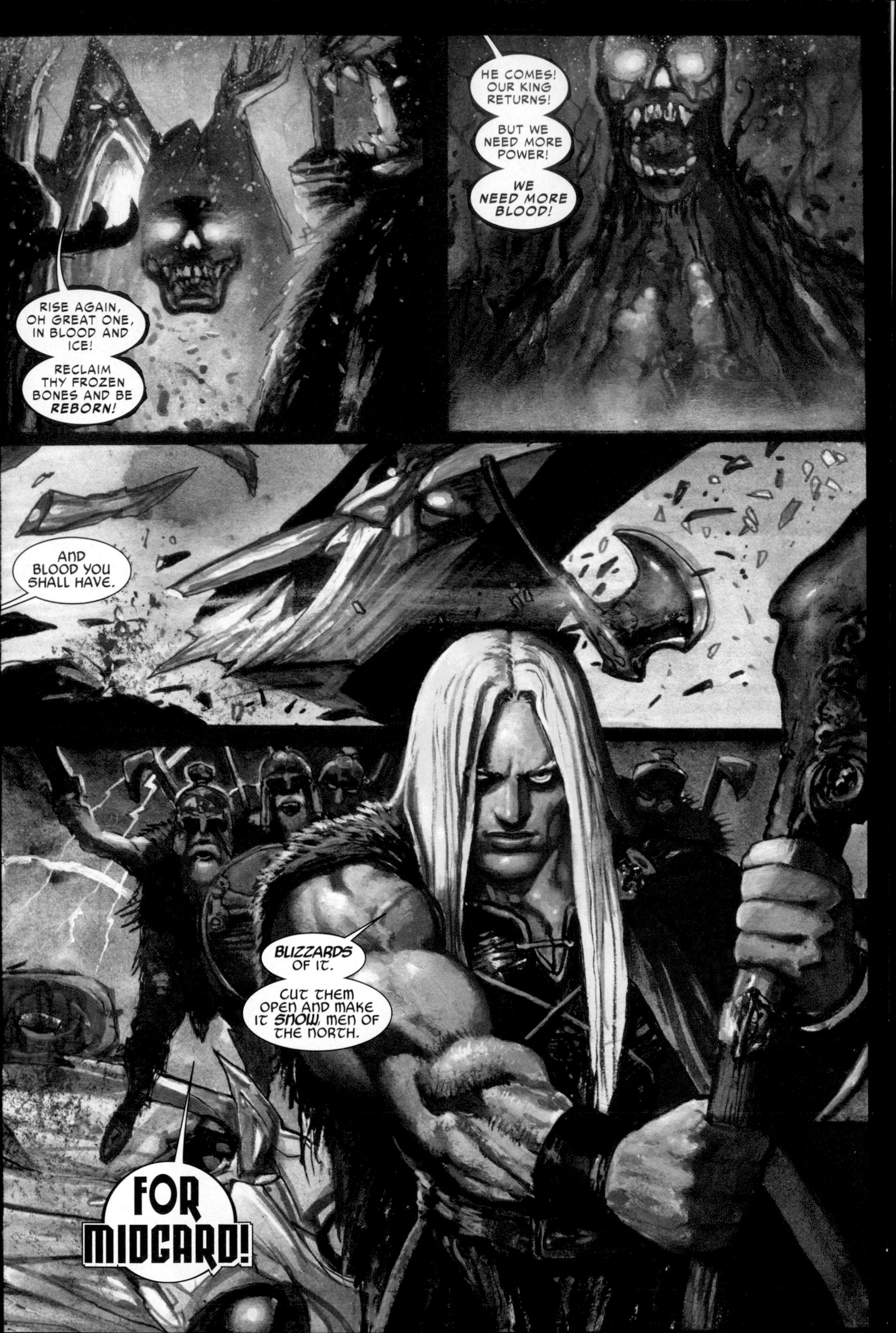
RISE AGAIN, OH GREAT ONE, IN BLOOD AND ICE!
RECLAIM THY FROZEN BONES AND BE *REBORN!*
HE COMES! OUR KING RETURNS!
BUT WE NEED MORE POWER!
WE NEED MORE BLOOD!
AND BLOOD YOU SHALL HAVE.
BLIZZARDS OF IT.
CUT THEM OPEN AND MAKE IT *SNOW*, MEN OF THE NORTH.
FOR MIDGARD!

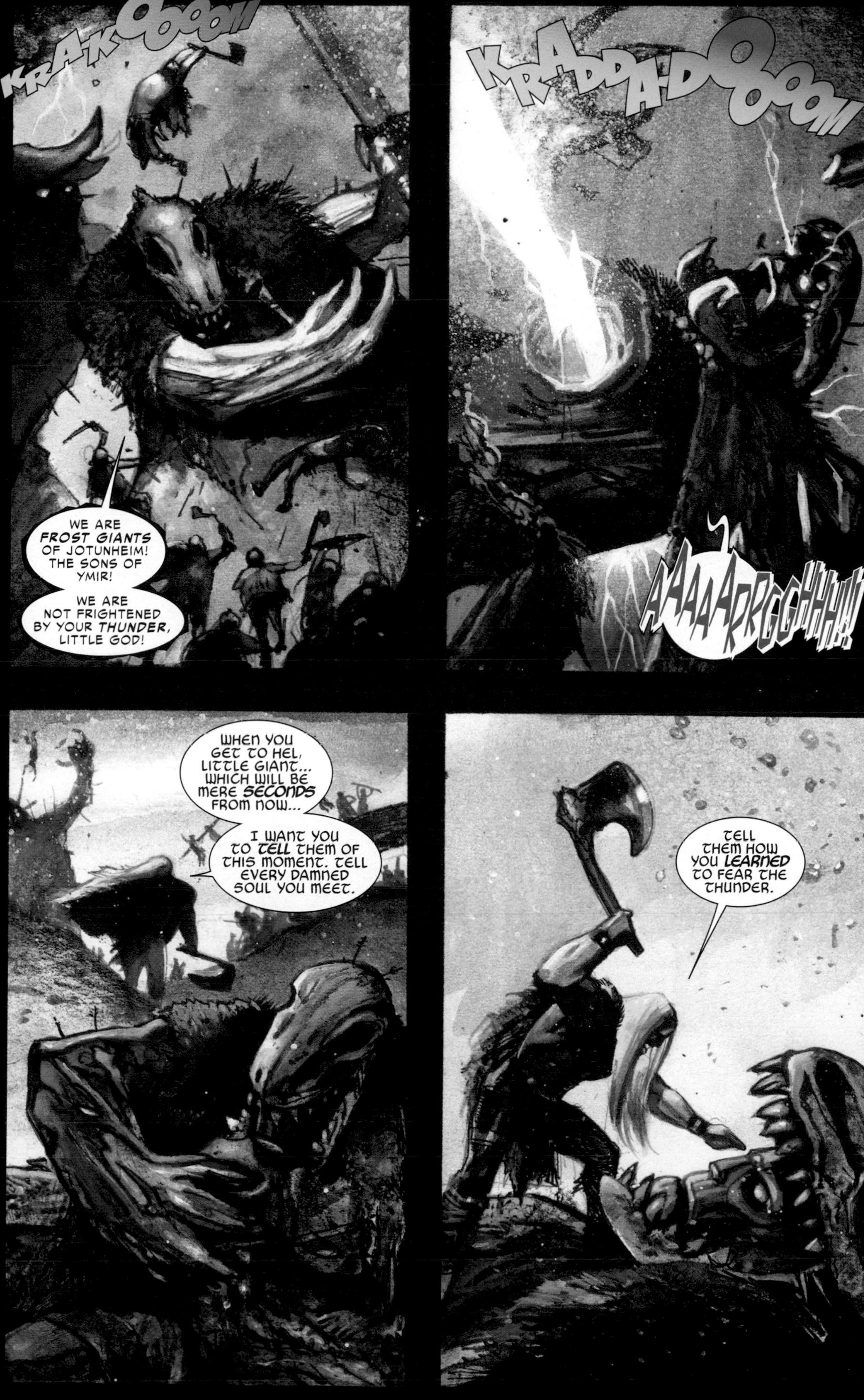
KRA-KOOOOM
WE ARE FROST GIANTS OF JOTUNHEIM! THE SONS OF YMIR!
WE ARE NOT FRIGHTENED BY YOUR THUNDER, LITTLE GOD!
KRADDA-DOOOOOM
AAAAARRGGHHH!!
WHEN YOU GET TO HEL, LITTLE GIANT... WHICH WILL BE MERE SECONDS FROM NOW...
I WANT YOU TO TELL THEM OF THIS MOMENT. TELL EVERY DAMNED SOUL YOU MEET.
TELL THEM HOW YOU LEARNED TO FEAR THE THUNDER.

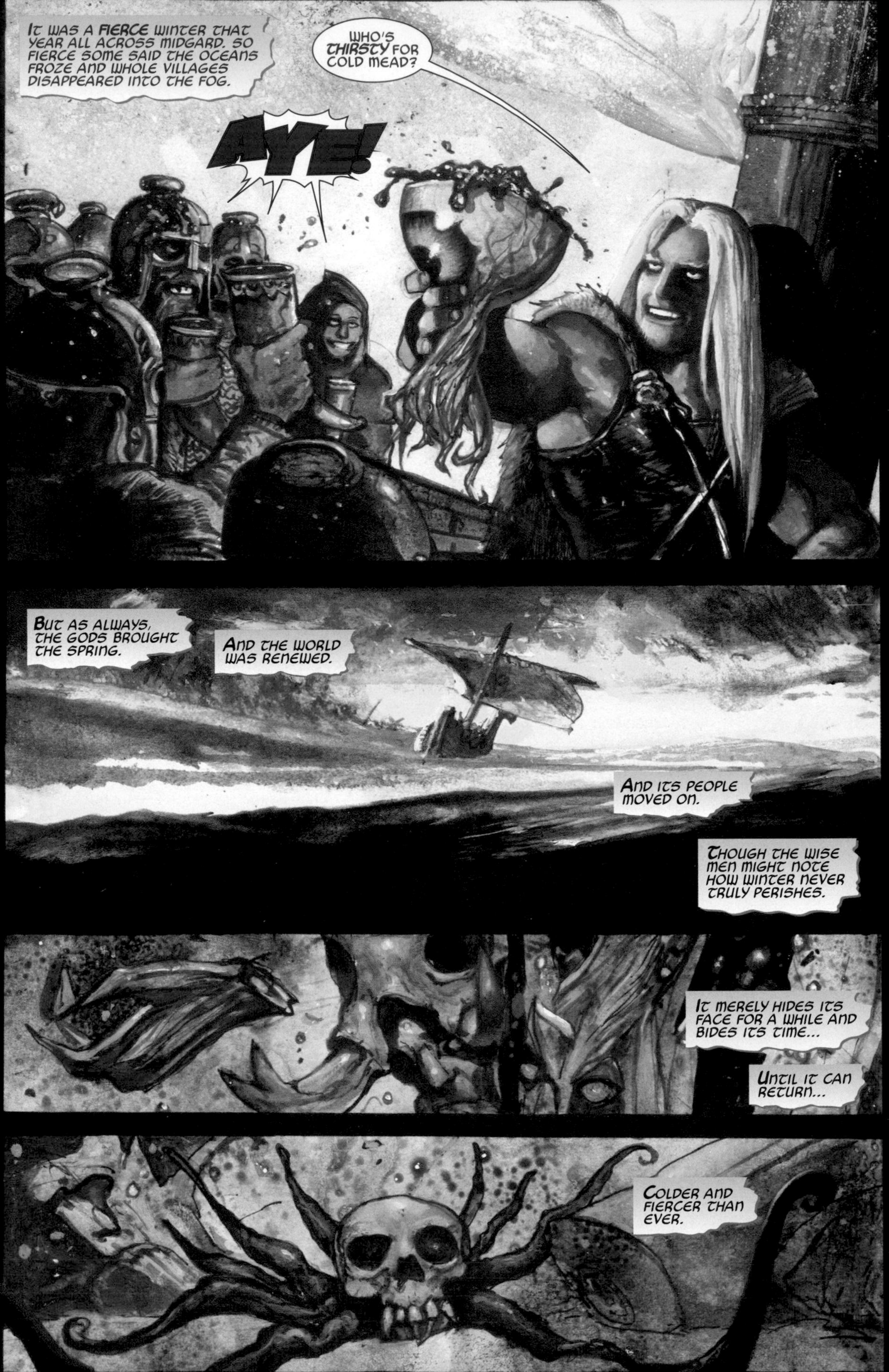
It was a FIERCE winter that year all across Midgard. So fierce some said the oceans froze and whole villages disappeared into the fog.
Who's THIRSTY for cold mead?
AYE!
But as always, the gods brought the spring.
And the world was renewed.
And its people moved on.
Though the wise men might note how winter never truly perishes.
It merely hides its face for a while and bides its time...
Until it can return...
Colder and fiercer than ever.

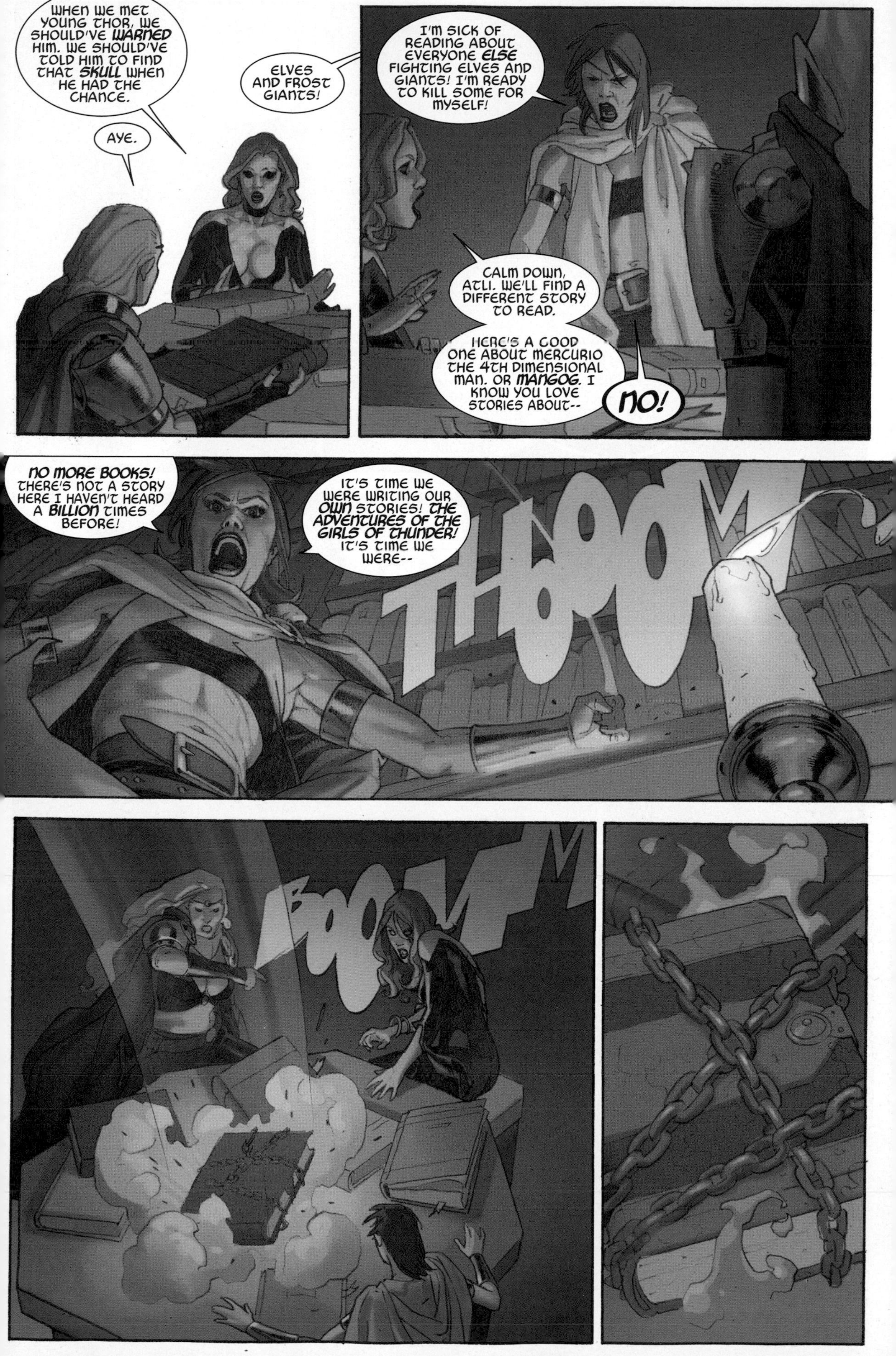
WHEN WE MET YOUNG THOR, WE SHOULD'VE WARNED HIM. WE SHOULD'VE TOLD HIM TO FIND THAT SKULL WHEN HE HAD THE CHANCE.
AYE.
ELVES AND FROST GIANTS!
I'M SICK OF READING ABOUT EVERYONE ELSE FIGHTING ELVES AND GIANTS! I'M READY TO KILL SOME FOR MYSELF!
CALM DOWN, ATLI. WE'LL FIND A DIFFERENT STORY TO READ.
HERE'S A GOOD ONE ABOUT MERCURIO THE 4TH DIMENSIONAL MAN. OR MANGOG. I KNOW YOU LOVE STORIES ABOUT--
NO!
NO MORE BOOKS! THERE'S NOT A STORY HERE I HAVEN'T HEARD A BILLION TIMES BEFORE!
IT'S TIME WE WERE WRITING OUR OWN STORIES! THE ADVENTURES OF THE GIRLS OF THUNDER! IT'S TIME WE WERE--
THOOM
BOOM

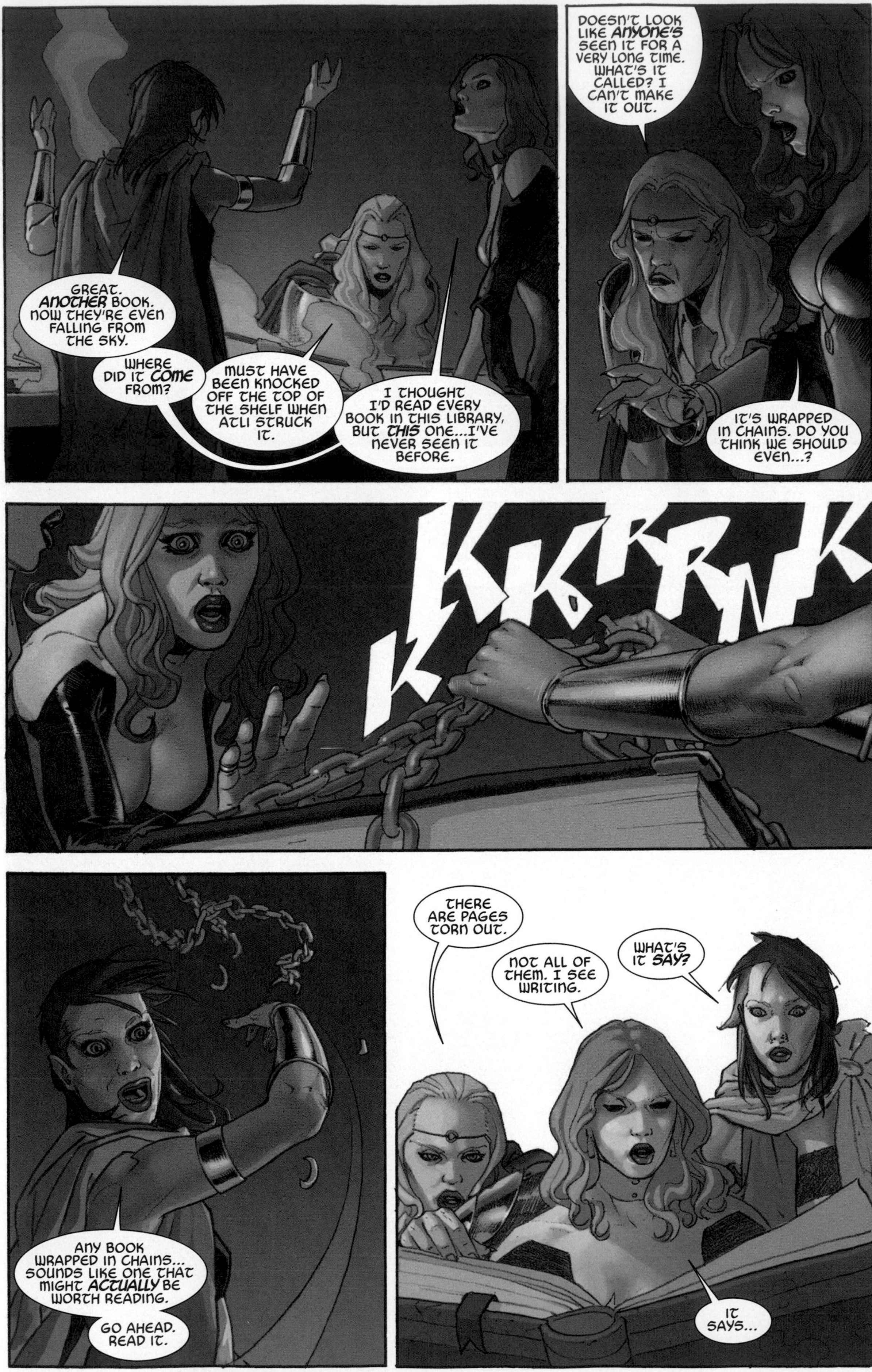
GREAT. ANOTHER BOOK. NOW THEY'RE EVEN FALLING FROM THE SKY.
WHERE DID IT COME FROM?
MUST HAVE BEEN KNOCKED OFF THE TOP OF THE SHELF WHEN ATLI STRUCK IT.
I THOUGHT I'D READ EVERY BOOK IN THIS LIBRARY, BUT THIS ONE...I'VE NEVER SEEN IT BEFORE.
DOESN'T LOOK LIKE ANYONE'S SEEN IT FOR A VERY LONG TIME. WHAT'S IT CALLED? I CAN'T MAKE IT OUT.
IT'S WRAPPED IN CHAINS. DO YOU THINK WE SHOULD EVEN...?
KKKRRNK
ANY BOOK WRAPPED IN CHAINS... SOUNDS LIKE ONE THAT MIGHT ACTUALLY BE WORTH READING.
GO AHEAD. READ IT.
THERE ARE PAGES TORN OUT.
NOT ALL OF THEM. I SEE WRITING.
WHAT'S IT SAY?
IT SAYS...

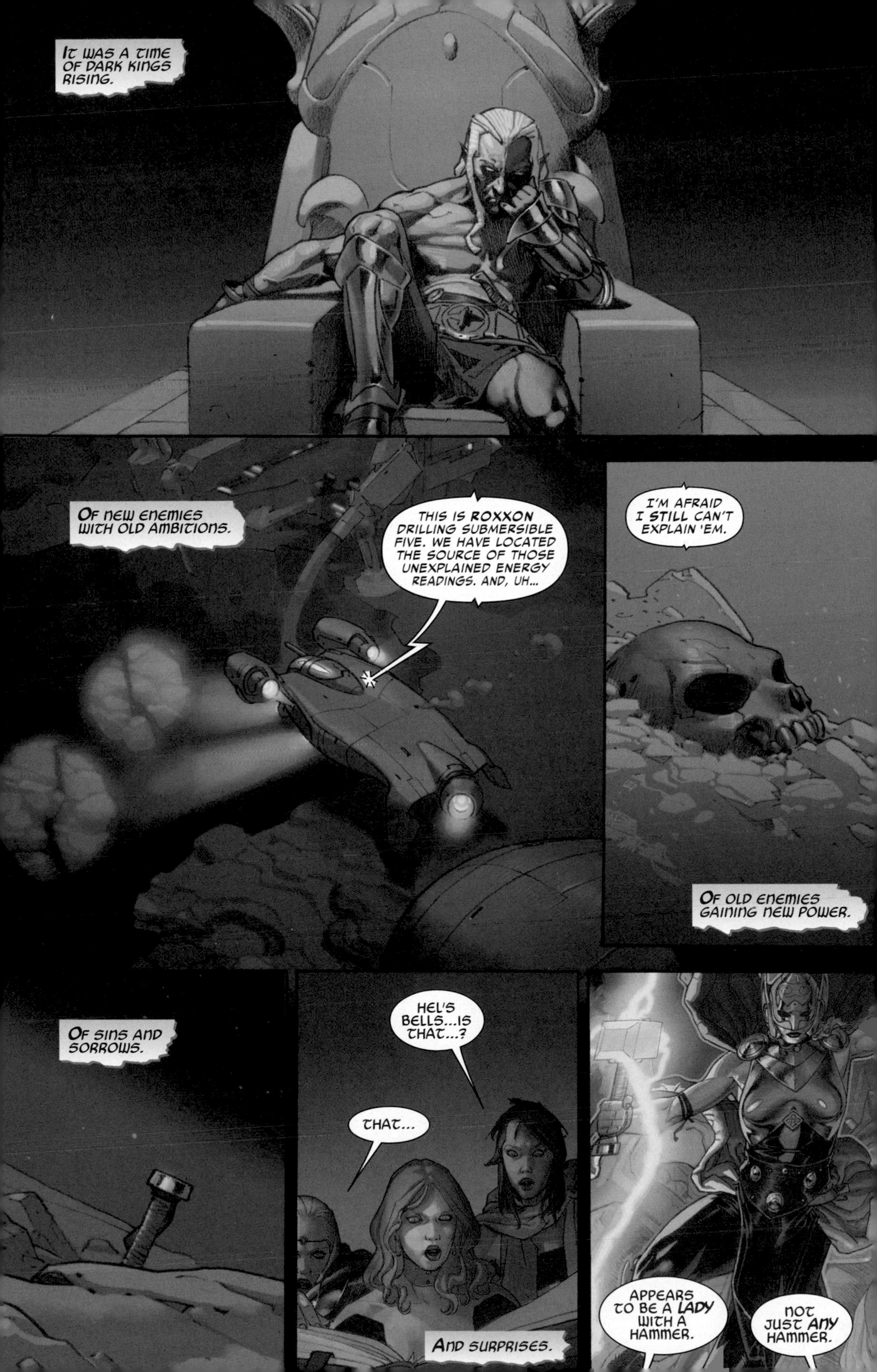

IT WAS A TIME OF DARK KINGS RISING.
OF NEW ENEMIES WITH OLD AMBITIONS.
THIS IS ROXXON DRILLING SUBMERSIBLE FIVE. WE HAVE LOCATED THE SOURCE OF THOSE UNEXPLAINED ENERGY READINGS. AND, UH...
I'M AFRAID I STILL CAN'T EXPLAIN 'EM.
OF OLD ENEMIES GAINING NEW POWER.
OF SINS AND SORROWS.
HEL'S BELLS...IS THAT...?
THAT...
AND SURPRISES.
APPEARS TO BE A LADY WITH A HAMMER.
NOT JUST ANY HAMMER.

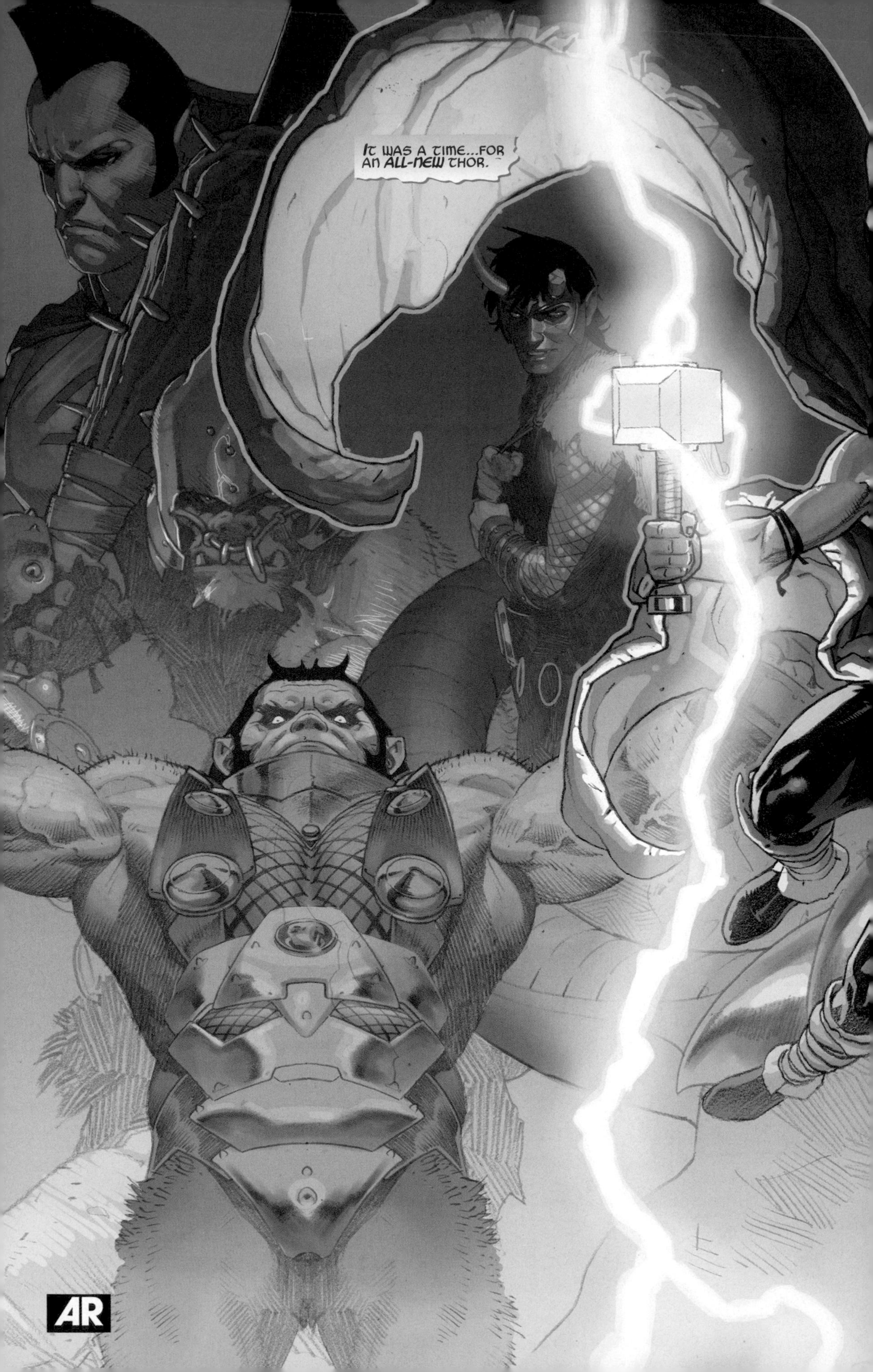
IT WAS A TIME...FOR AN ALL-NEW THOR.

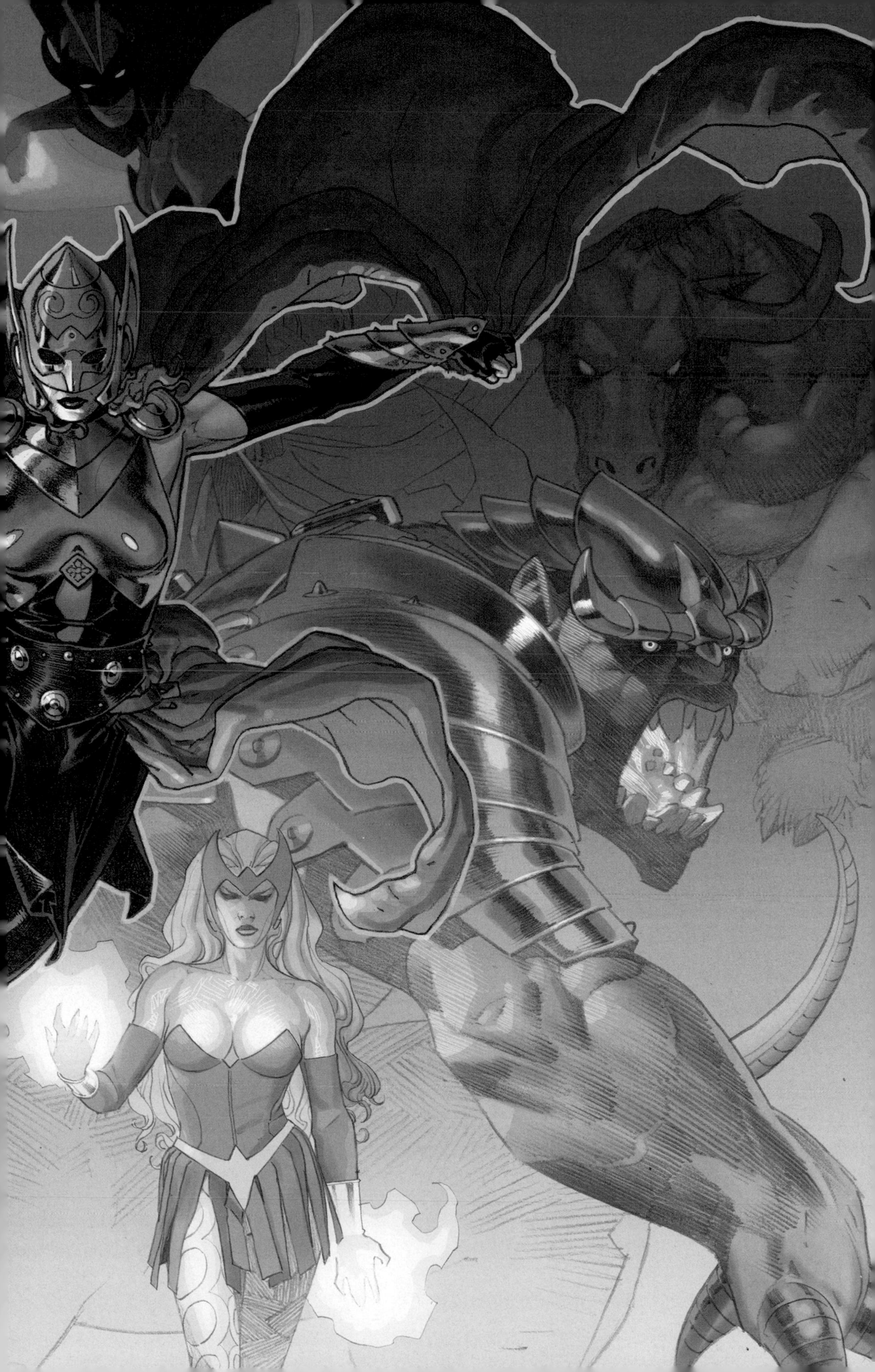

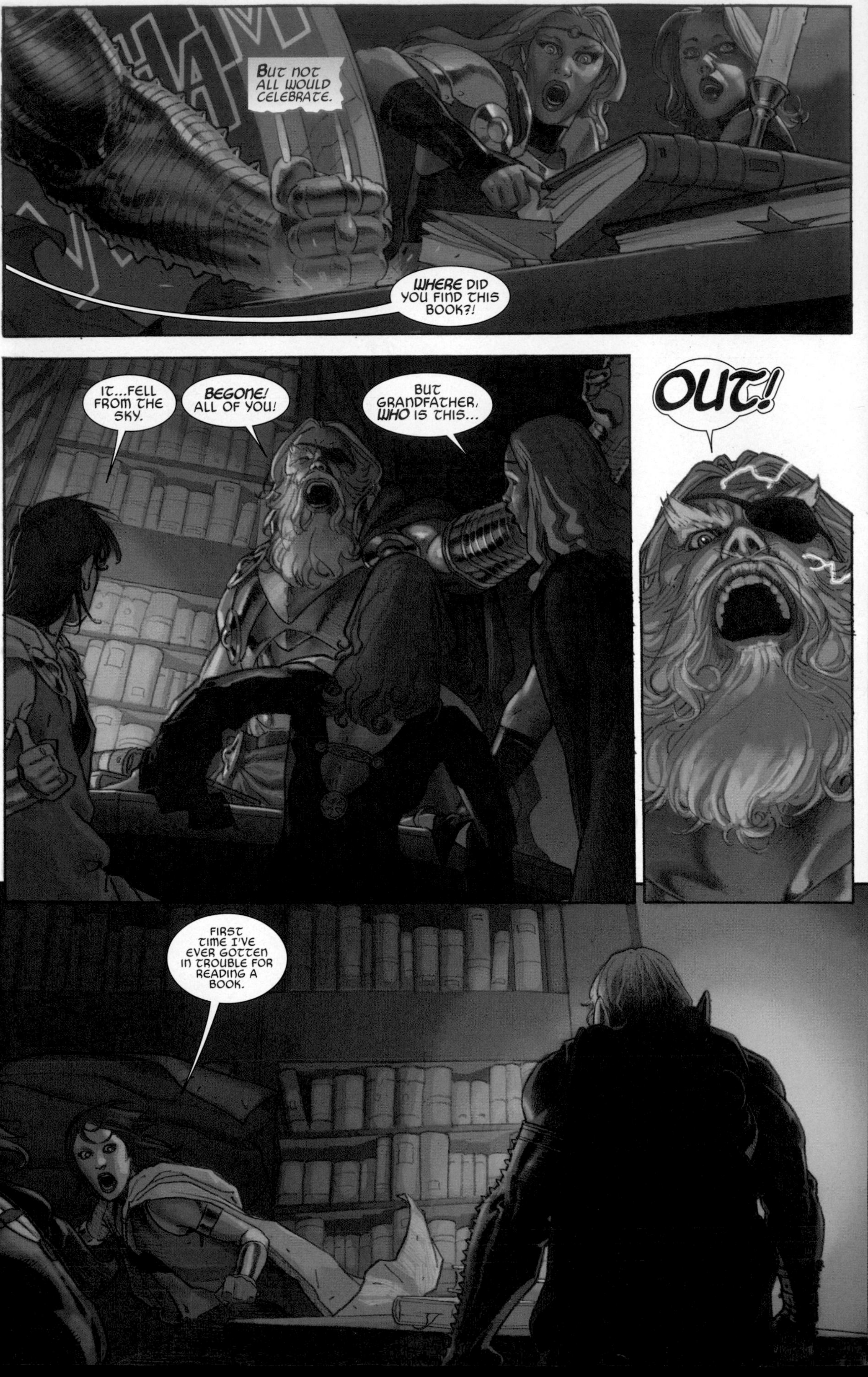

BUT NOT ALL WOULD CELEBRATE.
WHERE DID YOU FIND THIS BOOK?!
IT...FELL FROM THE SKY.
BEGONE! ALL OF YOU!
BUT GRANDFATHER, WHO IS THIS...
OUT!
FIRST TIME I'VE EVER GOTTEN IN TROUBLE FOR READING A BOOK.

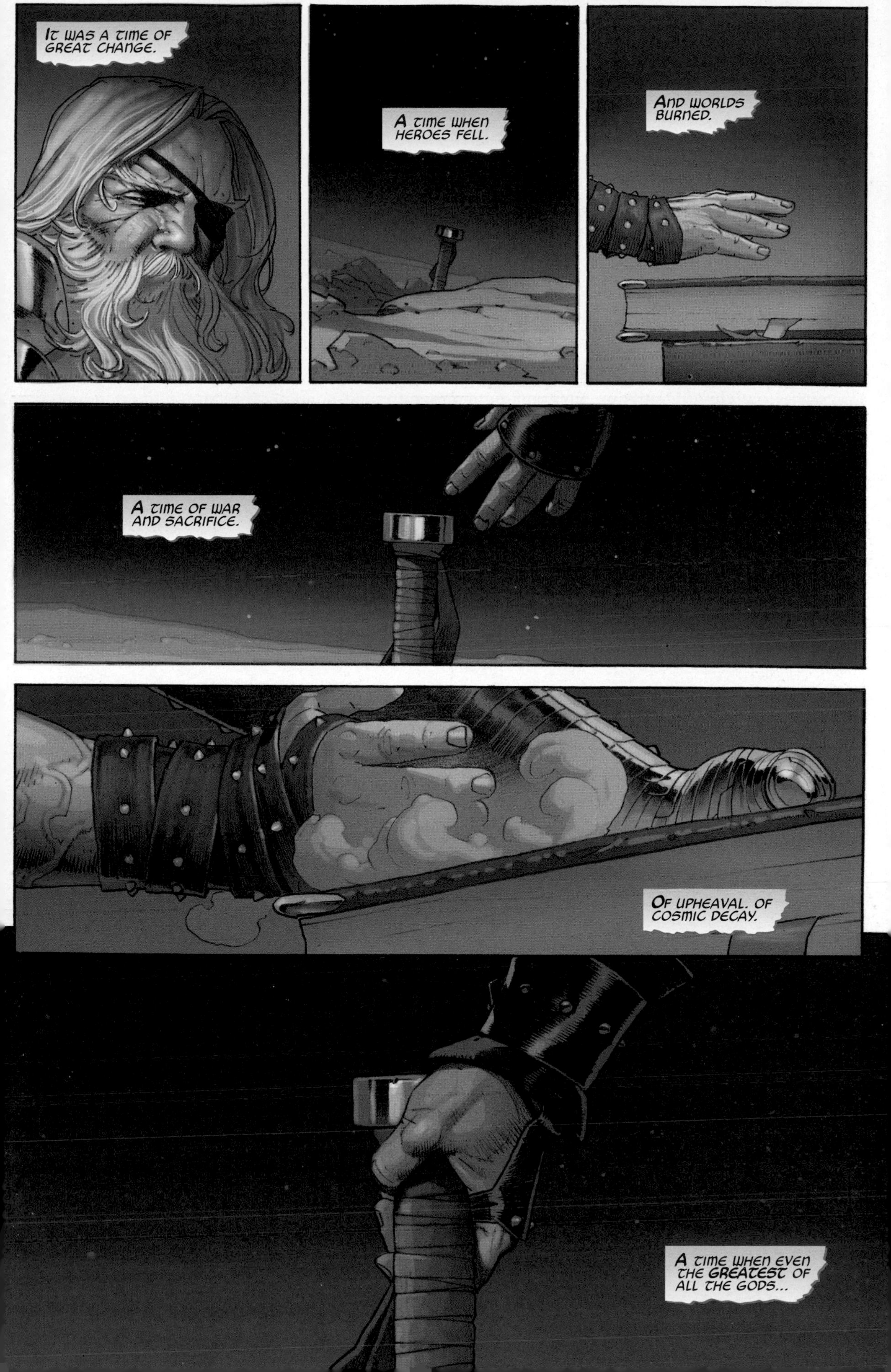
IT WAS A TIME OF GREAT CHANGE.
A TIME WHEN HEROES FELL.
AND WORLDS BURNED.
A TIME OF WAR AND SACRIFICE.
OF UPHEAVAL. OF COSMIC DECAY.
A TIME WHEN EVEN THE GREATEST OF ALL THE GODS...

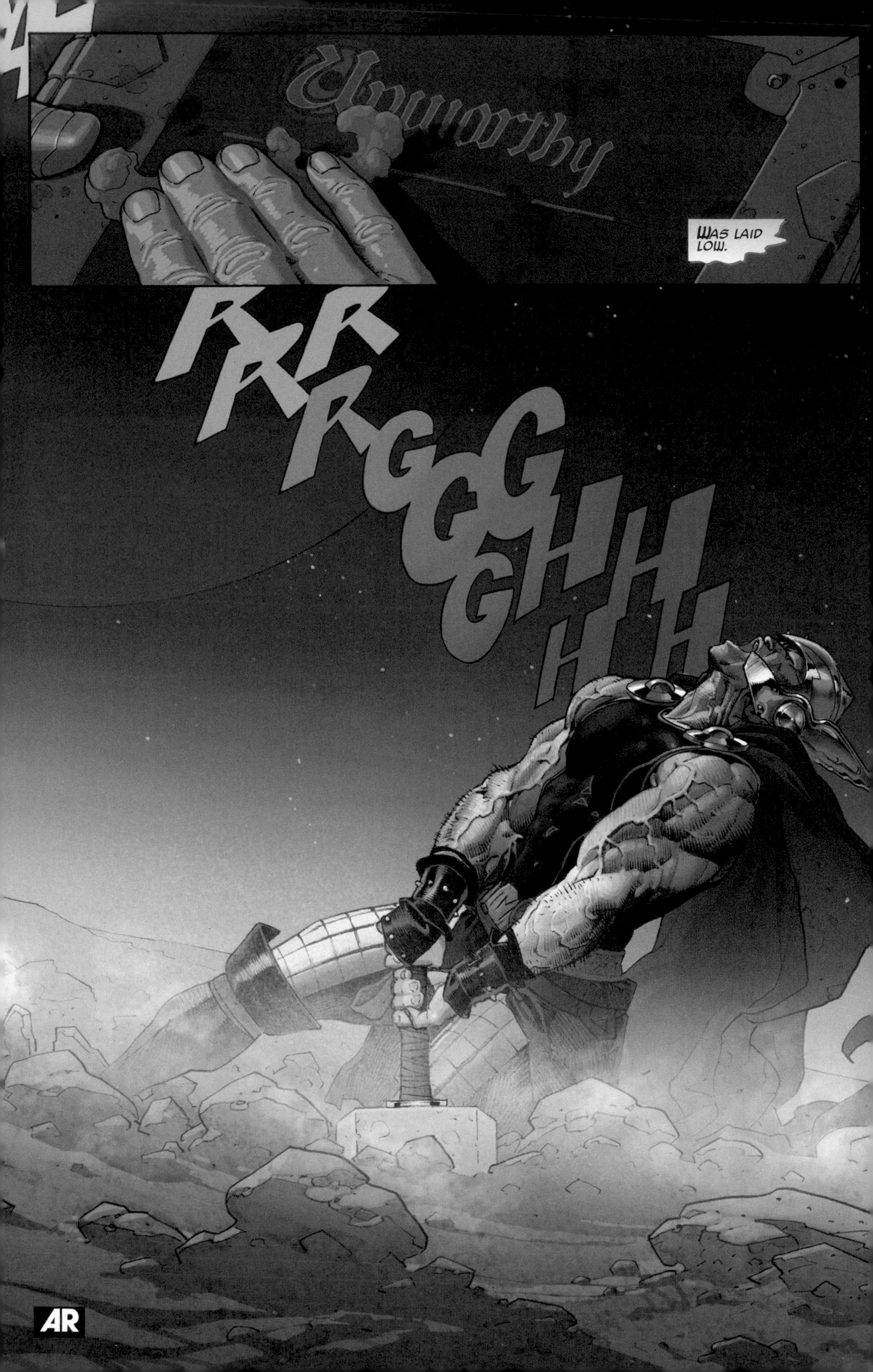
Unworthy
WAS LAID LOW.
RRRRGGGGHHHH

**#19 VARIANT
BY SIMONE BIANCHI**

**#19 VARIANT
BY CLAY MANN & IVE SVORCINA**

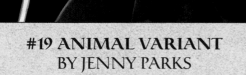

#19 ANIMAL VARIANT
BY JENNY PARKS

#20 VARIANT
BY NIC KLEIN

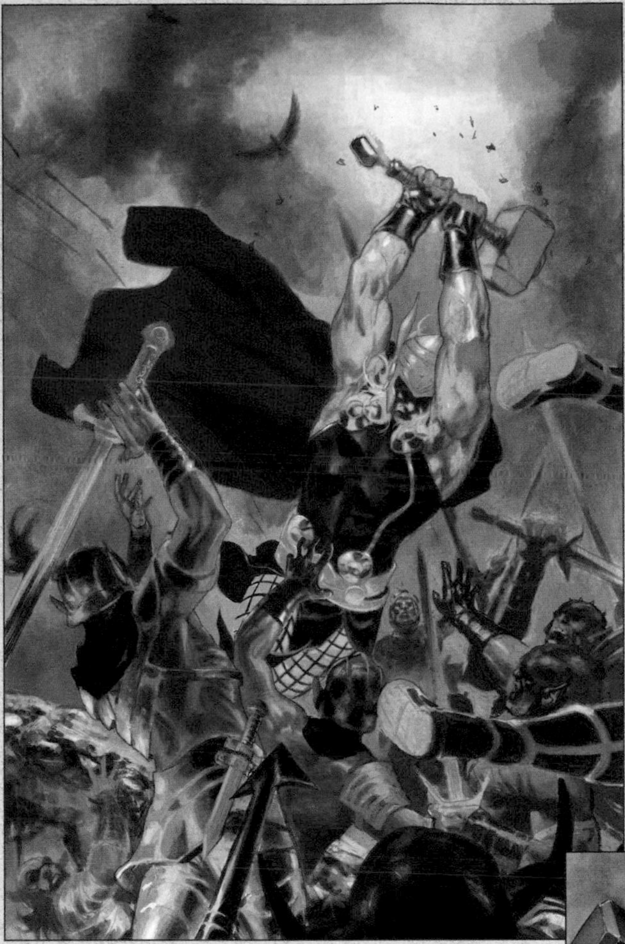

#21 VARIANT
BY RON GARNEY

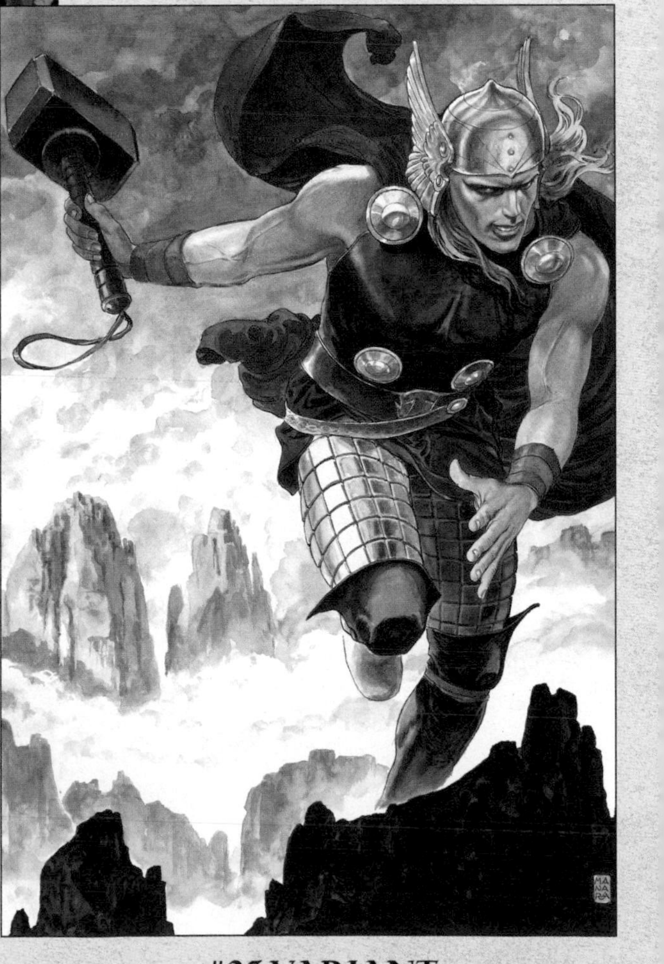

#25 VARIANT
BY MILO MANARA

#25 VARIANT
BY TOM RANEY
& CHRIS SOTOMAYOR

#25 VARIANT
BY R.M. GUERA

MARVEL AR AUGMENTED REALITY

MARVEL AUGMENTED REALITY (AR) ENHANCES AND CHANGES THE WAY YOU EXPERIENCE COMICS!

TO ACCESS THE FREE MARVEL AR CONTENT IN THIS BOOK*:

1. Locate the AR logo within the comic.
2. Go to Marvel.com/AR in your web browser.
3. Search by series title to find the corresponding AR.
4. Enjoy Marvel AR!

*All AR content that appears in this book has been archived and will be available only at Marvel.com/AR – no longer in the Marvel AR App. Content subject to change and availability.

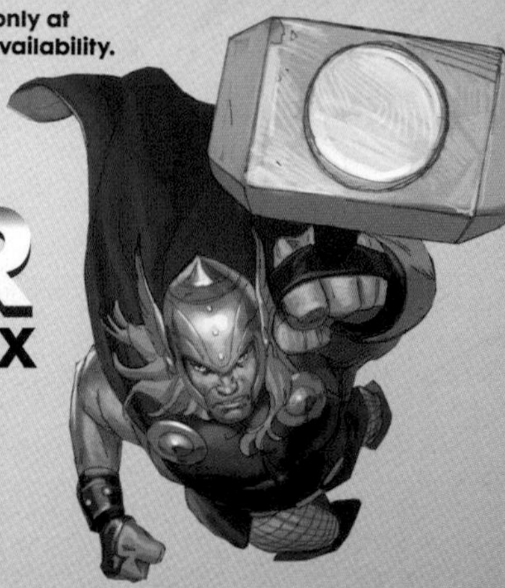

THOR GOD OF THUNDER AR INDEX

TMAB3DN9TN2S

TO REDEEM YOUR CODE FOR A FREE DIGITAL COPY:

1. GO TO MARVEL.COM/REDEEM. OFFER EXPIRES ON 11/19/16.
2. FOLLOW THE ON-SCREEN INSTRUCTIONS TO REDEEM YOUR DIGITAL COPY.
3. LAUNCH THE MARVEL COMICS APP TO READ YOUR COMIC NOW!
4. YOUR DIGITAL COPY WILL BE FOUND UNDER THE *MY COMICS* TAB.
5. READ & ENJOY!

YOUR FREE DIGITAL COPY WILL BE AVAILABLE ON:

MARVEL COMICS APP FOR APPLE® iOS DEVICES

MARVEL COMICS APP FOR ANDROID™ DEVICES